AP* SUCCESS

U.S. HISTORY

2001

Margaret Moran

W. Frances Holder

www.petersons.com

PETERSON'S
THOMSON LEARNING

Australia • Canada • Mexico • Singapore • Spain • United Kingdom • United States

PETERSON'S ™
THOMSON LEARNING

About Peterson's

Founded in 1966, Peterson's, a division of Thomson Learning, is the nation's largest and most respected provider of lifelong learning online resources, software, reference guides, and books. The Education Supersite[SM] at petersons.com—the Web's most heavily traveled education resource—has searchable databases and interactive tools for contacting U.S.-accredited institutions and programs. CollegeQuest[SM] (CollegeQuest.com) offers a complete solution for every step of the college decision-making process. GradAdvantage[TM] (GradAdvantage.org), developed with Educational Testing Service, is the only electronic admissions service capable of sending official graduate test score reports with a candidate's online application. Peterson's serves more than 55 million education consumers annually.

Thomson Learning is among the world's leading providers of lifelong learning, serving the needs of individuals, learning institutions, and corporations with products and services for both traditional classrooms and for online learning. For more information about the products and services offered by Thomson Learning, please visit www.thomsonlearning.com. Headquartered in Stamford, Connecticut, with offices worldwide, Thomson Learning is part of The Thomson Corporation (www.thomson.com), a leading e-information and solutions company in the business, professional, and education marketplaces. The Corporation's common shares are listed on the Toronto and London stock exchanges.

Special thanks to Rick Holder for his editorial assistance.

Photo Credits: p. 281, The Granger Collection, New York; p. 335, Culver Pictures, Inc.
Graphics by: Siren Design, Inc.

For more information, contact Peterson's, 2000 Lenox Drive, Lawrenceville, NJ 08648; 800-338-3282; or find us on the World Wide Web at: www.petersons.com/about

ISBN 0-7689-0500-1

Printed in the United States of America

10 9 8 7 6 5 4 3 2   02 01

CONTENTS

CONTENTS

CONTENTS

RED ALERT

10 STRATEGIES FOR ACING THE TEST

PREPARING FOR THE TEST

1. Read the *AP Course Description for History*, available from the College Board, and the *10 Facts About the AP U.S. History Test*, on pages 3–5 in this book.

2. Choose your Practice Plan from pages 9–14 in this book.

3. Choose a place and time to study every day. Stick to your routine and your plan.

4. Even though they are time-consuming, complete the Diagnostic and Practice Tests in this book. They will give you just what they promise: practice—practice in reading and following the directions, practice in pacing yourself, practice in understanding and answering multiple-choice questions, and practice in writing timed essays.

5. Complete all your assignments for your regular AP U.S. History class. Ask questions in class, talk about what you read and write, and enjoy what you are doing. The test is supposed to measure your development as an educated and thinking reader.

THE NIGHT BEFORE THE TEST

6. Assemble what you will need for the test: your admission materials, four number 2 pencils, two pens, a watch (without an alarm), and a healthy snack for the break. Put these items in a place where you will not forget them in the morning.

7. Don't cram. Relax. Go to a movie, visit a friend—but not one who is taking the test with you. Get a good night's sleep.

THE DAY OF THE TEST

8. Wear comfortable clothes. If you have a lucky color or a lucky piece of clothing or jewelry, wear it—as long as you won't distract anyone else. Take along a lucky charm if you have one.

9. If you do not usually eat a big breakfast, this is not the morning to change your routine, but it is probably a good idea to eat something nutritious if you can.

10. If you feel yourself getting anxious, concentrate on taking a couple of deep breaths. Remember, you don't have to answer all the questions, you can use EDUCATED GUESSES, and you don't have to write three "9" essays.

10 FACTS ABOUT THE AP UNITED STATES HISTORY TEST

1.   THE ADVANCED PLACEMENT PROGRAM OFFERS STUDENTS AN OPPORTUNITY TO RECEIVE COLLEGE CREDIT FOR COURSES THEY TAKE IN HIGH SCHOOL.

The AP program is a collaborative effort of secondary schools, colleges and universities, and the College Board through which students who are enrolled in AP or honors courses in any one or more of eighteen subject areas may receive credit or advanced placement for college-level work completed in high school. While the College Board makes recommendations about course content, it does not prescribe content. The annual testing program ensures a degree of comparability among high school courses in the same subject.

2.   MORE THAN 2,900 COLLEGES AND UNIVERSITIES PARTICIPATE.

Neither the College Board nor your high school awards AP credit. You need to find out from the colleges to which you are planning to apply whether they grant credit and/or use AP scores for placement. It is IMPORTANT that you obtain each school's policy IN WRITING so that when you actually choose one college and register, you will have proof of what you were told.

3.   THE AP UNITED STATES HISTORY TEST MEASURES FACTUAL KNOWLEDGE, ANALYTICAL SKILLS, AND THE ABILITY TO SYNTHESIZE INFORMATION.

According to the College Board, the multiple-choice section measures "factual knowledge, breadth of preparation, and knowledge-based analytical skills." The three-part essay section asks students "to demonstrate their mastery of historical interpretation and their ability to express their views and knowledge in writing." In answering the Document-Based Question (DBQ), students are asked not only to analyze the given documents, but to synthesize and evaluate the given materials during the process of analysis. Scoring of this particular essay is weighted toward the inclusion of "outside knowledge." All three essays are assessed on the strength of the thesis, the quality of the argument, and the validity of the supporting evidence.

4.   THE AP U.S. HISTORY TEST HAS TWO SECTIONS: MULTIPLE-CHOICE AND A THREE-PART ESSAY SECTION.

> **Study Strategy**
>
> *See Chapter 1 for multiple-choice strategies and Chapters 2 through 4 for strategies for writing essays.*

Section I: Multiple Choice has 80 questions testing your knowledge of U.S. history from the first explorers to current events. This section counts for 50 percent of your total score, and you have 55 minutes to complete it.

In Section II, you have three essays to write: a document-based question (DBQ) essay and two free response essays. To answer the DBQ part, you will be given a 15-minute mandatory reading time and 45 minutes to write the essay. You will have 70 minutes, approximately 35 minutes each, to write the two free response essays. The DBQ accounts for 45 percent of the total score for Section II.

5. THE AP U.S. HISTORY TEST COVERS AMERICAN HISTORY FROM THE FIRST EXPLORERS TO CURRENT EVENTS.

Study Strategy

See Chapters 5 through 10 for a brief review of U.S. history.

Although you will find questions from all time periods of U.S. history, most of them will be taken from the nineteenth and twentieth centuries. The College Board states that approximately

- 16 percent of the questions are based on history from the earliest explorers through 1789

- 50 percent are from 1790 to 1914

- 33 percent are from 1915 to the present.

There is an important qualifier for this breakdown. According to the College Board, neither the DBQ nor the free response essay questions are based on events after 1975. However, you may find a few multiple-choice questions on this period.

The College Board further breaks down the kinds of information that it tests. While noting that history is a complex entity that mixes many strands, the College Board states that the questions are divided according to the following categories:

- 35 percent on public policy and political institutions and behavior

- 35 percent on social change

- 15 percent on diplomacy and international relations

- 10 percent on economic developments

- 5 percent on cultural and intellectual developments.

6. THERE IS NO REQUIRED LENGTH FOR YOUR ESSAYS.

It is the quality, not the quantity, that counts. Realistically, a one-paragraph essay is not going to garner you a high mark because you cannot develop a well-reasoned analysis and present it effectively in a single paragraph. An essay of five paragraphs is a good goal. By following this model, you can set out your ideas with an interesting introduction, develop a reasoned middle, and provide a solid ending.

7. YOU WILL GET A COMPOSITE SCORE FOR YOUR TEST.

Test-Taking Strategy

See "Scoring High on the AP U.S. History Test," pp. 6–8.

The College Board reports a single score from 1 to 5 for the two-part test, with 5 being the highest. By understanding how you can balance the number of questions you need to answer correctly against the essay score you need to receive in order to get at least a "3," you can relieve some of your anxiety about passing the test.

8. EDUCATED GUESSING CAN HELP.

Test-Taking Strategy

See "Scoring High on the AP U.S. History Test," pp. 6–8.

No points are deducted for questions that go unanswered on the multiple-choice section, and don't expect to have time to answer them all. A quarter of a point is deducted for wrong answers. The College Board suggests guessing IF you know something about a question and can eliminate a couple of the answer choices. Call it "educated guessing."

9. THE TEST IS GIVEN IN MID-MAY.

Most likely, the test will be given at your school, so you do not have to worry about finding a strange building in a strange city. You will be in familiar surroundings, which should reduce your anxiety a bit. If the test is given somewhere else, be sure to take identification with you.

10. STUDYING FOR THE TEST CAN MAKE A DIFFERENCE.

Study Strategy

Turn to pp.9–12 and read "Practice Plan for Studying for the AP U.S. History Test."

The first step is to familiarize yourself with the format and directions for each part of the test. Then you will not waste time on the day of the test trying to understand what you are supposed to do. The second step is to put those analytical skills you have been learning to work, dissecting and understanding the kinds of questions you will be asked; and the third step is to practice "writing-on-demand" for the essays. So turn the page, and let's get started.

SCORING HIGH ON THE AP U.S. HISTORY TEST

Around early July, you and the colleges you designate will receive a score for your AP U.S. History Test, and your high school will receive its report a little later. The multiple-choice section is graded by machine, and your essays are graded during a marathon reading session by high school and college teachers.

A different reader grades each of your essays. None of the readers know who you are (that's why you fill in identification information on your Section II booklet and then seal it) or how the others scored your other essays. The grading is done on a holistic system; that is, the overall essay is scored, not just the development of your ideas, your spelling, or your punctuation. For each essay, the College Board works out grading criteria for the readers to use, much as your teacher uses a rubric to evaluate your writing.

What the Composite Score Means

The College Board refers to the composite score as weighted because a factor of 1.1250 for the multiple-choice section, a factor of 4.5000 for the DBQ essay, and a factor of 2.7500 for the two free response essays are used to determine a raw score for each section or part. That is, the actual score you get on the multiple-choice questions—say 48—is multiplied by 1.1250. The actual score that you get on the DBQ—say 6—is multiplied by 4.5000, and the actual score on the two free response essays—say 15—is multiplied by 2.7500. The two essay scores are then added to give you one weighted score for both parts of the essay section. This number and the weighted score from the multiple-choice section are added and the resulting composite score—somewhere between 0 and 180 (119, based on the above example)—is then equated to a number from 5 to 1. A score of 119 is good enough to get you a "5" for the test.

What Does All of This Mean to You?

You can leave blank or answer incorrectly some combination of 32 questions on an 80-question multiple-choice section, get a 6 for the DBQ and a 15 for your two free response essays, and still earn a score of 5. It is not as easy as it may seem or the majority of students would not fall into the 3 range, although a 3 may be good enough to get you college credit or advanced placement. A score of 4 certainly will.

Take a look at the charts on the next page. It takes work, but raising your score is not impossible. Sometimes, the difference between a 3 and a 4 or a 4 and a 5 is only a couple of points.

Study Strategy

Chapters 1 to 10 will help you raise your score.

POSSIBLE SCORE DISTRIBUTION FOR AN 80-QUESTION MULTIPLE-CHOICE SECTION

SCORE = 5			SCORE = 4			SCORE = 3		
MC	DBQ	Essays (2)	MC	DBQ	Essays (2)	MC	DBQ	Essays (2)
38	8	17	38	6	14	38	5	10
43	7	16	43	5	13	43	4	9
48	6	15	48	4	12	48	3	8
53	5	14	53	3	11	53	2	7
58	4	13	58	2	10	58	1	6

The highest score you can receive on an essay is a 9. It is possible to get a variety of scores on your essays—7, 5, 5, for example. The chances are that you will not get a wide range of individual essay scores like 6, 2, 5. Even if you did, you could still get at least a 3 and possibly a 4, depending on how many correct answers you have in the multiple-choice section balanced against how many wrong answers you have.

AP Grade	AP Qualifier	Composite Scores	Probability of Receiving Credit
5	Extremely Well Qualified	117–180	Yes
4	Well Qualified	96–116	Yes
3	Qualified	79–95	Probably
2	Possibly Qualified	51–78	Rarely
1	No Recommendation	0–50	No

According to the College Board, 50 percent of the 140,000 students who took the test in a recent year received at least a 3. The cut-off point for passing grades may change from year to year, but it remains in this range. This chart shows the actual conversion scale in a recent year. What it means is that you neither have to answer all the questions, nor do you have to answer them all correctly, nor write three "9" essays to receive your AP credit.

SOME THINGS TO REMEMBER

Red Alert!

These are important facts straight from the College Board.

1. The 80-question multiple-choice section is worth 50 percent of your total score.

2. The College Board says that students who do "acceptable work on the broader questions in the free response section" can receive a 3 if they answer about 60 percent of the multiple-choice questions correctly.

3. There is no deduction for unanswered questions.

4. There is a quarter-point deduction for wrong answers.

5. The DBQ and the two free response essays account for 50 percent of your total score. However, the DBQ is worth 45 percent of the total score for Section II while the two free response essays are each worth 27.5 percent of the total score for Section II.

WHY ARE WE TELLING YOU THESE FACTS?

Because you can use them to your advantage.

Study Strategy

See Chapter 1 for strategies.

1. It is important to spend time practicing the kinds of questions that you will find in the multiple-choice section because 50 percent of your score comes from that section. You do not have to put all your emphasis on the essay questions.

Test-Taking Strategy

The Diagnostic and Practice Tests will help you pace yourself in the exam.

2–3. You can leave some questions unanswered and still do well. Even though you will be practicing how to pace yourself as you use this book, you may not be able to complete all 80 questions on the day of the test. If you come across a really difficult one, you can skip it and still feel that you are not doomed to a low score.

Study Strategy

See Chapter 1 for strategies for "educated guessing."

4. There is a guessing penalty. If you do not know anything about the question or the choices, do not take a chance. However, if you know something about the question and can eliminate one or more of the answer choices, then it is probably worth your while to choose one of the other answers. Rather than calling it guessing, call it EDUCATED GUESSING. Even the College Board suggests this strategy.

Study Strategy

Chapter 3 offers strategies for answering the DBQ.

5. The DBQ is worth more points, but you can get a slightly lower raw score for it and still do well in Section II by getting a slightly better score on your two free response essay questions.

PRACTICE PLAN FOR STUDYING FOR THE AP U.S. HISTORY TEST

The following plan should be followed for nine weeks. The best study plan is one that continues through a full semester. A full-semester study plan means that you can apply what you are learning here to classwork—your essay writing—and apply your classwork—everything that you are reading—to test preparation. Then you have time to think about ideas and to talk with your teacher and other students about what you are learning, and you will not feel rushed. Staying relaxed about the test is important. The plan is worked out so that you should spend about 3 hours on each lesson.

Week 1

First: Take the *Diagnostic Test,* pp. 17–35, and complete the self-scoring process. List the areas that you had difficulty with, such as timing, question types, and writing on demand.

Then: Reread pp. 3–8 about the basic facts of the test and its scoring.

Week 2

Lesson 1
- Read *10 Strategies for Acing the Test,* p. 1.
- Reread *Scoring High on the AP U.S. History Test,* pp. 6–8.
- Review the list you made after the *Diagnostic Test* to see what you need to learn in order to do well on the multiple-choice section.
- Read Chapter 1, *Answering the Multiple-Choice Questions.*
- Do one set of practice questions at the end of the chapter and review the explanation of the answers.

Lesson 2
- Review Chapter 1, *Answering the Multiple-Choice Questions,* and do another set of practice questions at the end of the chapter.
- Review the answers for these practice questions.
- Read Chapter 5, *Reviewing the Colonial Period to 1789,* and find out more about any of the people, terms, and concepts that are unfamiliar to you.

Week 3

Lesson 1
- Read *10 Strategies for Acing the Test,* p. 1.
- Reread *Scoring High on the AP U.S. History Test,* pp. 6–8.
- Review Chapter 1, *Answering the Multiple-Choice Questions.*

- Review the list you made after the *Diagnostic Test* to see what you need to learn about the multiple-choice section.

- Do one set of practice questions at the end of the chapter, and review the answers.

Lesson 2
- Read Chapter 7, *Reviewing the New Nation to Mid-Century,* and find out more about any of the people, terms, or concepts that are unfamiliar to you. Read appropriate cases in Chapter 6, *The Constitution and Important Supreme Court Cases.*

Week 4
Lesson 1
- Read Chapter 2, *About Writing a "9" Essay.*

- Read Chapter 3, *Writing the DBQ Essay.*

- For practice, create an outline for an essay using the question on p. 85 about agrarian protests and the points suggested in the analysis of each document. Add your own ideas. Then develop a thesis for your essay.

- Write your essay. Complete the self-scoring process, and compare your score against your score on the *Diagnostic Test.*

- Ask a responsible friend, an AP classmate, or a teacher to evaluate your essay against the scoring guide. Where did you improve from the *Diagnostic Test?* What still needs improvement?

Lesson 2
- Read Chapter 8, *Reviewing the Events Leading to the Civil War and Its Aftermath,* and find out more about any of the people, terms, or concepts that are unfamiliar to you. Read appropriate cases in Chapter 6, *The Constitution and Important Supreme Court Cases.*

Week 5
Lesson 1
- Reread Chapter 2, *About Writing a "9" Essay*

- Read Chapter 4, *Writing the Free Response Essays,* and write from the simulated test at the end of the chapter.

- Complete the self-scoring process and compare the score with your score on the *Diagnostic Test* essays.

- Ask a responsible friend, an AP classmate, or a teacher to evaluate your essay against the scoring guide.

Lesson 2
- Read Chapter 9, *Reviewing Becoming an Urban and Industrial World Power,* and find out more about any people, terms, or

concepts that are unfamiliar to you. Read appropriate cases in Chapter 6, *The Constitution and Important Supreme Court Cases.*

Week 6

Lesson 1
- Answer the multiple-choice section of *Practice Test 1* and complete the self-scoring process.

- Compare the score to your score on the *Diagnostic Test.* Which question types continue to be a concern?

- Reread Chapter 1, *Answering the Multiple-Choice Questions,* as needed.

- Complete the DBQ on *Practice Test 1* and score your essay against the rubrics.

- Again, ask a responsible friend, an AP classmate, or a teacher to evaluate your essay against the scoring guide.

- Compare your scores to the scores on the *Diagnostic Test.* Where did you improve? Where does your writing still need work?

- Reread Chapters 2 and 3 as needed.

Lesson 2
- Read half of Chapter 10, *Reviewing the Twentieth Century: 1915 to the Present,* and find out more about any people, terms, or concepts that are unfamiliar to you.

Week 7

Lesson 1
- Answer the free response essay questions on *Practice Test 2* and score your essays against the rubric.

- Ask a responsible friend, an AP classmate, or a teacher to evaluate your essays on the scoring guide as well. Compare these scores to your scores on the *Diagnostic Test.*

- Reread Chapters 2 and 4 as needed.

Lesson 2
- Read the second half of Chapter 10, *Reviewing the Twentieth Century: 1915 to the Present,* and find out more about any people, terms, or concepts that are unfamiliar to you. Read appropriate cases in Chapter 6, *The Constitution and Important Supreme Court Cases.*

Week 8

Lesson 1
- Answer free response essay questions 3 and 4 from Chapter 4, *Writing the Free Response Essays,* and complete the self-scoring process.

- Compare the score to your scores for the two tests. Work on your strengths for the next two weeks by writing free response essay question 5 from Chapter 4, *Writing the Free Response Essays*.

Lesson 2
- Reveiw your notes on Chapters 5 through 10. Look for the significance of major events and trends.

Week 9

Lesson 1
- Take *Practice Test 2* and complete the self-scoring process. Check your results against the other two tests.

Lesson 2
- If you are still unsure about some areas, review those chapters and the practice activities.

- Reread *Scoring High on the AP U.S. History Test*, pp. 6–8, and *10 Strategies for Acing the Test*, p. 1–2.

THE PANIC PLAN

Eighteen weeks, nine weeks, how about two weeks? If you are the kind of person who puts everything off until the last possible minute, here is a two-week panic plan. Its objectives are to make you familiar with the test format and directions, to help you get as many right answers as possible, and to write the best DBQ and free response essays you can.

Week 1
- Read *10 Strategies for Acing the Test*, p. 1–2, and *Scoring High on the AP U.S. History Test*, pp. 6–8.
- Take the *Diagnostic Test*. Read the directions carefully and use a timer for each section.
- Complete the self-scoring process. You can learn a lot about the types of questions in the multiple-choice section by working through the answers.
- Read Chapter 5, *Reviewing the Colonial Period to 1789,*

Multiple Choice
- Answer the multiple-choice section on *Practice Test 1.*
- Complete the self-scoring process and see where you may still have problems with question types.
- Read all the answer explanations, including those you identified correctly.

Essays
- Complete Section II on *Practice Test 1.*
- Score your essays using the rubric. List your weaknesses.
- Read Chapter 2, *About Writing a "9" Essay,*
- Use the documents and question on agrarian protest on page 85 and Essays 2 and 3 in Chapter 4, *Writing the Free Response Essays,* p. 95, to gain practice in planning and writing the DBQ and two free response essays.
- Score your essays against the rubrics, noting areas for improvement.
- Ask a responsible friend, an AP classmate, or a teacher to evaluate your essays on the scoring guide as well. Compare it to your score on the *Diagnostic Test.*

Week 2
- Reread *Top 10 Strategies for Acing the Test*, p. 1–2, and *Scoring High on the AP U.S. History Test,* pp. 6–8.
- Complete *Practice Test 2* and score the multiple-choice and essay sections.

- Read Chapters 7, 8, 9, and 10. As you read these chapters, read along in Chapter 6, *The Constitution and Important Supreme Court Cases,* where appropriate.

Multiple Choice
- Work at least two practice sets of multiple-choice questions in Chapter 1, *Answering the Multiple-Choice Questions,* pp. 61–76.

Essays
- Write another set of essays—the DBQ and the free response essays from *Practice Test 1,* working on strengthening your weaknesses. Score them against the rubric.

- Ask a responsible friend, an AP classmate, or a teacher to evaluate your essays on the scoring guide.

WHY TAKE THE DIAGNOSTIC TEST?

What do you know about the format and questions on an AP U.S. History Test? If you knew all you needed to know, you would probably not be reading this book. Taking a practice test is one way to learn about the test and what it will be like taking it on the real test day. It is a long test, and you will need to pace yourself in answering the multiple-choice questions and in planning and writing your essays. Taking the *Diagnostic Test* will help you learn how much time to spend on each item.

Practice may not make perfect, but you can improve your score with practice. The more you learn about your strengths and weaknesses in test-taking abilities and in analytical skills, and the more you work on strengthening them, the better your score.

How should you take this test? Just as though it were the real test, so that means setting aside 3 hours and 5 minutes of uninterrupted, quiet time to take the test, plus the time to score your answers.

- Make a photocopy of an answer sheet at the back of this book.

- Assemble four number 2 pencils and two pens along with the answer sheet and six pieces of paper on which to make notes and write your three essays.

- Use a timer or a stopwatch to time each section of the test.

- Follow the directions for each section of the test—the multiple-choice section, the DBQ, and each of the other two essays. Set your timer for the allotted time for each section.

- When you have completed the test, check how many questions you were able to answer on the multiple-choice section and how far you got in completing each essay. This information will help you in pacing yourself for the other practice tests and for the real test.

- Then check the multiple-choice questions against the *Quick-Score Answers*, p. 36.

- Read the explanation for each answer, even if your answer was correct. You might learn something you didn't know about the content of the question.

- Score each of your essays against the rubrics. Be honest in your evaluation. Knowing your weaknesses is the only way to turn them into strengths.

- Turn to the *Practice Plan* and design your study plan from now until test day.

DIAGNOSTIC TEST

AP UNITED STATES HISTORY

On the front page of your test booklet, you will find some information about the test. Because you have studied this book, none of it should be new to you, and much of it is similar to other standardized tests that you have taken.

The page will tell you that the following exam will take 3 hours and 5 minutes—55 minutes for the multiple-choice section and 2 hours and 10 minutes for the three essays. Fifteen minutes of the time for Section II is a mandatory reading period, primarily for the DBQ. There are two booklets for this exam, one for the multiple-choice section and one for the essays.

The page in your test booklet will also say that SECTION I

- is 55 minutes.

- has 80 questions.

- counts for 50 percent of your total grade.

Then you will find a sentence in capital letters telling you not to open your exam booklet until the monitor tells you to open it.

Other instructions will tell you to be careful when you fill in the ovals on the answer sheet. Fill in each oval completely. If you erase an answer, erase it completely. If you skip a question, be sure to skip the answer oval for it. You will not receive any credit for work done in the test booklet, but you may use it for making notes.

You will also find a paragraph about the guessing penalty—a deduction of one-quarter point for every wrong answer—but also words of advice about guessing if you know something about the question and can eliminate several of the answers.

The final paragraph will remind you to work effectively and to pace yourself. You are told that not everyone will be able to answer all the questions and it is preferable to skip questions that are difficult and come back to them if you have time.

SECTION I

Time–55 minutes
80 questions

Directions: Each question or incomplete statement is followed by five suggested responses. Choose the best answer and fill in the correct oval on the answer sheet.

1. Great Britain's policy of governing its colonies to build up its own gold reserves and expand trade is known as

    (A) nationalism
    (B) favorable balance of trade
    (C) mercantilism
    (D) Navigation Acts
    (E) enumerated goods

2. All of the following were weaknesses of the Articles of Confederation EXCEPT

    (A) nine of the thirteen states had to approve all laws
    (B) a national court system ruled on the constitutionality of laws
    (C) Congress worked in committees without a chief executive
    (D) all states were required to approve amendments
    (E) Congress could raise money by borrowing or by asking states for money

3. In order to gain passage of the Assumption Bill, Alexander Hamilton agreed

    (A) to withdraw his tariff bill
    (B) to specify that speculators would be paid the full value of their bonds
    (C) to hold the bill authorizing the First Bank until Washington's second term
    (D) to support building the new capital city on Southern land
    (E) to support Madison's version of the bill

4. A major document of the women's rights movement was

    (A) Declaration of Sentiments and Resolutions
    (B) *The Feminine Mystique*
    (C) "Ain't I a Woman"
    (D) *Liberator*
    (E) *A Century of Dishonor*

5. Belief in the divinity and unity of people and nature and the supremacy of intuition over reason as a source of knowledge were characteristics of

    (A) the Hudson River School
    (B) Transcendentalism
    (C) nationalism
    (D) Deism
    (E) the Harlem Renaissance

6. During the Civil War, all of the following were true of the Union policy toward African Americans EXCEPT

(A) many African Americans saw duty only as teamsters, cooks, and laborers

(B) the Union refused to allow African Americans to enlist until there was a shortage of recruits

(C) African Americans fought in segregated units

(D) the Union commissioned some African Americans as officers, but most black troops fought under white officers

(E) African Americans were integrated into white regiments

7. The Sherman Antitrust Act of 1890 was difficult to enforce because

(A) it allowed the federal courts to determine its application

(B) it did not define certain key terms

(C) it needed additional legislation to give it force

(D) the 1890s were a time of consolidation in big business

(E) it did not have the support of the farmers who were most affected by it

8. The principle of separate but equal was established by

(A) *Brown* v. *the Board of Education of Topeka*

(B) *Wesbery* v. *Sanders*

(C) *Plessy* v. *Ferguson*

(D) *Bakke* v. *Board of Regents*

(E) *Heart of Atlanta Motel* v. *United States*

Questions 9 and 10 refer to the following cartoon.

9. The large cartoon figures represent Wall Street giants. Who does "Jack" represent?

(A) Herbert Hoover

(B) William McKinley

(C) Franklin Roosevelt

(D) Theodore Roosevelt

(E) Warren G. Harding

10. What would be the most appropriate label for the sword?

(A) In God We Trust

(B) In the Public Service

(C) Silver

(D) Gospel of Wealth

(E) Social Darwinism

11. Which of the following was not created during Roosevelt's first "Hundred Days" in office?

    (A) Public Works Administration
    (B) Agricultural Adjustment Administration
    (C) Civilian Conservation Corps
    (D) Social Security Administration
    (E) Tennessee Valley Authority

12. The General Court banished Roger Williams primarily because he

    (A) believed that the colonists should pay the Native Americans for their lands
    (B) preached separation of church and state
    (C) believed in the right of women to vote
    (D) challenged the rights of leaders to force people to attend religious services
    (E) was a secret Pilgrim

13. The Maryland Toleration Act of 1649 was significant because it

    (A) made it easier to fulfill the terms of indenture
    (B) granted religious freedom to Christian sects
    (C) provided for gradual emancipation of slaves in Maryland
    (D) was the earliest colonial statute related to religious freedom
    (E) allowed any male to hold office

14. Which of the following statements best describes the Lowell experiment of the 1820s?

    (A) The Boston Associates were more interested in profits than in the well-being of their workers.
    (B) Native-born women workers were replaced by lower-paid Irish immigrants.
    (C) The Boston Associates attempted to operate Lowell without the labor abuses of the English factory system.
    (D) Lowell women mill workers organized into successful unions.
    (E) Lowell was one of the earliest mills to use water power.

15. All of the following added to the growing tension between the North and the South EXCEPT

    (A) Uncle Tom's Cabin
    (B) Plessy v. Ferguson
    (C) raid on Harper's Ferry
    (D) California's request for statehood
    (E) Underground Railroad

16. The decision in Scott v. Sanford did all of the following EXCEPT

    (A) overturn the Missouri Compromise
    (B) outlaw the teaching of slaves to read and write
    (C) uphold the right of slave owners to their property in new territories
    (D) overturn the Compromise of 1850
    (E) call into question the validity of popular sovereignty

17. Which of the following is NOT an accurate description of the Knights of Labor?

 (A) The Knights championed the abolition of child labor.

 (B) Women, African Americans, and immigrants were admitted.

 (C) The Knights were organized into separate unions, according to crafts.

 (D) Because of the Haymarket Riot, the Knights became identified with radicalism.

 (E) The Knights advocated arbitration rather than strikes.

18. " . . . [C]onsider all surplus revenues which come to him simply as trust funds, which he is called upon to administer . . . in a manner which, in his judgment, is best calculated to produce the most beneficial results for the community."
The above reflects the philosophy of

 (A) Andrew Carnegie

 (B) Theodore Roosevelt

 (C) William Jennings Bryan

 (D) Frederick Douglass

 (E) Jane Addams

19. Which of the following was a victory for organized labor?

 (A) Taft-Hartley Act

 (B) AFL strike against US Steel in 1919

 (C) Wagner Act

 (D) Sherman Antitrust Act

 (E) Bonus Army

20. Which of the following was a direct consequence of United States involvement in Vietnam?

 (A) The United States ended diplomatic relations with China.

 (B) Nixon authorized an action that ended as the "Saturday Night Massacre."

 (C) Nixon authorized the Iran-Contra activities.

 (D) Congress passed the War Powers Act of 1973 over Nixon's veto.

 (E) The Cold War ended.

21. The Fundamental Orders of Connecticut

 (A) established representative government through election to the House of Burgesses

 (B) provided that any white man owning property could vote

 (C) separated church and state

 (D) established the General Court

 (E) outlawed slavery in the colony

22. Which of the following contradicts Thomas Jefferson's position as an advocate of states' rights and strict construction?

 (A) He opposed Hamilton's financial program during Washington's administration.

 (B) As president, he reduced taxes.

 (C) He maintained United States neutrality with Europe.

 (D) He authorized the Louisiana Purchase.

 (E) He employed a *laissez-faire* policy toward the economy during his administrations.

23. According to the principle of popular sovereignty used to deal with slavery,

   (A) no state admitted after 1850 would be allowed to legalize slavery

   (B) settlers within a territory had the right to determine for themselves whether the territory would be slave or free

   (C) a slave taken from a slave state to a free state was free

   (D) Congress, as the representative of the people, would decide whether a state would be free or slave

   (E) a territorial legislature could refuse to pass slave codes and thus keep slave owners out

24. Which of the following writers used a style known as "local color" or "regional"?

   (A) Stephen Crane

   (B) Theodore Dreiser

   (C) Mark Twain

   (D) Joseph Pulitzer

   (E) Thomas Eakins

25. All of the following were "push" factors for Southern and Eastern European immigration in the last half of the nineteenth century EXCEPT

   (A) tenant farms too small to support a family

   (B) financial panic and economic depression

   (C) high tariffs on foodstuffs

   (D) religious persecution

   (E) industrial development

26. Why was the election of Ronald Reagan in 1980 of major significance?

   (A) It demonstrated the importance of the economy in presidential elections.

   (B) It signaled a shift among voters to conservatism.

   (C) It reawakened interest in Richard Nixon's presidency.

   (D) It was the first time a movie star had been elected president.

   (E) It showed a weariness with Jimmy Carter's leadership style.

27. The colonial case against John Peter Zenger is considered a landmark in the development of which freedom?

   (A) speech

   (B) religion

   (C) the press

   (D) right to bear arms

   (E) right to assemble

28. Which of the following statements is correct about Pinckney's Treaty?

   (A) Canada and the United States agreed to a mutual disarmament of the Great Lakes.

   (B) The United States received the right of deposit at New Orleans.

   (C) Native Americans were banished from the Upper Midwest.

   (D) It set a boundary between Maine and New Brunswick, Canada.

   (E) The British agreed to leave their forts in the Old Northwest.

29. Which of the following was an example of sectional interests intervening in national politics?

(A) Hartford Convention
(B) New England Confederation
(C) Albany Congress
(D) Annapolis Convention
(E) Niagara Movement

30. Congress passed gag rules in 1836 to prevent

(A) free blacks from testifying in court
(B) publication of Frederick Douglass' *North Star*
(C) the organization of suffragist groups
(D) debate on antislavery petitions
(E) filibusters

31. The Freeport Doctrine of Stephen Douglas

(A) disagreed with the Dred Scott decision
(B) failed to address the rights of slave owners
(C) stated that a territorial legislature could discourage slavery by failing to pass slave codes
(D) restated the Republicans' position that slavery should not be allowed to spread
(E) repudiated popular sovereignty

32. The border states that remained in the Union were

(A) Ohio, Indiana, Illinois
(B) Tennessee, Kentucky
(C) Kentucky, Missouri
(D) Delaware, Maryland, Kentucky, Missouri
(E) Kansas, Missouri

33. The largest number of immigrants from one country to come to the United States in the years between 1860 and 1920 were

(A) Russians
(B) Austro-Hungarians
(C) Germans
(D) Canadians
(E) Mexicans

34. All of the following contributed to the development of the cattle industry in the West at the end of the nineteenth century EXCEPT

(A) replacement of longhorns by Herefords
(B) fencing in of the open range with barbed wire
(C) network of railroads
(D) new methods of meat processing
(E) Morrill Act

35. The United States acquired which of the following as a result of the treaty ending the Spanish-American War?

(A) Hawaii
(B) Alaska
(C) Panama
(D) Hispaniola
(E) the Philippines

36. Which of the following resulted in peace between Israel and Egypt?

(A) *perestroika*
(B) recognition of Palestine's right to exist
(C) Camp David Accords
(D) assassination of Anwar Sadat
(E) invasion of Kuwait

37. All of the following statements about colonial politics are true EXCEPT
    (A) the legislatures controlled taxes and expenditures
    (B) voting rights were limited to white male property owners
    (C) most colonies had bicameral legislatures
    (D) each colony elected its own governor
    (E) governors had limited authority

38. Which of the following was adopted to resolve the issue of representation in the House and Senate?
    (A) Three-Fifths Compromise
    (B) New Jersey Plan
    (C) direct election of senators
    (D) Great Compromise
    (E) Virginia Plan

39. Which of the following events is an example of the economic problems facing the government under the Articles of Confederation?
    (A) Whiskey Rebellion
    (B) Stono Uprising
    (C) Kentucky and Virginia Resolutions
    (D) Shays' Rebellion
    (E) Tariff of Abominations

40. The development of the United States as an industrial giant was implicit in the policies of
    (A) Hector St. John de Crèvecoeur
    (B) Thomas Jefferson
    (C) Alexander Hamilton
    (D) John C. Calhoun
    (E) Patrick Henry

41. American policy toward France during Washington's administration can best be described as an attempt to
    (A) honor the commitment to France the new nation had made in 1778 when they became allies
    (B) play France off against Great Britain
    (C) keep the United States out of a war it was ill-equipped to fight
    (D) protect United States trade with Great Britain
    (E) placate Napoleon in order to purchase Louisiana

42. All of the following contributed to the divisions in the antislavery movement in the 1840s EXCEPT
    (A) William Lloyd Garrison's linking of women's rights to abolition
    (B) Garrison's advocacy of nonviolence
    (C) the moderates' view that change could be effected through the political process
    (D) the publication of *Uncle Tom's Cabin*
    (E) the call to radical, violent change by former slaves who joined the abolitionist movement

43. Which of the following Union strategies did the most damage to the South's economy during the Civil War?
    (A) capture of Richmond
    (B) accepting escaped slaves into the Union lines
    (C) control of the Mississippi River
    (D) blockade of Southern ports
    (E) destroying Southern railroads

44. Who wrote the influential muckraking book *The History of the Standard Oil Company?*

(A) Ray Stannard Baker

(B) Ida B. Wells

(C) Frank Norris

(D) Upton Sinclair

(E) Ida Tarbell

45. The Roosevelt Corollary to the Monroe Doctrine was first applied

(A) to the British and German blockade of Venezuela

(B) in recognizing Panama's independence

(C) to the withdrawal from Nicaragua of United States troops who had been sent to collect debt payments

(D) to Cuba when the military occupation ended in 1901

(E) in the Dominican Republic when the United States assumed responsibility for collecting Dominican debts to pay off creditors

46. The major reason Prohibition was difficult to enforce was

(A) criminals took over the manufacture and sale of alcohol

(B) it was easy to smuggle alcohol into the United States because of its long, unguarded border

(C) communities continued to observe local option laws

(D) many Americans did not take the law seriously

(E) many Americans were embarrassed by the argument that Prohibition was a way to strike a blow at German Americans who dominated the brewery business

47. In the coalition Franklin Roosevelt put together, which of the following groups was new to the Democratic Party?

(A) Northern political machines

(B) Southern whites

(C) African Americans

(D) Southern political machines

(E) first- and second-generation immigrants

48. The Gulf of Tonkin Resolution was based on what false information?

(A) The North Vietnamese were sending troops into South Vietnam.

(B) North Vietnam had fired on United States destroyers that were aiding South Vietnam in electronic spying of the North.

(C) The Vietcong had little or no support in rural areas and, therefore, could be easily subdued.

(D) North Vietnam had fired on two destroyers in an unprovoked attack.

(E) The North Vietnamese were using napalm against United States soldiers.

49. The Stamp Act was significant because

(A) it was the first tax levied on goods imported from Great Britain

(B) it was to be strictly enforced by the British

(C) it was the first tax placed on goods made and sold in the colonies and, therefore, not part of mercantile policy

(D) if enforced it would drain colonial merchants of gold and silver

(E) it was the first instance of taxation without representation

50. A precursor to the Declaration of Independence was

   (A) the Proclamation of Rebellion
   (B) Lee's Resolution
   (C) Suffolk Resolves
   (D) Declaration of Rights and Grievances
   (E) Olive Branch Petition

51. All of the following were part of United States foreign policy under Washington EXCEPT

   (A) Pinckney's Treaty
   (B) Jay's Treaty
   (C) Proclamation of Neutrality
   (D) Treaty of Greenville
   (E) XYZ Affair

52. The Wilmot Proviso supported

   (A) popular sovereignty to determine whether a state created from the Louisiana Purchase would be free or slave
   (B) the argument of Southern senators that Congress had no constitutional power to forbid slavery in the territories
   (C) a moratorium on the admission of any new states to the Union until a permanent solution could be found
   (D) a ban on slavery in any state created out of land acquired from Mexico
   (E) a ban on the slave trade in Washington, D.C.

Questions 53 and 54 refer to the following chart.

Year	U.S. Exports to Europe	U.S. Exports to Asia
1890	684	20
1891	705	26
1892	851	20
1893	662	17
1894	701	22
1895	628	18
1896	673	26
1897	813	39
1898	974	45
1899	937	49

Source: *Historical Abstract of the United States*

53. In which year did the value of United States exports to Europe increase while the value of United States exports to Asia declined?

   (A) 1895
   (B) 1894
   (C) 1893
   (D) 1892
   (E) 1891

54. The trend in trade with Asia as shown on the graph appears to demonstrate the wisdom of

   (A) the Roosevelt Corollary
   (B) John Hay's Open Door policy
   (C) the Panama Canal Treaty
   (D) the annexation of the Philippines
   (E) a favorable balance of trade

55. "Nothing will do more to change the mental attitude and raise his status than a demonstration of intellectual parity by the Negro through his production of literature and art." The above statement was most probably written about

(A) the purpose of Tuskegee Institute

(B) the Harlem Renaissance

(C) Universal Negro Improvement Association

(D) *Crisis* magazine

(E) NAACP

56. Which of the following benefited African Americans the least during the New Deal?

(A) AAA

(B) SSA

(C) NYA

(D) CCC

(E) NRA

57. The right to privacy was expanded in

(A) *Heart of Atlanta Motel* v. *United States*

(B) *Roe* v. *Wade*

(C) Fourteenth Amendment

(D) Civil Rights Act of 1964

(E) Fair Credit Reporting Act of 1970

58. Which of the following colonies established the principle that local communities have a duty under the law to establish schools?

(A) Rhode Island

(B) Connecticut

(C) Georgia

(D) Pennsylvania

(E) Massachusetts

59. In the early 1700s, the Spanish decided to establish settlements in Texas to

(A) control the Apache

(B) keep Americans from settling the Plains

(C) keep the French from claiming the area

(D) convert the Native Americans

(E) provide stepping-stones into the interior for expeditions to find Cibola

60. In his Farewell Address, George Washington counseled Americans to avoid foreign alliances because

(A) they would make it difficult to carry on trade with a nation at war with a United States ally

(B) foreign alliances could lead to domestic insurrection over the issue of slavery

(C) foreign alliances could lead to curbs on United States exports and an unfavorable balance of trade for the United States

(D) the United States in time would be strong enough to choose its own course in foreign affairs without the need to rely on allies

(E) foreign alliances could revive the issue of mercantilism

61. Andrew Jackson opposed the Second Bank of the United States because

(A) he believed the bank concentrated too much power in the hands of a few wealthy men in the Northeast

(B) he believed the bank did not provide a sound basis for a national currency

(C) the bank would not accept federal deposits

(D) he believed the bank created an economic climate that fostered land speculation

(E) the bank closed state banks, known as "pet banks," run by Jackson supporters

62. In the presidential election of 1844, the principal issue was

(A) the qualifications of James K. Polk

(B) manifest destiny

(C) slavery

(D) the annexation of Texas

(E) Clay's refusal to promise to go to war against Mexico

63. In the economy of the New South,

(A) most African Americans found jobs in factories

(B) discrimination against African Americans lessened because there was more wealth

(C) most African Americans found they had no place in the South and moved north

(D) most African Americans remained tenant farmers

(E) African Americans found it easier to find work in a variety of jobs

64. The Pendleton Act was passed to regulate

(A) the banking system

(B) civil service

(C) railroads

(D) tariffs

(E) foreign policy toward Latin America

65. The primary reason that Mexicans immigrated to the United States between 1910 and 1920 was

(A) for better economic opportunities

(B) to participate in the bracero program that provided workers for the United States defense industry

(C) to flee the Mexican Revolution

(D) to be able to practice their religion as Roman Catholics without government interference

(E) the United States proposal to impose quotas on Mexican immigration

66. Which of the following movies was controversial at the time because of its portrayal of African Americans?

(A) *The Jazz Singer*

(B) *Gone with the Wind*

(C) *Inherit the Wind*

(D) *Birth of a Nation*

(E) *On the Road*

67. Because of isolationist opinions, Roosevelt developed which of the following strategies to help the Allies?

(A) Good Neighbor Policy

(B) gunboat diplomacy

(C) Neutrality Act of 1935

(D) Roosevelt Corollary

(E) Lend-lease

68. The purpose of Freedom Summer was to

    (A) call attention to segregation on interstate buses and in bus terminals in the South

    (B) protest the Vietnam War

    (C) register black voters in the South

    (D) call attention to the segregation of public facilities in the South

    (E) prepare students to integrate Southern schools

69. The only colony to recognize the land rights of Native Americans was

    (A) Massachusetts

    (B) Virginia

    (C) Pennsylvania

    (D) New Jersey

    (E) Maryland

70. The major reason that slavery did not develop in New England was

    (A) the presence of natural resources more suited to industrial development

    (B) the presence of a large pool of native-born women as workers

    (C) Puritan teachings that opposed slavery

    (D) that its climate and land features were less adaptable to large-scale farming

    (E) that New England merchants did not mind selling slaves but did not want to be reminded by the presence of slaves

71. Great Britain's interest in enforcing mercantilism after the French and Indian War revoked its previous policy of

    (A) right of self-determination

    (B) benign neglect

    (C) separation of powers

    (D) spheres of influence

    (E) salutary neglect

72. Which of the following is true about the Denmark Vesey Conspiracy?

    (A) Some 60 whites were killed.

    (B) The conspirators hoped to be reinforced from plantations along the Stono River.

    (C) A thunderstorm struck before the rebels could attack, and the state militia was called out to capture the rebels.

    (D) Laws limiting the rights of free blacks in Charleston were passed.

    (E) This was the last slave revolt in the Old South.

73. The Dawes Act can best be described as

    (A) a well-organized effort to strip Native Americans of their land

    (B) a bureaucratic plan to resettle and civilize Native Americans based on a false assumption that all Native Americans were farmers

    (C) a well-meaning attempt to rectify the wrongs of United States Indian policy

    (D) a policy of extermination

    (E) a get-rich-quick scheme for United States Indian agents

74. The Census Bureau's report in 1890 that the frontier was "closed" resulted in

    (A) the opening of Oklahoma to white settlement

    (B) concern that there would be nowhere for the "social discontent" to go

    (C) speculation in the remaining open land

    (D) a shift in power from rural areas to cities

    (E) forced removal of Mexican Americans from their lands in New Mexico and Arizona

75. The election of 1928 is significant because

   (A) it demonstrated the anti-Catholic prejudice that had been underground up to that time

   (B) Hoover broke the Democratic Party's hold on the "solid South"

   (C) Smith transformed the Democratic Party from a rural, small town party to an urban party

   (D) it showed a shift in the rural/urban alignment of the parties

   (E) the election repudiated the policies of Harding's "return to normalcy"

76. The primary reason that the TVA was controversial was that it

   (A) used government money to build factories

   (B) moved farmers off their lands

   (C) served as a yardstick to measure the fairness of electricity rates charged by private utilities

   (D) diverted the river through a series of twenty dams

   (E) aided large farmers at the expense of small farmers

77. During his two terms in office, Dwight Eisenhower did all of the following EXCEPT

   (A) break off diplomatic relations with Cuba

   (B) support a successful revolt by the Shah of Iran against Communist-leaning politicians

   (C) send United States troops under NATO into Hungary

   (D) provide economic support to the South Vietnamese under Diem

   (E) support nuclear disarmament

78. The counterculture of the 1960s was characterized by all of the following EXCEPT

   (A) antiwar protests

   (B) a sexual revolution

   (C) the reemergence of the women's movement

   (D) materialism

   (E) distrust of authority

79. The meaning of "black power" can be best characterized as

   (A) a call for separatism

   (B) a demand for equality

   (C) a political slogan with little meaning outside the African-American community

   (D) an appeal to black pride and for black leadership

   (E) a variation on Garvey's black nationalism

80. The major issue that cost George Bush the election in 1992 was

   (A) his relaxed manner of conducting the Presidency

   (B) a backlash over the invasion of Kuwait

   (C) his ineffective domestic war on drugs

   (D) inability to solve the Palestinian problem

   (E) the economy

END OF SECTION I.

If you have time, you may go back and review your answers.

SECTION II
PART A
(Suggested writing time—45 minutes)

> **Directions:** The following question asks you to write a cohesive essay incorporating your interpretation of Documents A through H and your knowledge of the period stated in the question. To earn a high score, you must cite key evidence from the documents and use your outside knowledge of United States history.

1. The rise of corporations transformed the United States in the late nineteenth century. Discuss the changes and determine if the transformations were for the better or for the worse.

   Use the following documents and your knowledge of United States history from 1880 through the turn of the century to construct your essay.

Document A

Source: Attorney for the defendants, Haymarket Riot prosecution, 1886

[The workers] assembled there, gentlemen, under the provision of our Constitution, to exercise the right of free speech, to discuss the eight-hour question, to discuss the situation of the workingmen. They assembled there incidentally to discuss what they deemed outrages at McCormick's [Harvester Company]. No man expected that a bomb would be thrown; no man expected that anyone would be injured at the meeting; but while some of these defendants were there and while this meeting was in peaceful progress, the police, with a devilish design, as we expect to prove, came down that body with their revolvers in their hand and pockets, ready for immediate use, intending to destroy the life of every man that stood upon that market square.

Document B

Source: Edward Bellamy, *Looking Backward: 2000-1887*, 1888

"That is just it," said Dr. Leete; "the organization of labor and the strikes were an effect, merely, of the concentration of capital in greater masses than had ever been known before. Before this concentration began, while as yet commerce and industry were conducted by innumerable petty concerns with small capital, instead of a small number of great concerns with vast capital, the individual workman was relatively important and independent in his relations to the employer. Moreover, when a little capital or a new idea was enough to start a man in business for himself, workingmen were constantly becoming employers and there was no hard and fast line between the two classes. Labor unions were needless then, and general strikes out of the question. But when the era of small concerns with small capital was succeeded by that of the great aggregations of capital, all this was changed. The individual laborer, who had been relatively important to the small employer, was reduced to insignificance and powerlessness over against the great corporation, while at the same time the way upward to the grade of employer was closed to him. Self-defense drove him to union with his fellows. . .

"The records of the period show that the outcry against the concentration of capital was furious. Men believed it threatened society with a form of tyranny more abhorrent than it had ever endured. They believed that the great corporations were preparing for them the yoke of a baser servitude than had ever been imposed on the race, servitude not to men but to soulless machines incapable of any motive but insatiable greed. . .

"[To solve the problem] The industry and commerce of the country; ceasing to be conducted by a set of irresponsible corporations and syndicates of private persons at their caprice and for their profit, were entrusted to a single syndicate representing the people, to be conducted in the common interest for the common profit. . . "

Document C

Source: Andrew Carnegie, "Wealth," 1889

There remains, then, only one mode of using great fortunes; but in this we have the true antidote for the temporary unequal distribution of wealth, the reconciliation of the rich and the poor—a reign of harmony—another ideal, differing, indeed, from that of the Communist in requiring only the further evolution of existing conditions, not the total overthrow of our civilization. It is founded upon the present most intense individualism, and the race is prepared to put it in practice by degrees whenever it pleases. Under its sway we shall have an ideal state, in which the surplus wealth of the few will become, in the best sense, the property of the many, because administered for the common good; and this wealth, passing through the hands of the few, can be made a much more potent force for the elevation of our race than if it had been distributed in small sums to the people themselves. Even the poorest can be made to see this, and to agree that great sums gathered by some of their fellow citizens and spent for public purposes, from which the masses reap the principal benefit, are more valuable to them than if scattered among them through the course of many years in trifling amounts.

Document D

Source: Samuel Gompers, "Letter on Labor in Industrial Society," 1894

You recognize that the industrial forces set in motion by steam and electricity have materially changed the structure of our civilization. You also admit that a system has grown up where the accumulations of the individual have passed from his control into that of representative combinations and trusts, and that the tendency in this direction is on the increase. How, then, can you consistently criticize the workingmen for recognizing that as individuals they can have no influence in deciding what the wages, hours of toil and conditions of employment shall be?

Document E

Source: William Graham Sumner, "The Absurd Effort to Make the World Over," 1894

The movement of the industrial organization . . . has brought out a great demand for men capable of managing great enterprises. Such have been called "captains of industry." The analogy with military leaders suggested by this name is not misleading. The great leaders in the development of the industrial organization need those talents of executive and administrative skill, power to command, courage, and fortitude, which were formerly called for in military affairs and scarcely anywhere else. The industrial army is also as dependent on its captains as a military body is on its generals. One of the worst features of the existing system is that the employees have a constant risk in their employer. If he is not competent to manage the business with success, they suffer with him. Capital also is dependent on the skill of the captain of industry for the certainty and magnitude of its profits. Under these circumstances there has been a great demand for men having the requisite ability for this function. As the organization has advanced, with more impersonal bonds of coherence and wider scope of operations, the value of this functionary has rapidly increased. The possession of the requisite ability is a natural monopoly. Consequently, all the conditions have concurred to give to those who possessed this monopoly excessive and constantly advancing rates or remuneration.

Document F

Source: *Journal of Social Science*, Volume XXXIII, November 1895

. . . [T]he best place to . . carry on any kind of business is where that business is already being done. For that reason we see different kinds of manufacturers grouping themselves together—textiles in one place, metals in another . . . and so on. The reason of this is obvious. In a community where a certain kind of business is carried on, the whole population become, to a certain extent, experts. . .

We must remember, too, that cities . . . have vastly improved within half a century. About fifty years ago neither New York nor Boston had public water, and very few of our cities had either water or gas, and horse railroads had not been thought of. . .

It would seem, then, (1) that for economic reasons a large part of the work of the world must be done in cities, and the people who do that work must live in cities. (2) That almost everything that is best in life can be better had in the city than elsewhere. . .

Document G

Source: Upton Sinclair, *The Jungle*, 1906

Of course Jurgis had made his home a miniature fertilizer mill a minute after entering. The stuff was half an inch deep in his skin—his whole system was full of it, and it would have taken a week not merely of scrubbing, but of vigorous exercise, to get it out of him. As it was, he could be compared with nothing known to men, save the newest discovery of the savants, a substance which emits energy for an unlimited time, without being itself in the least diminished in power. He smelt so that he made all the food at the table taste and set the whole family to vomiting; for himself it was three days before he could keep anything on his stomach—he might wash his hands and use a knife and fork, but were not his mouth and throat filled with poison?

And still Jurgis stuck it out! In spite of splitting headaches he would stagger down to the plant and take up his stand once more and begin to shovel in the blinding clouds of dust. And so at the end of the week he was a fertilizer man for life—he was able to eat again, and though his head never stopped aching, it ceased to be so bad that he could not work.

Document H

Source: John E. Rockefeller, "Random Reminiscences of Men and Events," 1909

I ascribe the success of the Standard Oil Company to its consistent policy of making the volume of its business large through the merit and cheapness of its products. It has spared no expense in utilizing the best superintendents and workmen and paid the best wages. It has not hesitated to sacrifice old machinery and old plants for new and better ones. It has placed its manufactories at the points where they could supply markets at the least expense. It has not only sought markets for its principal products but for all possible by-products, sparing no expense in introducing them to the public in every nook and corner of the world. It has not hesitated to invest millions of dollars in methods for cheapening the gathering and distribution of oils by pipe lines, special cars, tank-steamers, and tank-wagons. It has erected tank stations at railroad centers in every part of the country to cheapen the storage and delivery of oil. It has had faith in American oil and has brought together vast sums of money for the purpose of making it what it is and for holding its market against the competition of Russia and all the countries which are producers of oil and competitors against American products.

SECTION II
PART B AND PART C
(Suggested planning and writing time–70 minutes)
PART B

Directions: You are to answer ONE question from this group. The suggested planning time is 5 minutes with 30 minutes to write. State a thesis, cite relevant evidence, and use logical, clear arguments to support your generalizations.

2. Before 1763, economic issues rather than religious positions determined the development of American colonies. Explore the validity of this statement by discussing three of the following colonies:

   - Virginia

   - Maryland

   - Pennsylvania

   - Massachusetts Bay

   - Carolina

3. How did Britain's victory over France in the 1760s lead to problems with Britain's American colonies?

PART C

Directions: You are to answer ONE question from this group. The suggested planning time is 5 minutes with 30 minutes to write. State a thesis, cite relevant evidence, and use logical, clear arguments to support your generalizations.

4. Reconstruction governments made slow progress in rebuilding the South. Explain the consequences of this fact for Southerners.

5. President Truman was justified in using the atomic bomb against Japan. Evaluate the validity of this statement.

 **END OF TEST**

ANSWERS AND EXPLANATIONS

QUICK-SCORE ANSWERS							
1. C	11. D	21. B	31. C	41. C	51. E	61. A	71. E
2. B	12. B	22. D	32. D	42. D	52. D	62. B	72. D
3. D	13. D	23. B	33. C	43. D	53. D	63. D	73. C
4. A	14. C	24. C	34. E	44. E	54. B	64. B	74. B
5. B	15. B	25. E	35. E	45. E	55. B	65. C	75. D
6. E	16. B	26. B	36. C	46. D	56. B	66. D	76. C
7. B	17. C	27. C	37. D	47. C	57.B	67. E	77. C
8. C	18. A	28. B	38. D	48. D	58. E	68. C	78. D
9. D	19. C	29. A	39. D	49. E	59. C	69. C	79. D
10. B	20. D	30. D	40. C	50. B	60. D	70. D	80. E

EXPLANATION OF ANSWERS

1. **The correct answer is (C).** Mercantilism contributes to a sense of nationalism, choice (A), and can be a result of a strong sense of national identity, but it is an economic policy. A favorable balance of trade, choice (B), for the home country is a desired result of mercantilism. The Navigation Acts, choice (D), and enumerated goods, choice (E), were two ways Great Britain tried to enforce mercantilist policies on the American colonies.

2. **The correct answer is (B).** Under the Articles there was no national court system. Because there was no chief executive, choice (C), there was no unifying force for government policies. Because all thirteen states, rather than a majority, were required to ratify amendments, it was unlikely that small states and large states or Northern states and Southern states would agree on issues, choice (D). Although nine of the thirteen might agree on laws, it was difficult to get the representatives of any nine states to appear for sessions, choice (A). Congress was hampered in its duties because it could not levy taxes; it could only request money from the states or borrow it, which required approval, choice (E).

3. **The correct answer is (D).** The Assumption Bill was part of Hamilton's plan to put the new nation on a strong financial basis. Madison was the primary adversary of assuming all state debts related to the war and of repaying the war bonds at full value because speculators had bought them at deep discounts from the original bondholders, so choice (E) is illogical. Choices (B) and (C) are not true, and Congress declined to consider Hamilton's tariff plan, choice (A).

Test-Taking Strategy

Check the time frame of the question and the answers. Knowing that this question is about the early to mid-nineteenth century will help you eliminate choices (B) and (D).

4. **The correct answer is (A).** This document asked that all rights of U.S. citizens be extended to women, including the right to vote. It resulted from the first women's rights conference at Seneca Falls, New York, in 1848. Choice (B) is the title of Betty Friedan's book of the 1960s that reignited the women's movement. Choice (C) is a famous speech by Sojourner Truth, a former slave, an abolitionist, and a women's rights activist. Choice (D) was the name of Frederick Douglass's newspaper, and choice (E) is the title of Helen Hunt Jackson's book, published in the late nineteenth century, about the abuses of U.S. Indian policy.

Test-Taking Strategy

This is another question where knowing time frame will help you eliminate answer choices.

5. **The correct answer is (B).** The Hudson River School, choice (A), was a style of mostly landscape painting that was influenced by romanticism. Nationalism, choice (C), influenced the choice of subjects of the arts and literature in the United States of the early to mid-nineteenth century. Deism, choice (D), is a belief in a Supreme Being. A religion of nature and a religious movement of the seventeenth and eighteenth centuries, it influenced some of the founders of the new nation, such as Thomas Jefferson. Choice (E) was a literary and artistic movement among African Americans in the 1920s.

6. **The correct answer is (E).** It was not until 1862 that African Americans were allowed to enlist, choice (B). Lincoln had been against black enlistment, fearing that it would drive the border states into the Confederacy, and many whites considered it a "white man's war." Even when they joined, African Americans had to protest to be allowed to fight, choices (A) and (C), and to be paid the same as white soldiers. Only 75 to 100 African Americans became officers, choice (D).

Test-Taking Strategy

Be sure an answer is completely correct before choosing it.

7. **The correct answer is (B).** Choices (A), (C), and (D) are effects of the difficulty of enforcement, not the cause. In an ideal world, laws would be enforced whether the public agreed or not, but in this case, farmers supported the act and had lobbied for it, so choice (E) is at least partly inaccurate.

8. **The correct answer is (C).** Choice (A) is the landmark school
    desegregation case of the 1950s. Choice (B) is the "one man, one
    vote" case of the 1960s. Choice (D) is an affirmative action case
    relating to the use of race as an element in admissions policies in
    higher education. Choice (E) is a landmark interstate commerce
    case relating to serving African Americans.

9. **The correct answer is (D).** Theodore Roosevelt is known as
    the "trust buster." McKinley, choice (B), running on a platform of
    high tariffs and the gold standard, was elected through the efforts
    of Republican party boss Mark Hanna and big business interests.
    Harding's policies of normalcy, choice (E), meant little govern-
    ment regulation of business, high tariffs, and strike breaking.
    Hoover, choice (A), ran as a traditional pro-business Republican.
    Franklin Roosevelt, choice (C), courted business in the first New
    Deal, but he abandoned it in the second phase to build a
    coalition of traditional opponents of big business for the Demo-
    cratic Party.

10. **The correct answer is (B).** Silver, choice (C), as a political
    issue died out with the election of 1896. Choice (D) was the
    philosophy of big business philanthropists, so it is illogical as the
    tool of the president. Choice (E), a belief in the inevitability of
    social inequalities, would seem to contradict trust busting.
    Choice (A) is irrelevant.

11. **The correct answer is (D).** The programs of the first Hundred
    Days were dedicated to relief and recovery by getting people
    back to work and stimulating the economy. Reform programs
    like Social Security came later.

12. **The correct answer is (B).** Choices (A), (B), (C), and (D) are
    all true of Williams's beliefs, but choice (B) challenged the basis
    upon which the commonwealth rested. While his other teachings
    may have offended the Puritan leaders, it was choice (B) that was
    the most dangerous to their authority. Choice (E) is incorrect.

13. **The correct answer is (D).** Choices (B) and (D) are both true,
    but choice (D) puts the Maryland Toleration Act in the larger
    context of colonial history and is, therefore, a better choice.
    Choices (A) and (C) are distractors because although it seems to
    make sense that toleration could apply to either indenture or
    emancipation, think about this time in colonial history. Indenture
    for Africans was just beginning to be transformed into servitude
    for life, so choice (C) is illogical, and Maryland needed more
    workers, not fewer, so making it easier to end a term of inden-
    ture is also illogical. Choice (E) is incorrect.

14. **The correct answer is (C).** Choice (E) is true, but it is of less importance in the larger context than choice (C). In the beginning, native-born women workers lived in supervised boarding-houses, were served healthful meals, and had opportunities in the evening and on Sundays for recreation and to improve themselves. Wages were adequate for the time, and children were not employed. Choice (A) became true of factory owners in general in the late 1830s and 1840s, and choice (B) was also true of that period. Lowell workers organized unions in the 1840s, choice (D), but they were not successful.

15. **The correct answer is (B).** *Plessy* v. *Ferguson* is the post–Civil War (1896) landmark case establishing "separate but equal" facilities for African Americans. *Uncle Tom's Cabin,* choice (A), by Harriet Beecher Stowe, was an antislavery novel that provoked the South with its portrayals of the odious Simon Legree and faithful Uncle Tom. Choice (C) refers to John Brown's raid on the arsenal at Harper's Ferry and his plan to arm a slave insurrection in Virginia. Choice (D) set off the fiercest debate in Congress yet over the admission of slave and free states, and resulted in the Compromise of 1850. Choice (E) was a continual source of ill feeling and occasional violence.

16. **The correct answer is (B).** The Dred Scott decision stated that Congress did not have the power to determine whether a state could be slave or free, thus overturning choices (A) and (D) and upholding choice (C). It also called into question popular sovereignty, choice (E). Choice (B) is the answer and is also untrue because slave codes had already forbidden the teaching of reading and writing to slaves.

17. **The correct answer is (C).** The slightly later American Federation of Labor (AFL) under Samuel Gompers was organized into craft unions. The Knights were organized by industry, and this was one reason for their ultimate collapse, as was choice (D). Another difference between the two unions was the AFL's refusal to accept African Americans, women, and immigrants.

18. **The correct answer is (A).** This is from an article by Carnegie and states what has become known as the Gospel of Wealth. It is not consistent with the thinking of any of the other choices: Theodore Roosevelt, choice (B), who believed in "muscular Christianity"; Bryan, choice (C), who championed the cause of small farmers and silver miners; Douglass, choice (D), who worked for abolition; and Addams, choice (E), who worked for the betterment of poor urban immigrants.

19. **The correct answer is (C).** Also known as the National Labor Relations Act, the Wagner Act guaranteed the right to organize

and bargain collectively. Choice (A) greatly limited union activities. Choice (B) was one of many strikes that failed after World War I. Choice (D) was an attempt to regulate big business but was unsuccessful. Choice (E) failed in its attempt to have the government cash certificates issued to veterans for service in World War I.

20. **The correct answer is (D).** In an effort to curb the "imperial presidency" and regain some of its power, Congress passed this bill giving the president 48 hours to notify Congress after sending combat troops abroad or engaging in military action; if Congress did not agree, the president had 60 days to withdraw the troops. Choice (B) is true; the attorney general and then his top assistant resigned before Nixon was able to find a Justice Department official willing to fire special prosecutor Archibald Cox. However, this was in relation to Watergate, not Vietnam. The United States recognized China during Nixon's administration, so choice (A) is incorrect. Iran-contra, choice (C), occurred during the Reagan administration, and choice (E) occurred during the Bush administration.

Test-Taking Strategy

The chronological shift indicates a new, more difficult set of questions.

21. **The correct answer is (B).** Several of these responses are important and correct, but they do not relate to Connecticut. Choice (A) relates to Virginia, choice (C) to Rhode Island, and choice (D) to Massachusetts. Choice (E) is incorrect.

22. **The correct answer is (D).** Choices (A), (B), (C), and (E) are consistent with a strict constructionist view of the Constitution and a philosophy of limited federal power. Buying new territory stretched Jefferson's idea of the constitutional powers of the president.

23. **The correct answer is (B).** Choice (D) is a good distractor but not the definition of the term. Choice (E) is Stephen Douglas's Freeport Doctrine stated in the Lincoln-Douglas Debates. The Dred Scott decision established the opposite of choice (C), which is incorrect as a definition of popular sovereignty. Choice (A) is a partial restatement of the proposed Wilmot Proviso that would have outlawed slavery in lands ceded from Mexico.

24. **The correct answer is (C).** The novelists Crane, choice (A), and Dreiser, choice (B), were realists. Pulitzer, choice (D), was the influential publisher of the New York *World* that practiced "yellow journalism." Eakins, choice (E), was a painter of the realist school.

25. **The correct answer is (E).** Bulgarians, Hungarians, Romanians, and Poles emigrated after much of their nations were cut up into small tenant farms, choice (A). Choice (B) relates to Austria-Hungary in this period. High tariffs hurt Italian vineyard and

orchard workers, choice (C). Polish Catholics and Russian Jews emigrated because of religious persecution. Choice (E) was a pull factor.

Test-Taking Strategy

The key words are major significance. *What did this election say about the larger context of U.S. history?*

26. **The correct answer is (B).** Choices (A), (D), and (E) were all factors in the campaign, but the election's significance lay in the turn of many voters toward more limited government. Reagan was the first conservative elected President since Calvin Coolidge. Reagan campaigned on a platform of lower taxes, reduced government spending, and a strengthened military. Choice (C) is incorrect.

27. **The correct answer is (C).** Zenger published articles in his newspaper accusing the colonial governor of New York of election fraud, misappropriating public funds, and bribery. According to British libel law, it did not matter if the accusations were true. Zenger was indicted on the charge of seditious libel, but his lawyer argued that truth did matter and won his acquittal. Although British libel laws did not change, this case emboldened colonial newspapers to express opinions unpopular with the government and laid the foundation for freedom of press.

Test-Taking Strategy

Knowing the time frame of the question will help you eliminate two choices.

28. **The correct answer is (B).** Both choices (A) and (D) occurred after the War of 1812, the subject of question 29. Choice (A) refers to the Rush-Bagot Agreement. Choice (C) is partially true of the Treaty of Greenville; the Native Americans had to give up much of their lands in the Old Northwest. Choice (D) refers to the Webster-Ashburton Treaty, and choice (E) to Jay's Treaty.

Test-Taking Strategy

Recognizing the word national *in the question and the time frame of the question will help you eliminate all the answers but choice (A).*

29. **The correct answer is (A).** The Hartford Convention was called by New England Federalists who opposed the War of 1812 because it hurt trade. Choice (B) was an attempt at a colonial alliance to settle boundary disputes and for mutual defense, but it was marred by rivalries among the New England colonies. Choice (C) was called by seven colonies to seek the support of the Iroquois Confederacy but ended with a plan for colonial unity that was rejected by the colonial governments. Choice (D) was called to redress weaknesses in the Articles of Confederation and ended in the call for a convention to organize a new government. Choice (E) is the name of a group organized in 1905 and dedicated to improving the rights of African Americans.

30. **The correct answer is (D).** Choice (E) relates to a legislative tactic used by a minority to prevent the adoption of a measure or procedure by holding the floor and blocking a vote. It is used mostly in the U.S. Senate and has been used to block civil rights legislation. It is incorrect here, as are choices (A), (B), and (C).

31. **The correct answer is (C).** Douglas reluctantly agreed with the decision in Dred Scott, so choice (A) is incorrect. The basis for

the Doctrine was the right of slave owners to the protection of their property, so choice (B) is incorrect. Douglas was a Democrat, so choice (D) is illogical. Douglas built his career on championing popular sovereignty, and the Freeport Doctrine was an effort not to repudiate it, so choice (E) is incorrect.

32. **The correct answer is (D).** Choice (A) is a distractor, because those states were the seat of Copperhead power, opponents of the Civil War, many of whom were Democrats. Although Andrew Johnson was a senator from Tennessee and remained in the Senate after secession, Tennessee seceded, choice (B). Choice (C) is only partially correct. Kansas did not border the Confederacy and remained in the Union, choice (E).

33. **The correct answer is (C).** Choice (E) may confuse you, but large numbers of Mexican immigrants are a twentieth-century phenomenon, beginning during the Mexican Revolution of 1910–1920. Of the total 5.5 million Mexican immigrants between 1820 and 1996, more than 3.3 million immigrated between 1981 and 1996. Austro-Hungarians, choice (B), were the third largest group, with Russians, choice (A), fourth and Canadians, choice (D), eighth.

34. **The correct answer is (E).** The Morrill Act established land-grant colleges dedicated to agriculture and the mechanical arts and paid for by the sale or rental of public lands donated by the federal government. Herefords, choice (A), were hardier cattle; barbed wire, choice (B), enabled cattle ranchers to control the size of their herds and potential problems among themselves and with farmers and sheepherders; and choice (C) ended the need for long cattle drives. Choice (D) drove up the demand for beef.

35. **The correct answer is (E).** Hawaii, choice (A), was annexed at this time but not as a result of the war. The United States purchased Alaska, choice (B), in 1867 from Russia. Panama, choice (C), received its independence from Colombia in 1903 with U.S. help and the United States took control of the Panama Canal, but none of these came as a result of the war. The island of Hispaniola, choice (D), is home to Haiti and the Dominican Republic.

36. **The correct answer is (C).** Choice (A) refers to the economic policy of Mikhail Gorbachev in the Soviet Union, so it is incorrect. It was not until 1993 that Israel and Palestine signed a series of agreements recognizing the Palestinian right to self-rule in the Gaza Strip and parts of the West Bank. Sadat had been one of the signatories to the Accords, so choice (D) is illogical. Choice (E) is irrelevant.

37. The correct answer is (D). Through the power of the purse, colonial legislatures exercised control over taxes and expenditures, choice (A), which limited the authority of the governors, choice (E). Only Pennsylvania had a unicameral legislature, choice (C). Choice (B) was also true.

38. The correct answer is (D). According to the Great or Connecticut Compromise, there would be two legislative houses. In the lower house, each state would have representation based on population whereas in the upper house each state would have two representatives. Choice (A) refers to the compromise about counting slaves as part of the population, and choice (B), to a plan for allotting the same number of representatives for each state. Choice (E) was a plan to base representation on state population.

Test-Taking Strategy

The key words here are under the Articles of Confederation. *Knowing that, you could eliminate all the choices but (D).*

39. The correct answer is (D). Shays' Rebellion protested the high taxes after the Revolutionary War and the practice of confiscation and sale of farms to pay creditors. Choice (A) occurred on the frontier at the beginning of Washington's administration to protest a tax on whiskey. Choice (B) was an uprising by slaves in South Carolina in 1737. Choice (C) was written to protest the Alien and Sedition Acts and asserted the right of states to nullify federal laws. Choice (E) was the name given by Southerners to the high protective tariff of 1828.

40. The correct answer is (C). Choice (A) was a writer and farmer who wrote *Letters from an American Farmer,* which described rural life in the late eighteenth century. Jefferson, choice (B), believed the nation should be one of yeoman farmers. Calhoun, choice (D), championed policies that would aid the agrarian South. Choice (E) is irrelevant.

Test-Taking Strategy

The key words are best be described.

41. The correct answer is (C). There is some truth to both choices (B) and (D), but the most inclusive answer is choice (C). Choice (A) restates the argument that Jefferson made to Washington at the beginning of the French Revolution and with which Washington did not agree. Choice (E) is incorrect.

42. The correct answer is (D). Choices (A), (B), (C), and (D) are all true of the divisions that occurred in the abolitionist movement. The growth of slavery spurred some members to call for more dramatic and militant action. Choice (D) was one of the causes of this increased activity as well as an effect.

Test-Taking Strategy

The key words are most damage.

43. The correct answer is (D). By the end of the war, only about 200 ships a year were able to run the blockade, whereas some 6,000 entered and left Southern ports before the war. The blockade cut off the sale of cotton to Great Britain and France and kept the Confederacy from resupplying. Choices (B), (C), and (E) did damage to the economy but to a far less extent than choice (D), so choice (D) is the best answer. The capture of Richmond, choice (A), did not occur until the end of the war.

44. **The correct answer is (E).** Baker, choice (A), wrote *Follow the Color Line* about racial discrimination. Wells, choice (B), was a journalist and antilynching crusader. Norris was a novelist who wrote *The Octopus* about the railroad industry's hold on farmers. Sinclair, choice (D), wrote *The Jungle* about the meat-packing industry.

Test-Taking Strategy

The key word is first.

45. **The correct answer is (E).** The British and German blockade of Venezuela, choice (A), in an attempt to collect debts for their citizens, was one cause of the Roosevelt Corollary. Choice (C) occurred under Coolidge; the troops had been sent originally under Taft to install a pro-U.S. government and force the Nicaraguans to accept a loan from New York bankers. Choices (B) and (D) are both incorrect.

Test-Taking Strategy

The key word is major.

46. **The correct answer is (D).** Choices (A) and (B) are true, but neither is the most important reason why Prohibition, the "noble experiment," failed; the general public's ignoring of the law rendered it unenforceable. Choice (C) is incorrect because a constitutional amendment takes precedence over a local law. Some Americans may have been embarrassed by the argument, choice (E), but it was a major cause of the ratification of the amendment.

47. **The correct answer is (C).** From Reconstruction until Roosevelt, African Americans had traditionally voted the Republican ticket, the party of Lincoln. Southern small farmers, choice (B), had voted for Hoover in 1928, but returned to the Democratic Party under Roosevelt. Since the late 1800s, immigrants, choice (E), had traditionally voted for Democrats who ran the northern big city political machines, choice (A).

48. **The correct answer is (D).** Choice (A) did not occur until after the Gulf of Tonkin Resolution was passed. Choice (B) is the real reason that the North Vietnamese fired on one or possibly two U.S. destroyers. Choice (C) is the opposite of the true situation; the strongest support for the North Vietnamese was in the countryside. The United States used napalm, so choice (E) is incorrect.

Test-Taking Strategy

The key word is significant.

49. **The correct answer is (E).** Both choices (C) and (E) are true, but choice (E) relates the Stamp Act to the larger picture of the steps leading to the Revolution. Choice (A) is true, but it refers to the Townshend Acts. Choice (B) is true, but it relates to the Sugar Act. Choice (D) was true of the Currency Act.

Test-Taking Strategy

For a not/except *question, ask yourself if the answer is true. If it is, cross it off and go to the next answer.*

50. **The correct answer is (B).** In June 1776, Richard Henry Lee introduced a resolution calling for independence, and while it was debated, a committee worked on the Declaration of Independence. Lee's Resolution was approved by the Continental Congress on July 2, and the Declaration was adopted two days later. George III issued the Proclamation, choice (A), calling on his loyal subjects to oppose rebellion. Choice (C) was issued in response to the Intolerable Acts. Choice (D) listed the basic rights of British subjects and rejected Parliament's right to tax the colonists. Choice (E) was the colonists' attempt to find a peaceful solution to the increasing conflict with Great Britain.

51. **The correct answer is (E).** The XYZ Affair occurred during John Adams's administration when he sent John Marshall, Elbridge Gerry, and Charles Pinckney to France to negotiate disputes following Jay's Treaty. Three French agents demanded money loans and bribes before France would negotiate. Choice (A) opened the Mississippi River to U.S. citizens and gave them the right of deposit at New Orleans. Choice (B) ended British occupation in the Old Northwest and arranged for payment of prewar debts. Washington issued choice (C) to keep the nation out of the European wars. Choice (D) ended the Native American wars in the Old Northwest and forced Native American nations to give up most of their land in the region.

52. **The correct answer is (D).** This was an amendment to a bill authorizing the purchase of land from Mexico. While the House approved the amendment, the Senate did not, but the proviso created bitterness in the South. Choice (A) is incorrect because the question asks about Mexican lands. David Wilmot did not accept the argument stated in choice (B) or he would not have submitted his rider. Choice (C) is incorrect. Choice (E) relates to the Compromise of 1850.

53. **The correct answer is (D).**

54. **The correct answer is (B).** The Open Door Policy recognized the rights of all nations to trade in China. Choice (A) related to the Western Hemisphere and reserved to the United States the right to police chronic malefactor nations. Trade with Asia may have resulted in choice (E), but choice (E) would have been an effect, not a cause. Choices (C) and (D) are unrelated.

55. **The correct answer is (B).** This was written by James Weldon Johnson, an African-American author and statesman who wrote during the Harlem Renaissance. The words "art and literature" are clues. The purpose of Tuskegee was vocational education, so choice (A) is illogical. Choice (D) existed during the period, but it is incorrect. The NAACP focused on gaining rights for African

Americans, so choice (E) is incorrect. Choice (C), founded by Marcus Garvey, sought to foster political and economic as well as cultural independence.

56. **The correct answer is (B).** Nearly 60 percent of African Americans were tenant farmers and domestics. However, the Social Security Act excluded them, so the greatest inequality resulted from the SSA. AAA, choice (A), did not apply to tenant farmers either. Choices (C) and (D) provided jobs, but African Americans were discriminated against in the kinds of jobs they were assigned and in the amount they were paid. NRA codes, choice (E), provided for lower wages for workers in the South, many of whom were African American.

57. **The correct answer is (B).** Choice (C) defines the rights of citizens. Choice (D) prohibits discrimination in employment and created the Equal Employment Opportunity Commission. Choice (E) regulates the collection and dissemination of information about people's credit history, but it does not relate to the question.

58. **The correct answer is (E).** The Massachusetts General School Act of 1647 established this principle.

59. **The correct answer is (C).** When the Spanish discovered that a group of French traders had crossed Texas from Louisiana to the Rio Grande with the idea of opening a trade route to New Mexico, they decided to build settlements to discourage the French from taking Texas. Choices (A) and (D) would be effects of settlement but not causes. This was 150 years after the expeditions for Cibola, so choice (E) is illogical, as is choice (B). There was a vast French territory between the English colonists and Texas.

60. **The correct answer is (D).** Although choices (A) and (C) may seem reasonable, Washington was less concerned about trade than about the future of the nation. Choice (B) might be a possibility, except that in the late 1700s, slavery was not a very divisive issue. Choice (E) is illogical because the United States was an independent nation, not a colony.

61. **The correct answer is (A).** A sound currency, choice (B), was not a primary concern of Jackson's. The Second Bank was the depository of federal money, choice (C), until Jackson had all funds removed and placed in state banks that became known as "pet banks." Choice (E) jumbles these facts and is incorrect. It was Jackson's own policies that put millions of acres of land on the market and sparked land speculation, so choice (D) is incorrect.

Test-Taking Strategy

The key word is principal.
*Which is the most inclusive
answer?*

62. **The correct answer is (B).** All the answer choices figured in the election of 1844, but choice (B) is the most inclusive. Clay made Polk's lack of qualifications an issue, choice (A), but it appealed to only a small segment. Democrats joined the annexation of Texas, choice (D), to demands that the United States take control of all of Oregon, thereby balancing slave and free states, choice (C). Clay agreed to the annexation of Texas only if it could be achieved without a war with Mexico. With the exception of choice (A), the issues revolved around manifest destiny.

63. **The correct answer is (D).** Choices (A), (B), and (E) are incorrect, and they are the opposite of what occurred. Some African Americans did find jobs as laborers or street cleaners, menial jobs that white men did not want. In some areas blacks were not allowed to work in factories. They could not move off their tenant farms until they had paid off their debts. This was the time of lynch law and Jim Crow. The migration north did begin toward the end of 1800s, but it was only a trickle compared to what occurred after 1910.

64. **The correct answer is (B).** As a result of the growth of the spoils system (begun by Andrew Jackson), the rampant corruption in the Grant administration, and the assassination of President Garfield by a disappointed office seeker, Congress passed the Pendleton Act, which authorized the Civil Service Commission and the reform of the system.

Test-Taking Strategy

The key words are primary
reason.

65. **The correct answer is (C).** Choices (A), (C), and (D) are true, but choice (D) is an effect of choice (C), and choice (A) had been true for a long time before 1910. Choice (B) refers to a program in World War II to bring Mexicans to the United States for jobs as farm workers, not in defense plants. Choice (E) is incorrect.

66. **The correct answer is (D).** The movie by D. W. Griffith played on all the stereotypes and myths of Reconstruction and was picketed by the NAACP for its pro-Ku Klux Klan message. Choice (A) was the first talkie and showed Al Jolson in blackface as a minstrel, but neither it nor choice (B), with its stereotypes of enslaved African Americans, was as rabidly racist. Choice (C) is a later film about the Scopes trial and the teaching of evolution, and choice (E) is the title of a book by Jack Kerouac of the 1950s Beat Generation.

67. **The correct answer is (E).** Through lend-lease, Roosevelt was able to lend, sell, lease, and transfer to the Allies more than $50 billion in food, machinery, and supplies. The program continued through the war. Choice (A) was a Roosevelt policy of the 1930s

to improve relations with Latin America; among other things, he agreed to a resolution that "no state has the right to intervene in the internal affairs of another." Choice (C) was one of several laws that banned the sale or transfer of arms to belligerents. Choice (D) was Theodore Roosevelt's addition to the Monroe Doctrine and said that the United States could intervene to punish nations that were chronic wrongdoers.

68. **The correct answer is (C).** The summer of 1964 in the South saw the murder of three white voter registration workers from the North, firebombings, and mob violence, but African Americans registered in record numbers. Choice (A) was the goal of the Freedom Rides of 1961. Choice (D) refers to sit-ins at lunch counters. Choices (B) and (E) are incorrect.

69. **The correct answer is (C).** When William Penn established Pennsylvania, he insisted that Native Americans be paid for their land. This did not continue after Penn returned to England. With the exception of Rhode Island, settlers simply assumed that since the Native Americans did not have a settled way of life, the colonists could take any uninhabited land.

Test-Taking Strategy

The key words are major reason.

70. **The correct answer is (D).** Poor quality, rocky soil and a cold climate did not lend themselves to large-scale cotton, tobacco, rice, or indigo agriculture. Choices (A), (B), and (C) were true, but none was the major reason why slavery did not develop in New England. Choice (E) is illogical.

Test-Taking Strategy

Recognizing the time frame for the question will eliminate choices (B) and (D).

71. **The correct answer is (E).** Choice (A) is the right of people to determine their own government and to be free of foreign powers. Choice (B) is a term coined in the 1960s to describe the federal government's policy toward African Americans. Choice (C) is the system of government in which legislative, executive, and judicial powers are divided among three separate branches of government. Choice (D) were areas in China during the late 1800s where trade was controlled by a particular foreign power.

72. **The correct answer is (D).** Vesey had bought his freedom, so the city retaliated against free blacks. Choice (A) refers to the Nat Turner Rebellion. Choice (B) makes reference to the Stono Uprising near Charleston in 1739. Choice (C) is the Gabriel Prosser rebellion, and choice (E) is incorrect. Slave revolts continued until the Civil War.

Test-Taking Strategy

The key words are best be described.

73. **The correct answer is (C).** The Dawes Act was meant to end the extermination policy of the military, so choice (D) is incorrect. Some Indian agents turned the provisions of the act into choices (A) and (E), but that was not the intent of the law. Choices (B) and (C) are both true, but choice (C) is the more

inclusive answer of the two and reflects the concerns of the reformers who pushed for the law.

74. **The correct answer is (B).** Oklahoma was opened to settlement in 1889, so choice (A) is incorrect. The shift, choice (D), had occurred as a result of the transfer in the U.S.'s economic base from farming to industry. Choices (C) and (E) are incorrect.

75. **The correct answer is (D).** Choices (B), (C), and (D) are all true, but choice (D) is the most inclusive of the three answers, so it is the best choice. Anti-Catholic prejudice had been apparent since the mid-1800s with nativist activities aimed at Catholic immigrants, so choice (A) is incorrect. Choice (E) is also incorrect.

Test-Taking Strategy

The key word is significant.

76. **The correct answer is (C).** Choice (A) is incorrect. Farmers were moved off land, but it was marginally productive, so choice (B) was not controversial, nor was choice (D). The TVA did benefit large farmers to a greater degree than small farmers, many of whom were African American, but that did not cause much controversy. The use of TVA rates to measure the fairness of utility prices nationwide did cause controversy because private utility owners claimed that the TVA was tax-supported and paid no corporate income tax, so it could afford to charge less.

77. **The correct answer is (C).** Any intervention by the United States into Hungary was considered dangerous and impractical.

78. **The correct answer is (D).** Hippies dropped out and started communes. Although this was not a major movement, it was emblematic of a rejection of the values of the previous postwar generation that saw a dramatic rise in their standard of living. It went hand in hand with a distrust of authority, choice (E). Choice (C) may have confused you with the word *reemergence*, but after World War II, women retreated to the home and the ideal family became father as the breadwinner and mother as the homemaker. Betty Friedan's *The Feminine Mystique*, published in 1963, challenged this ideal.

Test-Taking Strategy

The key words are best characterized.

79. **The correct answer is (D).** Choices (A), (B), (D), and (E) are all true, but choice (D) is the most inclusive response. Choice (C) is incorrect. Black power, which generated anger and fear in parts of the white community, was a call to action to improve the conditions of African Americans.

Test-Taking Strategy

The key word is major.

80. **The correct answer is (E).** Choice (A) made Bush popular, so choice (A) is incorrect, as is choice (B). Choices (C) and (D) are both true, but Bush was not the only president to have difficulty solving these problems. It was the rapidly building deficit, slowing economic growth, and Bush's reneging on his promise of "no new taxes" that cost him supporters.

SUGGESTIONS FOR THE DOCUMENT-BASED QUESTION, PART A

Study Strategy

Revise your essay using points from this list that will strengthen it.

Be sure that you described changes and explained whether each was an improvement or a change for the worse. Notice that the articles are arranged in chronological order, but you do not need to write about them in that order. You should incorporate references to the documents into your essay in the order in which they best support your thesis. The following are points about Documents A through H that you might have included in your essay. Consider them as you complete your self-evaluation. Use the *Self-Evaluation Rubric* on pp. 58–59 to score your essays.

Document A

Since Document A is part of an opening statement by an attorney defending eight anarchists on trial for conspiracy to commit murder, some bias is to be expected. The basic facts are accurate: the day before the riot, four workers had been killed; the anarchists were protesting the killing; and the identity of the bomber was never uncovered.

The document highlights problems that developed as a result of the industrial system. In spite of a generally healthy economy, few workers could count on full-time employment; most were underpaid. The Knights of Labor was organized in 1869 to fight for better working conditions. The Haymarket Riot caused the decline and end of the union, but later unions, such as the American Federation of Labor, continued the fight. Strikes became common, and the upper and middle classes began to fear labor. Federal and state governments sided with business.

This and other documents point out that the new industrial order came with a high human cost. The benefits were unevenly distributed. While the U.S. economy gained overall, the gulf between the rich and poor grew wider. Ask yourself what changes this document reflects and whether those changes were for the better or for the worse. For whom were the changes better, and for whom were they worse?

Document B

Looking Backward is a utopian novel that describes a new social and economic order through the eyes of a young Boston man who has been placed in a hypnotic sleep. In Document B, he has just awakened in the year 2000 and is beginning to learn how the United States has changed. In contrast to the misery of the slums and the inequalities of the economic system of the 1880s, a new system of democratic capitalism has evolved. The collective organization has

Test-Taking Strategy

An opinion is acceptable as long as you support it with evidence.

eliminated crime, poverty, and welfare. People, especially workers, are no longer victimized by an evil system.

Tapping the feelings of mounting resentment against the excesses of wealth and big business, the ideas expressed in *Looking Backward* became immensely popular. Supporters founded Bellamy Clubs and the Nationalist Party, which hoped to institute Bellamy's concept of the future. Nationalists called for redistribution of wealth, civil service reform, and nationalization of utilities and the rail system. Here again is a negative response to industrialism, this time, by the middle class. What transformations does Bellamy's book predict? How would you evaluate those changes?

Document C

Review Strategy

Did you remember question 18 and the Gospel of Social Wealth?

Document C, from an essay by Andrew Carnegie, presents the author's thoughts about the responsibilities of the rich. In this selection, you see the industrialist's desire to understand and justify through action the immense wealth he has made. He believes strongly in the conditions that permit such huge fortunes to be made, but he also feels a great social responsibility. He sees it as his duty to spend his money for the public good. During his lifetime, he donated much of his wealth, over $60 million, for the establishment of libraries. More than any other person, he was responsible for the growth of free public libraries in this country.

Carnegie favored taxing huge fortunes. He felt that a high tax would encourage the wealthy to donate more generously, and he believed that it was disgraceful for an individual to die very rich. How does Carnegie's philosophy represent a difference from that of many other industrialists of the post–Civil War period? How did the steel tycoon's actions transform society? What, if any, implications do you see for the present?

Document D

Document D is an excerpt from a letter to Peter Grosscup, a federal judge who issued an injunction against the American Railway Union and Eugene V. Debs to prevent them from interfering with interstate commerce and the transportation of mail during a strike against the Pullman Company. Comparing unions to big business corporations and trusts, Gompers writes of the great social need for union organization. Gompers founded the American Federation of Labor as labor's answer to the corporation: a consolidated organization for controlling resources (in this case, labor) and competition (in this case, jobs). He presents this to the judge as a logical defense for union action against the Pullman Company.

Gompers, pragmatic and conservative, accepted capitalism and the wage system. He wanted higher wages, shorter workdays, improved safety, and better benefits. Through bargaining, strikes, and boycotts, he worked to win better conditions for skilled labor but not for unskilled workers. However, labor did not organize itself as systematically as the tycoons did. In fact, many workers regarded union activities as alien, subversive, and un-American. What does the lack of enthusiasm for union membership during this period indicate? In spite of that, how did the conditions of workers change?

Study Strategy

When you review Chapter 5 through 10, be sure to think about how this information can help you answer the essay questions.

Document E

Document E justifies the great wealth of the industrial tycoons of the Gilded Age. Sumner, an unabashed apologist for the status quo, argues that the law of supply and demand applies to the wealth commanded by leaders of corporations. Sumner's arguments set forth the adaptation of Darwinian concepts of natural selection to the social and economic system of the United States. Competition was natural and had to proceed without any restraints, including govern-ment regulation. Industrialists were simply products of natural selection.

Understandably, Sumner's concept of Social Darwinism was popular among businessmen, who cheered their own survival in the wilds of the business world. The same businessmen, however, worked hard to eliminate the very competition that they praised. Social Darwinism defended the status quo. How valid is the theory of Social Darwinism? How did it work against change? How might people argue against it?

Document F

Document F, taken from a magazine article written by a professor, argues for the importance of cities. As the document suggests, manufacturing played an important role in the growth of U.S. cities in the nineteenth century. Cities in the 1890s offered a population of workers convenient to factories, amenities not available in the 1850s, and homes to new immigrants.

The growth of cities created great changes in the society of the United States. Consider what changes resulted from larger cities. What about the negatives—noise, dirt, overcrowding, crime, corrup-tion? What reformers and reforms did urban conditions spawn? Were they always for the good? How did who you were influence whether you considered the reformers agents of good or bad change?

Document G

Document G, an excerpt from *The Jungle,* describes the horrible conditions the novel's main character experiences as he tries to make a living in the meat-packing industry. The environment of the stockyards was so shocking to readers that the public rallied to support pure food legislation then pending in Congress. The Meat Inspection Law and the Pure Food Act resulted.

Interestingly, Sinclair wrote to rally support for the laborers in the meat-packing plants, but readers became more upset about what they learned was in the products they ate. What changes did this book create? What does the success of this book say about the power of literature?

Document H

In Document H, Rockefeller attempts to justify his giant corporation, Standard Oil. Here he explains the organization of the industry that created the greatest trust in modern times.

While Rockefeller accumulated the largest fortune of his era, he also gave more to charitable causes than any other person. How did petroleum transform U.S. industry and transportation? How did petroleum products influence society? Why did critics disapprove of his business methods?

Other points to consider:

- Specific reforms and reformers

- Agriculture

- Labor activities

- Regulation or nonregulation by government, including court decisions

- Actions of industry

- Individual industrialists

SUGGESTIONS FOR FREE RESPONSE ESSAYS, PART B

ESSAY 2

Study Strategy

Be sure to complete the "Self-Evaluation Rubric" for each essay.

You might have chosen the following points to support your arguments about whether religious or economic issues drove the creation of any three of the five colonies listed. Consider these points as you complete your self-evaluation.

Massachusetts Bay Colony

- Puritans who were escaping from religious persecution in England founded the colony in 1630.

- Ministers had less authority than in the Anglican Church, although the colony was a theocracy for many years.

- The colony had begun as a joint-stock company.

- The first groups brought large supplies of food, clothing, and tools. The first settlers were skilled craftworkers, such as carpenters, masons, shipbuilders, and blacksmiths. There were also gentlemen who had graduated from Cambridge and Oxford.

- Within 10 years, some 20,000 people had migrated from England.

- The colony was built on a thriving business in shipbuilding and commerce.

Virginia

- In 1607, Jamestown was founded on the James River by the Virginia Company, a joint-stock company.

- The first settlers were gentlemen who did not work but searched for gold and would have starved had it not been for the Native Americans.

- Captain John Smith took over leadership and established rules that forced everyone to work in order to eat.

- In 1612, through the assistance of the Native Americans, colonists found a cash crop in tobacco, which was just beginning to be popular in Europe.

- By 1619, the colony had established a firm financial ground, had a growing population based on agriculture and trade, had received the right to self-government, and had accepted its first "shipment" of Africans.

Maryland

- The English king gave the land to George Calvert, Lord Baltimore, a Roman Catholic, who wanted to build a haven for Roman Catholics.

- As more Protestants settled in the colony, they attempted to take over the government from the Calverts. To forestall a crisis, the Toleration Act of 1649 was passed, granting religious freedom to all Christians.

- Tobacco became the leading cash crop, and slavery was introduced.

Pennsylvania

- In 1681, King Charles II gave land to William Penn, a Quaker, in payment of a debt to Penn's father.

- Penn set up the colony as a "Holy Experiment" and invited not only English settlers but also Dutch, French, and Germans to settle and live in peace.

- Penn provided free land grants to those who would build permanent homes in the colony.

- Slavery did not develop because many of the colonists were Quakers, who did not approve of slavery.

- The Quakers felt that all people were equal; therefore, the Native Americans were paid for their land, although this did not last long.

- Penn bought an additional land grant to give Pennsylvania a coastline, adding Delaware to the colony. Tobacco cultivation and slavery developed there.

Carolina

- The English king gave the area that became North and South Carolina to eight of his friends in 1663.

- Their goal was to make money.

- They wanted to set up manors similar to those in England and have people work for them, but colonists would not settle there under those circumstances.

- The proprietors then decided to give land to anyone who would live on it and bring in workers. Slavery was introduced.

- The area that is North Carolina developed plantations similar to those in Virginia.

- The area that is today South Carolina, with a warmer climate and a good seaport (Charleston), cultivated rice and indigo as cash crops.

ESSAY 3

Study Strategy

Revise each essay using suggested points from the list that will strengthen it.

You might have chosen the following points about how the British victory over the French in 1760 led to problems with its colonies. Consider them as you complete your self-evaluation.

- The Proclamation of 1763 forbid the colonists to settle beyond the Appalachian Mountains because of conflicts with Native Americans. This angered the colonists.

- Britain passed the Quartering Act, which required colonists to provide lodging for British soldiers.

- Britain imposed a series of taxes on the colonists to pay for its war debt: the Sugar Act, 1764; the Stamp Act, 1765; and the Townshend Acts, 1767.

- The addition of the taxes led to the cry of "no taxation without representation." This, claimed the colonists, was a fundamental right contained in the British Magna Carta.

- Opposed to this was Parliament's claim of virtual representation.

- The enforcement of the tax laws led to "writs of assistance," which allowed British agents to inspect cargo without giving a reason, another violation of British law.

- The colonists protested these new laws through "nonimportation agreements," pacts among groups of colonists to boycott the purchase of goods from British merchants.

SUGGESTIONS FOR FREE RESPONSE ESSAYS, PART C

ESSAY 4

Study Strategy

Be sure to complete the "Self-Evaluation Rubric" for each essay.

You might have chosen to discuss in your essay the following points about the causes and the consequences of the slow rebuilding of the South. Consider them as you complete your self-evaluation.

Causes

- The Radical Republicans imposed laws that were harsher than President Johnson's.

- The South lay in ruins after the war: lack of industry, lack of a functioning rail system, high inflation, and high death rate among men during the war. With the end of slavery came the end of a cheap, enforced labor pool.

- Government corruption—carpetbaggers and scalawags—was widespread.

- The South remained an agrarian society.

Consequences

- Southern taxes prior to the Civil War were not very high. After the war, taxes were increased greatly to pay for Reconstruction. This took resources out of the private sector and caused great resentment among white Southerners.

- Early in Reconstruction, some industry developed in the South, such as steel mills around Birmingham, Alabama, but manufacturing did not expand.

- In an effort to maintain a cheap labor supply, Southern landholders developed a system of tenant farming and sharecropping.

- To keep African Americans from exercising their rights, Southern states passed voting restrictions, such as poll taxes and literacy tests.

- Antiblack terrorist organizations and legislated segregation developed, as seen in Jim Crow laws and *Plessy* v. *Ferguson.*

ESSAY 5

Study Strategy

Check Chapters 5 through 10 to review content you are not sure about.

The following are some points about Truman's justification for the use of the atomic bomb that you might have included in your essay. Consider them as you complete your self-evaluation.

- Roosevelt told Truman little about the plans for the conduct of the war.

- Experts projected over a million Allied casualities as a result of an invasion of the Japanese islands.

- Japanese military and civilian casualities would be very high as well.

- Kamikaze fighters were inflicting heavy damage on Allied ships and personnel.

- Despite mounting losses, the Japanese leaders continued to tell their citizens to expect a great victory.

- The fire bombing of Japan was causing considerable civilian losses.

- Through the Soviets, Japan indicated that it would agree to an end to the war but not unconditional surrender.

- The Potsdam Declaration warned the Japanese of their total destruction if they did not surrender. The Suzuki government accepted it internally, but the military rejected it.

SELF-EVALUATION RUBRIC FOR THE ADVANCED PLACEMENT ESSAYS

	8–9	5–7	2–4	0–1
Overall Impression	Demonstrates excellent understanding of U.S. history and outstanding writing; thorough and effective; incisive	Demonstrates good understanding of U.S. history and good writing competence	Reveals simplistic or incomplete thinking and/or immature understanding of U.S. history; fails to respond adequately to the question; little or no analysis	Very little or no understanding of U.S. history; unacceptably brief; fails to respond to the question; little clarity
Understanding of U.S. History	Scholarly; excellent understanding of the question; effective and incisive; in-depth critical analysis; includes many apt, specific references; acknowledges opposing views	Mostly historically accurate; good understanding of the question; often perceptive; includes specific references and critical analysis	Some historical inaccuracies; superficial understanding and treatment of the question; some misreading of documents and lack of historical evidence; mechanical; overgeneralized	Serious historical errors; extensive misreadings and little supporting evidence; completely off the topic
Development	Original, unique and/or intriguing thesis; excellent use of documents and historical knowledge; thoroughly developed; conclusion shows applicability of thesis to other situations	Adequate thesis; satisfactory use of documents and/or historical knowledge; competent development; acceptable conclusion	Inadequate, irrelevant or illogical thesis; little use of documents and/or historical knowledge; some development; unsatisfactory, inapplicable, or nonexistent conclusion	Lacking both thesis and conclusion; little or no use of historical documents or knowledge; no distinguishable development
Organization/Conventions of English	Meticulously and thoroughly organized; coherent and unified; virtually error free	Reasonably organized; mostly coherent and unified; some errors	Somewhat organized; some incoherence and lack of unity; some major errors	Little or no organization; incoherent and void of unity; extremely flawed

Rate yourself in each of the categories below. Enter the numbers on the lines below. Be as honest as possible so you will know what areas need work. Then calculate the average of the four numbers to determine your final score. It is difficult to score yourself objectively, so you may wish to ask a respected friend or teacher to assess your essays for a more accurate reflection of their strengths and weaknesses. On the AP test itself, a reader will rate your essays on a scale of 0 to 9, with 9 being the highest.

Each category is rated 9 (high) to 0 (incompetent).

DBQ

SELF-EVALUATION

Overall Impression   _____

Understanding of U.S. History   _____

Development   _____

Organization/Conventions
  of English   _____

TOTAL   _____

    Divide by 4 for final score.   _____

DBQ

OBJECTIVE EVALUATION

Overall Impression   _____

Understanding of U.S. History   _____

Development   _____

Organization/Conventions
  of English   _____

TOTAL   _____

    Divide by 4 for final score.   _____

FREE RESPONSE 1

SELF-EVALUATION

Overall Impression   _____

Understanding of U.S. History   _____

Development   _____

Organization/Conventions
  of English   _____

TOTAL   _____

    Divide by 4 for final score.   _____

FREE RESPONSE 1

OBJECTIVE EVALUATION

Overall Impression   _____

Understanding of U.S. History   _____

Development   _____

Organization/Conventions
  of English   _____

TOTAL   _____

    Divide by 4 for final score.   _____

FREE RESPONSE 2

SELF-EVALUATION

Overall Impression   _____

Understanding of U.S. History   _____

Development   _____

Organization/Conventions
  of English   _____

TOTAL   _____

    Divide by 4 for final score.   _____

FREE RESPONSE 2

OBJECTIVE EVALUATION

Overall Impression   _____

Understanding of U.S. History   _____

Development   _____

Organization/Conventions
  of English   _____

TOTAL   _____

    Divide by 4 for final score.   _____

Chapter 1

ANSWERING THE MULTIPLE-CHOICE QUESTIONS

Study Strategy

Check the "Practice Plan for Studying for the AP U.S. History Test," pp. 9–12.

This chapter provides some basic information about Section I of the AP U.S. History Test as well as suggestions for developing a strategy for attacking the multiple-choice portion of the test. You have answered hundreds, probably thousands, of multiple-choice items during your time in school. The multiple-choice questions on the AP U.S. History Test are not that different, and like other tests, if you have studied and know some test-taking techniques, you can do well.

PRACTICE PLAN

Use the *Diagnostic Test* as a tool to improve your objective test-taking skills. Use the techniques explained in this chapter to practice answering the questions. Then correct your responses with the *Quick-Score Answers* provided for the test. If you do not understand why an answer is correct, refer to the explanations given after the *Quick-Score Answers*. It is generally a good idea to read the explanations to all the questions because you may find ideas or tips that will help you better analyze the answers to questions in the next *Practice Test* you take. The answers often have additional information about the topic that could come in handy to answer a future question.

After you have finished reviewing all the answers, ask yourself what your weak areas are and what you can do to improve, not just in test-taking techniques but in your knowledge of particular historical eras. Are there some periods that you need to spend time brushing up on? Review the strategies in this chapter and Chapters 5 through 10, which offer a brief review of U.S. history. Then try taking *Practice Test 1*.

BASIC INFORMATION

Test-Taking Strategy

Be sure to take a watch with you so you can pace yourself. Don't use the alarm.

1. Section I consists of 80 multiple-choice questions. There are five possible answer choices for each question.

2. You will have 55 minutes to answer the questions in Section I.

3. You will receive one point for each correct answer that you give. Points are not deducted for questions that you leave blank. If you

answer incorrectly, a quarter of a point is subtracted. This is the guessing penalty.

4. Section I counts for 50 percent of your final composite score.

5. Although the test covers U.S. history from exploration to the present, the majority of the questions will be taken from the nineteenth century:

   - 16 percent from the explorers through 1789

   - 50 percent from 1790 to 1914

   - 33 percent from 1915 to the present.

   Most of the twentieth-century questions will be pre-1975.

6. The College Board further breaks down the categories into:

   - 35 percent on public policy and political institutions and behavior

   - 35 percent on social change

   - 15 percent on diplomacy and international relations

   - 10 percent on economic developments

   - 5 percent on cultural and intellectual developments.

   Because history in reality does not break down into neat categories, you will find that any given question may span several categories.

7. The College Board states that the multiple-choice section is meant to test "factual knowledge, breadth of preparation, and knowledge-based analytical skills."

8. There are four question types: graphics (maps, cartoons, tables, graphs, and pictures), short quotations, and either statements to complete or questions to answer. The majority of items will be of the basic statement or question type. The graphics questions are straightforward read-and-interpret questions. Occasionally, you may find an additional question related to the graphic that asks for an answer that requires outside knowledge.

9. The College Board states that questions in the beginning of the test are easier and become more difficult as you progress through the test.

10. The questions are not randomly ordered. They are clustered in groups of six to twelve questions that go from the exploration through the twentieth century. That is, for every six to twelve questions, you will notice a progression from the colonial to the mid- to late-twentieth century, and then the questions will jump back to the colonial period.

11. You need to answer approximately 60 percent of the multiple-choice questions correctly (forty-eight) and do reasonably well on the essays to get at least a 3.

It is important to remember these last three facts. They mean (1) that you should try to answer as many of the questions at the beginning of the test as possible, (2) that you can use this knowledge of time frame to help you answer questions, and (3) that you do not have to answer all the questions.

ATTACKING THE QUESTIONS: PRACTICAL ADVICE

When you take the AP exam, you will want to have every advantage possible. Of course, the ideal is to know the correct answer as soon as you read the question and answer choices, but that does not always happen. Here are some methods to help you score well.

1. Read the question carefully. Circle or underline key words and phrases. You will find word prompts such as: *significant; direct result of, consequence of; true, correct; most characteristic of, best known for, best describes; primarily, primary reason.* These are qualifiers or descriptors that supply clues as to what you should be looking for in the answer choices.

   A word like *significant* means you should be looking for why something is important in the larger context of U.S. history. Words like *best describes* or *most characteristic of* are asking you to analyze the information and come up with an opinion based on facts. In both instances, one or more of the answer choices may be correct; you need to look for the one that is most inclusive, giving the broadest view of the subject.

2. Knowing that the questions are in chronological order can help you to eliminate answers that do not make sense for the time period. For example, identifying the Wilmot Proviso as having happened in the first half of the nineteenth century can help you eliminate any answers that refer to any other period.

3. Most of the questions are straightforward, but there are some *not/except* or reverse order questions. For these questions, read each answer and ask yourself if it is true about the subject of the question. If it is, cross it out and go to the next answer. You are looking for the choice that is **not** true.

4. One technique that is especially helpful is educated guessing. Use this strategy when you do not immediately know the correct answer.

   • Ignore answers that are absolutely wrong.

   • Eliminate choices in which part of the answer is incorrect.

40% Questions = 1790-1914

- Discard choices that are illogical or unrelated to the subject.

- Check the time period of the question and of the answer choices. Discard any responses that don't fit.

- Check the key words in the question again.

- Revisit remaining answers to discover which seems more correct.

- Choose the answer that feels right. Trust yourself. Your subconscious will usually guide you to the correct choice. Do not argue with yourself.

You are probably thinking about the quarter-point deduction for an incorrect answer, and you are wondering if taking a chance is worth the possible point loss. Recognize that if you use this strategy, your chances of scoring higher are excellent. You are not randomly guessing, but making an educated guess. You will have to answer four questions wrong to lose a single point. If you have an idea about which choice is correct, act on it. Even the College Board suggests you guess as long as you can eliminate some answer choices as wrong.

PRACTICING

Study Strategy

Check the "Practice Plan for Studying for the AP U.S. History Test," pp. 9–12.

Study Strategy

Read all the explanations. The reasoning involved and the additional historical information may help with later questions.

Read and answer *Practice Set 1* on the next page. Jot down your answers to the questions in the margin or on a separate sheet of paper. If you do not understand a question, you may check the explanation immediately. You may refer to the answers after each question, or you may wish to score the entire set at one time. Either is acceptable.

Follow the same procedure with *Practice Sets 2* and *3*. You might want to complete *Practice Set 2* and correct the answers before you do *Practice Set 3*. That way you will have another chance to work on any specific areas of weakness.

PRACTICE SET 1

1. The significance of the Massachusetts Bay Company was

   (A) its charter as a joint-stock company

   (B) its establishment of a flourishing colony

   (C) its transformation from a trading company into a commonwealth

   (D) its limitation on the number of men who could serve in the General Court

   (E) its merger with Plymouth Colony in 1691

2. The British reaction to the Boston Tea Party involved all of the following, EXCEPT

   (A) passage of the Massachusetts Bay Regulating Act

   (B) Edmund Burke's warning against blaming all Americans for the acts of some

   (C) the Boston Massacre

   (D) passage of the Boston Port Act

   (E) suspension of the Massachusetts legislature

3. *Marbury* v. *Madison* established

   (A) the scope of presidential war powers

   (B) the principle of judicial review

   (C) the principle of implied powers in the Constitution

   (D) Congress's right to regulate interstate commerce

   (E) the principle of separate but equal

4. Andrew Jackson's intention in issuing the Specie Circular was

   (A) to halt land speculation and inflation

   (B) to destroy the Second Bank of the United States

   (C) to shift the blame for the Panic of 1837 to Nicholas Biddle

   (D) to ensure that the federal government withdrew its deposits from state banks

   (E) to remove government controls over speculation and inflation

5. "The autumn of 1854 witnessed the erection of the first log-huts . . . by a few families of New England settlers. During the year 1855 its population increased rapidly, chiefly by the arrival of emigrants from the Northern States. Its log-hut existence gave way to a more advanced stage, . . . and the growing prosperity . . . early began to excite the jealousy of the abettors of slavery. Viewed as the stronghold of the Free-state party, it was made the point of attack . . ."

   The description above was most probably written about

   (A) the settling of Missouri

   (B) the settling on the frontier of Irish laborers who had left New England mill towns

   (C) the fight over the admission of Kansas as free or slave state

   (D) a settlement of New Englanders in the South

   (E) a settlement of Republicans in the South

6. Which of the following was true of the Emancipation Proclamation of 1863?

    (A) It immediately freed slaves in Southern states or parts of Southern states under Union occupation.

    (B) It freed slaves in Southern states still at war with the Union on January 1, 1864.

    (C) It freed slaves only in the border states.

    (D) It guaranteed freedom for slaves who escaped into the Union lines.

    (E) It freed all enslaved blacks when the war ended.

7. The National Origins Act of 1924 can best be described as

    (A) a necessary stopgap measure after World War I to control limitless immigration

    (B) an effort to remedy the Gentlemen's Agreement of 1907 between Theodore Roosevelt and Japan

    (C) having been passed in response to Sacco and Vanzetti

    (D) discriminatory against all those who did not come from Northern or Western Europe

    (E) an effort to equalize the flow of immigrants from all countries

EXPLANATION OF ANSWERS FOR PRACTICE SET 1

QUICK-SCORE ANSWERS	
1. C	5. C
2. C	6. B
3. B	7. D
4. A	

1. **The correct answer is (C).** The key word here is *significance.* When you see this word, ask yourself what is the significance of this event or person to the development of U.S. history. Massachusetts is not particularly significant in terms of choices (A) and (B) because the Virginia Company was also a joint-stock company, and for the most part, all the English colonies flourished except for Plymouth, which did merge with Massachusetts Bay, choice (E). But keep looking because although important, it is not particularly significant in a larger sense. That leaves choices (C) and (D). Considering the development of the colonies, would limiting participation in government be significant, or its opposite? The transformation of Massachusetts Bay from a trading company into a commonwealth made it the first self-governing political unit in what would become the United States.

2. **The correct answer is (C).** If you did not remember that the Boston Massacre preceded the Tea Party, you could try eliminating answers. The British reacted to the Tea Party by passing the Coercive Acts, called by the colonists the Intolerable Acts. Choice (A), also known as the Massachusetts Government Act, and choices (D) and (E) are elements of those laws. The Boston Tea Party caused some of the colonists' supporters in Parliament to speak out against them, but in so doing, Edmund Burke also warned his fellow Englishmen about the dangers ahead if they pursued war with the colonies, choice (B).

3. **The correct answer is (B).** If you did not know the answer, you could eliminate at least one answer, choice (E). Madison served as both secretary of state and president before cases began to come to the Supreme Court about the rights of African Americans, the most logical topic for a "separate but equal" court case.

4. **The correct answer is (A).** All these answers have some information relevant to Andrew Jackson's terms in office, so you need to read each one carefully. Jackson did set out to destroy the Second Bank, choice (B), of which Nicholas Biddle was president, first by vetoing the renewal of its charter and then by

Review Strategy

This is a not/except question. Ask yourself if each answer is a correct response to the question. If it is, cross it out and move on to the next answer.

removing federal deposits from it. There was a Panic of 1837, but Martin Van Buren was president by then, choice (C). Jackson had the federal government withdraw its money not from state banks but from the national bank, choice (D); he then had the money deposited in state banks, known as "pet banks." Jackson's intent in destroying the Second Bank was to make the federal government less powerful. He unwittingly accomplished choice (E) and set the groundwork for the Panic of 1837. His intention, however, had been to halt land speculation and inflation, choice (A), by requiring that public land be paid for in gold or silver.

5. **The correct answer is (C).** There are several clues in the reading: the years *1854* and *1855, New England, emigrants from Northern States, abettors of slavery,* and *Free-state party.* They all point to Kansas and the fight between the proslavery and antislavery forces who moved into Kansas to settle it before the territory was ready to request statehood. It might help you to know for other questions that the Emigrant Aid Society, an abolitionist organization in the North, subsidized antislavery settlers. The town being described is Lawrence, Kansas, which was burned by proslavery forces. John Brown and his supporters retaliated by killing five proslavery men at Pottawatamie Creek.

Test-Taking Strategy

Read the question prompts carefully and underline key words so you know clearly what you are looking for.

6. **The correct answer is (B).** This question asks you to look for what is true in the following list. The Emancipation Proclamation did not affect slaves in Southern states or parts of Southern states occupied by the Union, choice (A). It did decree that slaves in states still at war with the Union on January 1, 1864, would be free. It was a proclamation without any force, but it did help to sway the British away from supporting the South. Choice (C) is wrong because it was very important that the border states stay in the Union; Lincoln feared that freeing their slaves would drive them out. The Confiscation Act freed slaves who escaped into the Union lines, so choice (D) is wrong. The Thirteenth Amendment ended slavery.

7. **The correct answer is (D).** The key words here are *best describes.* Although nativists might agree with choice (A) and the Sacco and Vanzetti case, choice (C), probably added to interest in passing laws about immigration, the best—most inclusive—answer is choice (D). The law did more than close down the Gentleman's Agreement that allowed some Japanese immigrants into the country, and it favored immigrants from Western and Northern Europe, making choice (B) incomplete and choice (E) incorrect.

PRACTICE SET 2

1. All of the following spurred European interest in exploration, EXCEPT

   (A) the rise of nation-states

   (B) the Renaissance

   (C) development of a market for luxury goods from Asia

   (D) technological advances, such as the printing press and astrolabe

   (E) development of African slavery as a business

2. The Virginia and Kentucky Resolutions rest on the argument that the arbiter of the constitutionality of a law passed by Congress is

   (A) the Supreme Court

   (B) Congress

   (C) state legislatures

   (D) popular sovereignty

   (E) presidential veto

3. The major difference between Booker T. Washington's views and W.E.B. Du Bois's views was Du Bois's

   (A) emphasis on vocational training for African Americans

   (B) emphasis on a liberal arts education for African Americans

   (C) emphasis on the right of African Americans to demand whatever education they needed to gain full equality

   (D) support for the Niagara Movement

   (E) emphasis on continuing protests against injustice and appeals to black pride

4. All of the following are examples of reforms supported by progressives, EXCEPT

   (A) adoption of the Australian ballot

   (B) welfare reform

   (C) use of the initiative, referendum, and recall

   (D) direct election of U.S. senators

   (E) women's suffrage

Questions 5 through 7 refer to the following map.

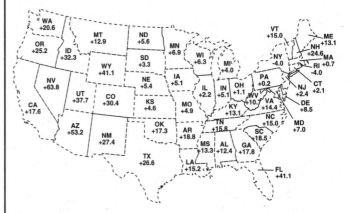

5. According to the map, which two Northeast states were the only states to lose population between 1970 and 1980?

   (A) New York and Pennsylvania

   (B) Massachusetts and Rhode Island

   (C) New York and Rhode Island

   (D) Pennsylvania and Rhode Island

   (E) Massachusetts and Pennsylvania

6. Which region of the 48 contiguous states had the greatest percentage increase in population between 1970 and 1980?

(A) New England

(B) Middle Atlantic states

(C) Midwest

(D) Southeast

(E) Southwest

7. Which of the following states experienced the greatest percentage increase in population between 1970 and 1980?

(A) New Hampshire

(B) Florida

(C) Nevada

(D) Arizona

(E) Texas

EXPLANATION OF ANSWERS FOR PRACTICE SET 2

QUICK-SCORE ANSWERS

1. E	4. B	7. C
2. C	5. C	
3. C	6. E	

1. **The correct answer is (E).** If you were not sure whether the other choices were correct, you could at least determine choice (E) is incorrect because the trans-Atlantic slave trade did not begin until the mid-1600s. European explorations occurred for the most part in the 1500s and early 1600s.

Test-Taking Strategy

Thinking about the time frame of a question can help you sort through the answer choices when you are not sure of the correct answer.

2. **The correct answer is (C).** Logic tips the scale toward choice (C) as the answer because these are state resolutions. Because the question is about the period of the early republic and these are Southern states, they would be trying to further states' rights and not the power of the president or of the Supreme Court. Therefore, logic indicates that choices (A) and (E) are incorrect. Popular sovereignty, choice (D), is a later development of the nineteenth century to solve the slavery question. Choice (B) does not make sense.

3. **The correct answer is (C).** The question asks for the *major* difference between Washington and Du Bois, so you need to look for the most inclusive correct answer. Choice (A) is incorrect because that was Washington's position. Choices (B), (C), (D), and (E) are all things that Du Bois supported in contrast to Washington, but choices (B) and (E) are elements of choice (C), so (C) is the best choice.

Test-Taking Strategy

There's more than one way to use except.

4. **The correct answer is (B).** The question is about a group that worked for change sometime between the late nineteenth and early twentieth centuries. You can tell this because of the time frame for question 3 and because the amendment for the direct election of senators was ratified in 1913 and for women's suffrage in 1920. Since this is an *except* question, you are looking for the choice that is not true. Choice (B) is the answer because there was no welfare program to reform in that period.

5. **The correct answer is (C).** Questions 5, 6, and 7 are straightforward questions that ask you to read the map and choose the correct answer based on what you see.

6. **The correct answer is (E).**

7. **The correct answer is (C).**

PRACTICE SET 3

1. Which of the following explored North America for Spain?

   (A) Cabot

   (B) DeSoto

   (C) Champlain

   (D) Magellan

   (E) La Salle

2. The Virginia Resolves are significant because

   (A) they were passed to protest the Stamp Act

   (B) they were based on the argument that the colonies could not be taxed by Parliament because they had no representation in Parliament

   (C) they laid the groundwork for Virginia's claim to Western lands

   (D) in passing them, the Virginia legislature seceded from the Union

   (E) in passing them, Virginia agreed to Congressional Reconstruction

3. Elizabeth Cady Stanton is most closely associated with which area of social reform in the nineteenth century?

   (A) abolition

   (B) the temperance movement

   (C) universal education

   (D) women's rights

   (E) prison reform

4. The direct cause of Congress's vote to impeach Andrew Johnson was

   (A) his opposition to Congressional Reconstruction

   (B) his opposition to the Fifteenth Amendment

   (C) corruption during his administration

   (D) his violation of the Tenure of Office Act

   (E) his veto of the Civil Rights Act of 1866

5. "I had opportunity to observe closely the operation of two powerful forces that were at work on the Negro's status—the exodus and the war. Negroes migrating to the North in great numbers, and I observed the anomaly of a premium being put on this element of the population that had generally been regarded as a burden and a handicap to the South."

   The above was most probably written about

   (A) contraband going behind the Union lines in the Civil War

   (B) movement of blacks to Northern cities during the Vietnam War

   (C) exodusters

   (D) migration of African Americans in the 1890s

   (E) Great Migration of 1915–1930

6. Which of the following laws of the New Deal was declared unconstitutional?

   (A) Civilian Conservation Corps

   (B) Works Progress Administration

   (C) Federal Housing Authority

   (D) National Industrial Recovery Act

   (E) National Youth Administration

7. Deficit spending advocates

   (A) protectionism

   (B) increasing the supply of goods and lowering taxes

   (C) increasing federal spending to stimulate the economy

   (D) stagflation

   (E) an increase in wages annually if the general level of prices in the economy rises above a certain level

EXPLANATION OF ANSWERS FOR PRACTICE SET 3

QUICK-SCORE ANSWERS		
1. B	4. D	7. C
2. B	5. E	
3. D	6. D	

1. **The correct answer is (B).** If you did not know, you could try eliminating choices. Although not always from the nation that employed them, many men explored for their own countries, so that eliminates choices (A), (C), and (E). The Italian Cabot sailed for England, while Frenchmen Champlain and La Salle explored for France. Magellan, choice (D), is credited as the first European to circumnavigate the globe, but he never set foot in North America.

2. **The correct answer is (B).** The key word here is *significant*. Choice (A) is true, but the meaning of the Virginia Resolves in the larger context of U.S. history is choice (B). They established the argument of "no taxation without representation" that became a rallying cry for the Revolution. Choices (C), (D), and (E) are incorrect. You could have eliminated choices (D) and (E) by checking for the time frame of the question. It comes after a question about exploration and before one on the mid-nineteenth century.

3. **The correct answer is (D).** The key words here are *most closely*. Stanton was involved in the abolition movement, choice (A), but she is best known for organizing the Seneca Falls women's rights conference in 1848 and her work for women's suffrage. The woman most closely associated with temperance, choice (B), is Frances Willard, who served from 1879 to 1898 as the president of the Women's Christian Temperance Association. Horace Mann is considered a pioneer in the fight for universal education, choice (C). Dorothea Dix is known for her work on prison and asylum reform, choice (E).

4. **The correct answer is (D).** The key words are *direct cause*. His enemies in Congress hated Johnson for choices (A) and (E), but his impeachment hearings directly resulted from choice (D), his firing of Secretary of State Edwin Stanton. Choice (B) is incorrect because it was the Fourteenth Amendment that he opposed; the Fifteenth Amendment was not ratified until after his administration. Choice (C) was not an issue in his administration but in that of his successor, Ullysses S. Grant.

5. **The correct answer is (E).** The word *war* is one clue, as is the phrase "the anomaly of a premium." The word *war* will help you eliminate choice (D). Although the United States did fight the Spanish-American War in the 1890s, it lasted only three months, not long enough to create an economy that would need additional workers. The time order of the questions in this group will help you eliminate choice (A). Question 4 is about Andrew Johnson's impeachment, so an answer about the Civil War for question 5 cannot be correct. (Contraband was the name given to slaves who escaped behind the Union lines.) You might think exodusters, choice (C), is correct, because the quotation uses the word *exodus* , but the exodusters moved west, not north, shortly after the Civil War. The phrase about a premium on African Americans indicates that they were in demand; this would equate with the need for workers in the North as the nation geared up for World War I, choice (E). No similar movement occurred during the Vietnam War because so many African Americans already lived in the North, choice (B). Don't be confused by the Great Migration that brought some 20,000 Puritans to Massachusetts Bay.

Review Strategy

See Chapter 6 for a discussion of Schechter *v.* United States.

6. **The correct answer is (D).** The NIRA was declared unconstitutional because the Supreme Court found that the Constitution gave the federal government the power to regulate interstate commerce but not all aspects of business. One provision of the law especially odious to employers was Section 7a, which gave employees the right to bargain collectively with their employers. Choice (A) provided work for youths between the ages of 18 and 25. They received food, clothing, shelter, and wages in exchange for outdoor work such as building fire trails and planting trees. The WPA, choice (B), cooperated with local and state governments to provide workers for useful public works projects such as building schools and roads. The three levels of government shared the cost and the administration of the program. The FHA, choice (C), still exists and helps people borrow money to buy homes. The NYA, choice (E), distributed money to needy students in exchange for performing work around their schools. The focus on the work programs was providing workers for "socially useful work" rather than "make-work" jobs. These programs kept young people from being unemployed and helped many of them continue their education.

7. **The correct answer is (C).** The objective of deficit spending is to create jobs. With greater employment, workers will have more money to spend. This stimulates demand, thus increasing production that creates even more jobs. It was the theory behind Roosevelt's economic policy and many presidents since. Choice

(B) is the definition of supply-side economics, the theory behind Ronald Reagan's economic policy; it states that by giving people more money, they will increase their savings and their purchasing power, thereby generating more economic activity. Stagflation, choice (D), is a condition of the economy in which inflation combines with low economic activity; it was the prevailing economic condition of the 1970s. Choice (E) is the definition of cost-of-living adjustment, which is also found in some government programs, such as Social Security. Choice (A) is a philosophy that underlies high tariffs.

Chapter 2

ABOUT WRITING A "9" ESSAY

Actually, this title is misleading because, as you read in *Scoring High on the AP U.S. History Test,* on pages 6–8, you do not need three "9" essays to get a "5" for your composite score. You need to believe that you will understand what the essay questions will ask you and that you will write clear and coherent essays in the time allotted. Now is the time to plan and practice, so you will have the self-confidence to excel, not panic.

Chapters 3 and 4 will help you to understand what the DBQ and the free response essay questions ask and how to answer each specific type of question. This chapter presents some basic information about Section II of the test and about good writing in general.

PRACTICE PLAN

Study Strategy

Check the "Practice Plan for Studying for the AP U.S. History Test," pp. 9–12.

In Chapters 3 and 4, you will explore the different types of questions that you may encounter with the DBQ and free response essay questions, and you will have ample opportunities to practice writing sample essays. Use the rubric, or scoring guide, to pinpoint your weaknesses and to improve as you write each subsequent essay.

Use the *Diagnostic Test* and *Practice Tests* as tools to improve your writing, too. Use the techniques described in this chapter and in Chapters 3 and 4 to plan and write your DBQ in 60 minutes and each of the free response essays in about 35 minutes. Then turn to the *Explanation of Answers* section after each test. Compare each essay with the list of suggested points that you might have developed in that essay. Score your essay with the *Self-Evaluation Rubric.* Ask a reliable friend, an AP classmate, or a teacher to evaluate your essay holistically. What are your weak areas? What can you improve? Take several of the points from the list and rework each of your essays using those points to strengthen the weak areas.

Reevaluate your essays. Again, compare the points you made with the ones we suggest. Did our suggestions help you to better understand what the questions were asking? Are your rewritten essays more tightly focused on the question and more clearly developed as a result of incorporating some of our points? Still need to work on your weak points? How much did you improve?

Now, stop. Do not keep working on the same essay to polish it to perfection. You won't have that opportunity during the test. The purpose of reworking an essay is to help you pinpoint what the question is really asking and how you can best answer it with a clear, coherent, and unified essay. Keep in mind what you learned on your first try and go on to the next essay.

BASIC INFORMATION ABOUT SECTION II

Study Strategy

See Chapters 3 and 4.

1. Section II has three parts: Part A, the DBQ; Part B, two free response essay questions on U.S. history up to and including the Civil War; and Part C, two free response essay questions on U.S. history from Reconstruction to the present.

2. You must answer the DBQ, one question from Part B, and one question from Part C.

3. The period of history from which the DBQ will be drawn varies from year to year.

4. You will have 1 hour to plan and write the DBQ and 70 minutes for the two free response essays. The College Board suggests you allot approximately 35 minutes to each free response essay. The 1 hour for the DBQ includes a mandatory 15-minute reading period in which you are to read and plan how you will answer the DBQ.

5. Each essay is scored from 1 to 9, with 9 being the highest.

6. Each of your essays will be evaluated holistically by a different reader, using a scoring guide developed by the College Board.

7. The essays together account for 50 percent of your final composite score. However, the DBQ is worth 45 percent of the total score for Section II, and the free response essays are worth 27.5 percent each.

What does all this mean? It means that you need to do some planning and practicing.

1, 2, 4. If you have 70 minutes to write the two free response essay questions, you cannot spend 50 minutes on one essay and 20 minutes on the other one. When you practice, take 5 minutes to read each question and to plan what you will say. Use the 30 minutes remaining to write your essay.

3. The time period from which the DBQ will be drawn is available both on the College Board Web site and in the College Board's booklet *Advanced Placement Course Description: History.* Order the booklet or visit the Web site. You cannot read every document and secondary source about the time period for your DBQ, but you can pay particular attention to events, trends, ideas, and

Study Strategy

The College Board Web site is www.collegeboard.org/ap

historiography about this time period as you read and study your regular AP course work.

5, 6, 7. For Parts B and C, skim the four choices. Choose one question from each part to answer. In making your decisions, look for the questions that you know the most about and can provide the most outside information to answer. Once you have decided, begin with the easier of the two. It will help to build your confidence, and because your three essays will be read by three different people, you do not have to worry that one weaker essay will pull down the scores for the other two essays. Instead, you can be confident that your clear, coherent, unified—and neatly written—essays will brighten each grader's pile of vague, incoherent, fragmented, and illegible essays.

Test-Taking Strategy

You will be able to make notes in your test booklet.

GOOD WRITING

You may have to plan and write your essays in a short period of time, but the characteristics of these essays are no different from those of any good writing exercise: unity, coherence, and adequate development.

First, who is your audience? Second, what is your purpose? Third, what is the appropriate tone?

AUDIENCE

You have an audience of one—a College Board–trained reader who teaches high school or college U.S. history and who will be reading hundreds of similar papers. She or he will have a scoring guide, or rubric, to aid in evaluating your paper. He or she will score your essay holistically, that is, there is no single score for things like grammar and punctuation. The reader will consider every aspect of your writing for its impact on the overall impression of your essay. (Our rubric singles out the various descriptors so you can pinpoint your weaknesses to work on and increase your overall score.)

PURPOSE

Your purpose is to get a score of 5 or better. To do that, you need to write a unified, coherent, and consistent essay that answers the question. A well-written essay that misses the point of the question will not get you a good score. That is why you need to read Chapters 3 and 4.

TONE

Your tone is the reflection of your attitude toward the subject of the essay. A writer's tone, for example, may be lighthearted, brusque, or serious. The safest tone to adopt is formal and persuasive, since you are being asked to take a position and support it. You do not want to be stuffy and pretentious by using phrases such as "one understands" or "we can surmise." On the other hand, do not be too casual by writing things like "you know what I mean." Most students, however, err on the side of "faux" erudition, using big words and convoluted constructions. When in doubt, write what you mean simply and directly.

STYLE

How do you develop the proper tone? Through style. Your style should be your own natural style that you use for school essays. That means

- using proper grammar and punctuation

- choosing words that convey your meaning in an interesting rather than a pedestrian or vague way: "The outcome hinged on the Speaker's ability to corral enough votes from the party's mavericks" versus "The Speaker tried for several hours to convince the recalcitrant members of his party."

- avoiding the use of several words when one will do: "There were a number of factors involved that added to the problem. . ." versus "The four factors most responsible for the problem were . . ."

- avoiding hackneyed phrases and clichés such as "The candidate was on cloud nine at the enthusiastic reception" versus "The candidate was smiling and waving at her well-wishers."

Your style adds interest to the paper. Interesting words and phrasing, as much as a unique point of view about a subject, can make a paper interesting to read.

UNITY AND COHERENCE

Unity is another word for clarity. A unified paper is one that is clearly developed. Each paragraph has a topic sentence, and all the sentences in the paragraph relate to each other and support the development of the topic sentence.

In the same way, each paragraph relates to every other, and every paragraph supports the overall thesis. This means, of course, that you need to have a thesis to develop. Chapters 3 and 4 will help you with developing thesis statements that answer the essay questions.

Remember that your thesis statement contains the central argument that you have developed from brainstorming ideas to answer the essay question. As the *Harbrace College Handbook,* that venerable college English manual, states: "[Your thesis statement] is basically a claim statement, that is, it indicates what you claim to be true, interesting, or valuable about your subject."

Although you can place your thesis statement anywhere in your essay, it is probably safest to put it in the first paragraph, so you can refer to it as you write to be sure that everything you are writing develops and supports it. Putting the thesis first also helps get you started writing.

ADEQUATE DEVELOPMENT

What is "adequate development"? You have a limited time to read, plan, and then develop your ideas—neatly. Using the five-paragraph structure will give you a format to work with: a one-paragraph introduction, a three-paragraph middle, and a one-paragraph ending. For your middle paragraphs, develop only one idea per paragraph, and be sure to include outside information. The body of your essay may actually be more than three paragraphs, but this format gives you direction.

PLANNING AND WRITING EACH ESSAY: PRACTICAL ADVICE

The following advice works both for the DBQ and for the free response essays.

- Read the question carefully and then the documents, if it is the DBQ.

- Underline what the question is asking you to do (compare, contrast, analyze, assess, and so on), and circle any terms, events, and people that the question mentions.

- Restate to yourself what the question is asking. Look at your underlined portions to verify that you understand the question.

- Do not take time to outline, but make a list by brainstorming ideas and supporting evidence as well as counterarguments that come to mind as you read.

- If you need to compare and contrast data or argue pros and cons, create a table to list the information.

Study Strategy

See Chapters 3 and 4 to learn how to determine what the question is really asking.

Test-Taking Strategy

Use the test booklet to jot down your quick list.

- Be sure to include relevant outside information, especially for the DBQ.

- Create a thesis statement from the ideas you generated.

- Turn this brainstorm into an informal working plan by numbering the items that you want to include in your essay in the order in which you want to include them. Do not be afraid to cross out some that no longer apply now that you have a thesis.

- Begin writing your first paragraph by clearly stating the thesis. Take a full 5 minutes to be sure that you are writing a clearly stated and interesting introduction.

- Once you have written the first paragraph, read it to be sure that your ideas follow one another logically and support the thesis.

- Write a transition into the second paragraph. Check your list of ideas.

- Keep writing until you have used all the RELEVANT ideas on your list. Check how well you are doing at incorporating supporting evidence and refuting counterarguments.

- Use transitions.

- Allow time to write a solid concluding paragraph. There are several ways to approach the conclusion: rephrasing the thesis, answering the questions by summarizing the main points of your argument, referring in some way back to your opening paragraph, or using an appropriate quotation.

- Pace yourself so that you have at least 3 minutes to reread your essay for proofreading and revision. Cross out any irrelevant ideas or words and make any additions. If you have been following your plan to develop your thesis, this time should be spent making sure your grammar and mechanics are correct and your handwriting is legible.

Chapter 3

WRITING THE DBQ ESSAY

After the five- to ten-minute break following the multiple-choice section, you will begin the hour-long document-based question (DBQ) portion. The DBQ is the first part of the essay section.

DEFINING THE DBQ

The DBQ requires that you use from eight to ten primary-source documents in order to answer a question about some issue in U.S. history. You may have to analyze and interpret diaries, news articles, photographs, speeches, legislation, maps, graphs, letters, cartoons, or any other type of material that can be printed. Usually the documents will be new to you, and although you may have seen one or two before, don't count on it. Most documents are one-quarter to half a page long. A few may be longer. No matter the length or the obscurity of the documents, the events they present will be familiar. Their issues deal with what the creators of the AP exam call the "mainstream" of U.S. history.

When the second portion of the test begins, you will receive a booklet in which you will find the question and the documents. After you fill out your identification information, you will be told that for the first 15 minutes of the session you are to read the documents and take notes. You may not start to write your essay until the 45-minute writing session begins.

All DBQs consist of the following three parts: the directions, the question, and the documents. Let's look at each part.

THE DIRECTIONS

The directions tell you to take 15 minutes to read and make notes about the documents. The papers given to you provide space to take notes and to organize what you want to say. You will write your DBQ during the remaining 45 minutes. The directions even tell you where to write your essay.

The directions also present the purpose of the DBQ. They read something like this:

> **Directions:** The following question asks you to write a cohesive essay incorporating your interpretation of Documents A through H and your knowledge of the period stated in the question. To earn a high score, you must cite key evidence from the documents and use your outside knowledge of U.S. history.

The directions clearly state that you are to analyze the documents and relate information to the mainstream of U.S. history in a well-written essay that expresses your opinion about the issues the question raises. That means you must state YOUR opinion as well as refer to historical events and developments that are not found in the documents. The College Board emphasizes that students must demonstrate outside knowledge of the issues involved "if the highest scores are to be earned" on the DBQ.

THE QUESTION

The second part of the DBQ is the question itself. Most probably the question is the shortest piece you will read in the DBQ. Read it carefully. Examine all its parts. Consider its implications. Do not fall into the trap of assuming you know what the question asks, skip a part. Underline, circle, or put brackets around the key words in the question.

Essays that thoroughly address all aspects of the question receive scores of 7, 8, or 9. Those that do not answer all parts will receive no higher than a 5. Later in this chapter you will learn about the types of questions that are likely to be in Section II and what those questions ask of you.

THE DOCUMENTS

The third section of the DBQ consists of the documents you are to read and analyze. The order in which the documents appear is not random. They are usually arranged chronologically. Other times the documents will be grouped by point of view. Not all documents will agree with one another. They will present different positions on important issues and opposing interpretations of historical events. In designing the question, the examination writers intend that you identify and resolve the varying assertions.

Peterson's AP Success: U.S. History

THE GAME PLAN

Now that you understand what the DBQ consists of, you need a game plan, or essay-preparation strategy, to help write a "9" paper. As obvious as this sounds, begin with the directions. Read them carefully. That strategy holds true in all examination situations.

1. ANALYZE THE QUESTION

As you read the question, consider two points: what your opinion is on the subject and what to discuss about the subject. Determine what issues to address and what documents to focus on. Consider the following question:

During the last three decades of the nineteenth century, farmers experienced severe difficulties. As the problems mounted, farmers pinned their hopes on political solutions.

Using the documents and your knowledge of U.S. history for the period from 1870 to 1900, evaluate the effectiveness of the agrarian protest.

Examine the question and query yourself about what the DBQ asks. The first thing to do is ensure you understand specific phrases in the question. Do you understand the word *agrarian?* You may wish to define the term in your essay.

Ask yourself what are the key points of the question. Be clear about the time frame—the 1870s to the turn of the century. Highlight in some way the key words in the question: *last three decades of the nineteenth century, farmers, problems mounted, evaluate, effectiveness, agrarian protest.*

The question revolves around farmers' difficulties and their efforts to solve their problems. Then the question goes on to ask you to express your opinion regarding the success farmers had at forcing political solutions. Therefore, you must explain the political steps they took and their results. In doing this, you must, of course, include a discussion of the documents as they relate to farmers' hardships and efforts for reform. In addition, you must use your historical knowledge of the agrarian and Populist movements during the latter half of the nineteenth century.

The DBQ you just analyzed is straightforward and easy to understand. It states directly that you must evaluate a situation. Other questions may be more difficult to discern. However, if you can identify the type of question, dissecting the DBQ becomes easier. The chart that follows shows question types you might encounter in

Section II. You will notice that certain words offer clues to the kinds of support you will need in order to develop an appropriate answer.

The AP United States history exam is demanding and you will find that some questions combine two or more types. However, by learning the clue words, you can apply the appropriate support and development strategies.

QUESTION TYPE	WORDS THAT OFFER CLUES	REQUIRED SUPPORT
Evaluation	Assess, evaluate, judge the validity	Look for evidence from the documents and your knowledge of U.S. history that substantiates your opinion.
Compare	Contrast, differ, differences	Look for and stress similarities with specific examples.
Contrast	Contrast, differ, differences	Identify and stress differences with specific examples.
Definition	Define, explain	Explain what something, such as a law or a policy, is or does.
Description	Describe	Provide the main features with specific details and examples.
Discussion	Discuss, explain	Make a general statement that shows you understand the concept in the question. Then support your main idea with examples, facts, and details.
Explanation	Explain, why, what, how	Offer examples, details, and facts that illustrate how something happened, what it is, or why it is so.
Illustration	Illustrate, show	Provide concrete examples and explain each one to demonstrate the truth or significance of the main idea.
Interpretation	Significance, meaning of quotations or events, influence, analyze	State a main idea about meaning. Give examples, facts, and reasons to explain and support your interpretation.
Opinion	What do you think, defend an idea or position, state your opinion	State your opinion clearly. Support and develop it with examples, facts, and reasons.
Prediction	If . . ., then; What if . . .	Predict and state a logical outcome based on your knowledge and evidence from the documents. Offer arguments to support your opinion.

2. TAKE NOTES

This step probably seems out of place to you, but it isn't. Most students want to read the documents immediately after reading the question. However, many students experience difficulty generating their own ideas because they focus exclusively on the documents. All they can think about is what they have read.

We suggest that before you begin to read the documents you brainstorm for the background and outside information you already know about the subject. Take a few minutes and jot down everything you can recall about the subject. Do not worry if it is relevant. Some of the information from your brainstorming may be included in the documents. Actually, that is a good thing because it shows your thinking is pertinent.

3. READ THE DOCUMENTS

Now you are ready to read the documents. The order in which the documents appear is important. Documents are usually arranged in chronological order. If the documents in your exam are in this order, this is a hint that suggests your essay should have some sort of chronological development. It does not mean that you have to include each document in this order. You should refer to the documents in the best way to support your thesis, but chronology is a useful principle of overall organization. You may find the documents in your exam are grouped around points of view. While this arrangement is not as common, it tells you that the focus of your essay should be a comparison or a contrast.

Test-Taking Strategy

You may find contradictions even within a document.

As you read, look for inconsistencies among the documents. Since the purpose of the DBQ is to assess your ability to combine historical research and analytical skill with factual recall, documents will present differing points of view and contradictory explanations of events. You must recognize and discuss these differences.

Be sure to read the source information for each document. A given writer or a time period may trigger important points to include in the DBQ. Sources can also provide insight into conflicting positions since different individuals have different perspectives. Ask yourself how gender, political beliefs, race, social class, and religion may contribute to the viewpoints expressed in the documents.

Study Strategy

Practice analyzing all types of documents as you review for the AP test and relate the information to the mainstream of U.S. history.

You will find that some documents are more valuable to you than others. However, do not simply ignore those that advocate opposing positions. Look for refuting evidence and incorporate it in your essay. By acknowledging it, you show that you understand the complexities of history.

The following documents relate to the question on page 3 regarding the agrarian protest of the latter part of the nineteenth century.

Document A

Source: Resolutions of a meeting of the Illinois' State Farmer's Association, April 1873

Resolved, That the railways of the world, except in those countries where they have been held under the strict regulations and supervision of the government, have proved themselves arbitrary; extortionate and as opposed to free institutions and free commerce between states as the feudal barons of the middle ages. . .

Resolved, That we hold, declare and resolve, that this despotism, which defies our laws, plunders our shippers, impoverishes our people, and corrupts our government, shall be subdued at whatever cost. . .

Resolved, That we urge the passage of a bill enforcing the principle that railroads are public highways, and requiring railroads to make connections with all roads whose tracks meet or cross their own, and to receive and transmit cars and trains offered over their roads at reasonable rates, whether offered at such crossings, or at stations along their roads, and empowering the making of connections by municipal corporations for that purpose, and for the public use. . .

Resolved, That we indorse most fully the action of those who tender legal rates of fare upon the railroads and refuse to pay more; and that it is the duty of the Legislature to provide by law . . . the right to ride on railroads at legal rates.

Analysis: Document A typifies the grievances of farmers against the railroads and their demands for effective state regulation. Such unified action shows that farmers were becoming increasingly vocal. They organized farmers' clubs and political parties. During this period, the National Grange exerted its greatest power and led the battle against the railroads. For a while the Grange movement was able to effect political change.

You should be able to easily incorporate Document A into an essay examining agrarian protests. This document would serve two purposes for you. First, it presents the farmers' position, emphasizing their economic problems, and second, it states their solution. The resolutions also offer you the opportunity to discuss the role of railroads in agriculture and their effect on agriculture. Implicit in a discussion of farmers versus the railroads is the role of government and government regulation.

You have probably thought of other issues related to this document. Remember, there is no one right answer. As long as you can support your thesis, you will do well. When you get to the actual writing of the essay, be sure to summarize, but not directly quote, a document.

Document B

Source: Chief Justice Morrison R. Waite, *Munn* v. *Illinois*, in his rejection of the argument that regulation violated the Fourteenth Amendment, 1877

The question to be determined in this case is whether the general assembly of Illinois can, under the limitations upon the legislative powers of the States imposed by the Constitution of the United States, fix by law the maximum charges for the storage of grain. . .

. . . Looking, then, to the common law, from whence came the right which the Constitution protects, we find that when private property is "affected with a public interest, it ceases to be *juris privari* only". . . Property does become clothed with a public interest when used in a manner to make it of public consequence, and affect the community at large. When, therefore, one devotes his property to a use in which the public has an interest, he, in effect, grants to the public an interest in that use, and must submit to be controlled by the public for the common good, to the extent of the interest he has thus created. He may withdraw his grant by discontinuing the use; but, so long as he maintains the use, he must submit to the control. . .

Analysis: Farmers, especially those in sparsely populated or newly settled regions, were overwhelmed by the high cost of shipping and grain storage. Railroads, grain elevators, and meat packers set their prices according to whim or monopoly rather than fair market value. *Munn* v. *Illinois* involved the right of the legislature to regulate prices for grain storage. However, the case had greater implications since it directly affected the constitutionality of state regulation of railroads. Document B presents the legal basis for regulating such property as grain elevators and railroads. Chief Justice Waite used a seventeenth-century English principle that property affecting the public interest is no longer affected only by private law but becomes subject to public regulation as well. The decision set a legal precedent for regulation.

Document B relates to Document A in that the case involves the farmers' interests. You might have remembered that the dissenting opinion of Justice Stephen J. Fields influenced later court decisions limiting state and federal regulation of railroads. You could use this document to support an argument that farmers' organizations were influencing state politicians who passed laws favorable to agriculture. In addition, you could maintain that the Supreme Court was also influenced by the farmers' position.

Document C

Source: Populist Party Platform, July 4, 1892

. . . [T]he forces of reform this day organized will never cease to move forward until every wrong is righted and equal rights and equal privileges securely established for all the men and women of this country. We declare, therefore-

First,—That the union of the labor forces of the United States this day consummated shall be permanent and perpetual; may its spirit enter into all hearts for the salvation of the Republic and the uplifting of mankind.

Second,—Wealth belongs to him who creates it, and every dollar taken from industry without an equivalent is robbery. "If any will not work, neither shall he eat." The interests of rural and civil labor are the same; their enemies are identical.

Study Strategy

Did you consider the Grange, the Bland-Allison Act, the Sherman Silver Act, and the "Cross of Gold" speech?

Analysis: Document C is an excellent statement of some of the goals of the Populist Party. This selection shows the new unity among southern and western farmers as well as radicals and reformers. All workers, whether rural or urban, shared common goals and had common adversaries.

Document C opens the door to discuss many topics. You could use it as a springboard to a discussion of farmers' alliances and political parties. The document lends itself to a discussion of the remaining elements of the Populist platform of sweeping reform— unlimited coinage of silver, an increase in the money supply, a progressive income tax, governmental ownership of railroads and the telephone and telegraph systems. Also, the excerpt suggests the possibility of including in your essay a discussion of the election of 1892 and Cleveland's second term.

Document D

Source: W. H. ("Coin") Harvey, *Coin's Financial School*, 1894

The money lenders in the United States, who own substantially all our money, have a selfish interest in maintaining the gold standard. They, too, will not yield. They believe that if the gold standard can survive for a few years longer, the people will get used to it—get used to their poverty—and quietly submit.—To that end they organize international bimetallic committees and say "Wait on England, she will be forced to give us bimetallism." Vain hope! Deception on this subject has been practiced long enough upon a patient and outraged people.

With silver remonetized, and gold at a premium, not one-tenth the hardships could result that now afflict us. . .

Analysis: Document D promotes the cause of free silver. It clearly states the demands of the free silver advocates and their hatred of the gold standard, bankers, and the British Empire. You will recall that the free silver concept advocated unlimited coinage of silver dollars. Harvey argues that those supporting the gold standard have no interest in stopping the deflation that has caused tremendous hardships for farmers and also the owners of small businesses.

Document D opens up several possibilities for your essay. It gives you the opportunity to discuss the plight of farmers, the switch in emphasis from government regulation to free silver, and the role of William Jennings Bryan. You might choose to write about the farmers' failure to compel Congress to enact a free silver policy. You could also mention that the Sherman Silver Purchase Act was re-pealed. The Democrats repudiated Cleveland and nominated William Jennings Bryan. What other points for discussion have you thought of including?

On the actual AP test, you will be given more documents, but these selections give you a taste of the critical analysis process. Did you notice the documents were arranged chronologically? This allows you to trace the agrarian movement through time.

4. ORGANIZE YOUR INFORMATION

After you have finished reading and note taking, it is time to organize your information. Review what you have written and delete repeti-tious or irrelevant information. Use a chart, columns, or a Venn diagram to order facts by topic or time period.

Now you are ready to create a thesis, or personal opinion, on the topic. Again, review your information. Ask yourself, "What do I think about the topic and how can I support that position?" Your answers provide ideas for your thesis. Before you make a final decision, reread the question to ensure your thesis addresses all parts of the question. When you begin to write, be sure to write your thesis in your first paragraph.

Only after the reading period will you be permitted to begin your essay. If you finish your reading, notes, and thesis statement early, create an informal outline. Number each of your ideas in the order you will write about them. Be sure to save your most powerful idea for the final paragraph before the conclusion.

If the reading period ends before you have created your informal outline, you must decide if using writing time to outline is advanta-geous. Consider circling, numbering, or underlining your notes as a time-saver.

Test-Taking Strategy

You do not have to take an all-true or all-false position on the topic.

Writing Strategy

Always express your own opinion and support it with evidence from the documents and mainstream history.

5. WRITE YOUR ESSAY

Reexamine Chapter 2 to review good writing techniques. The following are helpful hints for developing the DBQ essay:

- Remember that you can argue many different theses on a given DBQ. Choose the one that you can defend most successfully.

- Identify documents by letter or source.

- Include as many documents as you can.

- Do not quote directly from a document. Summarize.

- Remember you must include references to historical information from outside the documents.

- Write an essay that relates the documents to the events of the time period and supports your thesis.

- Use present tense in writing about what the documents say.

While understanding and interpreting the documents is critical in writing a "9" essay, the real test involves how well you relate the documents to the themes of U.S. history. Be positive and confident. You have prepared yourself well.

Chapter 4
WRITING THE FREE RESPONSE ESSAYS

Red Alert!

Each free response essay is worth 27.5 percent of your Section II score.

The free response section is the final part of your AP test. Like the DBQ, the free response essays are scored on a scale of 1 to 9. On the day of the test, you will begin Parts B and C immediately after you have finished the DBQ essay. (There is no break between the essay sections.) You will have 70 minutes to plan and write your essays.

DEFINING THE FREE RESPONSE QUESTIONS

The second part of Section II is made up of four essay questions. Two ask about the period before the Civil War, and two ask about the period after it. You must answer one question from each time period. These essays are similar to those you have written for your U.S. history classes, so the topics will be familiar to you.

Like the DBQs, the free response questions have no single correct answer. All the information must come from your knowledge and understanding of U.S. history. There are no documents to analyze or to stimulate your thinking. Most of the free response essays allow you to include a good deal of description. Be careful, however, that you do not simply describe. You also need to show relationships and make generalizations. You have about 35 minutes per essay, 5 minutes to make notes and prepare and 30 minutes to write. However, since there is less time per question, you will find that the free response questions are more focused and less comprehensive than the DBQ, thus requiring shorter answers.

Test-Taking Strategy

Remember to number the essay as it is numbered in the booklet (2. or 3. and 4. or 5.).

The free response questions have two parts: the directions and the questions. The directions tell you to choose the one essay question from Part B and the one question from Part C that you are best prepared to answer. Be sure you pick the questions you know the most about, not the ones that seem easier. The more you know and can show, the better you will score.

The directions continue by telling you to give supporting evidence for your thesis from relevant historical facts, events, and theories. Your essay is to be clear and logical.

You will find that the questions in Part B and in Part C fall into the same categories of questions that are defined in Chapter 3 for DBQ questions. Use the chart in Chapter 3, p. 86, to refresh your memory about question types and development.

THE GAME PLAN

You have already read a great deal about writing "9" essays in Chapters 2 and 3. To review, the following are the steps for structuring an AP essay:

1. Analyze the question. Circle, underline, and use brackets to highlight key words.
2. Jot down notes.
3. Evaluate your notes and develop a thesis.
4. Organize your information in a logical way in an outline.
5. Write your essay.
6. Check your work if you have time.

PRACTICAL ADVICE

Review Strategy

Reread Chapter 2 to review the suggestions for good writing and Chapter 3 to review types of questions.

Here are a few suggestions that may give your essays a final polish to help you score all the points you deserve.

- Remember to choose the questions you know the most about.

- Some essays may combine several question types.

- Plan your time well so you can divide the 70 minutes evenly between the two essays. Pace yourself to be sure you allow enough time to do a good job on both questions.

- The free response portion of the essay section is worth more than one quarter of your grade. Do not ease up or rush yourself even though you may be tired.

- Your introduction is one of the most important paragraphs in your essay. Make sure you state the topic and your opinion. If you do not, the evaluator may be confused. You do not need to write "In my opinion" or "I believe" in your opening paragraph. Just state your opinion or position clearly.

- Remember that you can argue many different theses on a given question. Choose the one that YOU can defend most successfully.

- Include as many facts and as much historical evidence as you can to support your essay.

- Remember, you must answer all parts of a given question.

- Write an essay that clearly, logically, and coherently answers the question with special insight or a unique point of view.

- Write clearly and neatly. If your cursive is difficult to read, print.

PRACTICE

Let's look at an example of the free response portion of Section II. For extra practice, write each essay and then review the suggestions that we provide after it. Evaluate your essay using the *Self-Evaluation Rubric* on pages 104–105.

PART B

Directions: You are to answer ONE question from this group. The suggested planning time is 5 minutes with 30 minutes to write. State a thesis, cite relevant evidence, and use logical, clear arguments to support your generalizations.

2. The Articles of Confederation created a government with a number of weaknesses. These problems manifested themselves in a number of key episodes. Discuss how three of the following events showed the strength or weakness of the new government.

   - Treaty of Paris
   - Land Ordinance
   - Shays' Rebellion
   - Annapolis Convention
   - Northwest Ordinance

3. Prior to the Civil War, politicians were associated with both their political stand and the region that they represented. Explain how each of the following represented a political position based upon the region of the country he represented.

   - Daniel Webster
   - John C. Calhoun
   - Henry Clay

PART C

Directions: You are to answer ONE question from this group. The suggested planning time is 5 minutes with 30 minutes to write. State a thesis, cite relevant evidence, and use logical, clear arguments to support your generalizations.

4. Social changes impact societies on an irregular basis. It has been said that the Jacksonian and post–World War I periods were times of great social change.

Support or refute the statement that those periods were a time of great social change.

5. When Franklin Roosevelt became president of the United States, he took a number of steps to jump-start the economy. Some experts have suggested that the steps taken by Roosevelt would not have turned the economy around without the impact of World War II. In a coherent essay discuss the validity of that claim.

SUGGESTIONS FOR FREE RESPONSE ESSAYS, PART B

ESSAY 2

Test-Taking Strategy

Create a thesis that shows you understand the concept in the question. Then support your main idea with examples, facts, and details.

Steps to the answer:

1. Note that this is a discussion question.

2. Think about what you know of the government under the Articles of Confederation. Most scholars believe that the lack of a unifying central government meant no decisions could be made for the states as a whole.

3. Using the ideas you developed in Step 2, create a thesis to serve as the core of your essay. Then select the three events that you believe you can best use to support your thesis. Keep in mind that the events you select may not be those you know the best. You are looking for the ones that support your ideas. Write about one main point in each paragraph.

4. Using the organizing and writing suggestions contained in Chapters 2 and 3 and in this chapter, write your essay. Use transition words to make your essay more cohesive.

5. Keep in mind that every fact and event may not support your thesis. Do not ignore these differing elements. Deal with counterpoints, acknowledging them and the issues that they raise while showing that support for your position is stronger. By doing so, you confirm that you understand the complexities of history.

You might have chosen the following points about the government and events in your essay on the Articles of Confederation. Consider them as you complete your self-evaluation.

- **Treaty of Paris:**

  - Britain failed to remove its troops from the Ohio Valley as had been agreed to in the Treaty of Paris.

- The government could do nothing because the Confederation gave the government no power to enforce the agreement.

- **Land Ordinance:**

  - The law divided the Northwest Territory into townships.
  - The survey and division were very specific, with thirty-six sections forming one township.
  - Land was to be sold to settlers for $1.00 per acre.
  - The law was one of the few positive outcomes of the Confederation.

- **Shays' Rebellion:**

  - Farmers who had made money during the Revolutionary War found that demand for food—and, as a result, prices—had dropped after the war.
  - They had incurred debt to pay for land and seed, but now could not pay for it.
  - Taxes were raised to pay the war debts.
  - Daniel Shays led a group of farmers in Massachusetts on a rampage against government buildings to prevent the sale of land that had been seized to repay debts.
  - Many Americans viewed this as a problem that came from the Articles of Confederation.

Test-Taking Strategy

If you use a historical term, title, or name, be sure to define it.

- **Annapolis Convention:**

  - Interstate commerce was a severe problem because there were no uniform standards, laws, or currencies.
  - Virginia called for a convention in Annapolis, but attendance was poor with only five states attending.
  - Out of the convention came a call for another meeting to address the problems with the Articles.

- **Northwest Ordinance:**

  - The Articles of Confederation did not define a means to admit new states to the government.
  - The Northwest Ordinance set up a government for the territory.
  - It provided for the division of the area into three to five territories in the future.
  - Slavery was outlawed in the Northwest Territory.
  - After 60,000 free settlers moved to a territory, they could ask Congress to admit them as a new state.

- The new states had all the rights and privileges of the old states.

- Ultimately, five states came from the Northwest Territory: Indiana, Wisconsin, Illinois, Michigan, and Ohio.

ESSAY 3

Steps to the answer:

1. Note that this is an explanation question.

2. You are asked to identify both the region and the political position of each of the politicians. Ask yourself what region each represented and what the key issues were for that area. You should immediately recognize that the men were going to have different views on the economy and states' versus federal rights and responsibilities. Consider using a chart or grid to organize your thoughts.

3. Using the ideas you developed in Step 2, create a thesis to serve as the core of your essay. Then select the three events that you believe you can best use to support your thesis. Keep in mind that the events you select may not be those you know the best. You are looking for the ones that support your ideas.

4. Using the organizing and writing suggestions contained in Chapters 2 and 3 and in this chapter, write your essay. Do not write excessively complex sentences. Readers have only a few minutes per essay, so you want your paper to be easy to understand.

5. Keep in mind that every fact and event may not support your thesis. Do not ignore these differing elements. Deal with counterpoints, acknowledging them and the issues they raise while showing that support for your position is stronger. By doing so, you confirm that you understand the complexities of history.

You might have chosen to include the following points about the political positions of Webster, Calhoun, and Clay in your essay discussing the regional politics of the time. Consider them as you complete your self-evaluation.

General Comments:

- All the men focused on economic issues

  - Foreign competition

  - A national bank

  - Tariffs on imported goods impacted the various regions of the nation differently

Daniel Webster:

- From Massachusetts

- A spokesman for the North

- A Whig

- Supported the Bank of the United States

- Supported the right of the federal government to make laws that superseded those of the states

- Advocated the use of tariffs to protect the nascent industries in the North

John C. Calhoun:

- From South Carolina

- A spokesman for the South

- A Democrat

- Advocated states' rights versus a federal government

- Said that the states had the right to nullify a federal law that the states deemed was illegal

- Opposed the Tariff of Abominations because it placed a hardship on Southern farmers

Henry Clay:

- From Kentucky

- A spokesman for the West

- A Whig

- Supported the Bank of the United States

- Proposed the American System

  - High tariffs to protect the developing industries in the North

  - Theory that the wealth of these Northern factories would be spent purchasing farm products from the South and West

  - Called for spending on internal infrastructure to make it easier and cheaper to ship goods to and from the South and West

  - Plan not approved

  - High tariffs, but funds not spent on the infrastructure

Study Strategy

Include information about the economic, political, and social interests of the different parts of the nation to add detail to your answer.

SUGGESTIONS FOR FREE RESPONSE ESSAYS, PART C

ESSAY 4

Test-Taking Strategy

Identify and stress differences or similarities with specific examples.

Steps to the answer:

1. Note that this question combines two categories: compare/contrast and evaluate.

2. You are asked to agree or disagree with the statement that the Jacksonian and post–World War I periods created significant social change. Ask yourself if you think the statement is true. Also, you might ask yourself if you think that the social changes during those periods were comparable in terms of their breadth and long-term impact.

3. Using the ideas you developed in Step 2, create a thesis to serve as the core of your essay. Then select the events that you believe you can best use to support your thesis. Keep in mind that the events you select may not be those you know the best. You are looking for the ones that support your ideas.

4. Using the organizing and writing suggestions contained in Chapters 2 and 3 and in this chapter, write your essay. Add a few "ten-dollar words" that you know you can use correctly.

5. Keep in mind that every fact and event may not support your thesis. Do not ignore these differing elements. Deal with counterpoints, acknowledging them and the issues they raise while showing that support for your position is stronger. By doing so, you confirm that you understand the complexities of history.

You might have chosen the following points to include in your discussion about social changes during the Jacksonian and post–World War I periods. Consider them as you complete your self-evaluation.

Jacksonian Period:

- The Jacksonian period is generally considered to be the years from 1824 to 1840.

- Jackson was considered the president of the common people. He was a popular frontier hero.

- Political changes:

    - New parties—Whigs or National Republicans and Democrats

    - Caucuses replaced by nominating conventions

Peterson's AP Success: U.S. History

- Suffrage extended to all white men whether or not they owned land

- Free African Americans were denied basic rights. Women were denied their rights.

- Settlers on the frontier were independent in thought and action.

- With the exception of the African Americans, there was a growing sense of equality among social classes.

- Jackson and his independent-minded constituents did not want a government that was too powerful.

- Jackson fought the Bank of the United States because of the concern that it had too much power. He believed that it favored the rich over the poor.

- Jackson advanced the "spoils system" in government by removing members of the Whig Party and replacing them with loyal Democrats.

- The Indian Removal Act pushed the Native Americans out of their traditional lands.

- The Panic of 1837 led to a depression and hard economic times. It also opened the door for the Whigs to win the presidency.

Study Strategy

You noticed that this question asks you about two different time periods. This often occurs on the AP exam.

Post–World War I Period:

- After World War I, Americans wanted a period of calm.

- Harding was elected president on a platform calling for a return to "normalcy."

- Harding's administration was plagued with scandals involving his friends. Among the most notable was the Teapot Dome scandal.

- The end of World War I brought a booming economy.

- Much of the economy was driven by the manufacture of affordable automobiles.

- Installment sales, buy-now-pay-later, fueled consumer spending.

- The stock market rose, in part, because of buying on margin.

- Prohibition was instituted.

- Women's roles changed:

    - Won the right to vote
    - Sought equal rights

- Continued to work in jobs held by men prior to World War I

- The movie, radio, and telephone industries developed and grew.

- African American culture expanded with the Harlem Renaissance.

- Racism was still widespread. The Ku Klux Klan achieved some political power in the South.

- Farmers had a difficult time.

- The Depression brought a halt to the free-spending of the 1920s.

ESSAY 5

Test-Taking Strategy

Look for and write about evidence that substantiates your opinion.

Steps to the answer:

1. Note that this is an evaluation question.

2. You are asked to identify both the steps taken by President Franklin Roosevelt to improve the economy and the economic impact of World War II. Once you have accomplished that, you need to evaluate the relative importance of the two to determine if you can establish which one was more important in improving the U.S. economy. It may be helpful to list some of the points on both sides of the question before you move to Step 3.

3. Using the ideas you developed in Step 2, create a thesis to serve as the core of your essay. Then select the topics and facts that you believe you can best use to support your thesis. Keep in mind that the events you select may not be those you know the best. You are looking for the ones that support your ideas.

4. Using the organizing and writing suggestions contained in Chapters 2 and 3 and in this chapter, write your essay. Take time to write a strong, satisfying conclusion. If you can do that, the last impression you leave on your reader will be a strong one.

5. Keep in mind that every fact and event may not support your thesis. Do not ignore these differing elements. Deal with counter-points, acknowledging them and the issues they raise while showing that support for your position is stronger. By doing so, you confirm that you understand the complexities of history.

You might have chosen the following points about the steps that Franklin Roosevelt took to improve the U.S. economy in your essay on the validity of the claim that World War II, and not his actions, was responsible for the economic turnaround. Consider them as you complete your self-evaluation.

Steps taken by Roosevelt:

- The New Deal

- "Fireside chats" to develop confidence

- The "Hundred Days" legislation

- "Bank holiday" to ease the pressure on the banking system

- Asked Congress for the Emergency Banking Relief Act; permitted only those banks with sufficient money to meet their customers' demands to reopen

- Created a series of programs to improve the economy on both a short-term and long-term basis: [You would select only some of the following to support your position.]

  - Civilian Conservation Corps
  - Social Security Act
  - Tennessee Valley Authority
  - Works Progress Administration
  - Federal Emergency Relief Administration
  - Rural Electrification Administration
  - Agricultural Adjustment Administration
  - Federal Deposit Insurance Corporation
  - National Recovery Administration
  - Public Works Administration
  - Minimum wage

- Second New Deal

- Recession of 1938

Impact of World War II:

- Full employment needed to produce war goods

- Women in the work force in great numbers

- Deficit spending used to fund the costs of war

- Investment in agriculture to provide food for the Allies

- Creation of a large industrial economy to design and build the weapons of war

- Spending on military research

SELF-EVALUATION RUBRIC FOR THE ADVANCED PLACEMENT ESSAYS

	8–9	5–7	2–4	0–1
Overall Impression	Demonstrates excellent understanding of U.S. history and outstanding writing; thorough and effective; incisive	Demonstrates good understanding of U.S. history and good writing competence	Reveals simplistic or incomplete thinking and/or immature understanding of U.S. history; fails to respond adequately to the question; little or no analysis	Very little or no understanding of U.S. history; unacceptably brief; fails to respond to the question; little clarity
Understanding of U.S. History	Scholarly; excellent understanding of the question; effective and incisive; in-depth critical analysis; includes many apt, specific references; acknowledges opposing views	Mostly historically accurate; good understanding of the question; often perceptive; includes specific references and critical analysis	Some historical inaccuracies; superficial understanding and treatment of the question; some misreading of documents and lack of historical evidence; mechanical; overgeneralized	Serious historical errors; extensive misreadings and little supporting evidence; completely off the topic
Development	Original, unique and/or intriguing thesis; excellent use of documents and historical knowledge; thoroughly developed; conclusion shows applicability of thesis to other situations	Adequate thesis; satisfactory use of documents and/or historical knowledge; competent development; acceptable conclusion	Inadequate, irrelevant or illogical thesis; little use of documents and/or historical knowledge; some development; unsatisfactory, inapplicable, or nonexistent conclusion	Lacking both thesis and conclusion; little or no use of historical documents or knowledge; no distinguishable development
Organization/Conventions of English	Meticulously and thoroughly organized; coherent and unified; virtually error free	Reasonably organized; mostly coherent and unified; some errors	Somewhat organized; some incoherence and lack of unity; some major errors	Little or no organization; incoherent and void of unity; extremely flawed

104

Peterson's AP Success: U.S. History

Rate yourself in each of the categories below. Enter the numbers on the lines below. Be as honest as possible so you will know what areas need work. Then calculate the average of the four numbers to determine your final score. It is difficult to score yourself objectively, so you may wish to ask a respected friend or teacher to assess your essays for a more accurate reflection of their strengths and weaknesses. On the AP test itself, a reader will rate your essays on a scale of 0 to 9, with 9 being the highest.

Each category is rated 9 (high) to 0 (incompetent).

ESSAY 2

SELF-EVALUATION

Overall Impression   _____

Understanding of U.S. History   _____

Development   _____

Organization/Conventions
of English   _____

TOTAL   _____
Divide by 4 for final score.   _____

ESSAY 2

OBJECTIVE EVALUATION

Overall Impression   _____

Understanding of U.S. History   _____

Development   _____

Organization/Conventions
of English   _____

TOTAL   _____
Divide by 4 for final score.   _____

ESSAY 3

SELF-EVALUATION

Overall Impression   _____

Understanding of U.S. History   _____

Development   _____

Organization/Conventions
of English   _____

TOTAL   _____
Divide by 4 for final score.   _____

ESSAY 3

OBJECTIVE EVALUATION

Overall Impression   _____

Understanding of U.S. History   _____

Development   _____

Organization/Conventions
of English   _____

TOTAL   _____
Divide by 4 for final score.   _____

ESSAY 4

SELF-EVALUATION

Overall Impression   _____

Understanding of U.S. History   _____

Development   _____

Organization/Conventions
of English   _____

TOTAL   _____
Divide by 4 for final score.   _____

ESSAY 4

OBJECTIVE EVALUATION

Overall Impression   _____

Understanding of U.S. History   _____

Development   _____

Organization/Conventions
of English   _____

TOTAL   _____
Divide by 4 for final score.   _____

ESSAY 5

SELF-EVALUATION

Overall Impression   _____

Understanding of U.S. History   _____

Development   _____

Organization/Conventions
of English   _____

TOTAL   _____
Divide by 4 for final score.   _____

ESSAY 5

OBJECTIVE EVALUATION

Overall Impression   _____

Understanding of U.S. History   _____

Development   _____

Organization/Conventions
of English   _____

TOTAL   _____
Divide by 4 for final score.   _____

Chapter 5

REVIEWING THE COLONIAL PERIOD TO 1789

Red Alert!

Check the College Board Web site (www.collegeboard.org/ap) for the time period for your DBQ.

The following review of European exploration and colonization, the expansion of the thirteen original English colonies, the movement toward independence, and the beginning of the new nation is meant as a tool to supplement your regular AP course. This review is based on the College Board's own AP history guide and focuses on political, economic, and social and cultural developments. The College Board's Guide for an AP United States History course lists six major topics, including the writing of the Constitution, for the period from exploration through 1789. According to the College Board, approximately one sixth (16 percent) of the multiple-choice questions are drawn from this period. It is also possible that the DBQ or a free response essay question could be based on some aspect of exploration, colonization, or the break from Great Britain. For example, the DBQ for the 1999 test was drawn from the period 1750 to 1800.

SECTION 1. DISCOVERY, SETTLEMENT, AND EXPANSION, 1492–1754

Review Strategy

See page 115 for the origins of slavery in the Americas.

The study of American history is the study of the intertwining of many different strands of historical development. A point at which to begin is Europe in the sixteenth century. The rise of nation-states, religious upheavals, and economic developments led Europeans to seek riches, territories, and dominion outside Europe to bolster their power on the continent. In studying American history, it is important to understand how and why these events interacted to create European colonies in the Americas. It is also possible to see in this early period the foundations of later developments in American history: not only political developments such as the beginnings of representative government but also social and cultural developments such as the subjugation of Native Americans and the institutionalization of slavery.

FAST FACTS

- Experts estimate that when Columbus reached the Americas, some 1 to 2 million Native Americans lived north of Mexico in six major culture areas: Northwest Coast, Plains, Plateau, Eastern Woodlands, Northern, and the Southwest. Another 20 million lived in Mexico and 30 million in South America. The First Americans are thought to have come across the **land bridge** now covered by the Bering Strait 15,000 to 30,000 years ago. Approximately 12,000 years ago, as the Ice Age animals disappeared, people turned to hunting smaller game, catching fish, and gathering plants. About 5,000 years ago, some peoples began to domesticate animals. With a stable food supply, groups established permanent settlements and the population increased. Specialization in arts and crafts resulted, and hierarchical organizations grew, often combining religious and secular power and a social structure. In some areas, monumental buildings were erected. The Native Americans who met the Europeans in the 1400s and 1500s had a wide range of cultures, dependent for the most part on the **environment.**

- The Spanish, French, and English handled their relations with Native Americans differently. With the establishment of the **encomienda system,** the Spanish in the Caribbean used the native people for forced labor. Many Native Americans died from small-pox and other European diseases and from brutal treatment. **Bartolomé de Las Casas,** a former conquistador turned priest, protested to the pope and Spanish king. In time, the encomienda system was ended, and enslaved Africans replaced the already dwindling native populations on the Spanish sugar plantations of the Caribbean. On the mainland in New Spain, the Spanish, supported by their military, set up **missions** and forced Native Americans to (1) give up their cultures, (2) wear European-style clothing, (3) learn Spanish, (4) convert to Christianity, and (5) labor for the priests.

- Because they had little military support, the French did not establish missions. Unarmed French missionaries went among Native Americans to preach and convert them and were often tortured and killed for their efforts. The English treatment of Native Americans varied from colony to colony but often began with good relations, as with the **Pilgrims** and **Wampanoags** and **William Penn** and the **Delaware** or **Leni-Lenape.** As more settlers moved to the colonies and encroached on Native American lands, fighting erupted between colonists and Native Americans, with Native Americans always losing.

KEY EXPLORERS AND THEIR ACHIEVEMENTS

DATE	EXPLORER	COUNTRY	ACHIEVEMENT
1487–1488	Diaz	Portugal	Sails around southern tip of Africa
1492–1504	Columbus	Spain	First European to explore the Western Hemisphere; explores the West Indies and the Caribbean
1497–1498	da Gama	Portugal	Sails around Africa to India
1497–1501(?)	Cabot	England	Explores Newfoundland and Nova Scotia
1499	Vespucci	Spain	Explores coast of South America
1500	Cabral	Portugal	Explores Brazil
1508–1509 1513	Ponce de Leon	Spain	Explores Puerto Rico Explores Florida
1516–1520	de Soto	Spain	Explores Central America
1519	Magellan	Spain	Circumnavigates the globe
1519	Cortés	Spain	Explores Mexico; conquers the Aztecs
1524	Verrazano	France	Explores northeastern coast of North America
1531	Pizarro	Spain	Explores Peru; conquers the Incas
1534–1542	Cartier	France	Explores St. Lawrence River
1539–1542	de Soto	Spain	Explores lower Mississippi River
1540–1542	Coronado	Spain	Explores southwestern U.S.
1542–1543	Cabrillo	Spain	Explores westn coast of North America
1603–1615	Champlain	France	Explores St. Lawrence River valley Founds Quebec
1609	Hudson	Netherlands	Explores east coast of North America, including Hudson River
1610–1611	Hudson	England	Explores Hudson Bay
1673	Marquette/Joliet	France	Explores Mississippi River
1679–1682	La Salle	France	Explores Great Lakes region; reaches mouth of the Mississippi River

Review Strategy

This "Fast Fact" and the table on page 109 relate to European exploration.

- Several factors spurred European interest in exploration: (1) The Crusades of the eleventh and twelfth centuries had interested Europeans in trade with Asia for luxury goods, such as spices, sugar, and silk. (2) European merchants, especially in trading cities such as Genoa and Venice and the Hanseatic League, a confederation of cities on the North and Baltic Seas, wanted new trade routes to Asia to cut out Middle Eastern middlemen. (3) Technological advances, such as the astrolabe and compass, made it possible for sailors to try new and dangerous water routes. (4) The rise of **nation-states** encouraged economic development and also rivalry among European nations for new territories and new wealth. (5) The **Renaissance** engendered a sense of curiosity and adventure among Europeans.

Review Strategy

These "Fast Facts" relate to the Spanish in the Americas.

- Spanish settlement in the Americas began in the Caribbean and moved north into what is now the United States and west and south into Central and South America. Between 1492 and 1800, Spain had conquered and colonized large sections of Central and South America and set up settlements in what are today California, New Mexico, Arizona, Texas, Mississippi, Louisiana, and Florida. The oldest permanent European settlement in the United States is **St. Augustine, Florida.** Settlements often began as a mission or a mission and **presidio**, a fort, with towns being established at a later stage of development. New Spain was divided into **viceroyalties** governed by **viceroys** appointed by the monarch.

- Long-term Spanish influences include (1) the use of Spanish as the dominant language in Central and South America; (2) the introduction of Roman Catholicism to Native Americans; (3) the subjugation and killing of Native Americans and taking of their lands and wealth; (4) the introduction of European crops, livestock, iron products, and firearms into native cultures; and (5) the introduction of Native American crops into Europe.

Review Strategy

This "Fast Fact" relates to the French in North America.

- The French did not attempt colonization until the early 1600s. In 1608, **Samuel de Champlain** founded Quebec in what is today Canada, but its northern climate attracted few colonists. By 1680, the French had established a line of settlements from Canada and the Great Lakes to the Gulf of Mexico. Unlike the Spanish, the French had not found gold but had found an abundant source of furs for export. Only about 10,000 settlers had come to New France by 1680 because (1) the colonies were not as rich as the sugar island colonies of the French, (2) most French monarchs were more interested in securing their power in Europe than in establishing American colonies, and (3) **Huguenots,** religious dissidents, were not allowed to emigrate. Government was by a

THE THIRTEEN ENGLISH COLONIES

NEW ENGLAND COLONIES

Colony	Date	Founded by	Reasons	Importance
Plymouth	1620	Pilgrims	Religious freedom	**Mayflower Compact**
Massachusetts Bay	1630	Puritans, Massachusetts Bay Company	Religious freedom; build **"a City on a Hill"**	Representative government through election to **General Court**
Plymouth and Massachusetts Bay joined	1691			
New Hampshire and Maine	1622	John Mason, Sir Ferdinando Gorges	Profit from trade and fishing	Colonists from Massachusetts move into area; by 1650s under Massachusetts' control
New Hampshire	1679	Royal charter from Charles II		
Connecticut	1636	Thomas Hooker	Expansion of trade, religious, and political freedoms; limited government	**Fundamental Orders of Connecticut:** (1) any man owning property could vote; (2) limited power of governor
	1662	Receives charter from king and becomes separate royal colony		
Rhode Island	1636	Roger Williams, buys land from Narragansetts	Religious **toleration**	Separates church and state, unlike Massachusetts Bay Colony

council appointed by the king, similar to the government of New Spain. In 1608, the French under Champlain had joined the Algonquins and Hurons in a fight against the **Iroquois.** The hatred of the French that this battle engendered among the Iroquois had significant consequences for later British colonists.

Review Strategy

These "Fast Facts" relate to Jamestown.

- The first permanent English settlement was **Jamestown,** founded in 1607 by **Captain John Smith.** The **Virginia Company** had received a **charter** from James I granting it the right to settle the area from the **lost colony of Roanoke,** off the coast of what is today North Carolina, to the Potomac River. The charter also

THE THIRTEEN ENGLISH COLONIES

MIDDLE COLONIES

Colony	Date	Founded by	Reasons	Importance
New Netherlands	1624	Dutch under Peter Minuit	Trade, religious freedom	Diverse population
New York	1664	Royal charter from Charles II to his brother, James, Duke of York	Takes valuable trade and land from rival	
Delaware	1638	Swedish settlers	Trade	
	1664	Seized by English	Take land from rival	
	1682	Land grant to William Penn, proprietary colony	Known as Lower Counties	Provides Pennsylvania with coastline
New Jersey	1664	Lord Berkeley, Sir George Carteret, **proprietary colony**	Division of New York because too large to govern; trade and religious and political freedoms	Few colonists; remains mostly Native American lands
	1702	Becomes royal colony		Protection of religious freedom and right of assembly to vote on local matters
Pennsylvania	1682	William Penn, proprietary colony	Religious and political freedoms	**Quakers' "Holy Experiment;"** attracts diverse population; pays Leni-Lenape for their land

Review Strategy

See page 115 for the origins of slavery in the Americas.

granted the colonists the same rights as English citizens. In order for the colonists to survive in the beginning, Smith established work rules and traded for food with nearby Native Americans, most notably **Powhatan,** the leader of the **Powhatan Confederacy,** whose daughter, **Pocohantas,** in time married **John Rolfe.** It was Rolfe who was responsible for establishing **tobacco** as a major **cash crop** for the Virginians. In 1619, the first Africans were brought to the colony, as were the first white women.

- The political significance of the Virginia Colony is in its establishment of the **House of Burgesses** in 1619. This was the first **representative government** in an English colony. Male colonists elected burgesses, or representatives, to consult with the gover-

THE THIRTEEN ENGLISH COLONIES

SOUTHERN COLONIES

Colony	Date	Founded by	Reasons	Importance
Jamestown	1607	Virginia Company	Trade, farming	Establishes self-government under the **House of Burgesses**
Virginia	1624	Becomes royal colony under James I		Continues House of Burgesses
Maryland	1632	Land grant from Charles I to Lord Baltimore; on his death to his son, Cecil, Lord Baltimore; first proprietary colony	Religious and political freedoms	Roman Catholics; elected assembly; **Act of Toleration** providing religious freedom to all Christians
The Carolinas	1663	Land grant from Charles II to 8 proprietors	Trade farming, religious freedom	Rice and indigo cultivation; need for large numbers of laborers leads to African enslavement
North Carolina	1712			
South Carolina	1729	Proprietors sold their rights to the king; became royal colonies		Establishes representative assemblies
Georgia	1732	James Oglethorpe, proprietary colony	Haven for debtors; buffer against Spanish Florida	Originally southern part of South Carolina; initially only small farms and no slavery; grows slowly, and Oglethorpe allows slavery and plantations

nor's council in making laws for the colony. Prior to 1670, colonists did not have to own property in order to vote. In that year, the franchise was limited to free, male property owners. In 1624, James I withdrew the charter from the **Virginia Company** and made Virginia a **royal colony** but allowed the House of Burgesses to continue.

- The **Pilgrims,** persecuted for their refusal to conform to the **Church of England,** received a charter from the **London Company** for land south of the Hudson River, but their ship was blown off course to the area that is today Cape Cod. Before landing in 1620, they wrote and signed the **Mayflower Compact,** the first document in the English colonies establishing **self-government.** Like the colonists at Jamestown, the Pilgrims relied initially on help from the local Native Americans. In time, the colonists became farmers and timber exporters, but few new colonists joined them and, in 1691, Plymouth Colony joined with the Massachusetts Bay Colony.

- **Massachusetts Bay Colony** was founded in 1629 by the **Puritans** under a charter from King Charles I. They, too, were seeking religious freedom, but, unlike the Pilgrims, they did not wish to separate from the Church of England but to "purify" it of practices they believed were too close to those of the Roman Catholic Church. With their charter, they set up the Massachusetts Bay Company and used it to establish a colony that would be a **commonwealth** based on the Bible. In the beginning, laws were passed by the **General Court** made up of freemen, those few male colonists who owned stock in the Massachusetts Bay Company. Very quickly, colonists rebelled, and in 1631, the leaders admitted to the General Court any Puritan man in good standing. As the colony continued to grow, the number became unwieldy, and the law was changed so that freemen in each town in the colony elected two representatives to the General Court. Like Jamestown, Massachusetts Bay had established a representative form of government—though limited in scope.

- Except for Pennsylvania, which had a **unicameral legislature**, the colonies had **bicameral legislatures** modeled on the upper and lower houses of Parliament. The upper chambers were made up of the governor, his advisers, and councillors appointed at the suggestion of the governor by the monarch or proprietor, depending on the kind of colony. In Rhode Island and Connecticut, the upper house was elected by the colonists, and in Massachusetts, the upper house was elected by the lower house. The lower houses were elected by the colonists, supposedly every two years, but some governors, such as Berkeley in Virginia, refused to call elections for years. This is why the **power of the purse** had become important. The legislatures had developed the right to levy taxes and pay the salaries of governors. By threatening to withhold his salary, the legislature could pass laws over a governor's objections.

- Voting requirements changed as the colonies grew. Originally, only Puritans could vote in Massachusetts Bay, and in royal colonies, only **Anglicans.** Catholics, Jews, Baptists, and Quakers were restricted from voting in certain colonies, and no colony allowed women, Native Americans, and slaves to vote. In all colonies, white males had to own land in order to vote. Over time, this changed so that men could own property other than land or pay a tax to be eligible to vote.

Review Strategy

This "Fast Fact" relates to the Dominion of New England.

- In 1686, following his accession to the throne as James II, the former Duke of York combined New York, New Jersey, and the New England colonies into the **Dominion of New England** with the intention of ending the region's illegal trading activities. Appointing **Sir Edmund Andros** as governor, James abolished the colonial legislatures and allowed Andros to govern with unlimited powers. In 1688, the English, angered by James's policies and his conversion to Catholicism, deposed him in the **Glorious Revolution,** installing William and Mary of Orange as monarchs. Andros was removed from office, and the charters were returned to the colonies along with their representative governments. An additional event of significance to the colonists was the drafting of an **English Bill of Rights** guaranteeing certain rights to every citizen, including the right to representative government.

Review Strategy

These "Fast Facts" relate to the origins of slavery in the Americas.

- **Slavery** in the Americas began with the Spanish on their sugar islands in the Caribbean. To replace Native Americans, the Spanish and later the English began to import Africans as slaves. In 1619, the first Africans to arrive in the colonies came off a Dutch ship at Jamestown and were treated as **indentured servants.** As it became more difficult to find the large number of workers needed for tobacco agriculture, the policy changed. In a court case in Jamestown in 1640, the indenture of an African was changed to servitude for life. In 1663, Maryland passed its first slave law. The plan for government for the Carolinas recognized Africans as slaves, and, therefore, as property. Slavery was legalized in Georgia when the colonists came to realize that they would make money only through plantation agriculture. New York and New Jersey began as a single Dutch colony, and Africans were recognized as indentured servants. After the English seized and divided the colony, slavery was legalized. However, the Northern colonies did not farm **labor-intensive crops,** such as tobacco, rice, and indigo, so there was little need for slaves. In the North, most slaves were household help.

- Estimates vary, but it is generally agreed that some 20 million Africans survived the **Middle Passage** of the **triangular trade route** between Europe, Africa, and the colonies. They came from the **West Coast of Africa,** and most were sold in the Caribbean or South America. After being captured by fellow Africans and force-marched to the sea in chains for sale to Europeans, Africans were kept in **slave factories**—warehouses, offices, the living quarters of Europeans, and pens—until ships were available. The Africans were then marched on board in chains and kept below decks where an average of 13 to 20 percent of the human cargo died during a voyage. On arrival in the colonies, the Africans were sold, without regard to keeping families together.

- The English institutionalized slavery because (1) they needed labor and (2) they viewed Africans with their foreign languages and ways as less than human. The English had found neither Native Americans—who died from disease or who, as runaways, melted into the forests—nor white indentured servants—who worked only for a specified time or who, as runaways, could melt into the general population—a satisfactory workforce.

KEY PEOPLE

Review Strategy

See if you can relate these to their correct context in the "Fast Facts" section.

- **Nathaniel Bacon, Bacon's Rebellion, Sir William Berkeley, Virginia**
- **William Bradford,** *History of Plimouth Plantation*
- **Iroquois League, Five Nations,** later **Six Nations**
- **Anne Hutchinson, doctrine of antinomianism, Rhode Island**
- **King Philip's War** or **Metacom's War, New England**
- **Jacob Leisler, Leisler's Rebellion, New York**
- **Pequot War, southern New England**
- **John Winthrop, Massachusetts Bay**

KEY TERMS/IDEAS

Review Strategy

See if you can relate these terms and ideas to their correct context in the "Fast Facts" section.

- **Chesapeake country, Chesapeake Bay**
- **Columbian Exchange of items and ideas among different cultures**
- **covenant, Massachusetts Bay Colony, congregations, saints or true believers**
- **Great Migration, England to Massachusetts Bay Colony, 1620–1640**
- **Halfway Covenant, Puritan compromise, 1662**
- **headright system, after 1618, Virginia Colony**
- **joint-stock company, Virginia Company and Massachusetts Bay Company**

- **New England Confederation; colonies of Connecticut, New Haven, Plymouth, and Massachusetts Bay; first attempt at union**
- **patroon system, Dutch colonies**
- **Restoration colonies, 1660–1688**
- **royal colony, proprietary colony**
- **Salem witch trials, 1692, Cotton Mather**
- **Treaty of Tordesillas, line of demarcation, Spain and Portugal in the Americas**

SECTION 2. COLONIAL SOCIETY AROUND 1750

By 1760, some 2 million people lived in the English colonies, with about half the population in the five Southern Colonies. The original colonists had settled along the coast, but, by the 1700s, settlers were moving inland to the **frontier or backcountry.** In the Northern Colonies, this meant the forests of northern New England, New York, and central Pennsylvania. In the Southern Colonies, settlers were leaving the **Tidewater,** that part of the Atlantic Coastal Plain between New Jersey and Georgia, for the **Piedmont,** an area that gradually slopes into the Appalachian Mountains. By the time of the American Revolution, colonists had settled the Piedmont and were moving across the Appalachians.

Review Strategy

This "Fast Fact" summarizes the social system in the colonies.

- Colonists, with the exception of slaves and free blacks, had an opportunity for **social mobility.**

SOCIAL STRUCTURE OF THE THIRTEEN ENGLISH COLONIES	
Gentry/Upper Class	Plantation owners (Southern Colonies), merchants, high government officials, clergy
Middle Class	Owners of small farms, skilled craftworkers, shopkeepers, and professionals such as doctors and teachers
Lower Class	Tenant farmers, hired farmhands, servants, unskilled workers, indentured servants, free blacks
Slaves	

- Most of the early colonists lived in villages or small towns and went out each day to farm their lands, especially in New England. Later, as the pattern of settlement grew and people moved to the frontier and the backcountry, a trading town would grow up here and there at an intersection of roads or waterways, but most people lived on their farms, far from one another and from town. Social life meant trips to town for shopping, to church, and to an occasional house-raising or barn dance. On the plantation, white women managed the house while their husbands or fathers managed the business of the plantation. A white overseer managed day-to-day operations in the fields where enslaved Africans—men, women, and children—supplied the unpaid labor. Some Africans were trained as skilled workers or as house servants.

- Philadelphia was the largest city in the 1750s, with a population of 20,000. New York and Boston ranked second and third. Charles Town, South Carolina, and Baltimore, Maryland, were the only large cities in the Southern Colonies. Although many immigrants stayed in the cities because they offered more opportunities, the cities were as foul and disease-ridden as they were in Europe. Over time, dirt streets were paved with brick or cobblestones, streetlights were installed, laws were passed to keep streets clean and to keep the peace, and parks and libraries were built.

- Colonial families of ten or twelve children were not unusual. Most women married in their early twenties and many died in their childbearing years, having had five or six children. In the rural areas, women took care of the children and the household chores: weaving cloth; sewing clothes; making soap, candles, and bread; cooking, cleaning, and washing; tending a small vegetable and herb garden; and doctoring the sick, often with medicines of their own making. On farms at planting and harvesting times, women and girls worked in the fields. Men worked in the fields, tended to the farm animals, and were responsible for selling or trading any **surplus.** Boys worked alongside their fathers as soon as they were big enough. In cities, work was still assigned by gender, but women and girls sometimes helped out in their fathers' or husbands' shops, and widows often took over their husbands' work.

- Women could learn trades and skills such as printing and silversmithing, but any money a woman earned working outside the home belonged to her husband or, if she was unmarried, to her father. Women could not vote, and married women could not own property. Single women, although not married women, could enter into business, sign contracts, and sue in court. Women had little opportunity for education, in part because there was little schooling available in the early colonies, and later because education was

ECONOMIC DEVELOPMENT IN THE THIRTEEN ENGLISH COLONIES

Colonies	Environment	Economy	Results
New England	Forested, rocky soil with long, cold winters and short growing seasons	Subsistence farming; manufacturing, shipbuilding, fishing; trade	Family-farmed land with an occasional hired hand or **indentured servant;** little use for slavery; trade with England and the West Indies, including **triangular trade** for slaves
Middle	Fertile soil; temperate climate with longer growing season	Major **cash crops:** wheat, corn, rye; **"breadbasket colonies;"** later trade and manufacturing centers	Some large estates; family farms large enough to hire farm workers or keep indentured servants; little slavery except for tobacco plantations in Delaware
Southern	Fertile soil; mild winters with a long growing season; abundant waterways for irrigation and transportation	Small farms for vegetables, grain; labor-intensive tobacco, rice, indigo agriculture on plantations; little manufacturing or Southern-owned shipping; few large cities	Most farms were small and worked by farm families at a **subsistence level;** almost self-sufficient plantations with hundreds of slaves were the exception; few free blacks in towns and cities

limited to boys. Note, however, that because of their importance to the colonies' development, women in the colonies had more rights, higher **status,** and greater economic independence than women in England.

Review Strategy

This "Fast Fact" relates to the First Great Awakening.

- By the early 1700s, the influence of Puritanism on the **Congregational Church** and on the New England **polity** was vastly reduced. A general lessening of interest in religion seemed to be spreading throughout the colonies, and in the 1730s and 1740s, an era of **religious revivalism** called the **First Great Awakening** engulfed the colonies. Spurred by charismatic preachers such as Englishmen **John Wesley** and **George Whitefield, Jonathan Edwards** of Massachusetts, and **William Tennent** and his son, **Gilbert,** thousands repented of their sins and joined Protestant churches, many of them new. The preachers taught that a person did not have to belong to an **established church** (Puritanism and Anglicanism) to be saved. A person had only to repent of his/her sins, believe in Jesus Christ as savior, and experience the Holy Spirit. The Great Awakening created (1) divisions among congregations and thus the rise of new congregations and sects, (2) a fear of education on the part of some while motivating others to found schools, and (3) a new sense of independence by encouraging people to actively choose their church.

Review Strategy

These "Fast Facts" relate to the "American mind."

- The mid-1700s is known as the **Enlightenment** or **Age of Reason.** Two of the most important influences of the time were **empiricist** philosopher **John Locke,** who wrote *Two Treatises of Government,* and scientist **Sir Isaac Newton.** Another major influence was **deism.** Based on the writings of men like **Voltaire** and **Jean-Jacques Rousseau,** deists believed in God but rejected Divine Providence and Divine Revelation, believing that everything was knowable through reason, including religious truth. Educated colonists such as Thomas Jefferson and Benjamin Franklin read the writings of the Enlightenment and were influenced in their political thinking by them.

- In his book, *The Americans: The Colonial Experience,* historian Daniel Boorstin has a part entitled "An American Frame of Mind" in which he states, "No American invention has influenced the world so powerfully as the concept of knowledge which sprang from the American experience." He explains this as the appeal to **self-evidence.** Colonists could "see" progress working. **Ben Franklin** and his *Poor Richard's Almanac(k)* as well as *The Autobiography of Ben Franklin* are good examples of how the Enlightenment translated into the American consciousness of the practical and the **pragmatic.**

Review Strategy

This "Fast Fact" relates to new immigrants to the colonies.

- The majority of original colonists were English, but by 1775 just under 50 percent of the colonists were English. While New England remained mostly English, the Middle and Southern Colonies gained diverse populations. Protestant Scotch-Irish, Scots, and Welsh; Irish Catholics; French Huguenots; **Sephardic Jews;** and German Protestants joined the Dutch, Swedes, and Finns already living in the Middle Colonies to make up about a third of the total colonial population. Africans made up the remaining 20 percent. New immigrants were motivated by the same **push/pull factors** as the original colonists: (1) to escape religious persecution, which often also meant (2) escaping curtailed civil rights, and (3) for economic gain.

Review Strategy

These "Fast Facts" relate to slavery.

- One reason that colonists used Africans as slaves was that the supply seemed limitless. In Virginia in the 1660s, there were only 300 Africans, but by 1756 there were 120,000 in a population of 293,000. About 3,000 were free blacks. In the forty years between 1714 and 1754, the total number of Africans in the colonies rose from 59,000 to almost 300,000. **Natural increase** accounted for some of this, but most slaves were newly arrived Africans. New

England and the Middle Colonies had few slaves in proportion to the overall slave population in the colonies. The climate and terrain were unsuited to plantation-style agriculture. In the early days of Massachusetts Bay, Puritans had banned slavery. However, in 1698, the **Royal African Company** authorized New England merchants to buy and sell Africans in the transatlantic slave trade.

- Slaves had no legal rights: (1) slave marriages were not recognized, (2) slaves could not own property (they *were* property), (3) they had little legal protection against a cruel owner, (4) they could be sold away from their families, and (5) it was illegal to teach a slave to read and write.

- Free blacks were few in number, although it was easier to be freed in New England and the Middle Colonies because there was less economic incentive to keep a slave. Blacks were free (1) if they were the descendants of the early indentured servants, (2) if their mothers were white, (3) if their owners freed them, or (4) if they bought their freedom with savings that their owners allowed them to keep from outside jobs they did.

KEY PEOPLE

- **Anne Bradstreet, poet, Massachusetts Bay Colony**
- **Phillis Wheatley, poet, former slave**
- **John Peter Zenger, trial for seditious libel, freedom of the press**

KEY TERMS/IDEAS

Review Strategy

See if you can relate these terms and ideas to their correct context in the "Fast Facts" section.

- **Massachusetts General School Act of 1647**
- **Presbyterianism**
- ***Sinners in the Hands of an Angry God*, Jonathan Edwards**

SECTION 3. THE MOVE TO INDEPENDENCE, 1754–1776

The world view of colonists in 1754 on the brink of the American Revolution was being shaped by a number of factors: (1) the experience of self-government, (2) the thinking of the Enlightenment, (3) belief in religious toleration and freedom to choose one's religious affiliation, and (4) social mobility, except for enslaved Africans. The catalyst for revolution would turn out to be actions of the British government intent on keeping its colonies in the service of mercantilism.

FAST FACTS

Review Strategy

These "Fast Facts" and the next table relate to mercantilism.

- Under the policy of **mercantilism,** European colonies existed for the purpose of building up **specie** or gold supplies and expanding trade for the home countries. To achieve these goals, nations had to build a **favorable balance of trade** by **exporting** more than they **imported.** England, later Great Britain, saw its colonies: (1) as sources of raw materials, (2) as markets for English goods, (3) as bases for the Royal Navy because a strong navy was needed to protect English interests much as the **Spanish Armada** had protected Spanish interests, and (4) as a way to develop a commercial navy.

- To enforce mercantilism, the English Parliament passed a series of **Navigation Acts** between 1651 and 1673. Among the laws were: (1) only English or colonial ships could transport goods to or from the English colonies (which greatly benefited New England shipbuilders), (2) certain goods such as tobacco, sugar, and cotton—**enumerated goods**—could be sold only to England, and (3) all goods bound for the colonies had to be shipped through England where they were unloaded, an **import duty** paid on them, and then reloaded for shipment to the colonies. The latter action increased the price of foreign goods in order to protect English manufacturers. Colonists found it easy to evade the Navigation Acts by smuggling. In 1673, England passed a law appointing **customs officials** to collect **customs duties** on goods brought into the colony, but they often remained in England and hired deputies who did little to collect taxes and could be bribed to ignore smuggling. It was also difficult to police the long coastline. As a result, the British government adopted a policy of **salutory neglect,** or noninterference, until 1764.
  Throughout the late 1690s and into the mid-1700s, the British government continued to pass laws aimed at controlling trade to and from the colonies.

MERCANTILE LAWS	
Woolen Act, 1699	Colonists could not export raw wool, yarn, or wool cloth to other colonies or to other countries, thus slowing colonial manufacturing but protecting English trade.
Hat Act, 1732	Colonial hatmakers could not sell their beaver hats outside the colonies.
Molasses Act, 1733	A tax was placed on sugar, rum, and molasses bought from the French West Indies rather than from the British West Indies.
Iron Act, 1750	Colonists were forbidden to build mills for smelting iron.

Review Strategy

The table on p. 124 and these "Fast Facts" relate to the French and Indian War.

- Mercantilism heightened the rivalries among European nations, especially between France and England. The immediate causes for conflict in North America were (1) conflicting claims to land, (2) fur trade with Native Americans, and (3) the arming of Native Americans for raids. The **Iroquois,** who traded with the British, were moving into areas where Native American allies of the French lived and trapped, while British colonists were moving across the Appalachians into territory the French claimed, especially the Ohio Valley where the French built a series of forts.

- The **Treaty of Paris, 1763,** officially ended the French and Indian War: (1) France ceded the Louisiana Territory to Spain to repay its debts, (2) France gave Canada and its land east of the Mississippi River to Great Britain, and (3) Spain, as an ally of France, turned over Florida to Great Britain. Only Great Britain and Spain retained land in North America.

- As the first conflicts in the French and Indian War were occurring, representatives from seven British colonies met at Albany, New York, in 1754 to ask the **Iroquois** for help. The Iroquois initially remained neutral, but as the war progressed and they saw the French losing, the Iroquois agreed to work with the British. At this Albany Congress, Ben Franklin suggested the **Albany Plan of Union,** based on the **Iroquois League of Six Nations.** The plan called for (1) a Grand Council of representatives chosen by the legislatures of each colony and (2) a president-general named by the British Crown (3) in order to make laws, raise taxes, and prepare for the defense of the colonies when the colonies needed to act together. The colonial legislatures rejected the idea because they did not want to give up power, even to their own representatives. Like the **New England Confederation,** however, the Albany Plan was a step toward uniting the colonies.

- The colonists experienced some unintended benefits from the French and Indian War: (1) colonial militias gained experience and skill in warfare, (2) the colonists saw that the British could be defeated, (3) militias had to accept blacks because there was a shortage of able-bodied men willing to fight, (4) colonists no longer feared Native Americans without the French to arm them, and (5) colonists learned more about people in other colonies, lessening their suspicions of them and at the same time learning the benefits of cooperation.

ANGLO-FRENCH WARS

War in Europe	War in North America	Result
War of League of Augsburg	King William's War, 1689–1697	French loss of Nova Scotia, Newfoundland, and Hudson Bay to Great Britain
War of Spanish Succession	Queen Anne's War, 1702–1713	
War of Austrian Succession	King George's War, 1742–1748	Loss of remaining French territory in North America to British: Canada and all land east of the Mississippi River
Seven Years' War	**French and Indian War,** 1754–1763	

Review Strategy

The table on pp. 126–27 and these "Fast Facts" summarize the steps to the American Revolution.

- In answer to **Pontiac's War** against forts on the frontier, the British government issued the **Proclamation of 1763** forbidding colonial settlement from west of the Appalachian Mountains to the Mississippi until treaties could be signed. Colonial trappers, traders, settlers, and **land speculators** protested the proclamation as unnecessary British intervention and ignored it. As a result of Pontiac's War, the British government decided that a British army should be sent to the colonies to protect its interests.

- The French and Indian War had cost Great Britain a great deal of money, and with the end of the war had come the responsibilities and costs of managing a new empire not only in North America but also in India. The British government pointed out that the colonists had gained much from the war: (1) the end of threats from the French and Native Americans and (2) the continued protection of the British army and navy. The British government expected the colonists to pay for these benefits. Not surprisingly, the colonists disagreed. The war was over, and they expected things to return to what they had been before—with one difference: the colonists saw a divergence between their interests and those of Great Britain.

- British policy toward the colonies changed significantly with the selection of **George Grenville** as Prime Minister in 1763: (1) the **Navigation Acts** were to be strictly enforced, (2) customs officials could no longer remain in England and send deputies to collect taxes, (3) **writs of assistance** were to be issued to allow officials to search for smuggled goods and collect unpaid taxes, (4) British warships were to patrol the coastline, and (5) smugglers were no longer to be tried in front of friendly juries of their peers but in front of **admiralty courts.** This violated one of the basic rights of the English people guaranteed in the **Magna Carta.**

- At the passage of the **Stamp Act, Patrick Henry** raised the cry of **taxation without representation** in his **Virginia Resolves,** which the House of Burgesses passed. According to his argument, each colonial charter guaranteed its citizens the same rights as people living in England. In England, the right to tax the people rested with the House of Commons, but the colonists had no representatives in the House and, therefore, the House could not levy taxes on them. Only their own colonial legislatures could tax them, and their legislatures had not passed the Stamp Act.

- Representatives from nine legislatures met in New York for the **Stamp Act Congress.** In a petition to **George III,** they (1) declared their loyalty and (2) agreed with the government's right to regulate trade but (3) argued that the Sugar and Stamp Acts were taxation without representation. Colonial merchants and planters signed **nonimportation agreements,** and colonists organized **boycotts** of British goods in which the **Daughters of Liberty** took part. **Sons of Liberty** attacked merchants willing to use the stamps as well as the tax collectors. In time, the boycotts caused rising unemployment and hurt British merchants who lobbied Parliament to repeal the Stamp Act, which was done in 1766.

- Although Parliament repealed the Stamp Act, it also passed the **Declaratory Act** in 1766. The act stated that Parliament had the power and right to make laws for the colonies "in all cases whatsoever." Thus, the basic question of whether Parliament, having no representatives from the colonies within its body, had the right to make laws taxing the colonies was answered to the satisfaction of Parliament and the monarch. Parliament based its position on the theory of **virtual representation.** The House of Commons was sworn to represent every person in England and the empire—whether or not he or she could vote. The colonists, however, were used to **direct** or **actual representation;** they had

BRITISH LEGISLATIVE ACTIONS LEADING TO THE REVOLUTION

LAW	PROVISIONS	CONSEQUENCES
Sugar Act, 1764	Reduced tax on molasses brought into colonies from British and non-British ports; meant to strengthen the Molasses Act, 1733	Colonists had been smuggling molasses from French colonies and not paying the tax. Strict enforcement meant paying the tax or not having molasses.
Currency Act, 1764	Forbid the colonies from issuing their own paper money; taxes to be paid in gold or silver coin, **specie,** rather than paper money	Because the **balance of trade** had shifted to Great Britain around 1750, colonial merchants had been sending large amounts of currency to Great Britain to pay their taxes, already making it difficult for merchants to do business.
Quartering Act, 1765	Passed as a way to save money on keeping the British army sent after the Proclamation of 1763; colonists to provide barracks and supplies for the soldiers	Colonists feared this was the beginning of a permanent British army that they would have to support.
Stamp Act, 1765	Provided that colonists must buy a special stamp to place on almost every kind of document: wills, marriage licenses, playing cards, newspapers, etc. (The English had been paying this tax since 1694.)	It was the first tax placed on goods made and sold in the colonies, and, as such, did not support **mercantilism.**
Townshend Acts, 1767	Placed **import duties** on such goods as glass, paint, paper, and tea; created more **admiralty courts;** suspended the New York legislature because it had refused to obey the Quartering Act	This was the first tax levied on goods imported from Great Britain. Revenue raised by the tax was to be used to pay salaries of royal governors and judges in the colonies, thus negating the **power of the purse.**
Tea Act, 1773	Continued tax on tea imposed by the Townshend Act; gave **monopoly** on selling tea in the colonies to the British East India Company; allowed company to choose merchants to sell its tea in the colonies	Tea merchants not chosen to sell the company's tea feared they would lose their businesses. There was also concern that in time the sale of other goods could be controlled in the same way.

been electing representatives to their assemblies since the earliest days of the colonies.

- Colonial resistance to the Townshend Acts took the form of writings, boycotts, and protests. **John Dickinson** wrote *Letters from a Pennsylvania Farmer* promoting unity of action among the colonists. The Massachusetts legislature drafted the

BRITISH LEGISLATIVE ACTIONS LEADING TO THE REVOLUTION—(cont'd)

LAW	PROVISIONS	CONSEQUENCES
Intolerable Acts, 1774 (also known as **Coercive Acts**)	Aimed specifically at Massachusetts as a result of the **Boston Tea Party:** • **Boston Port Act:** closed the port until the colonists paid for the tea • **Quartering Act:** required colonists to house troops sent to Massachusetts to enforce the Intolerable Acts • **Administration of Justice Act:** allowed a soldier or official accused of a crime to be tried outside the colony if the governor believed the person could not receive a fair trial in the colony • **Massachusetts Bay Regulating Act:** revoked the colony's charter	The acts, which took away rights that colonists believed were theirs as British subjects, angered not only colonists in Massachusetts but throughout the colonies.
Quebec Act, 1774	Extended the province of Quebec south to the Ohio River valley and west to the Mississippi River; British officials would govern it directly, but colonists could keep their laws; Roman Catholics could continue to practice their religion	Although the act was not meant to punish the English colonists, they viewed it as such because it negated the claims of Massachusetts, Connecticut, and Virginia to parts of the new province and allowed Roman Catholicism.

Massachusetts Circular Letter urging the other colonies to resist. Virginia, Maryland, and Georgia endorsed the letter, and Parliament retaliated by forbidding their legislatures and that of Massachusetts to convene. The House of Burgesses adopted a resolution that only colonial legislatures could tax the colonists. Mob violence broke out. In order to (1) ease tensions, (2) aid British merchants who were losing money again, and (3) end the drain on government revenues because of the costs of enforcement, Parliament, under the direction of the new prime minister, **Lord Frederick North,** repealed the tax provisions of the Townshend Acts—except for a small tax on tea as a symbol of the government's right to tax.

• The Townshend Acts were not repealed soon enough to prevent the **Boston Massacre,** in which five colonists were killed and six wounded after a detachment of British soldiers opened fired on a mob throwing rock-filled snowballs at them. One of the dead was **Crispus Attucks,** once a slave and now a free sailor and member of the Sons of Liberty.

KEY PEOPLE

Review Strategy

See if you can relate these to their correct context in the "Fast Facts" section.

- Samuel Adams, Committees of Correspondence
- Thomas Hutchinson, Townshend Acts, Boston Tea Party
- Louis Montcalm, James Wolfe, Quebec, Plains of Abraham
- William Pitt (the Elder), Prime Minister of England, French and Indian War

KEY TERMS/IDEAS

- direct tax, indirect tax
- *Gaspee Incident,* British revenue ship, trial in England

SECTION 4. THE AMERICAN REVOLUTION, 1775–1783

Although colonists in growing numbers had opposed the various taxation policies of Great Britain over the years, the number had always been relatively small and, to a certain extent, limited to the merchants and upper class. However, as the taxation policies became broader in scope and more widely enforced, the discontent spread among the colonists until mob violence erupted when new laws were passed. Tax collectors were tarred and feathered, shops of suspected British sympathizers ransacked, British revenue ships set afire, people who bought British goods intimidated, and British soldiers harassed. The Intolerable Acts added new reasons to the arguments of those openly espousing independence. Britain had expected that the other colonies would see the rightness of laws meant to punish Massachusetts for its lawlessness, but a number of colonists felt otherwise. That the new royal governor of Massachusetts, **General Thomas Gage,** began enforcing the Intolerable Acts did not help the cause of **Loyalists,** or **Tories.**

FAST FACTS

Review Strategy

These "Fast Facts" summarize the steps to independence.

- The **First Continental Congress,** proposed by the House of Burgesses, met in Philadelphia in fall 1774. Fifty-six male delegates assembled, representing all the colonies except Georgia, whose royal governor would not allow anyone to attend. **Patrick Henry** said, "Virginian, Pennsylvanian, New Yorkers, and New Englanders are no more. I am not a Virginian but an American." Still, there was no majority favoring independence within the Congress or among the colonists. About a third of the colonists, calling themselves **Patriots,** wanted independence from Great Britain, while another third wanted to remain loyal to Great Britain and work out their differences, and a third was indifferent. The First Continental Congress passed the **Suffolk Resolves** and the **Declaration of Rights and Grievances,** and called for another meeting in 1775.

- Even before the First Continental Congress met, fighting had broken out between colonists and the British army around Boston. Learning of arms caches at Concord and several other villages near Boston, General Gage sent soldiers on the night of April 18, 1775, to surprise them. An efficient network of spies dispatched **Paul Revere, Dr. Samuel Prescott,** and **William Dawes** to alert the towns. Reaching **Lexington** on the morning of April 19, the British were met by armed **Minutemen.** In the confusion, someone fired a shot ("the shot heard 'round the world"), and the British soldiers opened fire. Eight colonists were killed and ten wounded. The British went on to **Concord** where they exchanged fire with more Minutemen and then marched back to Boston with angry colonists shooting into the columns of retreating **Redcoats.** After Lexington and Concord, the Massachusetts militia, with reinforcements from other colonies, effectively hemmed the British in Boston until March 1776 when **General William Howe** and his army sailed for Canada, which allowed the **Continental Army** to enter Boston.

- The **Second Continental Congress** met in spring 1775. Between 1775 and 1781, it was to transform itself from an advisory body to the governing body of the new nation. Its original charge was to attempt to make peace with Great Britain while insisting on the rights of the colonists. The Second Continental Congress accomplished the following:

  - Passed the **Olive Branch Petition**

  - Passed the **Declaration of the Causes and Necessity of Taking Up Arms**

  - Established an army from the militia around Boston and placed **George Washington** in command

  - Established a navy

  - Authorized private ships, **privateers,** to attack British shipping

  - Sent representatives to France, Spain, and the Netherlands asking for military and economic support in the event of war against Great Britain

- Authorized and signed the **Declaration of Independence**

- Adopted the **Articles of Confederation**

- Acted as the national government (1) to prosecute the war, (2) conduct diplomatic relations with foreign governments, and (3) oversee ratification of the Articles of Confederation.

- In response to the Second Continental Congress' actions, George III issued the *Proclamation of Rebellion,* asking his "loyal subjects to oppose rebellion." He also ordered a naval blockade of the colonies and hired 10,000 German **(Hessian) mercenaries** to fight in the colonies.

- In April 1776, North Carolina instructed its delegates to the Second Continental Congress to support independence. A month later, Virginia followed suit. On June 7, **Richard Henry Lee** of Virginia introduced a resolution declaring "these United Colonies are, and of right, ought to be, free and independent states." While debate continued on **Lee's Resolution,** a committee composed of **John Adams, Roger Sherman, Benjamin Franklin, Robert Livingston,** and **Thomas Jefferson** began work on a declaration of independence, with Jefferson writing the first draft. Adams and Franklin contributed revisions, and the document was presented to Congress on June 28. Lee's Resolution was passed on July 2, and the Declaration adopted on July 4. All references to the monarch's part in the slave trade were excised so that the colonists would not lose the support of powerful and influential slave traders and slave owners.

Review Strategy

These "Fast Facts" relate to the Declaration of Independence.

- The **Declaration of Independence** has four major sections: (1) the **Preamble,** which describes why the colonists are seeking their independence; (2) the Declaration of Rights, (3) the List of Grievances, and (4) the formal Declaration of Independence. Jefferson drew on **Enlightenment** philosophers such as **John Locke** in his appeal to **self-evidence** and the **natural order (natural law).** He invoked the idea of a **social contract** between the ruled **(consent of the governed)** and their ruler. If the ruler abuses the contract **(absolute despotism),** then the ruled have the right to overthrow him/her. Although George III is listed as the cause of the separation, Parliament was as much to blame, but some members like William Pitt had supported the colonists. The signers formally declared their separation in the last section and asserted their rights "to levy war, conclude peace, contract alliances, establish commerce," and all other acts of an independent nation.

- The Congress had three purposes in adopting the Declaration of Independence: (1) certain generally accepted rules for conducting war would go into effect, (2) borrowing money to finance the war and governmental functions would be easier as a national entity, and (3) the Declaration was seen as a way to unite the colonists. However, colonists who remained loyal to Great Britain would be considered traitors.

Review Strategy

These "Fast Facts" relate to the conduct of the war.

Study Strategy

Don't bone up on the battles, because you will not be questioned on them.

- The new nation faced a number of disadvantages in its war with Great Britain: (1) difficulty in recruiting soldiers; (2) resistance to recruiting blacks for the army (although some 5,000 fought for the Patriots); (3) shortages of supplies for the military; (4) lack of a large, well equipped navy; (5) few Native American allies (most of the Iroquois League fought with the British in an effort to keep the Americans from their lands); (6) lack of European allies until late in the war; (6) lack of unity (Loyalists and those indifferent to the cause); and (7) a weak central government, for example, lack of power to levy taxes.

- As early as 1776, **France** had been secretly sending arms, supplies, and money to the new United States. In 1778, France recognized the colonies as a separate country and agreed to enter the war as an ally. France lent the new nation money and sent a large contingent of well-trained and well-equipped soldiers to reinforce the Continental Army as well as a fleet that effectively hindered British troop movements. Spain and the Netherlands joined the war against Great Britain. Russia, Prussia, Denmark, Sweden, and Portugal formed the **League of Armed Neutrality** against the British navy.

- Historians estimate that from 20 to 30 percent of colonists remained **Loyalists.** Although Loyalists lived in all states, the largest numbers lived in New York, Georgia, and South Carolina. Many were officeholders, wealthy landowners and merchants, and professionals—people who had financial ties to Great Britain. At the end of the war, some 80,000 fled, about half to Canada. Their property was confiscated by the states and sold.

- Although the fighting ended in 1781, the **Peace of Paris (Treaty of Paris)** was not ratified until 1783. **Benjamin Franklin, John Jay, John Adams,** and **Henry Laurens** negotiated the following concessions: (1) independence, (2) the territory between the Appalachians and the Mississippi River from the Great Lakes to Florida (the latter returned to Spain), (3) fishing rights in the Gulf of St. Lawrence and off Newfoundland, (4) payment by both countries of debts owed prior to the war, (5) agreement by Congress to ask states to allow Loyalists to sue for the value of their confiscated property, and (6) agreement by Great Britain to remove its troops from U.S. soil.

ARTICLES OF CONFEDERATION

WEAKNESSES	CONSEQUENCES
No chief executive; the Congress worked through committees	No coordination of committees and no uniform domestic or foreign policy
Required nine of thirteen states to approve laws (each state had one vote)	Rarely delegates from all thirteen states in Congress at once; often voted as blocs of smaller states (5) versus larger states (8)
Required all states to approve amendments	Never get agreement of all thirteen states, so Articles never amended
No power to levy or collect taxes; Congress could raise money only by borrowing or asking states for money	No reason for states to agree to requests; Congress always in need of money to fight the war
No power to regulate **interstate commerce**	Led to disputes between states and inability to regulate trade with foreign nations to protect American business
No power to enforce treaties	No power to force British to abide by the Peace/Treaty of Paris of 1783
No power to enforce its own laws	Only advise and request states to abide by national laws
No national court system; state courts interpreted national laws	Difficult to get states to abide by state court decisions

Review Strategy

These "Fast Facts" and the following table relate to the Articles of Confederation.

- From 1781 until 1789, when the U.S. Constitution was ratified, the new nation was governed under the **Articles of Confederation.** Because the former colonies were fighting against strong external control of their affairs, their leaders shaped a document that allowed each state a great deal of freedom, resulting in a **weak central government.** State governments were similar to their colonial governments and divided power among a governor, legislature, and judiciary with most power reserved to the legislature. Although each state constitution included a bill of rights, political power rested with the wealthy. Voting was restricted to propertied white men, and although slavery was prohibited in Northern states, the Southern economy continued to depend on it.

- Under the Articles of Confederation, the new nation accomplished the following: (1) signed the Peace of Paris ending the Revolutionary War, (2) established a policy for settling new lands and creating new states **(Land Ordinance of 1785, Northwest Ordinance of 1787),** and (3) established the departments of Foreign Affairs, War, Marine, and Treasury.

Peterson's AP Success: U.S. History

KEY PEOPLE

- **Abigail Adams, Mercy Otis Warren, James Warren**
- **Edmund Burke, Irish-born British politician**
- **Robert Morris, Haym Solomon, financial basis for the new nation**
- **Thomas Paine,** *Common Sense*

KEY TERMS/IDEAS

- **Continental Association, boycott, First Continental Congress**
- **battle at Saratoga, turning point**
- **Galloway Plan, Joseph Galloway, First Continental Congress, Loyalist**

SECTION 5. DRAFTING THE CONSTITUTION

The weaknesses of the Articles were soon apparent. Although the new government could, among other powers, establish post offices, borrow and coin money, declare war, ask states for recruits to build an army, and build and equip a navy, these powers meant little in reality. Each member of Congress was paid by his state and voted according to his state legislature's instructions. Most important to the new nation ravaged by recent war, the Confederation Congress did not have the power to deal with the **economic depression** that hit the nation after the war or the nation's growing sectional differences. Faced with mounting economic problems, including an **unfavorable balance of trade,** the states met several times to discuss solutions.

- In 1786, at the **Annapolis Conference,** delegates recommended a convention to make changes in the Articles. Meeting in Philadelphia, the fifty-five delegates soon saw that a new document was needed. Competing interests put forth different plans, and the major areas of compromise were:

- Other compromises included in the **U.S. Constitution** are: (1) **Three-Fifths Compromise** for counting slaves in determining taxes and representation for the House, (2) prohibition on importation of slaves after 1808, (3) right of Congress to regulate **interstate commerce** and foreign trade but not levy export taxes, and (4) four-year term for the president.

	VIRGINIA PLAN	NEW JERSEY PLAN	FINAL U.S. CONSTITUTION
Representation	Based on wealth or population	Equal representation for each state	**Senate:** two representatives per state **House:** based on population
Executive	National executive chosen by Congress	Executive Committee chosen by Congress	**President** chosen by **electors,** in turn elected by the people
Judicial	National judiciary chosen by Congress	National judiciary appointed by Executive Committee	**Supreme Court** appointed by the president with Senate confirmation; lower courts established by Congress
Legislative	Two houses: upper elected by the people with lower elected by the upper house	One house: appointed by state legislators	Two houses: upper chosen by state legislatures (changed to direct election by Seventeenth Amendment); lower elected by the people

- Advocates and opponents soon squared off over **ratification.** **Federalists** favored ratification because they claimed that without a strong federal government, the nation would be unable to protect itself from external enemies or solve internal problems. Initially, they argued against a **Bill of Rights** as unnecessary but agreed to its addition to gain support. **Anti-Federalists,** mainly farmers and others from the inland areas, claimed that the Constitution was extralegal because the convention had not been authorized to create a new document, that it took important rights away from the states, and that the Constitution needed a Bill of Rights to guarantee individual liberties.

- By June 1788, nine states had ratified the Constitution, but without Virginia and New York, the union would have little chance of survival. In Virginia, **Patrick Henry** led the fight against ratification. Only promises that Virginian George Washington would be the first president and that a Bill of Rights would be added convinced Virginians to vote "yes." The fight in New York enlisted **Alexander Hamilton, James Madison,** and **John Jay** to write a series of essays called *The Federalist* in defense of the Constitution. Once New York ratified and the new government took office in March 1789, Rhode Island and North Carolina became the last of the original states to ratify.

KEY PEOPLE

- **James Madison, account of the Constitutional Convention**

KEY TERMS/IDEAS

Review Strategy

See if you can relate these terms and ideas to their correct context in the "Fast Facts" section.

- **Great Compromise, Roger Sherman; New Jersey Plan, William Patterson; Virginia Plan, Edmund Randolph**
- **right of deposit, New Orleans, Spanish interference with trade**
- **sectionalism: social, cultural, economic, and political**
- **Shay's Rebellion, poor economic conditions in new nation**
- **Virginia Bill of Rights, U.S. Bill of Rights**

Chapter 6

THE CONSTITUTION AND IMPORTANT SUPREME COURT CASES

Review Strategy

For a review of the writing of the U.S. Constitution, see Chapter 5.

The chances are that you will not be asked any questions on the test about the structure of the U.S. Constitution, but you may be asked about what led to the passage of certain amendments or the consequences of certain amendments or about the significance of certain Supreme Court decisions. This chapter will give you the basic facts about the Constitution so that you have a context for understanding the significance of later events related to the Constitution. Pay particular attention to amendments related to large themes in U.S. history such as the Civil War (Thirteenth, Fourteenth, and Fifteenth Amendments).

FAST FACTS

- The U.S. Constitution consists of a **Preamble, seven Articles,** and **twenty-six Amendments.**

- The Constitution sets out the structure and powers of government but does not try to provide for every possibility. Knowing that they would not be able to provide solutions to all the circumstances the nation would face in the future, the Framers developed the amendment process to allow later generations to change the government as situations arose.

- The **amendment process** and the **system of checks and balances** enable the government to be both flexible and stable.

- The U.S. Constitution is based on six principles of government:

  1. **Popular sovereignty:** The people are the only source of governmental power.
  2. **Federalism:** Government power is divided between a national government and state governments.
  3. **Separation of powers:** Executive, legislative, and judicial powers are divided among three separate and co-equal branches of government.
  4. **Checks and balances:** The three branches of government have some overlapping powers that allow each to check, that is, restrain or balance, the power of the other two.

5. **Judicial review:** The courts have the power to declare unconstitutional the actions of the legislative and executive branches of government.

6. **Limited government:** The Constitution lists the powers granted to the federal government, reserved to the states, or shared concurrently; all other powers revert to the states.

- The first amendments to the Constitution are known as the **Bill of Rights** and were added to satisfy the Anti-Federalists, who opposed ratification because the proposed Constitution did not spell out the rights of the people.

- The **Thirteenth, Fourteenth,** and **Fifteenth Amendments** were passed after the Civil War to ensure the rights of newly freed slaves. These amendments figure prominently in the history of Reconstruction. Beginning in the 1960s, the Supreme Court used the Fourteenth Amendment as the basis for many **civil rights** decisions.

KEY PEOPLE

- **Anti-Federalists:** opposed ratification of the Constitution on a number of issues, centered on (1) the increased powers of the central government over those listed in the Articles of Confederation, and (2) the lack of a listing of the rights of individuals; Thomas Jefferson, Patrick Henry, John Hancock, and Samuel Adams among others

- **Federalists:** supported ratification, basing their arguments on (1) the weaknesses of the Articles of Confederation and (2) the need for a strong government to guide the new nation; James Madison, John Adams, and Alexander Hamilton as chief advocates

- **John Marshall:** Chief Justice of the Supreme Court from 1801–1835; known as the Great Chief Justice; would be called a judicial activist today. Under the Constitution, the powers of the Supreme Court were not spelled out. Marshall established the status and independence of the Supreme Court and led the Court in many rulings that set the basic principles of constitutional law for the United States.

- **Thurgood Marshall:** argued *Brown* v. *Board of Education of Topeka, Kansas* (1954) that overturned the decision in *Plessy* v. *Ferguson* (1896); became the first African-American Supreme Court Justice; liberal and judicial activist

- **Warren Court:** named after Chief Justice Earl Warren (1953–1969); judicial activist. The Warren Court wrote many landmark decisions in civil rights and individual rights, including *Brown* v. *Board of Education of Topeka, Kansas,* and *Miranda* v. *Arizona.*

Red Alert!

The "Supreme Court under John Marshall" is a topic listed in the AP guide from the College Board.

Red Alert!

The Warren Court is a topic in the AP guide from the College Board.

KEY TERMS/IDEAS

- **elastic clause:** Article I, Section 8; also known as the **"necessary and proper clause;"** grants Congress the right to make all laws "necessary and proper" in order to carry out the federal government's duties; this is an expressed power and the constitutional basis for implied powers

- **supremacy clause:** part of Article VI; the Constitution, laws passed by Congress, and treaties of the United States have superior authority over laws of state and local governments

- **concurrent powers:** powers, such as the right to tax and to establish and maintain courts, that are shared by the federal and state governments but exercised separately and simultaneously

- **denied powers:** powers denied to all governments; Article I, Sections 9 and 10

- **enumerated powers:** powers stated directly in the Constitution as belonging to the federal government; Article I, Section 8; Article II, Section 2; Article III; Sixteenth Amendment

- **expressed powers:** same as **enumerated powers**

- **implied powers:** based on the "necessary and proper" or elastic clause; powers required by the federal government to carry out its duties as stated in the Constitution; not listed but based in expressed powers, such as the power to collect taxes implies the power to establish the Internal Revenue Service

- **inherent powers:** belong to the federal government by virtue of being the federal government

- **reserved powers:** powers that belong to the states; Tenth Amendment

- **judicial activism:** theory that the Supreme Court through its decisions should shape national social and political policies

- **judicial restraint:** theory that the Supreme Court through its decisions should avoid an active role in shaping national social and political policies

- **loose constructionist:** one who argues that the Constitution needs to respond to changing times; the **Warren Court,** for example

- **strict constructionist:** one who argues that the judiciary's decisions need to be based on the Framers' intent; Justice Clarence Thomas, for example

139

PROVISIONS OF THE UNITED STATES CONSTITUTION

ARTICLES	
Article I	Establishes the Legislative Branch Make up of the House of Representatives and the Senate, elections and meetings, organization and rules, passing of laws, powers of Congress, powers denied to the federal government, powers denied to the states; Three-Fifths Compromise for apportionment was repealed by the Fifteenth Amendment; **"necessary and proper clause;" "commerce clause"**
Article II	Establishes the Executive Branch Term, election, qualifications of the president and vice president; powers of the president; duties of the president; impeachment
Article III	Establishes the Judicial Branch Federal courts, jurisdiction of federal courts; defines treason
Article IV	Relations among the states Honoring official acts of other states; mutual duties of states; new states and territories; federal protection for states
Article V	The amendment process
Article VI	Public debts, supremacy of national law, oaths of office; **"supremacy clause"**
Article VII	Ratification process
AMENDMENTS	
First Amendment	Freedoms of religion, speech, press, assembly, petition
Second Amendment	Right to bear arms
Third Amendment	Restrictions on quartering of troops
Fourth Amendment	Protection against unlawful search and seizure
Fifth Amendment	Rights of the accused in criminal proceedings, due process
Sixth Amendment	Right to a speedy, fair trial
Seventh Amendment	Rights involved in a civil suit
Eighth Amendment	Punishment for crimes **(cruel and unusual punishment)**
Ninth Amendment	Powers reserved to the people **(nonenumerated rights)**
Tenth Amendment	Powers reserved to the states
Eleventh Amendment	Suits against states by a resident or by another state must be heard in state courts, not federal courts: repealed part of Article III

PROVISIONS OF THE UNITED STATES CONSTITUTION—(cont'd)

Twelfth Amendment	Election of president and vice president
Thirteenth Amendment	Ratified as a result of the Civil War; abolishes slavery
Fourteenth Amendment	Ratified after the Civil War; defines the rights of citizens; replaces part of Article I by requiring that African Americans be fully counted in determining apportionment; sets out punishment for leaders of the Confederacy; promises payment for federal debt as a result of the Civil War but not for debts of the Confederacy. This amendment's **"equal protection under the law"** provision figures prominently in later civil rights decisions by the Supreme Court.
Fifteenth Amendment	Ratified after the Civil War; grants the right to vote regardless of race, color, or previous servitude. Southern states defied the amendment until the 1960s when Congress passed various voting rights acts.
Sixteenth Amendment	Grants federal government the ability to tax income
Seventeenth Amendment	Provides for direct election of senators; replaces Article I, Section 3, paragraphs 2 and 3
Eighteenth Amendment Twenty-first Amendment	Prohibits manufacture, sale, or transportation of alcohol Repealed Eighteenth Amendment
Nineteenth Amendment	Grants women the right to vote
Twentieth Amendment	Modified sections of Article I and the Twelfth Amendment relating to when the terms of office begin for members of Congress and the president and vice president; known as the **"Lame Duck" Amendment** because it shortened the time that a defeated legislator/official served between the election and the new term of office
Twenty-second Amendment	Limits presidential term to two terms if elected on his/her own and to one term if serving out the term of a predecessor for more than two years
Twenty-third Amendment	Provides three presidential electors for the District of Columbia
Twenty-fourth Amendment	Abolishes the poll tax for federal elections; part of the civil rights legislation of the 1960s
Twenty-fifth Amendment	Provides for presidential disability and succession if the president is unable to perform his/her duties
Twenty-sixth Amendment	Expands the right to vote to include 18-year-old citizens

TWELVE IMPORTANT SUPREME COURT DECISIONS

The Constitution can be changed formally by the amendment process, but it can also be changed informally through legislation, executive action (Executive Orders), party practices (as one example, the Constitution does not mention political conventions to nominate presidential and vice-presidential candidates, but parties hold conventions every four years), custom (secretaries of the Executive Departments make up the president's Cabinet), and court decisions. The Supreme Court is the major shaper of judicial change. Since John Marshall's tenure as chief justice, the tension between strict constructionist and loose constructionist views has existed on the Court and between its supporters and opponents.

Several Supreme Court cases appear in the College Board outline for an Advanced Placement course in U.S. history. These cases are summarized below to provide a capsule description of the case and its significance in the evolution of the nation's law. You might have questions directly related to these cases on the test.

The other cases discussed below relate to broad issues in U.S. history and are considered important Supreme Court decisions that have shaped national policies. Several of them are representative of the Marshall and Warren Courts, which are highlighted in the AP course guide. Knowing about these cases could help you in writing your free-response essays or in answering the DBQ by providing you with outside information to bolster your argument. There are other Supreme Court decisions that are important to particular events in the nation's history, such as Indian removal (*Cherokee Nation* v. *Georgia;* 1832), but these are not considered **landmark cases.** They did not establish or expand principles for later generations.

The cases are listed chronologically and arranged by historical period according to the College Board guide for an AP course in U.S. history.

THE AGE OF JEFFERSON

Red Alert!

The "Supreme Court under John Marshall" is a topic in the AP guide from the College Board.

- *Marbury* v. *Madison* (1803; principle of judicial review)

  Case: In January 1801, with less than three months left in his term, President John Adams appointed a number of Federalists as justices to lesser federal courts for terms of five years each. The Senate confirmed the appointments, and Adams signed their commissions in the last hours of his term, the so-called midnight judges. Several of these commissions were not delivered, and the new president, Thomas Jefferson, an Anti-Federalist, had Secretary of State James Madison withhold them. William Marbury asked the Supreme Court to issue a writ of mandamus to force Madison to give him his commission. Marbury based his suit on a section of the Judiciary Act of 1789 that created the federal court system.

Decision: The Supreme Court ruled that the section of the Judiciary Act that Marbury cited conflicted with the Constitution and was, as a result, unconstitutional. Marshall based the Court's opinion on the premise that the Constitution is the supreme law of the land. As a result, all other laws are subordinate to it. Judges take an oath to uphold the Constitution and, therefore, cannot enforce any act ruled to be in conflict with the Constitution.

Significance: In this decision, John Marshall led the Court in establishing its power to review laws and declare them unconstitutional, if necessary.

- **McCulloch v. Maryland** (1819; principle of implied powers)

  Case: In 1816 as part of a political fight to limit the powers of the federal government, Maryland placed a tax on all notes issued by banks that did business in the state but were chartered outside of the state. The target was the Second Bank of the United States. In a test case, the bank's cashier, James McCulloch, refused to pay the tax. Maryland won in state court, and McCulloch appealed.

  Decision: In upholding the constitutionality of the Second Bank, the Court cited the **"necessary and proper clause."** The Court ruled that the Bank was necessary to fulfill the government's duties to tax, borrow, and coin money.

  Significance: The Court's opinion broadened the powers of Congress to include implied powers in addition to those listed in the Constitution. This ruling has had a major impact on the development of the government, allowing it to evolve as needed to meet new circumstances.

- **Gibbons v. Ogden** (1824; interstate commerce)

  Case: The case revolved around the Commerce Clause, Article I, Section 8, Clause 3, of the Constitution. The state of New York had awarded Aaron Ogden an exclusive permit to carry passengers by steamboat between New York City and New Jersey. The federal government had issued a coasting license to Thomas Gibbons for the same route. Ogden sued

Gibbons and won in a New York court. Gibbons appealed to the Supreme Court.

Decision: The Supreme Court ruled in Gibbons' favor that a state cannot interfere with Congress's power to regulate interstate commerce. It took a broad view of the term *commerce*.

Significance: Marshall, dealing a blow to the arguments of states' rights advocates, established the superiority of federal authority over states' rights under the Constitution. This ruling, which enlarged the definition of commerce, became the basis of the Civil Rights Act of 1964 prohibiting discrimination in public accommodations.

BACKGROUND TO THE CIVIL WAR

Red Alert!

The Dred Scott decision is a topic in the AP guide from the College Board.

- *Scott* v. *Sanford* (1857)

   Case: Dred Scott was a slave of Dr. John Emerson, a doctor in the U.S. Army who moved from army post to army post. During his postings, Scott accompanied him and had lived in a free state and a free territory, although they had returned to Missouri, a slave state, before Emerson's death. Scott sued his owner's widow in Missouri court for his freedom, contending that he had been freed when he was transported into a free state and free territory to live. A lower court agreed with Scott, but the Missouri Supreme Court ruled against him as did a lower federal court. His lawyers appealed to the Supreme Court.

   Decision: The Southern majority on the Court held that Congress had no power to forbid slavery in U.S. territories. The Court also ruled that a person descended from a slave had no rights as a citizen and, therefore, could not sue in court.

   Significance: This ruling struck down (1) the Missouri Compromise, by which Congress had determined which states would be free and which slave, and (2) the Kansas-Nebraska Act that used the principle of popular sovereignty to determine whether the two territories would be admitted to the Union as free or slave states.

NEW SOUTH

Red Alert!

Plessy *v.* Ferguson *is a topic in the AP guide from the College Board.*

- ***Plessy* v. *Ferguson*** (1896; principle of separate but equal)

  Case: In a test of the Jim Crow laws, Homer Plessy, an African American, was arrested in Louisiana for riding in a whites-only railroad car. Plessy was found guilty in state court, and appealed to the U.S. Supreme Court on the basis of the Fourteenth Amendment's "equal protection under the law" guarantee.

  Decision: The Court ruled that as long as the facilities were equal, it was not unconstitutional to segregate whites and blacks.

  Significance: The Court's ruling led to new and more comprehensive segregation laws across the South.

WORLD WAR I

Red Alert!

One of the topics in the AP guide is civil liberties during World War I.

- ***Schenck* v. *United States*** (1919; principle of a clear and present danger)

  Case: Under the Espionage Act of 1917, Charles Schenck, general secretary of the Socialist Party in the United States, was convicted of printing and distributing leaflets urging men to resist the draft during World War I. The Espionage Act forbade people from saying, printing, writing, or publishing anything against the government. Schenck appealed on the grounds that the First Amendment's guarantee of freedom of speech protected him.

  Decision: The Court ruled against Schenck, holding that during peacetime, the First Amendment would have protected him, but during wartime, his words presented a danger to the nation.

  Significance: This decision meant that the First Amendment does not protect freedom of speech when it presents an immediate danger that it will incite a criminal action.

EISENHOWER AND THE 1950s

Red Alert!

Brown *v.* Board of Education *is a topic in the AP guide from the College Board.*

- ***Brown* v. *the Board of Education of Topeka, Kansas*** (1954; equal protection under the law)

  Case: African Americans had won several Supreme Court cases involving segregation in colleges and universities but needed a case involving public elementary and secondary schools. In 1954, Thurgood Marshall and the National Association for the Advancement of Colored People (NAACP) found their case in *Brown* v. *Board of Education of Topeka, Kansas,* filed on behalf of Linda Brown by her father. According to the law, Linda could not attend her neighborhood school, which was all-white, but had to go across town to an all-black school. Marshall based his argument on expert testimony demonstrating that segregated schools damaged the self-esteem of African-American children. As such, segregated schools violated the equal protection clause of the Fourteenth Amendment.

Decision: The Warren Court agreed with Marshall's argument.

Significance: The Court ordered schools to desegregate "with all deliberate speed." It would take court orders, more laws, and the civil rights movement to desegregate public education in the South and the North. This ruling reversed *Plessy* v. *Ferguson.*

KENNEDY AND JOHNSON ERAS

Red Alert!

Heart of Atlanta *and the next two cases relate to the topic of the Warren Court in the AP guide from the College Board.*

- *Heart of Atlanta Motel* v. *United States* (1964; interstate commerce)

Case: In 1964, Congress, using its power to regulate interstate commerce under Article I, Section 8, passed the Civil Rights Act banning discrimination in public accommodations and in employment. A motel owner challenged the law, contending that his business was local—even though it was convenient to exits for an interstate—and, therefore, should not be regulated under interstate commerce.

Decision: The Warren Court ruled against the owner. It based its decision on the theory that public accommodations, places that sell lodging (hotels, rooming houses, etc.), food (restaurants, lunch counters, etc.), and entertainment (movie theaters, auditoriums, etc.) serve transients and/or have moved a large portion of their goods by interstate commerce. In its opinion, the Court found "overwhelming evidence of the disruptive effect [of] racial discrimination" on commerce.

Significance: The Court's ruling upheld Congress's use of the commerce clause as the basis for civil rights legislation.

- ***Wesbery* v. *Sanders*** (1964; one man, one vote)

  Case: As a result of the 1960 Census, Georgia's ten congressional districts were reapportioned. The Fifth District had over 800,000 people while the other nine districts had just under 400,000 on average. Several members of the Fifth Congressional District joined in a suit against Sanders, their representative, claiming that the size of the district deprived them of equal representation.

  Decision: The Court, citing Article I, Section 2, ruled that the disparity in size of the population of the ten congressional districts violated the Constitution.

  Significance: This case was one in a series of cases dealing with apportionment of state and congressional seats that the Court agreed to hear. The decisions in these cases, known collectively as "one man, one vote," ended the pattern of rural overrepresentation and urban underrepresentation in legislatures.

- ***Gideon* v. *Wainwright*** (1963; right to be represented by counsel)

  Case: Clarence Earl Gideon was charged with robbing a Florida pool hall—a felony. Indigent, Gideon asked for a court-appointed lawyer and was denied. Convicted and sentenced to five years in jail, Gideon crafted his own appeal and sent it to the Supreme Court.

  Decision: The Court overturned the conviction stating that the **due process clause** of the Fourteenth Amendment protects individuals against state encroachments on their rights. Represented by counsel, Gideon was retried and acquitted.

  Significance: Florida as well as other states had to release prisoners who had not been represented by an attorney. As a result of *Gideon,* everyone accused of a crime must be represented by an attorney. If a person is too poor, then the state must provide one. This is one of several cases dealing with the rights of the accused the Warren Court agreed to hear. Many of the decisions have been controversial among conservatives, because they think the Warren Court was soft on criminals.

- *Miranda* **v.** *Arizona* (1966; Miranda Rule)

  Case: Ernesto Miranda was arrested on charges of kidnapping and rape and identified by the victim. He was not informed of his right to have an attorney present during questioning. After 2 hours of interrogation, Miranda confessed and voluntarily signed a confession, which was later used in court. Miranda was convicted and appealed. His lawyer argued that Miranda's right under the Fifth Amendment to avoid self-incrimination was violated when he was not informed of his right to have a lawyer present.

  Decision: The Warren Court reversed the conviction in a 5–4 decision. It ruled that a suspect must be "read his rights": the right to remain silent, that anything the suspect says may be used against him/her in a court of law, the right to have a lawyer present during questioning, the right to have a court-appointed attorney if the person cannot afford one, and the right to end questioning at any time.

  Significance: The Warren Court stated that the Court would not uphold any convictions on appeal if the suspects had not been informed of their constitutional rights before questioning.

NIXON

- *Roe* **v.** *Wade* (1973; right to privacy)

  Case: Looking for a case to test state laws against abortion, advocates found it in *Roe* v. *Wade*. A Texas law banned all abortions except those to save the life of the mother. An unwed pregnant woman sought an abortion and was denied. Her case was appealed to the Supreme Court.

  Decision: In their opinion, the justices ruled that the state may not ban abortions in the first six months of pregnancy. A fetus is not a person and, therefore, not protected by the Fourteenth Amendment. However, the amendment does protect a *woman's* right to privacy, and, therefore, the state may not interfere in a woman's decision to have an abortion. At the same time, the right to an abortion is not absolute. After the first trimester, the state may regulate abortion procedures to protect women who elect to have the procedure. During the final three months, the state may regulate and even ban abortions in the interest of the unborn, except in cases to save the life of the mother.

Significance: The Court's decision expanded the right to privacy, which is not explicitly stated in the Constitution. The Court based its opinion on personal property rights found in the Fourteenth Amendment. The decision sparked a campaign to add an anti-abortion amendment to the Constitution.

SOME ADDITIONAL SUPREME COURT CASES WITH IMPACT ON HISTORICAL EVENTS

AGE OF JACKSON

Red Alert!

Cherokee Nation *and* Worcester *relate to the topic of Indian removal in the AP guide.*

- *Cherokee Nation* v. *The State of Georgia* (1831)

  The Cherokee Nation, besieged by white settlers who wanted their land, sued in Supreme Court to prevent the seizure of their land by the state of Georgia. The Court under John Marshall found that the Cherokee were not a sovereign nation but a dependent one and, as such, had no standing to bring a lawsuit to the Supreme Court. However, the Court found that they did have the right to their land. Georgia, supported by President Andrew Jackson, ignored the ruling.

- *Worcester* v. *Georgia* (1832)

  The Cherokee tried again to win recognition of their claims with *Worcester* v. *Georgia,* citing treaties with the federal government. This time the Court under John Marshall agreed with the Cherokee and declared Georgia's laws in regard to the Cherokee unconstitutional. "The Cherokee Nation then is a distinct community, occupying its own territory . . . in which the laws of Georgia can have no force, and which the citizens of Georgia have no right to enter without the assent of the Cherokee themselves or in conformity with treaties and the acts of Congress." Again, Georgia—and Andrew Jackson—ignored the ruling.

ROOSEVELT AND THE NEW DEAL

Red Alert!

Schecter *relates to the topic of the New Deal in the AP guide.*

- *Schechter Poultry Corp.* **v.** *United States* (1935)

  The National Recovery Administration (NRA), one of the alphabet agencies of the New Deal, had been established under the National Industrial Recovery Act (NIRA). It was extremely unpopular with the public—large employers, small business owners, consumers, and labor. The Supreme Court found the law unconstitutional because, among other reasons, it attempted to regulate intrastate commerce, a violation of the commerce clause of Article I.

WORLD WAR II

Red Alert!

Korematsu *relates to the topic of Japanese internment in the AP guide.*

- *Korematsu* **v.** *United States* (1944)

  This is one of several cases that dealt with the internment of American-born citizens of Japanese descent. In May 1942, all Japanese people in California were ordered to report to evacuation centers for relocation to internment camps. Fred Korematsu, intending to move to the Midwest voluntarily, did not report. However, when the authorities found him in California at the end of the month, they arrested him. He was convicted of ignoring the evacuation order. On appeal, the Supreme Court upheld the conviction. They found that the evacuation was a lawful exercise of the war powers granted to the president and Congress under the Constitution.

Chapter 7

REVIEWING THE NEW NATION TO MID-CENTURY

Study Strategy

Check the College Board Web site (www.collegeboard. org/ap) for the time period for your DBQ.

According to the College Board's guide for the United States History AP Test, approximately half of the 80 multiple-choice questions are drawn from the period from 1790 to 1914. We have divided the material into three chapters. The DBQ may also be drawn from this period. For the year 2000 AP test, for example, the College Board Web site began listing the DBQ the previous summer as based on documents for the period from 1875 to 1925.

Red Alert!

See "10 Facts About the AP United States History Test" for basic information about the test format, pp. 1–3.

As you review the information on the concepts, trends, events, and people who were important in the nation's history between 1790 and 1914, remember that the College Board asks questions about "political institutions and behavior and public policy, social and economic change, diplomacy and international relations, and cultural and intellectual developments." As you review your course materials and read this book, look for trends, cause-and-effect relationships, differences and similarities, and the significance of events and actions on the evolution of the nation. Be prepared to analyze events and people's motives and to evaluate outcomes. Memorizing the who, when, and why is only part of what you need to learn.

SECTION 1. THE NEW NATION, 1789–1800

Once nine states had ratified the Constitution, the members of the **electoral college** assembled in their states in February 1789 and voted for president and vice-president. **George Washington** was unanimously chosen president, and **John Adams,** who received the next highest number of votes, was elected vice-president. They took their oaths of office on April 30, and thus began the new nation.

FAST FACTS

Review Strategy

These "Fast Facts" relate to George Washington's presidency.

- The new government had to deal with (1) the national debt, (2) foreign affairs, and (3) its own frontier. However, it had to deal with these in the context of realizing the promises of the new Constitution for the new nation. The government under Washington had to determine how to establish and maintain a balance between the powers of the federal government and the rights of the people and the states.

- The **Washington presidency** is as important for the **precedents** it set as for the business of the nation that it conducted. Washington established, among other precedents, (1) that the president was to be addressed as "Mr. President," (2) that a president should serve only two terms (in 1940, Franklin Roosevelt was the first president to seek a third term, and the Twenty-Second Amendment later turned Washington's precedent into law), (3) that the president should be advised by able and experienced leaders, (4) that the president can grant or withhold diplomatic recognition to foreign governments, (5) that federal troops can be used to enforce the law by virtue of the president's power as commander in chief, (6) that the president is, in essence, the leader of his political party, (7) that the president should deliver the State of the Union speech before a joint session of Congress, (8) that Senate approval of presidential appointments refers only to confirmation, not removal from office, (9) that the Senate's role of "advise and consent" means ratifying or rejecting treaties, not negotiating them, and (10) that, although Congress's role is to make laws, the president should take an active role in shaping and urging the passage of laws he deems worthwhile and necessary.

- According to the Constitution, the heads of the **executive departments** are to report to the president, but it does not state the number of departments and what they should be. In 1789, Congress created the **Departments of Treasury, State,** and **War** (in 1949, the Departments of War, Navy, and the U.S. Air Force were combined into the Department of Defense). Washington selected experienced leaders to fill these posts: as secretary of state, **Thomas Jefferson,** who had written the Declaration of Independence and been minister to France under the Articles of Confederation; as secretary of war, **General Henry Knox,** who had held the same post under the Articles of Confederation; and as secretary of the treasury, **Alexander Hamilton,** who had written part of *The Federalist*. Along with the attorney general, these men became known as the **Cabinet.** By the middle of his first term, Washington was consulting with them almost weekly, a custom that has continued.

- The **Judiciary Act of 1789** filled in another piece of the new government by establishing the **federal court system**. The Act created (1) the positions of chief justice and five associate justices for a national Supreme Court and (2) thirteen district courts and three circuit courts. (The number of associate justices and lower courts has increased with the increase in the size of the nation.) Washington chose three Southerners and three Northerners for the Supreme Court positions, naming **John Jay** of New York, a co-author of *The Federalist,* as the first **chief justice.** (3) The Judiciary Act also gave the Supreme Court the **power of judicial review,** enabling the Court to declare void any state laws and any decisions of state courts that the Court held to violate the U.S. Constitution or federal laws and treaties made under the Constitution.

- The first Congress established the position of **attorney general** to advise the president and the government on legal matters. (The Department of Justice was not established as a separate Executive Department until 1870.) **Edmund Randolph,** a lawyer who had drafted the **Virginia Plan** during the Constitutional Convention, was named to the post.

Review Strategy

See Chapter 6 for a listing of the first ten amendments.

- The **Anti-Federalists** urged passage of the promised **Bill of Rights.** In September 1789, the first Congress passed and sent to the states for ratification twelve proposed amendments to the Constitution. Ten were ratified by 1791 and added to the Constitution as the first ten amendments.

Review Strategy

These "Fast Facts" relate to Hamilton's financial program.

- A major problem facing the new government was debt from the war—$50 million owed to foreign countries and to U.S. citizens. The states owed about $25 million. The Constitution gave the new nation the power to levy taxes and create a money system. It was up to Hamilton to make these powers a reality. Hamilton proposed a four-part plan: (1) repayment of the entire war debt owed by the national government and by the states, (2) establishment of a **national bank,** (3) adoption of a **protective tariff,** and (4) adoption of an **excise tax on whiskey.** Hamilton set out his plan in a two-part report: ***Report on the Public Credit*** and ***Report on Manufactures.***

Review Strategy

Note the sectional rivalries that are beginning to take shape in the new nation.

- As the first step, Hamilton planned to sell government **bonds** that had a 20-year payback period to repay both federal and state debts. The money from the new bonds would be used to buy back at face value the bonds issued during the war. These bonds were now valued at little more than the paper they were printed on, but Hamilton's plan had two goals: (1) to establish the new nation as a good credit risk by paying off its debts, especially to France and the Netherlands, and (2) to encourage support for the nation through the self-interest of the bondholders, mostly wealthy people. Opposition came from those states, mainly in the South, whose debts were small or who had repaid their creditors. Opponents led by **James Madison** also argued that it was **speculators,** many of them New England merchants, who would profit from repayment. Hamilton argued successfully that the nation must establish itself as creditworthy. To placate the Southerners in Congress, Hamilton agreed to support the proposal to have the new nation's capital built in Southern territory. The compromise resulted in the building of **Washington, D.C.,** on land along the Potomac River that was donated by Virginia and Maryland.

- The second part of Hamilton's program called for creation of the Bank of the United States, a **national bank** with branches in major cities. The bank would serve as the depository of government tax revenues, and operating capital for the bank would come from those reserves as well as from the sale of shares in the bank. The bank would also issue **currency** for the nation that would in time replace local and state bank notes, thus stabilizing the value of the nation's money system. This would benefit the nation as a whole and business in particular.

Review Strategy

See Chapter 6 for a discussion of the Constitution's powers.

- Opposition was strong, not only in Congress where Madison again led the fight, but within the Cabinet, where Jefferson was a powerful opponent. The arguments were that (1) the sale of shares in the bank at $400 a share meant that only the wealthy could afford to invest; (2) government money would be deposited only in branches of the national bank, thus depriving private banks of business; and (3) the Constitution gave the federal government no power to create a banking system. The last argument was based on the **enumerated powers** in the Constitution.

- Hamilton countered by arguing that the **"elastic and proper clause"** of the Constitution gave the government the power "to make all laws which shall be necessary and proper for carrying into execution the foregoing powers," among which were the powers to tax and to borrow money. Hamilton persuaded Washington of the legitimacy of his argument based on the **implied powers** of the Constitution, and the Bank of the United States, the **First Bank,** was chartered in 1791 for 20 years.

- The next step in Hamilton's fiscal program was to increase the modest **tariff** levied by Congress in 1789. Congress saw the tariff as a way to generate a little revenue for the government, whereas Hamilton saw the tariff as a way not only (1) to raise revenue for the government but also (2) to protect the nation's nascent industries by raising the price of foreign goods. Hamilton, an advocate of a strong central government that favored wealthy businesspeople, had a vision of the United States as an industrial power. He realized that the nation would have to manufacture much of what it needed if it were not to remain dependent on other nations. Hamilton's vision clashed with those in Congress who saw the nation as one of small farms, and his tariff was never acted on.

- In 1791, Congress passed Hamilton's excise tax on whiskey. The tax fell hardest on frontier farmers whose major crop was corn. Because of the difficulty of transporting corn to market, Western farmers turned their corn into whiskey that they then sold for cash. The frontiersmen refused to pay the new excise tax, and in 1794, federal marshals attempted to enforce the law in Pennsylvania but were routed. Hamilton convinced Washington to send militia from neighboring states, and the **Whiskey Rebellion** ended at the sight of 15,000 troops converging on the Pennsylvania frontier. The unintended result was the shift in loyalty of frontiersmen from the Federalists to the Democratic-Republicans.

Review Strategy

These "Fast Facts" relate to the rise of the political party system.

- Another unintended result of Hamilton's fiscal program was the rise of the **political party system** by 1794. Those who sided with Hamilton believed in a broad interpretation of the Constitution (**loose constructionists**) that allowed for expansion of the federal government. Hamilton distrusted the ability of ordinary people to manage government and attracted to the **Federalists** wealthy merchants, manufacturers, lawyers, and church leaders from New England and New York who believed that the federal government should help underwrite the nation's industrial development. (The party slowly died as a result of its opposition to the **War of 1812.**)

- The **Democratic-Republicans** who did not support expansion of governmental powers beyond what the Constitution stated (**strict constructionists**) opposed the Federalists. Jefferson became leader of the Democratic-Republicans, or simply **Republicans** (in the mid-1820s, they became known as Democrats). Jefferson and the Republicans believed in (1) limited federal power, (2) strong state governments, and (3) guarantees of individual rights. To them, the best society was one based on small farms. The Republicans' strength lay in the South and on the frontier.

- Washington's administration also dealt with the addition of new states: Kentucky, Tennessee, Ohio, and Vermont. The Mississippi River became the nation's western boundary. The new nation alternated between fighting the Native Americans on its western flank and making treaties with them. The British in the upper Midwest and the Spanish to the south armed Native Americans in an attempt to keep the new nation from expanding.

- To keep the new nation out of the European conflict that developed after the **French Revolution,** in 1793 Washington issued the **Neutrality Proclamation.** He was concerned that the nation was still too weak to defend itself and too dependent on British trade to enter the war on the side of the French against the British. Jefferson and the Democratic-Republicans favored honoring the U.S. treaty with the French and entering the war. Congress agreed with Washington and passed the **Neutrality Act,** which made the proclamation law.

- A number of problems with Great Britain remained for Washington's administration to resolve: (1) the British were still occupying some of their forts and trading posts in the area between the Ohio and Mississippi Rivers, (2) the British were apparently arming Native Americans for raids against Americans, (3) the United States was now refusing to repay Loyalists for property lost in the American Revolution, (4) the British, at war with the French, were capturing U.S. ships that traded with French colonies in the Caribbean, and (5) the British were **impressing** U.S. sailors suspected of deserting the British navy.

- **Jay's Treaty** solved the most important issues. The British agreed (1) to leave the frontier in 1796 and (2) to grant the United States trading rights with British islands in the Caribbean. (A joint committee was to work out the other issues, but the capture of U.S. ships and impressment were not resolved.) The treaty was ratified despite opposition from Republicans who wanted to honor the alliance of 1778 with the French and who saw the treaty as an attempt by the Federalists to increase trade with Great Britain.

Review Strategy

See Chapter 6 for a listing of the amendments to the Constitution, especially the Twelfth Amendment.

- Opposition to Jay's Treaty figured in the election of 1796, the first presidential election in which members of opposing parties competed. Because the person with the highest number of votes would become president and the person with the next highest number would be named vice-president, John Adams, a Federalist, became president, and Thomas Jefferson, a Republican, was chosen vice-president.

Review Strategy

These "Fast Facts" relate to the Adams presidency.

- As president, Adams was faced with increasing hostilities from the French who were seizing U.S. ships in the Caribbean in retaliation for Jay's Treaty. Adams sent **Charles Pinckney, Elbridge Gerry,** and **John Marshall** to France to negotiate a solution. **Charles Talleyrand,** the French foreign minister, sent three agents to the Americans to demand money, which they refused to pay. The Americans referred to the agents only as X, Y, and Z. News of the **XYZ Affair** angered Americans who claimed "Millions for defense but not one cent for tribute." Talleyrand claimed the situation was all a mistake, and Adams sent a new delegation. The sea war continued until 1800, when the French agreed that the **alliance of 1778,** which had made allies of France and the fledgling United

States, was null and void. The Republicans' support for the French severely damaged the party.

- Party rivalry led to passage of the Alien, Naturalization, and Sedition Acts. The **Alien Act** gave the president the power to expel any alien believed to be dangerous to the nation. The **Naturalization Act** extended the time an alien had to live in the United States before being eligible for citizenship from five to fourteen years. The **Sedition Act** made it a crime to oppose the laws or make false or critical statements about the government or any official. The first two laws were aimed at French immigrants, many of whom supported the Republicans. The last law affected a number of Republicans, including several members of Congress.

- The laws backfired and increased support for the Republicans, who protested the Sedition Act on the grounds that it violated the **First Amendment**'s guarantees of freedom of speech and freedom of the press. Believing that the states had the right to declare laws of the federal government unconstitutional, Jefferson urged the states to **nullify** the Alien and Sedition Acts. Jefferson himself wrote the **Virginia Resolution,** and James Madison wrote the **Kentucky Resolution,** which declared the laws unconstitutional.

KEY PEOPLE

Review Strategy

See if you can relate these people to their correct context in the "Fast Facts" section.

- **Benjamin Banneker, Washington, D.C.**
- **Citizen Edmond Genet**
- **Pinckney's Treaty, right of deposit at New Orleans, 31st parallel as boundary between Georgia and Spanish Florida**

KEY TERMS/IDEAS

Review Strategy

See if you can relate these terms and ideas to their correct context in the "Fast Facts" section.

- **Assumption Bill, Thomas Jefferson**
- **Battle of Fallen Timbers, General Anthony Wayne, Blue Jacket, Northwest Territory, Treaty of Greenville**
- **French Revolution**
- **Washington's Farewell Address: warnings against political parties, sectionalism, and foreign alliances**

SECTION 2. THE AGE OF JEFFERSON, 1800–1816

Jefferson called the election of 1800 the **"Revolution of 1800"** because it quietly handed the reins of government from the Federalists to the Republicans. The election also demonstrated the need for a better way to elect the president and vice-president. It took seven days and thirty-six ballots in the House of Representatives to break the tie and select Jefferson as president and **Aaron Burr** as vice-president. As a result, the **Twelfth Amendment** was ratified in 1804 to change the process so that candidates were clearly designated as being nominated either for president or for vice-president.

FAST FACTS

Review Strategy

These "Fast Facts" relate to the presidency of Thomas Jefferson.

Review Strategy

See Chapter 6 for information on Marbury *vs.* Madison *and the doctrine of judicial review.*

- In seeking the presidency, Jefferson sought to increase the power base of the Republican party by attracting New England merchants. Once in office, Jefferson had the Naturalization Act and the excise tax on whiskey repealed, and the Alien and Sedition Acts were allowed to expire. He chose to allow the First Bank to continue undisturbed, but he sought to reduce the size of the government and of the federal budget and to pay down the debt. Jefferson believed in a **laissez-faire** philosophy of government in which the government's role would be limited.

- Jefferson's strict constructionist views were put to the test over the **Louisiana Purchase.** In 1800, Spain had signed over Louisiana to France. By 1802, the French, intent on creating an empire in North America, were no longer allowing Western farmers to use the port of New Orleans. Jefferson sent **James Monroe** and **Robert Livingston** to France to offer to buy New Orleans and West Florida for $10 million. The French countered with an offer of $15 million for all of Louisiana. Concerned that the Constitution did not authorize the president to purchase land, Jefferson believed an amendment was needed. Livingston then warned that **Napoleon** might renege if kept waiting. With misgivings, Jefferson asked the Senate to ratify the **treaty of cession,** which authorized the purchase. On the other side of the debate, Federalists protested that the treaty violated the Constitution. Jefferson finally based the purchase on the **implied powers** of the Constitution that required the president to protect the nation. The Louisiana Purchase (1) almost doubled the size of the United States, (2) gave the United States control of the Mississippi River and New Orleans, and (3) removed the French threat from the frontier.

Review Strategy

This "Fast Fact" relates to the Burr conspiracy.

- Having defected from the Republicans to run as a Federalist for governor of New York in 1804, **Aaron Burr** was defeated. A major factor in his defeat had been the opposition of Alexander Hamilton, who did not trust Burr and had blocked his bid for president in 1800. After the governor's election, the ill feeling continued, and Burr challenged Hamilton to a duel in which he shot and killed Hamilton. Indicted for murder, Burr fled west, where he began to talk vaguely of plans to have the Western territories secede or to conquer Mexico and make himself emperor. Finally, Jefferson ordered his arrest. Captured in 1807, Burr stood trial for treason. The government was unable to find two trustworthy witnesses to an "overt act" of treason, the strict test of treason in the Constitution, and Burr was acquitted and went into exile.

Review Strategy

These "Fast Facts" relate to the causes of the War of 1812.

- In the early 1800s, a Shawnee holy man named **the Prophet** and his brother, the chief **Tecumseh,** tried to unite Native Americans from the Great Lakes to the Gulf of Mexico to block any more U.S. settlers from entering their lands. Tecumseh and the Prophet built a village along **Tippecanoe** Creek in Indiana Territory, where many Native Americans came to hear the Prophet. In 1811, **General William Henry Harrison,** governor of the Indiana Territory, led a force of some 1,000 against Tippecanoe. The Prophet staged a surprise attack, and each side suffered heavy losses, but Harrison burned the village and claimed victory. His soldiers also claimed to have found British weapons in the village.

- When Napoleon came to power after the French Revolution, war dragged on in Europe between France and its enemies for a number of years. The new nation was caught between the warring factions who would not honor its **neutrality**. Both sides continued to capture U.S. ships for trading with the other side. In 1807, after the **HMS *Leopard*** fired on, boarded, and seized four crewmen from the **USS *Chesapeake,*** Jefferson ordered an **embargo** on trade with all foreign nations. Jefferson hoped that France and Great Britain would be forced to respect U.S. rights in exchange for U.S. goods; however, the embargo had little effect on those nations but caused a **depression** in the United States that affected not only merchants, ship owners, sailors, and manufacturers, but also farmers who lost their foreign markets. The **Embargo Act** became a major issue in the election of 1808, but the Republicans were able to elect **James Madison,** Jefferson's choice, as president. At the end of Jefferson's second term, Congress, with Jefferson's approval, repealed the Act.

- Madison signed **Macon's Bill No. 2** in 1810 that stated that if either France or Great Britain would agree to respect U.S. rights as a neutral nation, the United States would cut off trade with the other country. Napoleon agreed, and Madison cut off trade with Great Britain in 1811, only to find that the French continued to seize U.S. merchant ships. The British began to **blockade** some U.S. ports and continued to impress U.S. sailors. Then, on June 16, 1812, the British decided to suspend attacks on U.S. ships because it needed U.S. foodstuffs, and its merchants needed markets and trade goods. However, not knowing this, the United States declared war on Great Britain on June 18.

Review Strategy

Note the sectionalism that divided support for the War of 1812.

- The **War of 1812** had a number of causes, many of them championed by the **War Hawks** in Congress, young men from the West and the South. The causes were (1) impressment of sailors, (2) attacks on U.S. merchant ships, (3) arming of Native Americans on the frontier by the British, (4) the desire to expand U.S. territory to include British Canada and Spanish Florida (Spain was an ally of Great Britain), and (5) a strong sense of **nationalism**. New Englanders did not share the enthusiasm for this war and referred to it as **"Mr. Madison's War."**

Review Strategy

These "Fast Facts" relate to the conduct of the War of 1812.

- The Americans began the war thinking they could easily invade and capture **Canada** because the population was sparse, and most settlers were French, not British. However, the U.S. army was small—less than 7,000—and ill prepared. When Madison asked for state militia, some New England governors refused to send troops. Lacking a commanding general and an overall strategy, the Americans at first lost Detroit and Fort Dearborn and were repulsed in an attack across the Niagara River in New York State. The Americans were able to take **Lake Erie** and then won the **Battle of the Thames,** holding the British off along the western end of the Canadian front. But in the East, the Americans failed in several attempts to invade Canada.

- After the British defeated Napoleon in 1814, they turned their full attention to the war with the United States and planned a three-pronged attack: (1) invasion from Canada, (2) an attack on Washington, D.C., and (3) an attack on New Orleans. The British sent some 14,000 troops from Montreal to invade New York State. Engaged by Americans near Plattsburg on **Lake Champlain,** the British were driven back and did not invade the United States from Canada again. The British captured and burned Washington but were stopped at Fort McHenry. **General Andrew Jackson** soundly defeated the British at the **Battle of New Orleans**—two weeks after the war had ended.

Review Strategy

This "Fast Fact" relates to the Hartford Convention.

- In December 1814, a group of disgruntled Federalists from New England met secretly at what became known as the **Hartford Convention** to discuss their dissatisfaction with government policies. The group wrote seven constitutional amendments meant to redress these grievances by increasing the political power of the region. One of the reasons that the New England governors had not sent militia for the invasion of Canada was because they feared the power that any new territories created from an annexed Canada would wield. A committee of delegates arrived in Washing-

Peterson's AP Success: U.S. History

ton to present their demands to Madison as the end of the war was announced. Although the Hartford Convention had discussed secession and the members had rejected it, opponents of the Federalists were able to taint them with suspicions of secession and thus effectively ended the Federalists' influence.

Review Strategy

This "Fast Fact" relates to the Treaty of Ghent.

- The **Treaty of Ghent,** negotiated by **John Quincy Adams, Albert Gallatin,** and **Henry Clay,** ended the War of 1812 but did not settle the problems of neutrality, impressment, and boundaries between the two nations. The issue of the border with Canada was sent to a commission to resolve. After the war, however, Native Americans in the upper Midwest were no longer a threat to U.S. westward expansion. The war also changed the relationship between the United States and Great Britain. Although neither nation had won, the United States had held at bay the strongest nation in the world.

KEY PEOPLE

Review Strategy

See if you can relate these people to their correct context in the "Fast Facts" section.

- **John C. Calhoun, Henry Clay as War Hawks**
- **Albert Gallatin, secretary of the treasury under Jefferson**
- **Francis Scott Key, "The Star-Spangled Banner"**
- **Meriwether Lewis, William Clark, Lewis and Clark expedition, York, Sacajawea, *Journal of Meriwether Lewis*, Columbia River**
- **Toussaint l'Ouverture, Haiti, slave revolt**
- **Oliver Hazard Perry, battle for Lake Erie, "We have met the enemy and they are ours"**
- **Zebulon Pike, Spanish territory**

KEY TERMS/IDEAS

Review Strategy

See if you can relate these terms and ideas to their correct context in the "Fast Facts" section.

- **Berlin and Milan decrees, French laws restricting trade with ships that carried British goods or entered British ports**
- **Jefferson's Inaugural Address**
- **Nonintercourse Act, trade with nations other than Great Britain and France**
- **Orders of Council, British laws restricting trade by neutral nations unless they stopped in British ports first**

SECTION 3. NATIONALISM: PROSPERITY AND CHANGE

The period from 1815 to 1828 marked great changes for the new nation—both at home and abroad. **James Monroe's** two terms as president are known as the **"Era of Good Feelings,"** a time characterized by geographic expansion of the republic and, for a time, economic expansion. Monroe, a Republican from Virginia and Madison's former secretary of state, made a tour of the country shortly after his election and spoke about national unity. He promised to look out for the interests of all Americans—New Englanders as well as Southerners and Westerners. This was one example of the growing spirit of **nationalism** that was an outcome of the War of 1812. The Republicans over time usurped the position of the Federalists so that for 10 years the Republicans were the only political party. As a result, Monroe ran unopposed for reelection in 1820.

FAST FACTS

Review Strategy

See Chapter 6 for Chief Justice John Marshall's influence on the role of the federal government versus the states in this period.

Review Strategy

These "Fast Facts" relate to the politics of the "Era of Good Feelings."

- Even before Monroe took office, Congress was considering legislation that would spur economic growth in every section of the country and economic independence from other countries. Known as the **American System** and sponsored by **John C. Calhoun** and **Henry Clay,** the program included (1) a **protective tariff** for American manufacturing that had grown up during the embargo and the war; (2) **internal improvements,** a national system of roads and canals paid for by revenue from the tariff to aid commerce between farmers in the southern and frontier states and their markets on the coast; and (3) authorization of a **Second National Bank.**

- Expiration of the First Bank's charter in 1811 because of the opposition of Republicans had severely hampered efforts to finance the War of 1812. Without the National Bank, there was no stable national currency; people had little confidence in the state-chartered banks and in their currency. Because it was good for the country, Republicans approved a charter for the Second National Bank in 1816.

- Congress also passed the **Tariff of 1816.** Westerners and people from the Middle Atlantic states supported the tariff. Even some of those, like Thomas Jefferson, who had opposed Hamilton's tariff plan in 1789, approved of this protective tariff. New Englanders were divided, with **Daniel Webster** arguing for no tariff. At this point, some Southerners, such as **John C. Calhoun,** expected that their region would develop manufacturing and were willing to live with the tariff.

- The plan for internal improvements fared less well. In 1806, Congress had approved money to build a road from Cumberland, Maryland, across the mountains into what is today West Virginia. The **National** or **Cumberland Road** was begun in 1811, and by Madison's administration had reached into Ohio. In 1816, Congress passed a bill for internal improvements at federal expense. Madison vetoed it because he did not believe the Constitution allowed expenditures to improve transportation. Monroe also vetoed the bill.

Review Strategy

This "Fast Fact" relates to the Panic of 1819.

Review Strategy

See McCulloch *v.* Maryland *in Chapter 6 for John Marshall's decision on states' rights versus the federal government.*

- The prosperity brought about by the postwar boom sparked a frenzy of borrowing to buy land and to build factories. Banks eager to make money were willing to offer loans with little collateral. In 1818, to stem the **speculation,** the Bank of the United States ordered its branch banks to tighten credit. Many of the state banks had been issuing their paper money without the gold or silver to back it, so the notes were worthless. Unable to back their paper, state banks closed; unable to repay their loans, farmers and manufacturers went bankrupt. A **depression** ensued that lasted for three years.

Review Strategy

This "Fast Fact" relates to the Missouri Compromise.

- The first serious controversy over slavery since the Constitution arose over admission of Missouri, part of the Louisiana Purchase, to the Union as a slave state. There were eleven free states and eleven slave states with twenty-two votes each in the Senate. Admitting Missouri would tip the balance in favor of slave states. The House passed and the Senate rejected the **Tallmadge Amendment** that would have outlawed the further importation of slaves into Missouri and freed all people on their twenty-fifth birthdays who were born into slavery after Missouri became a state. Then Maine petitioned to be admitted as a free state, thus restoring the balance of slave and free states. Henry Clay was able to reach a compromise in which (1) Maine would be admitted as a free state and Missouri as a slave state and (2) any future state created from the Louisiana Purchase north of the 36° 30' line would be free. Known as the **Missouri Compromise,** it only delayed resolution of the problem of slavery.

Review Strategy

These "Fast Facts" relate to foreign policy in the Monroe administration.

- After the War of 1812, the United States and Great Britain signed the **Rush-Bagot Agreement** by which they agreed not to keep warships on the Great Lakes. In 1818, they set the boundary between the Louisiana Territory and Canada at the 49th parallel. However, the issue of the boundary line for Oregon would continue unresolved until the 1840s.

- After the Revolutionary War, Spain received **Florida—East and West**—from Great Britain, and the areas remained under Spanish rule until 1819. In the thirty intervening years, many Americans had moved into the Floridas: white settlers, slaves escaping from servitude, Native Americans forced from their lands in the new states, and escaped criminals. They paid little attention to Spanish colonial government, and Spain, entangled in European wars, had few soldiers to send to Florida to subdue the settlers. In 1810, Americans in West Florida declared their independence and were admitted as a territory into the United States. When Madison offered to buy East Florida, the Spanish refused. In 1818, President Monroe sent **General Andrew Jackson** into East Florida in what became known as the **First Seminole War** to stop raids by Native Americans into U.S. territory. The following year, Spain agreed to give up East Florida in return for the United States's abandonment of claims to Texas. The **Adams-Onis Treaty** also recognized U.S. claims to the Oregon Territory.

Review Strategy

See p. 227 for the Roosevelt Corollary to the Monroe Doctrine.

- With the exception of Cuba and Puerto Rico, between 1810 and 1824 the Spanish colonies of **Latin America** had won or were in the process of winning their independence from Spain. As a result, both the United States and Great Britain had found profitable trading partners among these new nations. They did not wish to lose them if Spain regained its colonies now that it was no longer bogged down in the long war against Napoleon. In addition, the United States was concerned about **Russia**'s activity along the Pacific Coast where it was setting up trading posts and had claimed **Alaska**. The British urged the United States to join it in issuing a declaration that opposed intervention by any European nation in the new nations of Latin America and that agreed that neither Great Britain nor the United States would attempt to annex any part of the hemisphere. President Monroe consulted his secretary of state, John Quincy Adams, who advised issuing a statement alone, which Monroe did. The **Monroe Doctrine,** issued in 1823, was a warning to European nations to stay out of the affairs of the Western Hemisphere and, in turn, the United States would not interfere in European affairs. It was a bold statement by a nation that did not have the military power to back it up, but it showed the nation's desire to be considered a world power. Had the European nations decided to call the United States's bluff, it would have been British warships that would have intervened.

Review Strategy

This "Fast Fact" relates to the election of 1824.

- Although by the election of 1824 the Federalist party was dead, the Republicans were split into several groups, usually along sectional lines, so that four Republicans ran for president in 1824. William H. Crawford of Georgia was picked by the Republican **caucus** to run for president. **John Quincy Adams** of Massachusetts, son of the second president, was a favorite son of New England. **Henry Clay,** building a reputation as the **Great Compromiser,** represented the West. Because of his role in the War of 1812, **Andrew Jackson** of Tennessee, also a Western state, was popular across all sections. When the election was over, Jackson had the most electoral votes (and popular votes), but not a majority. According to the Twelfth Amendment, the House of Representatives was to decide the election. Clay was disqualified because he had the fewest number of electoral votes. He threw his support to Adams, and Adams was elected president. When Adams made Clay his secretary of state, Jackson and his supporters claimed that a **"corrupt bargain"** between Clay and Adams had cost Jackson his rightful victory. Clay had blocked Jackson's election to keep a rival Westerner from the presidency. Adams chose Clay because they shared certain beliefs, such as the necessity for a strong federal government and the importance of the American System.

Review Strategy

These "Fast Facts" relate to canal building and railroads.

Review Strategy

See Chapter 6 for a discussion of Gibbons v. Ogden, John Marshall's landmark decision on interstate commerce.

- Although federally supported internal improvements had been voted down, the nation saw a **transportation revolution** in the 1800s. The **Canal Era** began with the building of the **Erie Canal** in New York State to connect the Northeast and the Great Lakes. By 1840, a network of canals linked the waterways of the Northeast with those of the newer states of the West. The western parts of New York and Pennsylvania were joined with eastern ports and with the Great Lakes, while canals in Ohio, Indiana, Kentucky, and Illinois linked the Ohio and Mississippi Rivers with the Great Lakes. In addition to speeding goods to customers, the canals created new markets. Canals made it possible for people—both the native-born who felt the older states were getting too crowded and the increasing waves of immigrants—to move quickly from the Eastern seaboard to the new frontier to settle. No canals were as financially successful as the Erie Canal, and the **Panic of 1837,** along with the advent of the railroad, ended the Canal Era.

- Although the first **railroads** were operating in the 1830s, a safe and reliable steam engine was needed before railroads could overtake canals, and that did not occur until the early 1850s. Railroads were a more satisfactory means of transporting goods and people than canals because (1) they did not rely on waterways for their routes, (2) they could operate in all kinds of weather, and (3) they were cheap to operate. Even more than canals, the railroads spurred the growth and settlement of the Western territories and the development of the nation's **market economy.**

Review Strategy

These "Fast Facts" relate to the factory system and early labor organizing.

- The **factory system** replaced the **domestic system** in the United States in the early 1800s. A major impetus to this development was the embargo of 1897 and the War of 1812. The first mills were located in New England and operated by water power. Later, the large turbines were powered by coal or steam. Francis Cabot Lowell and his **Boston Associates** formed a corporation to build **Lowell, Massachusetts,** a company town whose factories produced textiles. In time, **entrepreneurs** learned how to transfer the factory system to other industries, such as manufacturing woolen goods and firearms. As a result, more and more jobs once done by skilled workers were taken over by machines. Areas in the Mid-Atlantic states, with the same resources of energy and cheap labor as New England, grew into industrial cities.

- The first workers in the textile mills were native-born women recruited from New England farms. They lived in supervised boarding houses and viewed millwork as a way to help out their families by sending money home, to save for their future marriage, or to see something of the world before they married and settled down. The original **Lowell System** was an experiment in running factories without the abuses of the English factory system. By the 1830s, however, these women were being replaced by families of new immigrants, including children. Penniless, these families would work for less than the women. Conditions in the mills deteriorated as mill owners demanded more work for a greater return on their investment. When times were bad, such as during the Panic of 1837, mill owners cut the already low wages.

- In the 1790s, the first **labor unions** organized skilled workers, such as printers. As early as the 1820s, factory workers organized to demand (1) higher wages, (2) a 10-hour workday, (3) better working conditions, and (4) an end to debtors' prisons. Several times in the 1830s and 1840s, the women workers in Lowell went out on **strike.** Each time, the mill owners threatened to replace them, and the women returned to work without winning their demands. The influx of immigrants beginning in the 1830s, and especially the large numbers of Irish in the 1840s, impeded the growth of the labor movement.

Review Strategy

This "Fast Fact" relates to the cotton revolution in the South. For more on the development of the South, see pp. 168–170.

- Because most labor, land, and capital in the South were dedicated to farming, little industry developed in that region. Because of the growing demand for cotton to feed the textile industry in the North and in England, the South had the potential to make money from cotton agriculture. However, removing cotton seeds from cotton bolls was labor intensive. With the invention of the **cotton gin** in 1793 by **Eli Whitney,** based on a suggestion by **Catherine Greene,** cotton bolls could be cleaned quickly. Raising cotton immediately became more profitable. As a result, cotton agriculture and **slavery,** which provided the labor, spread across the South.

KEY PEOPLE

Review Strategy

See if you can relate these people to their correct context in the "Fast Facts" section.

- Richard Arkwright, Samuel Slater, spinning machine
- Sarah Bagley, Lowell Female Labor Reform Organization
- John C. Calhoun, Vice-President, election of 1824
- Edmund Cartwright, power loom
- De Witt Clinton
- Robert Fulton, *Clermont*
- Samuel F. B. Morse, telegraph
- Daniel Webster, "defender of the Constitution," nationalist
- Eli Whitney, interchangeable parts

KEY TERMS/IDEAS

Review Strategy

See if you can relate these terms and ideas to their correct context in the "Fast Facts" section.

- clipper ships, China trade; steamships
- *Commonwealth* v. *Hunt*, Massachusetts court ruling on legality of unions
- Factory Girls' Association
- Natchez Trace; turnpikes
- National Trades Union
- trade societies, closed shop
- Virginia dynasty of presidents
- Waltham System

SECTION 4. SECTIONALISM

While the War of 1812 engendered a sense of nationalism in politicians and ordinary citizens alike, the economic changes that occurred after the war brought a growing sense of **sectionalism.** The nation was being divided by the economic self-interests of the Northeast, the South, and the quickly expanding Western states and territories.

FAST FACTS

Review Strategy

These "Fast Facts" and the chart relate to the South and the development of the cotton culture.

Review Strategy

See Chapter 5 for information on how the slave trade was banned.

- As a result of the cotton gin, **cotton agriculture** spread widely across the South from the coastal states to the Mississippi River, the **Deep South.** Because of the need for large numbers of workers, **slavery** spread with it. Although the importation of enslaved Africans had ended in 1808, a thriving **internal market** for slaves developed between the old states and the new states of the South. By 1860, there were almost 4 million slaves, four times the number in 1808.

- Because slaves were considered property, slave owners thought nothing of selling individuals, thus splitting families apart. The worst fear was to be "sold down the river," meaning the Mississippi, to toil in the **cotton factories** of the **Deep South** (Alabama, Mississippi, Arkansas, Louisiana, and, later, Texas). Slaves worked from sunup to sundown in gangs supervised by a white **overseer** and a **slave driver**—often an African American—planting, hoeing, weeding, picking, and ginning cotton, depending on the season. Women and children worked alongside the men. A few slaves were trained as house servants to work in the planters' houses as butlers, cooks, or maids. A few learned skills such as blacksmithing and carpentry.

- From the earliest times, slaves had rebelled. In the 1600s and 1700s in New York and New England, slaves plotted against their owners but were caught and executed. Passage of a series of **slave codes** followed each incident. In the **Stono Uprising,** which took place in South Carolina in 1739, some twenty slaves tried to escape to St. Augustine in Spanish-held Florida but were captured. The Spanish were offering freedom to any slave who escaped to Florida. Other uprisings that frightened Southern slaveholders were (1) **Gabriel Prosser's Conspiracy** in Virginia, (2) **Denmark Vesey's Conspiracy** in South Carolina, and (3) **Nat Turner's Rebellion,** also in Virginia. In addition to outright rebellion, slaves used other ways to resist: they worked slowly and sabotaged tools and machinery.

- Although the phrase **"Cotton Kingdom"** has come to symbolize the **antebellum South,** in reality the South was more than big cotton plantations. Virginia, Kentucky, Tennessee, and North Carolina raised tobacco; Louisiana's main crop was sugar; and the swampy areas of Georgia and South Carolina cultivated rice. There were only about 50,000 large plantations in the South, but hundreds of thousands of small farms raised food crops and livestock, much of it for the farmers' own use. Most Southerners lived at the **subsistence level.**

- Because cotton was the major export of the South, the region had little industry—about 10 percent of the nation's total number of factories—few canals, major roads, or railroads and few large cities. Planters hesitated to put their money into factories because farming was more profitable. What industry existed, such as milling wheat or making iron tools, developed to satisfy local needs. These mills and factories were not part of any large national trading network, so there was little reason to build a transportation system. The economy of the South remained **rural** until the Civil War, so there was little reason to develop, or need for, a number of large cities.

- The **"cotton culture"** gave rise to a rigid class system:

Planters	Owned from 20 to 200 slaves, lived on the best lands, were the leaders of the region
Small slaveholders	Owned fewer than 20 slaves and might own only 1 or 2, worked medium-size farms, had little influence
Small farmers	Owned no slaves, raised their own food and livestock, usually raised some **cash crop,** such as cotton or tobacco
Tenant farmers	Worked poor land, often exhausted soils that planters no longer could use, generally in debt
Poor whites	Frontier families living in the mountains on rocky soil that was difficult to farm, also hunted for food; might hire out as day laborers
Free blacks	Nearly half of all blacks in the United States; after 1830, Southern legislatures passed laws severely limiting their freedom (could not vote, have a trial by jury, testify against whites, attend public schools, or assemble in a group without a white person present); earned livelihoods as craftworkers
Slaves	No rights, considered **chattel**

- To the Southern way of thinking, a number of economic factors supported slavery: (1) the increasing demand for cotton, (2) the labor-intensive nature of cotton agriculture, (3) the cheap source of labor in slaves, and (4) the climate of the South, especially the Deep South, that allowed almost year-round farming, so slaves did not have to be supported during slack time. To justify their use of human beings as slaves, Southerners developed the argument that slavery actually helped slaves. According to the explanation, the system guaranteed slaves food to eat, a roof over their heads, clothes to wear, and a home in sickness and old age. Planters contrasted this secure life with the precarious existence of employees in Northern factories. Led by wealthy planters, this **proslavery argument** took hold in the antebellum South and infused the thinking of small farmers who wanted to own more slaves, farmers who hoped to own slaves some day, and even those with no hope of owning slaves. It created a sense of who Southerners were and what they stood for.

Review Strategy

These "Fast Facts" relate to immigration.

- The North during this period was developing into an urban, industrial region. Swelling **immigration,** especially from Ireland beginning in the 1840s, provided the labor to turn the engines of commerce. Between 1790 and 1815, about 250,000 Europeans immigrated to the new nation. Between 1820 and 1860, some 4.6 million came, mostly to port cities of the Northeast, where many stayed.

- Immigrants came for a variety of reasons. **Pull factors** included economic opportunities created by industrialization, the transportation revolution, and westward expansion. Jobs and the possibility of owning land brought many people. **Push factors** depended on the immigrant group, but in general included (1) lack of economic opportunities at home, including the inability to afford to own land; (2) crop failures; and (3) political instability.

- Immigrants were not always welcome. **Nativist** sentiment ran against immigrants because native-born Americans were concerned that the immigrants (1) would take their jobs, (2) were threats to the American way of life because they established their own separate communities, (3) were revolutionaries because of the revolutions of 1830 and 1848 in Europe, and (4) were Roman Catholics. **Anti-Catholic prejudice** was strong before the Civil War and directed mostly toward the Irish. Most other immigrant groups were Protestant, as were most native-born Americans.

- Between 1790 and the 1820s, the **Western frontier** had been pushed from the Appalachians to the Mississippi. The land between the Mississippi and the Rocky Mountains, the Great Plains, today the major farming area of the country, was considered the **Great American Desert** until after the Civil War. In the 1830s and 1840s, it was simply the area that settlers had to get through on their way to the **Oregon Territory.** The first Americans into

Oregon had been **fur traders, Mountain Men** who blazed the **Oregon Trail.**

Review Strategy

This "Fast Fact" relates to the Upper Midwest.

- By 1840, the fertile lands between the Ohio and Mississippi Rivers had been settled, and five states had been carved out of the **Northwest Territory** (Michigan, Ohio, Indiana, Illinois, and Missouri). Large farm families worked the land. In the beginning, the families were **self-sufficient,** but the invention of the **steel plow** and the **mechanical reaper** allowed them to raise **cash crops.** The upper Midwest became the major grain-producing region of the United States. An efficient transportation system of waterways, canals, and, later, railroads developed to move goods to market. To serve these farmers who now had money to spend, villages and towns grew, especially at the junctions of transportation routes. A number of these towns grew into major American commercial and industrial cities.

Review Strategy

These "Fast Facts" relate to Native American removal.

- As white settlers moved into the land beyond the Appalachians, they came into contact with Native Americans already living there. As early as the 1790s, the nation had fought Native Americans in the Northwest Territory **(Battle of Fallen Timbers).** The **Treaty of Greenville** forced Native Americans to give up most of their lands, thus opening the area for white settlement. In 1831, as a result of the **Black Hawk War,** the **Sauk** and **Fox** were forced to move from Illinois and Wisconsin across the Mississippi to Iowa.

Review Strategy

See Chapter 6 for Cherokee Nation *v.* The State of Georgia *and* Worcester *v.* Georgia.

- In the 1820s and 1830s, the battle for Native American land shifted to the South and the **Old Southwest,** the area south of the Ohio River and between the Appalachians and the Mississippi (the modern states of Kentucky, Tennessee, Alabama, and Mississippi). The **Five Civilized Tribes,** as they were called because they had been converted to Christianity and had become farmers, stood in the way of settlers. The **Indian Removal Act of 1830** gave President Andrew Jackson the power to remove the Native Americans by force to the **Indian Territory,** what is now Oklahoma. One by one, the nations were removed, sometimes forcibly. The **Cherokee** were recognized as a separate nation by the United States since 1790 and fought back through the court system. Even when they won, it made no difference to Georgians who wanted their land. In 1838, **President Martin Van Buren** sent the army to move the Cherokee to Indian Territory, a journey known as the **Trail of Tears.**

KEY PEOPLE

Review Strategy

See if you can relate these people to their correct context in the "Fast Facts" section.

- John Deere
- Charles Goodyear
- Cyrus McCormick
- Solomon Northup, *Twelve Years a Slave*
- squatters, government lands

KEY TERMS/IDEAS

Review Strategy

See if you can relate these terms and ideas to their correct context in the "Fast Facts" section.

- American Colonization Society, Liberia
- Irish potato famine
- Know-Nothings, Order of the Star-Spangled Banner

SECTION 5. THE AGE OF JACKSON, 1828–1848

The years between 1828 and the Mexican War of 1848 saw rapid change in both the political life of the country and its size. Sectional rivalries came to dominate politics and affect the nation's economy as well. The major change was in the size and nature of the electorate. The **"Age of Jackson"** has come to be synonymous with the **"Age of the Common Man."**

FAST FACTS

Review Strategy

These "Fast Facts" deal with increased political participation.

- The election of 1828 was run not on issues but on the personalities of the candidates, **John Quincy Adams** and **Andrew Jackson.** The election is significant in that (1) for the first time a candidate born west of the Appalachians was elected president, (2) the political center of the nation was shifting away from the Atlantic seaboard, (3) leaders were no longer necessarily to be chosen from among the ranks of the educated and wealthy, (4) the number of voters increased threefold from the 1824 election, (5) the **Democratic Party** (supporters of Jackson) came into existence, and (6) the Republicans (the old Democratic-Republicans) were replaced by the **National Republicans** (supporters of Adams).

- The increased **political participation** evident in the election of 1828 came about because of the change in **voting requirements.** The growth of the West, with its sense of social equality and the change in ways of making a living in all sections, prompted the states to drop property qualifications. Religious tests were also dropped. Some states substituted the payment of a tax, but this too was eventually eliminated. By the 1820s, all free white male taxpayers could vote, and free black men could vote in some Northern states. Women and slaves were excluded. The removal of property requirements meant that **suffrage** was extended down into the middle and lower classes—**the common man.**

- **Jacksonian Democracy** manifested itself in other ways. People now expected their leaders to ask their opinions and represent their views. More offices became elective rather than appointive, especially local positions such as judge and sheriff. People took more interest in politics, and political parties began to organize at the **grassroots** level. Rather than use the **caucus** to choose candidates for public office, parties began to use **nominating conventions.** These changes led to **political patronage** and the **spoils system** ("to the victor belongs the spoils"), which Jackson used widely to reward his friends with jobs in the federal government. But the changes also reflected a belief in the ability of ordinary people to govern—a logical outgrowth of the American Revolution.

Review Strategy

These "Fast Facts" deal with new political parties.

- During the election of 1828, Jackson's supporters began calling themselves **Democrats** after the Democratic-Republican Party of Jefferson. Jackson's appeal widened the traditional base of the party to include Westerners and ordinary people.

- The **Whig Party** was formed during the election of 1832 by the National Republicans and Jackson's opponents in the Democratic Party. Henry Clay was their presidential candidate. The party took its name from those who had opposed King George III; the new Whigs called Jackson **"King Andrew."** Jackson had very strong views of what the role of president should be. The Whigs in general supported the protective tariff and the National Bank. Whig candidates were elected president in 1840 and 1844, but sectional differences (slavery and economic policy) divided the party. After the deaths of Clay and **Daniel Webster,** who had kept the party together, it disappeared in the 1850s.

Review Strategy

These "Fasts Facts" deal with states' rights and nullification.

- The issue of **internal improvements** came up in Jackson's first term and became enmeshed with the issue of **states' rights.** Congress had passed a bill authorizing the expenditure of federal funds to extend the Cumberland Road within the state of Kentucky. Jackson appeared to support states' rights by vetoing the bill on the grounds that the Constitution did not allow the use of federal funds for local transportation. This became known as the **Maysville Road veto.**

Review Strategy

The Kentucky and Virginia Resolutions and the Hartford Convention took the same stand.

- In the early 1820s, Northeastern manufacturers began to lobby for a higher tariff, arguing that the **Tariff of 1816** was not enough. Although Southerners had supported the earlier tariff, they opposed the **Tariff of 1824,** fearing that if Europeans could not sell their goods to Americans, they would stop buying raw materials from the South. The tariff was raised again in 1828 over their protests and was called by them the **Tariff of Abominations.** As Southerners feared, cotton exports fell, and some planters faced serious losses. In 1832, Congress passed a new tariff bill that lowered the tax on some items. South Carolinians protested that the bill was not enough. They also believed that the tariff controversy showed that the federal government was becoming too strong, and that the next step would be the end of slavery. The South Carolina legislature called a convention and passed an **Ordinance of Nullification** stating that the tariff was "null, void, and no law; nor binding upon this state, its officers, or its citizens." The state threatened to secede if the federal government attempted to collect the tariff in South Carolina.

- Based on the Maysville Road veto, Southerners thought Jackson, a fellow Southerner and slave owner, would agree with the South Carolina position. However, Jackson stood behind the Constitution. While warning South Carolinians that secession was treason, he tried to persuade the leaders of Congress to pass a new tariff bill that would reduce taxes. He also requested that Congress pass the **Force Bill** to allow him to use the army and navy to collect the tariff and put down any insurrection. **Henry Clay,** the **Great Compromiser,** negotiated a new tariff that was acceptable to South Carolina, and South Carolina repealed the nullification ordinance, thus ending the **Nullification Crisis.**

Review Strategy

This "Fast Fact" deals with the break between Jackson and Calhoun.

- In 1828, **John C. Calhoun** had published the ***South Carolina Exposition,*** anonymously arguing that the Constitution gave the federal government the power to levy taxes to raise revenue but not to protect segments of the economy. Therefore, the Tariff of 1828 was unconstitutional, and states could declare it null and void. Although he was Jackson's vice-president in 1832, Calhoun was vehemently opposed to Jackson's stand on nullification. He resigned and ran for election as senator from South Carolina. Calhoun remained a strong advocate of Southern interests and **states' rights** in national politics until his death in 1850.

Review Strategy

These "Fast Facts" deal with the Bank War.

- Jackson distrusted the **Second Bank** because he believed it (1) was run by the wealthy for their own self-interests and (2) had too much influence in economic policy. The Bank's charter was to come up for renewal in 1836, but **Nicholas Biddle,** the Bank's president, requested early renewal in 1832, hoping to make the Bank a major issue in the election of 1832. **Henry Clay,** the presidential candidate on the Whig ticket, introduced the bill. Congress voted to recharter the Bank, but Jackson vetoed it. Congress could not override the veto. During the campaign, Clay, **Daniel Webster,** and the Bank's advocates called for renewal of its charter, arguing that the nation's economy depended on it. The voters, especially Westerners, Southerners, and the working class in the East, agreed with Jackson, and he was reelected.

- Regardless of the law, Jackson destroyed the Bank in 1833 by having all federal money withdrawn from it. Jackson went through three Secretaries of the Treasury before one would agree to remove the funds. Jackson deposited the money in various state banks that the Whigs called **"pet banks,"** because they were supposedly run by loyal supporters of Jackson. Biddle countered by restricting credit to state banks and withdrawing money from circulation. As a result, credit dried up, and the nation teetered on the brink of an economic depression. Biddle sought to blame Jackson for the depression, while Democrats claimed that Jackson had been right to veto the Bank if it could cause so much damage. The people again agreed with Jackson, seeing his veto as an affirmation of democracy. Feeling the pressure from the fierce attacks, Biddle reissued credit to state banks.

Review Strategy

This "Fast Fact" deals with the Panic of 1837.

- After the break with Calhoun, Jackson turned to **Martin Van Buren** to succeed him as president. Shortly after taking office, Van Buren found himself faced with the **Panic of 1837.** There were a number of causes for the panic and ensuing depression: (1) the **Specie Circular,** Jackson's attempt to halt the speculation and inflation that followed the release for sale of millions of acres of government land by requiring gold or silver, rather than bank notes to purchase the land, (2) the withdrawal of British investments as Great Britain suffered through its own economic hard times, and (3) the lack of a national banking system with stable currency.

Review Strategy

This "Fast Fact" deals with the Independent Treasury System.

- Van Buren did not want a central bank either, but he realized that the government's money had to be deposited somewhere. After having seen so many fail, he believed that small commercial banks were not safe. Van Buren proposed the **Independent Treasury Act** as a way to separate the federal treasury from the banking system. Vaults were installed in selected sites around the country to hold federal tax revenues, which were to be backed by gold. Congress approved the system in 1840, repealed it in 1841, and reinstated it in 1846. The system ended in 1913 with passage of the **Federal Reserve Act.**

KEY PEOPLE/TERMS

Review Strategy

See if you can relate these people and terms to their correct context in the "Fast Facts" section.

- John Jacob Astor, American Fur Company

- James Beckwith

- Peggy Eaton, John Eaton

- Rachel Jackson

- Robert G. Hayne, South Carolina senator, governor

- Alexis de Tocqueville, *Democracy in America*

- Webster-Hayne Debate, public lands, issue of nullification

- wildcat banks

SECTION 6. A CHANGING SOCIETY AND AN EMERGING CULTURE

The sense of nationalism that informed politics found voice in an emerging cultural identity as well. Desirous of developing their own subjects and styles, American writers and artists set about creating an American culture. Mindful of the promises of the Declaration of Independence, some Americans also sought to reform a society that they felt was not living up to its founding ideals.

FAST FACTS

Review Strategy

This "Fast Fact" relates to the religious revival of the early 1800s.

- Part of the impetus to the reform movements was a resurgence in religion. Like the Great Awakening of the mid-1700s, the **Second Great Awakening,** which began in the 1790s, was accompanied by revival meetings, the erection of new churches, and the founding of new colleges and universities. In response to the needs of waves of new immigrants, Roman Catholics built churches and schools and founded charitable organizations.

Review Strategy

These "Fast Facts" relate to public education.

- The growth in political participation both encouraged the **movement for public education** and was an outgrowth of increased educational levels. Before the 1830s, only New England supported public elementary schools to any extent. Reformers called for public schools (1) to educate future voters and (2) to prevent social ills like poverty and crime. However, not everyone agreed with the reformers. Levying taxes to pay for public schools was an issue in part because of a dislike of taxes and in part because some religious groups that ran their own schools did not see why they had to pay to send other people's children to public school. If and how to educate African Americans remained an issue. Some people, especially in the West, saw no particular need for anything but the basics of education.

- By the 1850s, most free states had established public school systems. The **Northwest Ordinance** had required that each township set aside land for a school, so free public education grew quickly in the Midwest. In the South, because it was an agrarian society, little headway was made in establishing free public education. The children of planters, merchants, and professionals had tutors, or their sons were sent to private schools. While Americans might have supported elementary schools, there was little support for public high schools, although private **academies** for secondary education thrived.

- Some reformers wanted to remake all of society. These **Utopian experiments** were small communities of like-minded individuals who lived apart from society in self-sufficient enclaves. Some groups were based on the principles of **socialism;** that is, all members would work together and own all property in common. Other groups, like the **Mormons,** based their communities on religious principles.

- The Mormons, or the **Church of the Latter-Day Saints,** had communities in Ohio, Illinois, and Missouri before settling in Utah. In each location, they were resented by their neighbors (1) who took offense at the Mormon teaching that they had received revelations from God **(Book of Mormon),** (2) who did not approve of the Mormon practice of **polygamy,** and (3) who feared the Mormons would oppose slavery (Missouri). After an attack on their community of Nauvoo, Illinois, the Mormons went west, settling in Utah, which was still under Mexican control. After the Mexican War, the Mormons requested statehood, but they were caught in the controversy over slavery. Utah did not become a state until 1896.

- **Transcendentalism** was very much an American literary movement. Centered in New England, it took its inspiration from **Immanuel Kant** and the **German Idealists** as well as from the works of such English authors as **Samuel Taylor Coleridge** and **William Wordsworth.** Transcendentalists emphasized (1) the unity and divinity of human beings and nature, (2) the value of intuition over reason, (3) self-reliance, and (4) individual conscience. Authors such as **Ralph Waldo Emerson, Henry David Thoreau, Bronson Alcott,** and **Margaret Fuller,** who edited their journal *Dial,* were prominent Transcendentalists.

Review Strategy

These "Fast Facts" relate to the development of a national literature and art.

- Transcendentalism also influenced the development of such literary greats as **Herman Melville, Nathaniel Hawthorne,** and later, **Walt Whitman.** The writers of the 1820s, 1830s, and 1840s created a **national literature**—that is, a literature that took its themes, its settings, and its characters from the new nation. The purpose was, in the words of one historian, "to reform America's attitude toward itself." No longer would Americans think of themselves as poor relations of Europeans when it came to culture. For example, **James Fenimore Cooper** used the recent frontier past to create heroic figures. **Washington Irving** turned the Dutch history of the Hudson River Valley into literature, while Nathaniel Hawthorne used Puritanism as the backdrop for his stories. **Romanticism** played a role in the development of American literature of this period, but the context was purely American.

- The art of the period used American themes and subjects and was also inspired by romanticism. The **Hudson River School** used the landscape of the river valley for its paintings just as the **Knicker-bocker School** used the area for its literary themes. Among its most famous artists are **Thomas Cole** and **Asher B. Durand.** Earlier artists of the 1800s, such as **John Trumbull, Gilbert Stuart,** and **Charles Wilson Peale,** used the battles of the Revolutionary War and its heroes as the subject matter for their paintings. Later painters **George Caleb Bingham** and **George Catlin** used the new frontier's Native Americans and ordinary people, such as fur traders floating down the Missouri River, as subjects for their paintings.

Review Strategy

These "Fast Facts" relate to women's rights.

- A major reform movement of the nineteenth century dealt with **women's rights.** At that time, (1) education for girls was limited, especially for poor girls; (2) women could not train for a profession other than teaching, and that only because women were more likely to work for less than men; (3) married women could not own property, although single women could; (4) mothers had no legal rights to their children; (5) married women could not make a contract or sue in court; (6) married women who worked outside the home had no right to their wages; (7) women could not vote; (8) women could not hold public office; and (9) public speaking in front of an audience of men and women was not considered proper for women, although they could work in reform movements under the direction of men.

- At the **Seneca Falls Convention** in 1848, the first **women's rights conference, Lucretia Mott** and **Elizabeth Cady Stanton** led the delegates in drafting the **Declaration of Sentiments and Resolutions,** modeled after the Declaration of Independence. At mid-century the reformers were able to effect few changes, although some states passed laws allowing women to own and manage property.

Review Strategy

These "Fast Facts" relate to abolition.

- There was a crossover between the women's rights movement and **abolition,** with many women active in both. **Sojourner Truth** spoke both for enslaved Africans and women, while **Frederick Douglass,** perhaps the best known of the African-American abolitionists, seconded Stanton's call for voting rights for women.

- In the early 1800s, the **antislavery movement** had supporters in all sections of the country, but as cotton became more profitable, fewer Southerners were willing to speak out against slavery. Abolitionist activities increased in the 1830s, and petitions began to pour into Congress. To stop debate on these petitions, Southerners pushed through **gag rules** in both the House and the Senate in 1836 that rejected all petitions without debate. The gag rules were repealed in 1844.

Review Strategy

These "Fast Facts" relate to other reform movements.

- The **temperance movement** developed in answer to the growing problem of drinking and drunkenness. Reformers laid the blame for such social ills as poverty, crime, and mental illness on heavy drinking, and launched a campaign to convince people to give up drinking and to ask governments to **prohibit** the sale of alcohol. Temperance meetings resembled religious revival meetings, and in fact, many of the movement's leaders were clergy. As a result of the clamor raised by the movement, a number of politicians supported it, and about a dozen states passed laws prohibiting the sale of alcohol. Other states passed laws giving local governments the option of banning the sale of liquor in their jurisdiction.

- Through the efforts of **Dorothea Dix** and like-minded reformers, a number of reforms were made to help the mentally ill and criminals. When Dix began her work, those who were mentally ill went untreated and were sent to prisons with criminals. By the 1850s, (1) hospitals for the mentally ill had been opened in a number of states, (2) male and female prisoners were segregated, (3) youthful offenders were separated from adults, (4) the poor were no longer imprisoned for debt, and (5) the whipping of prisoners had been abolished by a number of states.

KEY PEOPLE

Review Strategy

See if you can relate these people to their correct context in the "Fast Facts" section.

- **Susan B. Anthony, Lucy Stone, Pauline Wright Davis**
- **Catherine Beecher, Emma Hart Willard**
- **Thomas Gallaudet, hearing impaired, sign language**
- **Henry Highland Garnett**

- William Lloyd Garrison, *Liberator,* New England Anti-Slavery Society, American Anti-Slavery Society

- Angelina Grimké, Sarah Grimké

- F. E. W. Harper (Frances Ellen Watkins), free African-American abolitionist

- Samuel Gridley Howe, New England Institution for the Blind

- Elijah Lovejoy

- James Russell Lowell, Henry Wadsworth Longfellow

- Horace Mann, secretary of education, Board of Education, Massachusetts, normal schools to train teachers, professionals

- Herman Melville, Edgar Allan Poe

- Sarah Peale, John James Audubon

- David Ruggles, William Still, free African-American abolitionists

- Shakers

- Joseph Smith, Brigham Young

- David Walker, *Walker's Appeal*

- Theodore Weld, *American Slavery As It Is*

KEY TERMS/IDEAS

Review Strategy

See if you can relate these terms and ideas to their correct context in the "Fast Facts" section.

- Amana Colony, Iowa; social experiment

- American Temperance Union

- Brook Farm, Transcendentalists

- Bowdoin College, first to admit African Americans

- higher education for professions such as medicine and law; apprenticeships

- Federal style, Charles Bulfinch, U.S. Capitol building

- Greek Revival, Virginia State Capitol

- Lincoln University, first African-American college

- Mount Holyoke Female Seminary, Mary Lyon

- New Harmony, Indiana; Robert Owen, social experiment

- *The North Star*

- Oberlin Collegiate Institute, coeducation, University of Iowa

- **Oneida Community, New York; religious experiment; considered themselves the family of God; very successful manufacturing business**

- **Unitarian Church**

Chapter 8

REVIEWING THE EVENTS LEADING TO THE CIVIL WAR AND ITS AFTERMATH

Study Strategy

Check the College Board Web site (www.collegeboard.org/ ap) for the time period for your DBQ.

The study of U.S. history in the nineteenth century revolves to a large extent around the events leading to the Civil War, the fighting of the war, and then Reconstruction of the South. The essay section of the AP U.S. History Test divides its questions into before and after the Civil War. Chapter 8 provides a brief summary of the period for your review. Remember that half the questions on the multiple-choice section ask about events and people from 1789 to 1914. Consider that a number of the questions will deal with the years from 1845 to 1877 and the people and events that brought about the Civil War and its resolution.

SECTION 1. TERRITORIAL EXPANSION AND SECTIONAL CRISIS

By 1840, the United States had enjoyed more than two decades of peace. The frontier had been pushed back to the Mississippi, and Americans who were eager for land and/or adventure were traveling through the **Great American Desert** to the Pacific Northwest. **Commercial agriculture** was coming to dominate the Midwest. The **transportation revolution** and the **factory system** had transformed the Northeast and Middle Atlantic states into centers of commerce. Cotton was king in the South. What next?

As the land between the Atlantic seaboard and the Mississippi filled with people and farms and more immigrants came to the country, some people looked to move farther west. However, the British and the Spanish blocked the way. In 1845, an editor at the *New York Morning News* wrote that the nation had a "**manifest destiny** to overspread the continent allotted by Providence." Americans used this idea of manifest destiny as their justification for expansion into the Southwest (Arizona, New Mexico, Texas, and Oklahoma) and the Far West (California, Oregon, and Washington). It was also a sense of **mission,** what Providence had deemed the direction of their future to be, that drove Americans west.

FAST FACTS

- Between 1845 and 1853, the United States grew to its current size of the forty-eight contiguous states, adding Alaska and Hawaii later.

ACQUISITION	PRESENT STATES
Texas by resolution of Congress in 1845	Texas, parts of Oklahoma, Kansas, Colorado, and New Mexico
Oregon Territory by treaty with Great Britain in 1846	Oregon, Washington, Idaho, and parts of Montana and Wyoming
Mexican Cession by treaty with Mexico in 1848	California, Nevada, Utah, Arizona, and parts of Colorado, Wyoming, and New Mexico
Gadsden Purchase from Mexico in 1853	Parts of Arizona and New Mexico
Alaska purchased from Russia in 1867	Alaska
Hawaii annexed by the United States in 1898	Hawaii

Review Strategy

These "Fast Facts" relate to the annexation of Texas.

- Mexico had achieved its independence from Spain in 1821. With few Mexicans living in Texas, Mexico was interested in settling the vast area. The Mexican government accepted **Moses Austin's** request to settle in East Texas, provided that the settlers (1) became Roman Catholics and (2) obeyed Mexican law, including the banning of slaves. Under the leadership of his son, **Stephen Austin,** some 300 families immigrated to Texas in 1822. By 1830, when Americans outnumbered Mexicans in Texas by more than five to one, the Mexican government (1) refused entrance to any more Americans and (2) reiterated the ban on slavery. This occurred because many Americans who had come to Texas were slave owners who brought their slaves to work on cotton and sugar plantations. Austin protested and was jailed.

- When **General Antonio Santa Anna** became president of Mexico and assumed dictatorial powers, the Americans in Texas rebelled. Fighting broke out **(Battle of the Alamo),** but Santa Anna was unable to stop the rebels under **General Sam Houston (Battle of San Jacinto).** Santa Anna signed a treaty acknowledging Texas's independence but later refused to recognize it. However, the Mexicans could do nothing to stop Texas from declaring itself the **Lone Star Republic.**

- When Texans voted to ask the United States for admission as a state, Southerners readily agreed, but those who opposed slavery were against **annexation.** Jackson chose to delay the issue until after the 1836 election, and the new president, Martin Van Buren, refused to recommend annexation, thus delaying the issue again. By 1843, concern had grown that Texas would compete with the U.S. South as a source of cotton for British markets. The Senate defeated a bill to annex Texas, and **President John Tyler,** seeking reelection as a Whig, determined to make annexation a campaign issue. The antislavery Whigs, however, opposed annexation and nominated Henry Clay. The Democrats favored annexation of Texas and acquisition of Oregon, and their **dark horse** candidate, **James K. Polk,** running on a **platform of annexation,** won. By a **joint resolution** of Congress, Texas was annexed in 1845.

Review Strategy

This "Fast Fact" relates to the Mexican War.

- Annexation did not settle the question because Mexico and the United States claimed different boundaries for Texas. When U.S. troops in the disputed area were attacked by Mexican forces, the United States declared war. The **Mexican War** was waged on three fronts: northern Mexico, New Mexico and California, and Mexico City. The **Treaty of Guadalupe Hidalgo** (1) settled the boundary between Mexico and the United States at the Rio Grande, (2) gave the U.S. territory known as the **Mexican Cession** in exchange for $15 million, and (3) settled claims against Mexico for $3.5 million.

Review Strategy

This "Fast Fact" relates to the Wilmot Proviso.

- Fearing that the Mexican War would result in additional slave states, many Northerners opposed the war. **David Wilmot** from Pennsylvania proposed a bill in the House of Representatives banning slavery in any territory acquired from Mexico. **John C. Calhoun** vigorously opposed the **Wilmot Proviso** on the grounds that it was unconstitutional. Congress had a duty to protect the property rights of citizens, and that included slave owners' right to carry their property into new territory. The Senate rejected the bill.

Review Strategy

This "Fast Fact" relates to statehood for California.

- After 1821, the Mexican government gave away land in **California** to attract settlers as it had in Texas. In the beginning, Americans adopted Spanish culture, became Mexican citizens, and married native-born Californians. By the 1840s, the Americans who came hoped for annexation by the United States. In 1845, President Polk offered to buy California from Mexico but was refused. Polk countered by encouraging the Americans in California to rebel. Once the Mexican War began, a group of Americans rose up in the **Bear Flag Revolt** and declared California independent. The Treaty of Guadalupe Hidalgo gave California to the United States as part of the Mexican Cession. The **gold rush** intervened, but in 1849, California drafted a constitution banning slavery and requested statehood.

- The debate over the admission of California sparked one of the most acrimonious disputes in Congress over slavery. There were then fifteen free and fifteen slave states. Admitting California as a free state would destroy this balance, and the nation would face the same problem every time a territory carved from the former Mexican lands requested statehood. **Henry Clay** proposed a compromise: (1) California would be admitted as a free state; (2) the peoples of New Mexico and Utah would decide by **popular sovereignty** whether they would be free or slave; (3) Texas would give up its claim to part of this territory in exchange for $10 million; (4) the slave trade, but not slavery, would be abolished in the District of Columbia; and (5) Congress would pass a Fugitive Slave Law. **John C. Calhoun** opposed the **Compromise of 1850** because he believed it would diminish the South's influence in national affairs. Both he and **President Zachary Taylor,** who also opposed the Compromise, died, and the new president, **Millard Fillmore,** supported it. Influenced by the arguments of **Daniel Webster,** who pleaded with Northerners to preserve the Union, and **Stephen A. Douglas,** the Compromise was passed.

- In addition to the former Mexicans in Texas and California, there were Spanish-speaking settlers in the New Mexico Territory, which included the present states of Arizona and New Mexico. Altogether, about 75,000 Hispanics became citizens of the United States. Americans considered the Hispanic culture inferior. Because Hispanics spoke Spanish, they were considered "foreigners" in what had been their land first. All too often their rights were ignored. Costly legal battles were fought to take their lands. Tensions remained high between Hispanics and Anglos throughout the 1800s.

- At one time, **Spain, Russia, Great Britain,** and the **United States** claimed **Oregon,** which stretched from the northern border of California to the southern border of Alaska. Spain gave up its claim in the **Adams-Onis Treaty,** and Russia withdrew as a result of the **Monroe Doctrine.** Great Britain and the United States held the area jointly. Originally an important source of furs, in the 1840s Oregon became a destination for settlers and a political problem. Great Britain and the United States disagreed over the boundary. Polk offered to set the boundary at the 49th parallel, but Britain refused. Faced with the prospect of war (**"Fifty-four forty or fight!"**), Britain agreed to Polk's proposal, and Oregon was divided into the Oregon and **Washington Territories.**

Review Strategy

These "Fast Facts" relate to other expansionist efforts.

- Additional land was acquired from Mexico in 1853 for $10 million. Known as the **Gadsden Purchase,** this strip of land allowed the United States to have a southern route for a transcontinental railroad.

- In 1867, the United States bought Alaska from Russia. Secretary of State **William Seward,** a strong advocate of manifest destiny, pressed for the purchase because of the area's natural resources. At the time, however, it was called **Seward's Folly.** In 1899, gold was found, and a new gold rush was on.

KEY PEOPLE

Review Strategy

See if you can relate these people to their correct context in the "Fast Facts" section.

- **Captain John C. Fremont, the Pathfinder, California**
- **Colonel Stephen Kearny, New Mexico campaign**
- **General Winfield Scott, Veracruz, Mexico City**
- **General Zachary Taylor, Battle of Buena Vista**
- **Dr. Marcus Whitman, Narcissa Prentice Whitman, Henry Spalding, Elizabeth Hart Spalding, Samuel Parker**

KEY TERMS/IDEAS

Review Strategy

See if you can relate these terms and ideas to their correct context in the "Fast Facts" section.

- **Columbia River, fishing rights**
- **Mexican Borderlands**
- **Oregon Trail**
- **Santa Fe Trail**
- **Sutter's Mill, Forty-Niners, three routes west**

SECTION 2. PRELUDE TO THE CIVIL WAR

Review Strategy

See p. 186 for how the Compromise of 1850 came about.

Although the **Compromise of 1850** delayed the Civil War for eleven years, it settled nothing. Using **popular sovereignty** in Utah and New Mexico to decide whether the states would be slave or free did not address the central issue of whether slavery should be allowed to spread to new areas. Response to the **Fugitive Slave Law,** however, was immediate.

FAST FACTS

Review Strategy

These "Fast Facts" relate to the antislavery movement.

- The Fugitive Slave Law (1) authorized federal marshals to hunt escaped slaves and return them to their owners and (2) provided heavy fines against law officers and ordinary citizens who aided an escaped slave or failed to assist in the capture of one. The law was passed to undermine support for the **Underground Railroad.** However, the law drove many Northerners to join the **antislavery movement.** Angry Northerners sometimes went so far as to attack slave catchers and free their prisoners. Northern legislatures passed **personal liberty laws** that provided for trials to determine the status of apprehended blacks who might be fugitive slaves and forbid state officials to aid slave catchers. Southerners reacted angrily, claiming that Northerners were ignoring the Compromise of 1850 and the rights of Southern property owners.

- Based on information from escaped slaves, the novel ***Uncle Tom's Cabin*** by **Harriet Beecher Stowe** added fuel to the controversy. The book angered Southerners who said it painted an unfair and untrue picture of plantation life. Northerners accepted it at face value. Published in 1852, some 300,000 copies had been sold within a year.

Review Strategy

These "Fast Facts" relate to the Kansas-Nebraska Act.

Review Strategy

See p. 163 for more on the Missouri Compromise.

- The **Kansas-Nebraska Act** added to the tension. **Stephen A. Douglas** introduced the bill in 1854, claiming he was interested in (1) encouraging the settlement of the **trans-Missouri region,** (2) building a transcontinental railroad along a route from Chicago west to connect the nation (rather than on a southerly route using the land in the Gadsden Purchase), and (3) piercing the "barbarian wall" of Native Americans. The Act provided that (1) the trans-Missouri area be divided into Kansas and Nebraska, (2) popular sovereignty decide the issue of slavery, and (3) the ban on slavery north of the 36° 30', the **Missouri Compromise,** be repealed. Settlers, speculators, **pro-slavery** advocates, and **antislavery** forces rushed to control Kansas.

- When it came time to draft a constitution for Kansas, proslavery forces rigged the election for members to the constitutional convention and adopted a proslavery constitution, known as the **Lecompton Constitution.** Antislavery forces then held their own convention and drafted their own constitution. When the Lecompton Constitution was sent to Congress, **President James Buchanan** advised Congress to accept it, believing it would reinstate equanimity between North and South. His fellow Democrat Douglas argued strongly against it. Congress finally sent the constitution back to Kansas for a **popular referendum,** in which it was soundly defeated ten to one.

- Casualties of the Kansas-Nebraska Act were party unity and the Whig party itself. Southern Democrats and Southern Whigs voted for the bill, whereas Northern Democrats and Northern Whigs voted against it. The **Whigs** had been more a party of personalities—Henry Clay and Daniel Webster—than programs, and it could not mend its sectional split. After 1852, it ran no more presidential candidates. In an effort to unite their forces, antislavery supporters from both parties, abolitionists, and members of the **Free-Soil Party** formed, in 1854, the **Republican Party,** taking its name from the Jeffersonian Democratic-Republican Party.

Review Strategy

This "Fast Fact" relates to the election of 1856.

- In the presidential election of 1856, the sectional divisions were very clear. The Democrats supported the Kansas-Nebraska Act and nominated James Buchanan, a Northerner who sympathized with the South. The new Republican Party ran on a platform that called for the prohibition of slavery but not its abolition. Their platform offered something for everyone (except Southerners): a protective tariff, free Western lands, and a national banking system. **John C. Frémont,** of Mexican War fame, was their candidate, winning 33 percent of the popular vote and two thirds of the free states' electoral votes. The Republicans were looking at the very real possibility that in the next election, a candidate with the backing of the free states alone could win the presidency.

Review Strategy

See Chapter 6 for Scott *v.* Sanford.

- Another factor that added to the growing division between North and South was the **Dred Scott** case. Buchanan had hoped it would settle the issue of the legality of slavery in new territories, but it only inflamed the situation.

Review Strategy

This "Fast Fact" relates to the Lincoln-Douglas debates.

- The Republicans' opposition to the decision in the Dred Scott case attracted new members, including **Abraham Lincoln,** a lawyer in Illinois. The Illinois Republican Party nominated him to run against Stephen A. Douglas for senator in the 1858 election. A clever debater, Lincoln challenged Douglas to a series of seven debates throughout the state. In the debates, Lincoln denied being an abolitionist and said that Republicans would not interfere with slavery where it already existed, but that Republicans would not allow slavery to spread into new territories. He asked Douglas if he supported popular sovereignty or the Dred Scott decision, a question that put Douglas on the spot. In the **Freeport Doctrine,** Douglas chose to answer in a way that he thought would cause him the least damage. He said that by failing to pass **slave codes,** a territorial legislature could discourage slavery, thus in effect rendering the Dred Scott decision null and void. The debates attracted national attention, and although Lincoln lost, he had made a reputation for himself as a leader of the Republican Party.

Douglas's answer probably cost him the support of Southern Democrats and the presidency in the election of 1860.

- Another incident that increased North-South tensions was **John Brown's raid** on the federal arsenal at Harper's Ferry, Virginia. Brown and his followers were captured before they could carry out their plans to arm slaves and wage war on slave owners. Southerners were horrified at the thought of a general slave rebellion and then outraged when they found that Northern abolitionists had supplied Brown with money.

- In 1860, realizing that popular sovereignty did not guarantee that a territory would allow slavery, Southern Democrats refused to endorse Douglas for president because he ran on a platform supporting popular sovereignty. They wanted a platform that supported the Dred Scott decision and federal protection of slavery in the territories. Northern Democrats and Southern Democrats met separately; Northern delegates nominated Douglas, and Southern Democrats chose Buchanan's vice-president, **John C. Breckinridge** of Kentucky. Republicans chose Lincoln and a platform that would appeal to Western farmers and Northern workers. It pledged to continue slavery where it existed but to stop its spread into new territories. The **Constitutional Union Party** avoided the issue of slavery and its candidate, **John Bell** of Tennessee, ran on the Union, the Constitution, and enforcement of U.S. laws. Lincoln won in both popular vote and electoral vote, carrying all eighteen free states.

- South Carolina had warned that if Lincoln were elected, it would secede. In December 1860, South Carolina passed an **ordinance of secession** and a statement explaining its reasons: (1) abolitionist propaganda, (2) the Underground Railroad, (3) Northern personal liberty laws, and (4) the formation of the Republican Party. Other reasons that have been given for the Civil War are (5) states' rights versus a strong central government, (6) the struggle for political power between the North and the South, and (7) the end of slavery.

- After the November election results were known, South Carolina, Georgia, Louisiana, Mississippi, Florida, Alabama, and Texas seceded. By February 1861, the states had formed the **Confederate States of America (C.S.A.),** written a constitution, and chosen **Jefferson Davis** as president. Lame-duck President Buchanan claimed that secession was unconstitutional, but he did nothing. Lincoln became president on March 4, 1861, and in his inaugural address, he said that no state can decide on its own to leave the Union. He appealed to the Southern states to reconsider. When the

South Carolinians surrounded **Fort Sumter** in Charleston Harbor and attacked a federal ship coming to supply the fort, the Civil War had begun. Four more states, Virginia, Tennessee, Arkansas, and North Carolina, seceded and joined the Confederacy.

KEY PEOPLE

Review Strategy

See if you can relate these people to their correct context in the "Fast Facts" section.

- Anthony Burns
- Franklin Pierce
- Charles Sumner, Preston Brooks, Andrew Butler
- Harriet Tubman, "Go Down, Moses"

KEY TERMS/IDEAS

Review Strategy

See if you can relate these terms and ideas to their correct context in the "Fast Facts" Section.

- American Party, election of 1856, ex-Whigs and Know-Nothings, anti-immigrant party
  "Bleeding Kansas," burning of Lawrence, John Brown, Emigrant Aid Society, Blue Lodge
- Ostend Manifesto, Cuba, manifest destiny, Southern interest in acquiring additional slave territory

SECTION 3. THE CIVIL WAR

The **Union** had a strong government already in place to conduct the war, whereas the **Confederacy** had to build its government. The Union also had a population of 22 million. Slightly more than one third of the Confederacy's 9 million people were slaves. The North had many more advantages, especially economic, than the South, but the war was not the short, easy victory that either side expected before the fighting began.

FAST FACTS

Review Strategy

These "Fast Facts" relate to the mobilization of the Union and the Confederacy.

- Both sides faced the problems of **mobilization** and **financing** the war. The North (1) had twice as many soldiers though its army was small, (2) had a small navy, and (3) needed to invade and conquer the South to win. The Confederacy (1) had more and better officers, (2) had to use private ships for its navy, but (3) had only to fight a defensive war.
- At first, both the North and the South used volunteers who were paid a **bounty** to fight, but eventually both sides passed **draft laws.** The South allowed draftees to hire substitutes, and anyone who owned twenty or more slaves was exempted. New draft laws

in 1863 and 1864 eliminated the substitutes and some of the exemptions. The age limits were also changed from 18 to 35 to 17 to 50 as the supply of able-bodied men dwindled. The Union also allowed a draftee to hire a substitute or to pay $300 to the government. **Draft riots** broke out to protest the unfairness of the law but soon turned to racial violence.

- The Union did not accept African Americans into the army and navy until 1862, when it was becoming difficult to recruit enough white soldiers. Black soldiers found discrimination in pay, training, medical care, and the work. They were often cooks, drivers, or laborers rather than soldiers. When white soldiers refused to serve with blacks, a few states, like Massachusetts, formed all-black regiments, often led by white officers. Altogether, some 186,000 African Americans served in the army and 29,000 in the Union navy. In addition, about 200,000 of the half million slaves, called **contraband,** who escaped to the Union lines worked as laborers, cooks, and teamsters. The **Confiscation Act of 1861** provided a uniform policy regarding slaves who escaped from their owners to the Union lines; they were to be free forever.

- The Confederacy did not enlist slaves in its army, but it did force them to work on war-related construction projects, such as building fortifications and producing munitions. Slaves also worked as teamsters, cooks, and ambulance drivers for the army.

Review Strategy

These "Fast Facts" relate to how the Union and the Confederacy financed the Civil War.

- The Union (1) had 80 percent of the industry in the United States; (2) had almost all its deposits of coal, iron, copper, and gold; (3) had the better railroad system since almost all tracks ran outside the Confederacy; (4) was the center for almost all banking and finance; and (5) continued throughout the war to trade with European nations. The Confederacy was still an agrarian economy in 1860. Its ability to sell its cotton for English goods was severely hampered by the Union blockade.

- The Union financed the war by (1) raising the **tariff,** (2) levying **excise** and **income taxes,** (3) issuing paper money, and (4) selling government **bonds.** The Confederacy (1) levied a **direct tax** on slaves and land, (2) passed an excise tax, (3) adopted a tax to be paid in goods rather than cash, and (4) printed paper money. These taxes raised little money, and unlike the Union, the Confederacy found it difficult to raise money by selling bonds. Most Southern capital was tied up in land and slaves. Foreign investors were dubious about the future of the Confederacy. Although **inflation** became a problem in the North, it was far worse for the Confederacy. By the end of the war, the value of Confederate money was about 5 cents on the dollar.

Review Strategy

This "Fast Fact" relates to civil liberties in the North.

- Not all Northerners were eager to support the war. Lincoln took action against opponents, most of whom were Democrats, that violated **civil liberties,** including shutting down hostile newspapers and jailing Confederate sympathizers without benefit of **habeas corpus.** Private telegraph lines and railroads near war zones were confiscated and run by the government.

Review Strategy

These "Fast Facts" relate to the Confederate Constitution and states' rights.

- Although based on the U.S. Constitution, the **Confederate Constitution** had several provisions that addressed the issues of the prewar Southern position. Among them were the ideas that (1) the sovereignty of the individual states was paramount over the central government, (2) slave property was protected, and (3) protective tariffs and internal improvements were banned.

- The issue of states' rights came up quickly. North Carolina refused to obey the draft law, arguing that the Confederate government had no right to force the citizens of a state to serve in the military. At one point, Jefferson Davis suspended habeas corpus, but the courts denied his right to do so. South Carolina and, later, Georgia talked about seceding from the Confederacy.

Review Strategy

This "Fast Fact" relates to foreign policy.

- Achieving recognition of the **C.S.A.** as a sovereign nation was the focus of Confederate **foreign policy,** while the Union worked to deny the Confederacy this recognition. For the first two years of the war, both Great Britain and France were sympathetic to the Confederacy, hoping that if the Confederates won (1) they would be a source of cotton and other raw materials without, in turn, imposing tariffs on imported manufactured goods and (2) that the Northeastern and Mid-Atlantic commercial interests would be less of a competitive threat. In addition, Lincoln's claim at the war's beginning that he wanted to preserve the Union rather than free the slaves put off many Europeans who had abolished slavery earlier in the century. Several incidents between Great Britain and the Union almost resulted in war, but the offending side always stepped back.

Review Strategy

This "Fast Fact" relates to the role of women in the war.

- On the home front, women in both the Confederacy and the Union learned to run the family farm and manage the family business. They took the place of drafted men in factories but found their wages cut to less than what men had been paid. Women raised money for the war, rolled bandages, knitted, and sewed. Women also acted as spies, smugglers, and scouts. Some even disguised themselves as men and fought as soldiers.

Review Strategy

These "Fast Facts" relate to the conduct of the Civil War.

- The Union had three military objectives: (1) to capture the Confederacy's capital, **Richmond;** (2) to gain control of the Mississippi; and (3) to **blockade** Southern ports. These three goals would (1) weaken Southern morale, which was a time-honored war strategy; (2) split the South and close an important route for carrying reinforcements and supplies from Texas and Arkansas to the rest of the Confederacy; and (3) keep the South from trading raw cotton for much needed supplies from Europe. The South had little in the way of manufacturing before the war, and although the South had opened some factories to produce war materials, it badly needed supplies from abroad.

Study Strategy

Remember that the details of the battles are not important, but the significance of the battles is.

- The Union Army was divided into two parts: an army east of the Appalachians and one west of the mountains. After the **First Battle of Bull Run (Manassas),** no major fighting took place until 1862. The army in the East battled for Richmond in a series of brutal engagements, with huge casualties on both sides. After a particularly costly defeat for the Union at **Chancellorsville, General Robert E. Lee** in July 1863 took his troops into the North. At **Gettysburg,** they met Union forces and in the ensuing battle, Lee was forced to retreat. This defeat showed that Lee's strategy of taking the war into the Union for a speedy end would not work. It is also significant because it ended any hope of assistance from the British.

- In pursuit of the second goal, **Admiral David Farragut,** who was Hispanic, captured New Orleans, Baton Rouge, and Natchez, putting the lower part of the Mississippi under Union control by the end of 1862. From May to July 1863, **General Ulysses S. Grant** laid siege to **Vicksburg** on the Mississippi. With its surrender, the Union was in control of all the Mississippi. The victory won Grant command of all army forces in the West. When he took **Chattanooga** later in the year, Lincoln put him in command of the entire Union Army.

- Grant moved east and engaged Lee's army in a series of battles. Lee stopped at **Petersburg** near Richmond, and Grant surrounded the city. In the meantime, **General William Sherman** burned **Atlanta** and made his victorious and ruinous **"march to the sea"** from Atlanta to Savannah, then turning north to Richmond. Lee moved out of Petersburg with Grant in pursuit. Richmond fell, and Lee surrendered at **Appomattox Court House** on April 9.

- The third goal, the blockade, was very effective in the last two years of the war, cutting the number of ships entering Southern ports from around 6,000 a year to around 200. Although some **blockade runners** operated, the Union navy tightened its cordon so that by the end of the war, Southern factories were melting church bells for cannon, and Southern women were making a coffee substitute from sweet potatoes.

Review Strategy

This "Fast Fact" relates to the Emancipation Proclamation.

- Lincoln was reluctant to make emancipation a war goal for the Union because (1) he was concerned that the **border states** would join the Confederacy, (2) he knew that Northern workers feared the loss of their jobs to ex-slaves who would work for less, and (3) he believed that slave owners should be paid for the loss of their property. By 1863, however, the pressure to declare emancipation, especially from **Radical Republicans,** was growing in order (1) to punish the Confederacy, (2) to incite a general slave insurrection that would end the war quickly, and (3) to ensure that the British, who had outlawed slavery, would not support the Confederacy. In September 1862, Lincoln issued the **Emancipation Proclamation,** announcing that on January 1, 1863, all slaves in states or parts of states still in rebellion would be free. In reality, the Proclamation freed no one. Slaves in border states or in Union-occupied areas were unaffected, as were slaves in Confederate territory. Lincoln's purpose was to try to end the war by pressuring the rebellious states to make peace before January 1.

Review Strategy

This "Fast Fact" relates to the election of 1864.

- For the election of 1864, Democratic supporters of the war joined the Republicans to form the **Union Party.** They nominated Lincoln, and for vice-president, Andrew Johnson, a Democrat and the only Southern senator who had not joined the Confederacy. The Democrats chose war hero **General George McClellan.** McClellan refused to run on the Democrats' platform that called the war a failure and demanded it be stopped. Lincoln believed he would win or lose depending on how well the Union Army was doing. When **General William Sherman** captured Atlanta, many people thought the war would end soon. The Republicans had also managed to run the nation while managing the war: (1) the tariff had been raised in 1861 with some rates as high as 40 percent, (2) the banking system had been strengthened, and (3) vast amounts of **cheap Western land** had been made available—something for every section in the Union. Lincoln won reelection easily.

Key People

Review Strategy

See if you can relate these people to their correct context in the "Fast Facts" section.

- **Clara Barton, American Red Cross**
- **Dr. Elizabeth Blackwell**
- **General Ambrose Burnside, Union commander in the East, failure to take Richmond**
- **Copperheads, Northern Democrats**
- **Dorothea Dix, supervised all Union Army nurses**

- General Henry Halleck, command of Union army in the West, commander of entire army

- Hinton Helper, *The Impending Crisis of the South*

- General Joseph Hooker, Union commander in the East, retreated at Chancellorsville

- General Thomas "Stonewall" Jackson, nicknamed for his stand against the Union at the First Battle of Bull Run, Shenandoah Valley campaign

- General John Johnston, Confederate

- George McClellan, General of the Union army in the East, twice removed from command

- Emperor Maximilian, Napoleon III, French Mexican empire, violation of the Monroe Doctrine

- General George Meade, commanded Union at Gettysburg, did not follow rout of Confederates

- Ely S. Parker, Seneca, aide to General Grant, U.S. Commissioner of Indian Affairs

- John Slidell, James M. Mason, HMS *Trent*

- Clement Vallandigham, critical of Lincoln, *Ex parte Vallandigham*

- Stand Watie, Cherokee, Brigadier General, Confederacy, Cherokee Mounted Rifles

Key Terms/Ideas

Review Strategy

See if you can relate these terms and ideas to their correct context in the "Fast Facts" section.

- Battles of Shiloh, Chickahominy, Second Bull Run, Antietam Wilderness, Spotsylvania Court House, Cold Harbor

- Central Pacific, Union Pacific, transcontinental railroad, northern route, land grants

- *Ex parte Milligan*, presidential war powers

- Homestead Act of 1862, 160 acres, resident and work requirements

- *Florida, Alabama,* Confederate warships, British shipyards

- *Monitor, Merimac,* ironclads

- Morrill Land Grant Act of 1862, federal land grants, establish colleges of agriculture and mechanical arts

- National Banking Act of 1863

SECTION 4. RECONSTRUCTION

At the end of the Civil War, the South lay in ruins. One in twenty whites had been either wounded or killed. Yankee soldiers had taken, destroyed, or burned anything they could find that might have been useful to the Confederates. Two thirds of the Southern railroad system was unable to operate because of track damage. **Inflation** was as much as 300 percent, and Confederate-issued war bonds were worthless. The federal government confiscated any cotton left in warehouses, so there was nothing to export. All this affected not just white Southerners but also their former slaves. At the same time, the nation needed to determine how to readmit the former Confederate states to the Union and how to deal with their leaders.

FAST FACTS

Review Strategy

This "Fast Fact" relates to the Freedmen's Bureau.

- The **Freedmen's Bureau** was set up under the control of the War Department in March 1865 to help Southern blacks who were homeless and jobless because of the war. The bureau (1) helped them find homes and jobs, (2) negotiated labor contracts between African Americans and their employers, (3) built hospitals, (4) set up schools and provided teachers, and (5) provided legal help. Because a provision in the law setting up the bureau stated that former slaves could rent land that was abandoned or confiscated by the federal government for failure to pay taxes and after three years buy it, blacks believed that the government was going to give them **"forty acres and a mule."** In the fight with Congress over Reconstruction, Johnson ordered all land returned to its former owners.

Review Strategy

These "Fast Facts" relate to Lincoln's Reconstruction Plan.

- Before the war was over, Lincoln announced his plan for **Reconstruction.** (1) A state could be readmitted when the number of men who had taken a **loyalty oath** to the Union equaled one tenth the number of voters in the 1860 presidential election (**"ten percent plan"**). (2) Most ex-Confederates would be granted **amnesty** if they took the loyalty oath. (3) High-ranking ex-Confederate officials would have to ask the president for a **pardon** to be granted amnesty. (4) The new state constitutions had to ban slavery. (5) States had to provide free public education to blacks. Once readmitted, a state would have to (1) form a government, (2) hold a constitutional convention, and (3) write a new constitution. Under Lincoln's plan, Tennessee, Arkansas, Virginia, and Louisiana set up new governments before the end of the war. Although not in his original plan, Lincoln came to believe that the right to vote should be given to African Americans who had fought for the Union or who had some education.

- Congress refused to allow the newly elected members of Congress from these four states to take their seats. In 1864, the **Radical Republicans** had introduced their proposal for Reconstruction, the **Wade-Davis Bill.** (1) The South would be placed under military rule. (2) A majority of those who had voted in the 1860 election would have to take the loyalty oath for a state to be readmitted. (3) Only those white men who had not fought voluntarily against the Union could vote and attend their state's constitutional convention. (4) The new constitutions had to ban slavery. (5) Former Confederate officials would not be allowed to vote. Lincoln used a **pocket veto** on the bill. He based his veto on the argument that Reconstruction was part of the war effort and as commander-in-chief, according to the Constitution, it was the president's duty to deal with it.

- The Radical Republicans and others, like Northern business interests, disagreed with Lincoln for a variety of reasons: (1) The conditions of readmission were not harsh enough. (2) Reconstruction was Congress's job, not the president's. (3) The Southern white electorate would become Democrats. (4) Former Confederate members of Congress might vote against Republican programs. (5) The president's program did not address the rights of newly freed slaves.

Review Strategy

These "Fast Facts" relate to Johnson's Reconstruction Plan.

- After Lincoln's assassination, **Vice-President Andrew Johnson,** who had been the only Southern senator not to leave Congress after secession, became president. He was a Jacksonian Democrat who favored states' rights and the interests of the small farmer, which he had been. He believed that it would be the small Southern farmer who would remake the South into a democratic region loyal to the Union. While Congress was in recess, he went ahead with Reconstruction, following Lincoln's plan, for the most part, with a few changes: (1) Amnesty was offered to all former Confederates, except the highest officials and those whose property was worth more than $20,000. (2) These men were prohibited from voting or holding state or federal office, unless they asked the president for a pardon. (3) The ordinances of secession had to be revoked. (4) Confederate war debts could not be collected. (5) The states had to ratify the **Thirteenth Amendment.**

- In January 1865, Congress had passed the Thirteenth Amendment outlawing slavery, and by December, the necessary twenty-seven states had ratified it.

- While Congress was in recess, all the former Confederate states except Texas had followed the steps of Johnson's Reconstruction plan and were ready to seat their members in Congress when

Congress reconvened in December 1865. However, none of the states had provided for voting rights for former slaves. The Radical Republicans refused to accept the supposedly reconstructed states. The Radicals argued that only Congress had the power to make laws and that many of the new members had been officials of the Confederacy, including fifty-eight members of the Confederate Congress and **Alexander H. Stephens,** the Confederacy's vice-president. Congress appointed a committee to investigate whether the Southern states should be reinstated. The committee reported that **Presidential Reconstruction** was not working, and that Congress should oversee the process.

Review Strategy

These "Fast Facts" relate to the civil rights of newly freed slaves.

- One of the actions of the South that had enraged Radical Republicans and others in the North was the passage of **black codes** by Southern legislatures in 1865 and 1866. These laws in reaction to the Freedmen's Bureau and the Thirteenth Amendment varied from state to state but in general:

  (1) allowed former slaves to

    - marry fellow blacks

    - own personal property

    - sue and be sued

  (2) forbade former slaves to

    - serve on juries

    - vote

    - carry weapons without a license

    - hold public office

    - own land

    - travel without a permit

    - be out after curfew

    - assemble in groups without a white person in attendance

  (3) required a former slave to buy a license to work in a craft
  (4) authorized the arrest and fining of unemployed blacks
  (5) allowed an employer to pay the fine of an unemployed black in exchange for the person's labor.

The South claimed it needed these powers to enforce public safety. Northerners saw them as an attempt to reinstate slavery by ensuring a supply of cheap, unskilled labor that working plantations still required.

In response, Congress passed the **Civil Rights Act of 1866** and the Fourteenth Amendment. The Civil Rights Act granted citizenship to all people born in the United States and gave African Americans the rights to (1) testify in court, (2) own land, (3) make contracts, and (4) exercise all the rights of white Americans. Johnson vetoed the bill, arguing that it violated the rights of the states. Moderate Republicans joined Radical Republicans and overrode the president's veto.

Review Strategy

See Chapter 6 for more on the Constitution.

- Johnson was not alone in considering the Civil Rights Act unconstitutional. To avoid the possibility of having it struck down by the Supreme Court, Congress passed the **Fourteenth Amendment.** It provided that (1) all persons born in the United States or naturalized were citizens of the United States and of the state in which they lived, (2) states were forbidden to deny citizens their rights without **due process of law,** (3) all citizens were to enjoy **equal protection under the law,** (4) a state that denied voting rights to any adult male would have its representation in Congress reduced in proportion to the number of citizens who had been denied the vote, (5) former Confederate officials could not hold federal or state office unless pardoned by a two-thirds vote of Congress, (6) Confederate debts would not be paid, and (7) former slave owners could not sue for payment for loss of their slaves.

- Congress added the **Fifteenth Amendment** in 1869. This amendment replaced part of the Fourteenth Amendment by removing from the states the power to deny the right to vote based "on race, color, or previous condition of servitude."

Review Strategy

These "Fast Facts" relate to Radical Reconstruction.

- Johnson made the Fourteenth Amendment the major issue of the Congressional elections of 1866. He urged the Southern states not to ratify it, and except for Tennessee, none did. Voters agreed with the Republicans and sent more than a two-thirds majority of Republicans to both houses, enough to overturn presidential vetoes. The Radical Republicans now established **military Reconstruction** using a series of **Reconstruction Acts.** (1) Except for Tennessee, which had ratified the Fourteenth Amendment, the other ten state governments were declared illegal. (2) The ten states were divided into five military districts. (3) The army could use force in these districts, if necessary, to protect civil rights and maintain the peace. (4) Each state was to call a convention to write a new constitution. (5) The members of the constitutional convention were to be elected by all adult males—white and African American. (6) Former Confederate officials could not participate in the conventions (a provision similar to the Fourteenth Amendment). (7) The new constitutions were to guarantee **suffrage** to

African-American males. (8) The former Confederate states had to ratify the Fourteenth Amendment that accorded the rights of citizens to African Americans.

- Congressional Reconstruction called for the military governor of each district to oversee the organization of state governments. (1) The governor was to see that former slaves were able to vote for members of the new constitutional conventions and that ex-Confederate officials were not. (2) The new constitutions were to guarantee the right to vote to African Americans. (3) Voters in each state had to approve their new constitution. (4) Congress would then vote on the constitution. (5) The state legislature would ratify the Fourteenth Amendment. Once these conditions were met, the state could apply for readmission to the Union. By 1868, six of the states had been readmitted, and by 1870, Texas, Georgia, Mississippi, and Virginia had been reinstated. These last four states had to ratify the Fifteenth Amendment also.

Review Strategy

This "Fast Fact" relates to the impeachment of Johnson.

- During this battle for power, Congress passed the **Tenure of Office Act** in 1867 that required the president to get Congressional approval before removing any federal official, including Cabinet members who had been approved by the Senate. The president vetoed the bill, but Congress overrode his veto. Johnson then fired **Edward Stanton,** Secretary of War, who had opposed Johnson's Reconstruction plan and supported the Radical Republicans. The House voted to **impeach** Johnson for violating the Tenure of Office Act. The Senate trial lasted six weeks, and in three separate votes, the Senate was always one vote short of conviction. Johnson was acquitted, but his political career was effectively over.

Review Strategy

These "Fast Facts" relate to Southern government under Reconstruction.

- While former Confederate officials were banned from holding office, many Southern men who would have been political leaders had been killed during the war. Other Southerners refused to cooperate with the federal government and resented its support for the rights of blacks. Three groups were primarily involved in reconstructing state governments in the South: (1) Northerners who wanted to help the newly freed slaves or who were interested in what they could gain for themselves, (2) Southern whites who were originally **Unionists** or were interested in what they could gain for themselves by working in the new governments, and (3) free-born and newly freed African Americans. Some African Americans were well educated, but most were poor, uneducated, and lacking in political experience. With the exception of South Carolina, where blacks controlled the lower house until 1874, no other state legislature—upper or lower house—was controlled by blacks. No African American was ever elected a governor. Most important offices were held by Northerners or by Southern whites.

- The record of the Reconstruction governments is mixed. While there was certainly corruption, considered in the context of **Boss Tweed** in New York, the **Whiskey Ring** in St. Louis, and scandal in the federal government, it was not unusual for the period. Tax rates rose dramatically, but 80 percent of state monies was put to use rebuilding transportation networks. In addition, state governments (1) in an area that had had little public education built schools to educate not only white children but also black children, (2) allowed black and poor white men to vote and hold office for the first time, (3) abolished imprisonment for debt, and (4) built hospitals and orphanages. However, Reconstruction did not help freed slaves to improve their economic status. In time, even the political rights that African Americans had gained were lost.

Review Strategy

These "Fast Facts" relate to the end of Reconstruction.

- By the early 1870s, Northerners were tiring of Reconstruction. (1) The tales of corruption and **graft** assiduously spread by Southern newspapers were turning some Northerners against it. (2) **Moderate Republicans** who had gained ground in Congress did not agree with the Radicals' harsh approach. (3) Radicals lost influence with the deaths of **Charles Sumner** and **Thaddeus Stevens,** two major supporters, and the departure from office of Andrew Johnson, who had angered many politicians. (4) The **Panic of 1873** deflected the attention of some Northerners from concern for the rights of Southern blacks, who had now been free for eight years, to financial concerns. (5) Northern business interests wanted to regularize business with the South.

- The end of Reconstruction began with passage of the **Amnesty Act** in 1872, which returned the right to vote and hold office to most ex-Confederates. Only Louisiana, Florida, and South Carolina remained under Reconstruction governments by 1876.

- For the presidential election of 1876, the Republicans had nominated **Rutherford B. Hayes** and campaigned on **"the bloody flag."** Democrats nominated **Samuel B. Tilden** and ran on a platform to end corruption in the federal government. Tilden had apparently won, but the Republican leaders in Florida, Louisiana, and South Carolina challenged a number of votes in their states, and Hayes was ultimately declared the winner in those states. A committee of eight Republicans and seven Democrats was appointed to investigate. The committee compromised (**Compromise of 1877).** In exchange for an end to Reconstruction, a Southern appointee to the Cabinet, and money to build the Texas and Pacific Railroad, Hayes was declared the winner.

KEY PEOPLE

Review Strategy

See if you can relate these people to their correct context in the "Fast Facts" section.

- Blanche K. Bruce, African American, senator, Mississippi
- Ulysses S. Grant, President, 1868–1876, corruption in government
- Horace Greeley, Liberal Republicans
- P. B. S. Pinchback, African American, lieutenant governor, Louisiana
- Hiram Revels, African American, senator, Mississippi

KEY TERMS/IDEAS

Review Strategy

See if you can relate these terms and ideas to their correct context in the "Fast Facts" section.

- Conquered provinces, Stevens' theory, seceded states were not even territories
- Force Acts, federal laws, combat anti-black groups in the South
- Ku Klux Klan, Knights of the White Camellia, terrorist groups opposed to Reconstruction
- scalawags, carpetbaggers, myths
- rebellion of individuals, Lincoln's theory; since individuals had rebelled, the president could use his pardon power to reinstate Southern states
- Second Freedmen's Bureau Act, Johnson's veto, civil authority
- state suicide theory, Sumner's view, in secession Southern states became similar to any unorganized territory and, therefore, Congress had the power to establish terms for readmission

Chapter 9

BECOMING AN URBAN AND INDUSTRIAL WORLD POWER

Study Strategy

Check the the College Board Web site (www.collegeboard-.org/ap) for the time period for your DBQ.

The study of history of the latter portion of the nineteenth century and the turn of the century is usually divided into the building of the New South, the settling of the Plains, the influx of immigrants, the rise of cities, and the emergence of the United States as an industrial nation. As the nation became used to its new wealth, it turned its political interests outward and began to flex its muscles in the arena of world affairs. Chapter 9 describes the shift of the United States from an agrarian to an industrial nation with imperial interests.

Remember that the AP United States History Test asks questions about "political institutions and behavior and public policy, social and economic change, diplomacy and international relations, and cultural and intellectual developments." As you read and review for the test, look for trends and the significance of events and people, analyze and determine cause-and-effect relationships, and compare and contrast motives and outcomes. Knowing the how and why is especially important in crafting answers for the DBQ and essay questions.

SECTION 1. THE NEW SOUTH

The period from 1865 to 1866 is called "Confederate" Reconstruction by some because presidential plans for Reconstruction called for ex-Confederates to remake their governments themselves. At the same time, Southern whites began their campaign of terror against African Americans and their white supporters. The **Freedmen's Bureau** was singled out for attack. The **Ku Klux Klan** and other white supremacist groups like the **White Camellia** sprang up. When Radical Reconstruction took over and ousted former Confederates from office—replacing them with Northerners, Southern "scalawags," and African Americans—the Klan and similar groups increased their activities.

FAST FACTS

Review Strategy

These "Fast Facts" relate to government in the New South.

- It was against this background of terror and racism that the **Fifteenth Amendment** was drafted and ratified and the **Enforcement Acts of 1870** and **1871** were passed. These two Acts made it a federal crime to interfere with any man's right to vote. However, the ability of the Klan to terrorize African Americans and their supporters made the laws ineffective.

- By the end of Reconstruction in 1877, **Redeemers** had taken over the state governments in all the former Confederate states. "Redeemer" was the name Southern whites gave to those politicians who restored white supremacy in the South. Most Redeemers were businessmen, not old-time Southern plantation owners, and making money was their goal. They reduced taxes such as corporate income taxes on the private sector and cut spending on the public sector, such as funding universal public education.

Review Strategy

These "Fast Facts" relate to African Americans in the New South.

- While Southern whites rejoiced at the end of the federal occupation of the South, Southern African Americans faced a bleak future—economically, politically, and societally. Although the end of slavery meant that African Americans were no longer bound to a plantation, it also meant that they were on their own to find employment, food, shelter, and clothing. They had no education and little understanding of contracts and commercial transactions, so white farmers and shopkeepers were able to take advantage of them. Immediately after the war, the Freedmen's Bureau helped blacks, but it was closed down in 1872. By the 1880s, the **sharecropping system** had replaced slavery as the dominant socioeconomic institution in the South.

- After the war, because Southern planters had little cash, they could not pay workers. Yet field hands, both blacks and poor whites, needed to work. The Freedmen's Bureau worked out a system in which the landowner would give the sharecropper (and his family) land, tools, a mule, seed, and a shack to live in. The sharecropper would work the land and give one third to half of the harvest to the landowner. This was known as the **crop lien system.** In time the sharecropper would be able to save enough money to buy land. The system turned out to be very different in practice.

- The sharecropper's plot was usually too small to grow much surplus. Repeated use of the land without any knowledge of good farming practices resulted in poor yields and exhausted soil. As a result, there was little to return to the landowner as rent for the use of the land, seed, tools, mule, and house. In addition, the sharecropper had to repay a shopkeeper, who was often the landowner, for food, clothing, and other supplies that the share-cropper and his family had bought on credit in expectation of a good harvest. Often the sharecropper found he had nothing left once he had repaid his debts. The cycle began all over again as he borrowed to keep his family fed over the winter.

- The African Americans' options were few. Attempting to get legal redress in a Southern white community was futile. Even if African Americans could save enough money to buy land, most white landowners would not sell land to them. Bargaining for better terms for sharecropping was impossible because white landowners in many areas joined together to determine the terms they would offer to sharecroppers. Because white workers would not work alongside African Americans, the latter were barred from employment in the new mills and factories of the industrialized South. The threat of hiring blacks was often enough to end any strike threat by white workers.

- Politically, African Americans continued to vote and hold public office during Radical Reconstruction. Beginning in 1890 in Mississippi, the Southern states began to write new constitutions and new laws that effectively kept African Americans from voting. The new laws did not violate the Fifteenth Amendment but used other means to bar blacks from the voting booth: **poll taxes, literacy tests, grandfather clauses, property requirements,** and **the direct primary.** The grandfather clause was declared unconstitutional in 1915.

- The **Civil Rights Act of 1875** had established that all persons within the United States regardless of "race and color . . . [and] previous condition of servitude" were eligible to the "full and equal enjoyment" of public accommodations. In 1883, the Supreme Court declared the Act unconstitutional on the basis that the Fourteenth Amendment applied only to states.

Review Strategy

Check Chapter 6 for more information on Plessy v. Ferguson.

- Any hope for social equality ended with **Jim Crow.** The first Jim Crow law, requiring separate railway cars for African Americans and whites, had been passed in 1881 in Tennessee. After the Supreme Court ruling on the Civil Rights Act of 1875, other Southern legislatures followed with similar laws until railroad stations, streetcars, schools, parks, playgrounds, theaters, and other public facilities across the South were segregated. In 1896, the Supreme Court institutionalized segregation with its ruling in ***Plessy* v. *Ferguson.***

- African Americans responded by developing their own communities and their own businesses. Mutual aid societies, insurance companies, funeral parlors, and banks sprang up. Black churches became a focal point of life and would, along with the NAACP, become the base for civil rights activities in the next century.

- White supremacist groups continued to spread terror among African Americans. **Lynching** was a favored tactic. **Ida Wells Barnett,** a former teacher turned journalist, campaigned to end "lynch law." **Frederick Douglass** emerged to lead protests against the treatment of African Americans in the South.

Review Strategy

These "Fast Facts" relate to the economy of the New South.

- While African Americans were struggling to survive, the general economy of the **"New South"** was slowly improving until, by 1890, cotton production and the amount of railroad tracks were twice what they had been in 1860. The latter aided the South in developing its industrial base. One of the factors that had caused the end of Radical Reconstruction had been the desire of business interests to get back to business. Northern financiers and Southern businessmen joined together to provide capital to rebuild the South's infrastructure and to develop industry.

- Southern industrial production quadrupled between 1860 and 1900. Birmingham, Alabama, and Chattanooga, Tennessee, became centers of the Southern iron and steel industry. Tobacco processing developed in North Carolina and Virginia. Cotton textile mills appeared in South Carolina and Georgia, and sugar refineries in Louisiana. All an area needed for industrial development was a mix of (1) water power, (2) a supply of cheap labor, (3) raw agricultural products or (4) natural resources such as coal and iron deposits, and (5) access to transportation. Because of the distance to Northern markets and the amount of competition for Southern goods, wages were usually low, and unions made little progress because of the threat to hire African-American workers.

KEY PEOPLE/TERMS

Review Strategy

See if you can relate these people and terms to their correct context in the "Fast Facts" section.

- **Henry Grady, term "New South"**
- **Exodusters, Henry Adams, Benjamin "Pap" Singleton**
- **convict-lease system**
- **disenfranchisement**

SECTION 2. THE LAST FRONTIER

While the South was rebuilding itself, settlers were finding that the **Great American Desert** was in reality a vast fertile plain. The region around the Mississippi had been settled and people were looking for new land. As miners, ranchers, sheepherders, and farmers moved into the Great Plains and the mountains beyond, they came up against the claims of the Native Americans who had lived there for centuries.

FAST FACTS

Review Strategy

These "Fast Facts" relate to Native Americans.

Review Strategy

See "Trail of Tears" on p. 171.

- While engaged in the Civil War, Lincoln and his Republican Congress had also passed legislation that was important to the development of the Great Plains. Settlers needed two things to move west: cheap land and access to cheap land. The **Homestead Act of 1862** provided the cheap land. The Act granted plots of 100 acres to individuals—citizens or immigrants—who would live on and work the land for five years.

- **The Pacific Railway Acts of 1862** and **1864** subsidized the **Central Pacific** and the **Union Pacific** to build the first **transcontinental railroad.** The companies were given vast tracts of land along their routes to divide and sell to pay for laying the track. Work did not begin until 1865, and the two branches of the railroad met at Promontory Point, Utah, in 1869. Additional railroads were built including the **Southern Pacific** along a right-of-way through the land bought from Mexico in the **Gadsden Purchase.**

- In the early days of the Republic, the federal government had forced Native Americans in the Upper Midwest to sign treaties that ceded large tracts of land to the United States. The Native Americans were then confined to small reserves. Beginning in the 1830s with the establishment of the **Indian Territory** in what is today Oklahoma, Native Americans from the Southeast were moved onto **reservations** in the Indian Territory.

- Around 1850, the **Bureau of Indian Affairs (BIA)** adopted a policy known as **concentration.** Native Americans were to be confined to certain areas of the West away from the settlers travelling to California and Oregon. The Native Americans would be free to continue their own ways of life.

- As more settlers came, the BIA decided to resettle on **reservations** all Native Americans on the Plains and in the Southwest. Reservations greatly restricted the traditional way of life of Native Americans. Some of the reservation lands were suited to farming, but much of it was poor. In addition, most of the Native American groups were **hunters and gatherers,** not farmers. By the late 1880s, the buffalo were gone from the Plains. As a result, Native Americans had to rely on the BIA for food, clothing, and shelter. Bureau agents were often corrupt. Sometimes they stole the food and supplies meant for the Native Americans and resold them, and sometimes the agents took bribes from suppliers to accept shoddy goods.

- Among the Native American leaders who resisted resettlement were **Chief Joseph** of the **Nez Perce; Mangas Coloradas, Cochise,** and **Geronimo** of the **Chiricahua Apache; Black Kettle** of the **Cheyenne; Red Cloud** and **Crazy Horse** of the **Oglala Sioux;** and **Sitting Bull** of the **Hunkpapa Sioux.** The last major battle between Native Americans and the U.S. Army was the massacre at **Wounded Knee,** South Dakota, in which the army in a surprise attack charged a camp of men, women, and children at dawn, killing several hundred Native Americans.

- Two voices raised in protest were **Sarah Winnemucca,** a Paiute, who wrote and lectured about the government's mistreatment of her people, and **Helen Hunt Jackson,** who wrote *A Century of Dishonor,* which outlined the government's mistreatment of Native Americans and the corruption in the BIA. The book also sought to correct the many stereotypes that whites had about Native Americans.

- In an effort to quiet the protests that arose with the publication of Jackson's book, the federal government passed the **Dawes Act.** It (1) broke up reservations, (2) gave 160 acres of land to the head of each household and lesser amounts to bachelors and women, (3) restricted the sale of the land or use of it for collateral for twenty-five years in an effort to protect Native Americans from unscrupulous land speculators, (4) granted citizenship after twenty-five years to those who received land, and (5) sold to whites any land not given to Native Americans, the proceeds of which were to be used to educate Native American children. As an attempt to assimilate Native Americans into white culture, the Act failed for several reasons: (1) many Native Americans were not farmers; (2) the land was often poor; (3) many families sold their land, and when the proceeds were gone, they had nothing to live on; and (4) many were cheated out of their land. In time Native Americans lost their own culture, traditions, much of their lands, and their means of financial support without being accepted into the dominant white culture. Native Americans remained wards of the government and were increasingly dependent on it for the means of survival.

Review Strategy

These "Fast Facts" deal with the settling of the Plains.

- The **open-range** cattle industry began on the Texas plains in the 1840s and 1850s with cattle that had been driven up from Mexico. The land the cattle ranged over was unfenced government property that the cattleranchers neither rented nor owned. By the 1870s, cattle ranching had spread to the Northern Plains. The early cattle drives had either New Orleans or the gold fields of California as their destination. After the Civil War, the cattle drives moved across several trails to railheads in Kansas and Nebraska, where the cattle were sold and shipped to meat-packing plants in Chicago. With the building of rail lines south into Texas in the 1870s, the long cattle drives were over.

- By 1890 open-range cattle ranching itself was over, coincidentally the year the Census Bureau declared the **frontier** closed. As early as the 1860s, farmers, and, in the 1880s, sheepherders were moving onto the Plains, buying up land, building **barbed-wire** fences, and damming rivers. When a decline in the price of beef in the 1880s combined with two winters of blizzards and severe cold and a summer of drought between 1885 and 1887, many ranchers were forced into bankruptcy. To combat these problems, ranchers (1) formed cooperative associations, (2) bought or rented government land to end the range wars that had erupted between the ranchers and the farmers and sheepherders, (3) introduced sturdier **Hereford** cattle, (4) kept herds small to keep prices up, and (5) grew hay to feed cattle in severe weather.

- Farmers began moving onto the Plains after the Civil War. Some were African Americans escaping the black codes and hoping to own their own land. Others were newly arrived immigrants. Farming on the Plains involved a number of problems: (1) less than 20 inches of rain a year, (2) low yield per acre, (3) free-roaming cattle, and (4) a lack of trees for fencing. The problems were solved by (1) developing "dry" farming techniques; (2) the invention of various farming implements, such as steel plows and threshing machines combined with harvesters, that made possible the cultivation of vast acres of land; and (3) the invention of barbed-wire for fencing.

Review Strategy

Silver miners had a great influence on national politics during the late 1800s. See Section 6, p. 224.

- Beginning in the 1850s, miners trickled and then flooded into the Rockies and the Southwest looking for silver and gold. In 1891, Cripple Creek, Colorado, marked the last big gold and silver strike. In the approximately thirty-five years of the mining bonanza, many towns and cities had grown from tent cities. Although few miners struck it rich, many people stayed to build new lives and make their living from selling goods and providing services to their fellow townspeople and the outlying farmers and ranchers. A number of large cities developed from mining camps, such as Virginia City, Denver, and Helena, Montana.

- By the end of the century, mining had shifted from the solitary gold panner to big business. In addition to gold and silver for currency, the nation needed metals like copper, tin, and lead for industry.

KEY PEOPLE

Review Strategy

See if you can relate these people to their correct context in the "Fast Facts" section.

- **Buffalo Soldiers**
- **Joseph Glidden**
- **James J. Hill, Great Northern, "empire builder"**
- **Leland Stanford, Collis Huntington**
- **Frederick Jackson Turner, U.S. frontier, individualism, democracy,** *The Frontier in American History*

KEY TERMS/IDEAS

Review Strategy

See if you can relate these terms and ideas to their correct context in the "Fast Facts" section.

- **Ghost Dance, Sioux, celebration of traditional way of life**
- **Indian Appropriation Act, end of sovereignty of Native American nations, no new treaties**
- **Indian Territory, Dawes Commission, Oklahoma Land Rush**
- **Morrill Land Grant Act**
- **Treaty of Fort Laramie, 1868, Great Sioux Reservation**

SECTION 3. INDUSTRY, LABOR, AND BIG BUSINESS

While the South was rebuilding and the West was being settled, the Midwest and Northeast were growing quickly as a result of new inventions and new industries. Industrial growth was fueled by a wave of immigrants from Southern and Eastern Europe and by rural Americans looking for opportunity. During the last part of the nineteenth century, the United States changed from a rural, agrarian society to an industrial, urban one.

FAST FACTS

Review Strategy

These "Fast Facts" relate to the nation's industrial development.

- For the **Industrial Revolution** to take hold and develop in the United States, certain requirements had to be met. The nation needed (1) a national transportation system; (2) large deposits of iron and coal and later, oil; (3) new sources of power such as **electricity, steam turbines,** and **diesel engines;** (4) surplus agricultural production for textile factories, meat-packing plants, and canneries; (5) a supply of labor; (6) capital for investment; and (7) a stable banking system.

- The late 1800s saw a consolidation in the **railroad industry.** Until then, railroads were small independent lines meant to link relatively small areas. For example, when the **Pennsylvania Railroad** began to absorb competitors, it bought up several hundred companies. Because of the number of companies, there was no uniformity in rail widths. With the consolidation of lines, a standard for rails was set. (1) The merging of rail lines, (2) the building of several transcontinental lines, (3) the standardization of rails, and (4) the establishment of three standard time zones helped to bring about a **national rail system.** The growth of railroads made it possible to move raw materials to factories and finished goods to markets easily—but not cheaply.

- The early factories had been powered by water wheels. The **industrial revolution** required vast amounts of energy and the flexibility to build factories close to raw materials or transportation hubs. **Coal** to power the new **steam turbines** was one answer. The United States had the largest deposits of anthracite coal in the world and large fields of bituminous coal as well. Coal mining became big business in the second half of the nineteenth century, especially to feed the furnaces of the growing steel industry.

Review Strategy

These "Fast Facts" deal with philosophies of the late 1800s.

- **Social Darwinism** applied to human society the theories of natural selection and evolution that **Charles Darwin** developed while observing nature. According to Darwin, a constant competition for survival exists in the natural world in which the weak vie for a place with the strong who always win, thus ensuring the continuity of the species. Social Darwinists transferred this competition to the human species and pointed to successful businessmen as proof. The poor were poor because they were unfit and, therefore, had to suffer the consequences. The most notable Social Darwinists were English philosopher and social theorist **Herbert Spencer** and Yale philosopher **William Graham Sumner.**

- Social Darwinism greatly influenced social thinking in the late 1800s. Its supposed reliance on science and scientific fact provided proof for the rightness of the principle of **laissez-faire government.** Social Darwinism suggested that poverty and failure were the result of laziness, inefficiency, and lack of ability. (There was a certain similarity to Puritanism in the belief that hard work and success were a sign of being one of the chosen.) According to this rationale, government should not interfere in the workings of society by providing assistance to the poor or to faltering businesses. Competition—even cutthroat competition—should be applauded because it showed that the fittest were winning and ensuring the survival of the nation. With this philosophy as a backdrop, neither the federal government nor state governments attempted to check the ruthless competition and exploitation of the industrial era.

- **Andrew Carnegie** was a Social Darwinist who allowed his managers to cut wages and demand 70-hour workweeks. But he also espoused what is known as the **"Gospel of Wealth."** He believed that those who made great sums of money had a duty to use part of that money to help those who would help themselves to better their lives. True to his word, he established the Carnegie Foundations that today continue to provide philanthropy to a wide variety of organizations such as public libraries and research institutions.

- One dissenting voice was the **Social Gospel** movement that developed among Protestant churches around the turn of the century. Proponents believed that the desire to achieve heaven did not rule out improving life on earth. Christians had a sacred duty to work toward the eradication of social and economic abuses in society. Social Gospelers advocated an end to child labor, a shorter workday, and a six-day workweek.

Review Strategy

These "Fast Facts" and the chart relate to labor in the late 1800s.

- The **Knights of Labor** was founded as an **industrial union** in 1869 to organize all skilled and unskilled workers in an industry. African Americans were welcome and made up about 10 percent of the membership. Women and immigrants were also members. Under **Terence V. Powderly,** the Knights worked for an 8-hour workday and health and safety regulations, including limits on the kinds of jobs that children could perform. Powderly believed in the power of negotiation rather than the strike. The **Haymarket Riots** severely damaged the Knights, and they rapidly lost members. By 1900 the union had disappeared.

- The **American Federation of Labor (AFL)** was organized the year of the Haymarket Riots and was led by **Samuel Gompers** for thirty-seven years. It was an affiliation of **craft unions** for skilled workers, thus leaving out women, immigrants, and African Americans, most of whom were unskilled. Each craft union within the AFL bargained for its own workers and managed its own affairs. The central organization lobbied for an 8-hour workday and a six-day workweek, higher wages, better working conditions, protection for workers on dangerous jobs, and compensation for workers and their families for injuries or death on the job.

- There were a number of strikes in the late 1800s, but three were especially damaging to labor. The strike was not a particularly effective bargaining tool until strikers began using the **sit-down strike** in the 1930s.

Peterson's AP Success: U.S. History

LABOR UNREST	CAUSES	RESULTS
Haymarket Riots, Chicago, 1886	Begins as a general strike in support of the 8-hour day for all trade unions in the city; after three days of peaceful demonstrations, crowd at an outdoor meeting ordered to disperse; bomb thrown, killing seven police officers and four workers	Eight anarchists tried and convicted; four hanged Effectively kills the Knights of Labor; nation horrified by violence and fearful of labor
Homestead Strike, Carnegie Steel Company, Homestead, Pennsylvania, 1892	Strike of Amalgamated Association of Iron, Steel, and Tin Workers to protest wage cut and 70-hour workweek demanded by management	Pinkerton guards called in to break up strike; ten die; national guard called in by order of President Harrison; strike broken Effectively kills unionism in steel industry until 1930s Tarnishes reputation of Carnegie and Harrison
Pullman Strike, Pullman Palace Car Company, Pullman, Illinois, 1894	Strike by Pullman workers and American Railway Union to protest wage cut and dismissal of union workers who had protested wage cut	Stops railway traffic in and out of Chicago for two months; twenty-seven states affected; twenty-two workers killed Company owners granted **injunction;** workers in violation of **Sherman Antitrust Act** Federal troops ordered in by President Cleveland; strike broken; adds to public's fear of labor

- All of these strikes, plus others like the **Baltimore and Ohio Railroad Workers strike** in 1877, hurt organized labor. A major weapon used by company owners was the **injunction.** According to the courts at this time, union members in determining to strike entered into "a conspiracy in restraint of trade." This violated the Sherman Antitrust Act of 1890. That the Act had been written to regulate big business rather than unions was ignored. In general, the courts and governments favored business over labor.

- Despite the negative impact of strikes and hostile court rulings, labor made a number of gains in the years between 1877 and 1917. Government employees won the 8-hour workday in 1892, and the 8-hour workday was extended to railroad workers in 1916. The Erdman Act, passed in 1898, provided for arbitration of labor disputes involving interstate carriers. Ten years later the Employers' Liability Act made railroads responsible for employees' injuries while on the job. States, often pressured by progressives, also passed laws protecting workers.

KEY PEOPLE/TERMS

Review Strategy

See if you can relate these people and terms to their correct context in the "Fast Facts" section.

- Horatio Alger, Jr., *Ragged Dick,* "poor boy works hard and makes good"

- Andrew Carnegie, Carnegie Steel Company, Henry Frick

- J. Pierpoint Morgan, J.P. Morgan & Co.; Northern Securities Company

- John D. Rockefeller, Standard Oil

- Cornelius Vanderbilt, New York Central; "Commodore"

- Bessemer process; open-hearth process; skyscrapers

SECTION 4. URBAN SOCIETY

As the introduction to Section 3 noted, the late 1800s saw the nation shift from an agrarian and rural society to an urban and industrial one. Because the Northeast was the oldest region of the nation, it had the most cities and the most industry. The fastest growing cities were in the Midwest where rail lines fed the burgeoning factories with both raw materials and workers. The railroads also aided in the building of western cities. Southern cities grew more slowly because industrial development played less of a role in the South.

FAST FACTS

Review Strategy

These "Fast Facts relate to how cities developed.

- A variety of reasons sent people to the cities: (1) farm workers lost their jobs to the new farm equipment, (2) small farmers could not afford to buy the new equipment and without it could not compete with large **commercial farms,** (3) farmers lost their land during the **Panic of 1873,** (4) African Americans were escaping from Jim Crow, and (5) immigrants were looking to make a better life for themselves. Many of the immigrants had been farmers in their native countries and were tired of trying to scrape by on too little land with too few resources. The excitement, bright lights, and educational and cultural opportunities as well as the freedom that cities seemed to offer also lured some restless rural people to the big city. The isolation and loneliness of rural life pushed others.

- The quality of urban life depended on whether a person was wealthy, middle class, or poor; and white and native-born, African American, or an immigrant. Being poor or an immigrant consigned a person to life in a **tenement** in the **slums,** while the middle class and the wealthy moved farther and farther from a city's downtown as **cable cars** and **electric streetcars** made it possible to commute from the outskirts of a city.

- With the growth of the cities came numerous problems and some solutions. In the place of horse-drawn streetcars and cabs came elevated trains, cable cars, and subways to carry workers along the crowded streets. Because business transactions demanded fast communications, telephone and telegraph systems developed locally and then nationwide. To light crowded streets and to take advantage of as much working time as possible, some form of illumination was needed. The dynamo, electricity, the arc light, and Edison's light bulb together solved the problems. Less easily solved were the problems of safe water, disposal of sewage, and adequate housing.

Review Strategy

These "Fast Facts" relate to immigration.

- Most immigrants who came to the United States from the first days of the republic to 1890 were from Northern and Western Europe, the largest number from Germany. In the ten years between 1890 and 1900, however, 70 percent of all immigrants came from **Eastern** and **Southern Europe:** Italians, Russians, Austro-Hungarians, Poles, Bulgarians, Serbs, Romanians, Greeks, and Turks.

- Economic reasons caused many of these people to leave their homelands. Large landholdings across much of the regions had been subdivided into tenant farms that were too small for farmers to support their families. Austria-Hungary suffered an economic depression in 1873. Italy saw its markets for fruit and wine decline sharply in this period. Political reasons also figured in the **push factors** that sent people to the United States. Poland had been carved up, so that it ceased to exist. Polish Catholics and Russian Jews emigrated because of religious persecution in their native lands. Although some immigrants moved to the Plains to farm and others found jobs as miners or on construction crews, most became city dwellers and went to work in factories and **sweatshops.**

These "Fast Facts" relate to politics.

See Section 6 for political reforms.

See Section 6 for social reforms.

KEY PEOPLE/TERMS

See if you can relate these terms to the correct context in the "Fast Facts" section.

- One of the first people that a new immigrant family would probably meet was the local **ward boss.** He would help a family find housing and work and see that they were taken care of if they got sick. The ward leader would help them navigate the American legal system, including filing for citizenship. In exchange, the male members of the family were expected to vote the way the ward leader told them to.

- The ward boss was at the bottom of the city and/or state **political machine.** The period from the late 1860s to the turn of the century was marked by political corruption at the local, state, and federal government levels and in both the Republican and Democratic parties. The **party boss** for a city or state (1) controlled his party, (2) decided who would run for office, (3) influenced the decisions and actions of officials once elected, and (4) doled out **patronage** jobs. At the city level, Democrat **William "Boss" Tweed** in New York was one of the most corrupt party bosses. As Superintendent of Public Works, he took millions of dollars in bribes in exchange for awarding city contracts.

- Social reformers opened **settlement houses** to help immigrants make the transition to their new lives more easily. **Lillian Wald,** through New York's **Henry Street Settlement House,** and **Jane Addams,** with Chicago's **Hull House,** provided (1) classes to teach immigrants to read and write English, (2) health care for families, and (3) recreational, sports, and cultural activities.

- **Jacob Riis, journalist, social reformer**
- **spoils system, merit system**

SECTION 5. INTELLECTUAL AND CULTURAL MOVEMENTS

The period after the Civil War brought many changes not only to the South but also to the Northeast, Midwest, and Far West. Not the least of these changes had to do with the intellectual and cultural life of the nation. There was greater access to higher education simply because there were more colleges and universities. Great advances were made in science and technology, much of it related to practical applications for business, industry, and the home. A new phenomenon—**leisure time**—developed among the middle class.

FAST FACTS

Review Strategy

These "Fast Facts" relate to education.

- As the nation entered the **Industrial Age,** some people saw the need for a new kind of education. Responding to the need to train people for office work, the number of high schools increased tenfold between 1870 and 1900. High school courses of study included such practical business subjects as bookkeeping, typing, and manual arts. The natural sciences were also added to the curriculum. Education also began earlier with the introduction of **kindergarten** in 1873.

- The **Morrill Act** resulted in the building of a number of so-called **land-grant colleges,** which were to teach agricultural and mechanical arts. These new colleges and universities admitted women and African Americans. Established colleges like Princeton and Harvard added more science and foreign languages other than classical Greek and Latin to their traditional courses of study. Law and medicine became professional courses of study. In the past, new doctors and lawyers were trained through apprenticeships. Several all-black institutions of higher education were also founded during this post–Civil War period, among them **Tuskegee Institute,** Howard University, and Bethune-Cookman College. While **coeducation** in higher education was the norm west of the Appalachians, in the Northeast, women were founding all-women's colleges such as Vassar, Mount Holyoke, and Bryn Mawr.

Review Strategy

This "Fast Fact" relates to inventions.

- The late 1800s saw Americans making great advances in science and the practical applications of scientific discoveries. Among the discoveries and inventions of this period were the harnessing of electricity, the light bulb, the telephone, the elevator, the escalator, air brakes for trains, the linotype machine for setting type, and the ballpoint pen. Driven by the needs of industry, most of the discoveries that occupied American scientists were in the field of **applied science** rather than pure science.

Review Strategy

These "Fast Facts" relate to cultural developments at the turn of the century.

- **Realism** and to a lesser extent **naturalism** were the predominant influences on U.S. writers at the turn of the century. Among the realists were **Hamlin Garland, Frank Norris, Willa Cather,** and **William Dean Howells. Stephen Crane** and **Theodore Dreiser** were naturalists who had been influenced by Howells. There were also **regional** or **local color** writers, among whom **Mark Twain** was the best known. Others in the genre were **Edward Eggleston, Sarah Orne Jewett,** and **Joel Chandler Harris.** Nonfiction writers of note were **Oliver Wendel Holmes, Henry Adams,** and **Edward Bellamy.** Writers who transcended labels were the poet **Emily Dickinson, Henry James,** and **Edith Wharton.**

Review Strategy

See Section 8 for more on the influence of journalism on social reform.

- In many cities in the late 1800s, general interest newspapers, foreign-language newspapers, and newspapers for African-American readers were being published. Magazines developed as a response to a better educated middle class that had more time for leisure activities. Women's magazines, such as the ***Ladies Home Journal*** and ***Godey's Lady's Book,*** appeared along with ***Atlantic Monthly, Harper's Weekly,*** and ***McClure's.*** These magazines published articles that highlighted the serious problems of the day and called for social and political reforms.

- **Impressionists** and **realists** vied for the attention of the art world during the late 1800s. **Mary Cassatt** and **James McNeil Whistler** were well-known American impressionists who studied and worked in Europe. Among the realists were **John Singer Sargent, Thomas Eakins,** and **Henry Ossawa Tanner.** Sculptors of the period included **Edmonia Lewis, Daniel Chester French, Augustus Saint-Gaudens,** and **Frederic Remington.**

- At the end of the nineteenth century, about 12 percent of the nation's families controlled about 88 percent of the nation's wealth. However, a growing middle class found that they too had a little **discretionary income** and time to enjoy themselves. In addition to reading newspapers and magazines, people attended vaudeville shows and nickelodeons. Baseball, basketball, and football became major spectator sports. In rural areas and farm states, people went to state fairs, had square dances, and attended quilting bees.

Key People/Terms

Review Strategy

See if you can relate these people and terms to their correct context in the "Fast Facts" section.

- **George Washington Carver, impact on Southern farming**

- **John Dewey, "learn by doing"**
  Thomas Edison, light bulb, phonograph

- **William Randolph Hearst, social reform**

- **Joseph Pulitzer, human-interest stories**

- **Centennial Exposition**
- **World's Columbian Exposition**

SECTION 6. THE GILDED AGE

The term **"Gilded Age"** was coined from the title of a novel by Mark Twain and C. D. Warner. It came to represent the period from around 1877 to the 1890s. It was a time characterized by corruption in government and unbridled competition in business.

FAST FACTS

Review Strategy

This "Fast Fact" relates to the conservative nature of the Presidency in the late 1800s.

Review Strategy

This "Fast Fact" relates to the tariff issue that split the parties.

- As one historian has noted, this was a time of undistinguished occupants of the White House. Presidents tended to be "of modest intellect, vision, and resourcefulness." **Party men,** they were elected by conservative financial and business interests who wanted the status quo maintained. In general, the five men who sat in the president's seat between 1877 and 1897 (Rutherford B. Hayes, James A. Garfield, Chester A. Arthur, Grover Cleveland, and Benjamin Harrison) were conservatives in fiscal policy, foreign affairs, and social reform. Although like Ulysses S. Grant, they were personally honest, they were heedless of the corruption and **"influence-peddling"** that went on in their administrations.

- A major issue of the 1880s was the **tariff.** As Arthur took office, a number of people, from politicians to ordinary citizens, thought the time had come to lower tariff rates on certain items. These people were not arguing against using import duties to protect infant industries, but they saw no need to protect industries that were among the largest in the world. In fact, advocates of lower tariff rates argued that the lack of competition from foreign companies was enabling some U.S. manufacturers to charge higher prices. However, Republicans balked when the commission established to study the issue recommended a general reduction in tariff rates, and the **Tariff Act of 1883,** also known as the **Mongrel Tariff,** was the result. It offered little relief to consumers. The significance of the law, however, lay in the division it created between the Republican and Democratic Parties. After passage of this Act and until the latter part of the twentieth century, the Republicans consistently defended high tariffs and the Democrats opposed them. From the Civil War until 1883, there had been little difference between the two parties on the tariff.

- Scandals like **Crédit Mobilier, manipulation of railroad stocks,** discrimination in the establishment of **freight rates, free passes, pooling,** and **rebates** finally pushed farmers into organizing to protest the practices of the railroads. For farmers, the issue was not only the cost of shipping their grain, but also the high fees the railroads charged to store grain in railroad-owned elevators and warehouses. The railroads insisted the farmers store their grain with them as a condition of shipping.

- The fight to regulate railroad practices began in the Midwest with state laws, known popularly as **Grange laws,** prohibiting rebates and discrimination in setting rates. Railroads argued that they were being deprived of their property without **due process,** which was in violation of the Fourteenth Amendment. In *Munn v. Illinois,* one of six **Granger cases,** the U.S. Supreme Court upheld the right of the people to regulate railroads, which in effect had become **public utilities.** The Court ruled that property in which the public had an interest must expect to be controlled by the "public interest."

- While *Munn* was a victory, the Supreme Court ruled in the 1886 **Wabash Case** that the states had no power to regulate traffic that crossed state boundaries. That ended all attempts by states to regulate railroad traffic. In response, Congress passed the **Interstate Commerce Act** establishing the **Interstate Commerce Commission,** the nation's first federal regulatory agency. The Act also declared illegal (1) pooling, (2) rebates and lower rates to favored customers, (3) charging higher fees for short hauls than for long hauls on the same line, and (4) charging unreasonable rates. Railroads had to post their rates and give ten days' notice when changing rates. The Act, however, had little practical effect because the Commission had no power to enforce its provisions other than filing lawsuits. In sixteen cases brought before the Supreme Court in eighteen years, the decisions in fifteen cases favored the railroads. The law is important, however, because it established the principle of federal regulation of business.

- By the end of the 1870s, larger companies—manufacturing, railroad, and financial—began to find ways to reduce their competition. Sometimes they acquired smaller companies in **mergers.** The mergers might result in **horizontal combinations** or **vertical combinations,** depending on the nature of the businesses bought. In some industries, competing companies banded together in **pools** to restrain competition among themselves. Because there was no way to enforce these **"gentlemen's agreements,"** they were not very satisfactory. In the 1880s, beginning with **John D. Rockefeller's** Standard Oil, companies turned to **trusts** to formalize their agreements to act together in such a way as to remove competition. In practice, trusts became **monopolies.** Having crushed their competitors, monopolies felt free to raise prices, break labor unions, and exploit the nation's natural resources.

- In response to the public outcry against trusts, both the Republicans and the Democrats promised in the election of 1888 to curb trusts. The **Sherman Antitrust Act of 1890** was the result. It declared illegal "every contract, combination in the form of a trust . . . or conspiracy, **in restraint of trade** or commerce." Unfortunately, the lawmakers did not define terms such as trust and combination so that it was difficult to enforce the law. The greatest defeat for the law was *United States* **v.** *E.C. Knight Company,* in which the Supreme Court ruled that merely owning sugar refineries and controlling the sugar refining process did not constitute restraint of interstate commerce. Some historians view passage of the Sherman Antitrust Act as a way to placate the public, while others see it as a way to control labor unions. The law is important because it established the principle of federal regulation of big business.

- The **National Grange** was begun in 1867 as a fraternal order, but women, because of their vital roles in farm life, were welcomed as equal members. During the 1870s, the **Granger Movement** organized farmers in the South, West, and Midwest to fight railroad monopolies and their storage businesses. The Grange used political clout to elect sympathetic members to several state legislatures who then passed what were known as Grange laws to regulate the business practices of the railroads. The railroads fought the laws in the courts in what became the basis of the Granger cases.

- The second organization that supported farmers was the **Populist Party**, which was formed by the **Southern Alliance** and the **Northwestern Alliance** of farmers. In the election of 1892, the Populists drafted what is known as the **Omaha Platform.** It called for (1) government ownership of railroads; (2) free and unlimited coinage of silver at the rate of 16-to-1 with gold; (3) direct election of U.S. senators; (4) the secret ballot, also known as the Australian ballot; (5) a graduated income tax; (6) government storage of crops and advances to farmers on the price of those crops until farm prices improved [**subtreasury**]; (7) 8-hour workday; and (8) limits on immigration. The last two planks were meant to attract urban workers to the party. James B. Weaver, the Populist candidate for president, won one million popular votes and twenty-two electoral votes. Much of the vote appeared to be in response to the Party's monetary plank.

- In the aftermath of the **Panic of 1873,** people who owed debts wanted to expand the currency supply, thus reducing the value of the dollar and their debts. Although interest in **greenbackism** as a remedy faded, **free and unlimited coinage of silver** at the ratio of 16-to-1 with gold took its place. Farmers united with Western miners, who were suffering from an oversupply of silver as a result of various silver strikes, to lobby Congress. Congress, however, fearful of a glut of silver coins, had **demonetized** silver, that is, had ordered the coinage of silver halted. To proponents of free silver, this became known as the **Crime of 1873.**

- In 1878, Congress passed the **Bland-Allison Act** ordering the purchase and coining of two- to four-million dollars worth of silver a month. The law had little effect on the money supply and provided little relief to debtors or miners.

- In 1890, Congress passed the **Sherman Silver Purchase Act,** which required the purchase of four and a half million ounces of silver every month. To pay for the silver, the Treasury had to issue new notes. This Act provided cheap money and satisfied the Populists. In the **Panic of 1893,** President Cleveland asked Congress to repeal the law, and the Populists reacted angrily when Congress agreed with the president. Cleveland lost more support among farmers when he negotiated with J. P. Morgan and other Wall Street financiers for a bailout of the government. Gold reserves had dipped to a dangerous low during the depression that followed the Panic of 1893, the worst the nation had yet seen.

- The silver controversy became the central issue in the election of 1896. Democrats chose **William Jennings Bryan** after his rousing **"Cross of Gold"** speech. He ran on a platform similar to the Populists' Omaha Platform. Populists split over whom to back but eventually supported Bryan. Republicans nominated William McKinley who ran on a platform supporting a high tariff, the gold standard, annexation of Hawaii, and a strong foreign policy. Dissident Republicans bolted from the party, formed the National Silver Republicans, and supported Bryan. Although Bryan did well in the South and West, McKinley held the Northeast and won.

- The Populist Party declined and collapsed after the 1896 election, in part because the depression that followed the Panic of 1873 was lifting and in part because the Democratic Party had usurped its platform. Many of the ideas of the Populists were realized: (1) the secret ballot, (2) a graduated income tax through passage of the Sixteenth Amendment, (3) direct election of U.S. senators through passage of the Seventeenth Amendment, (4) the Federal Reserve Act of 1913 that reorganized the monetary policy of the nation, (5) the Warehouse Act of 1916 that was based on the subtreasury principle, and (6) strengthening of the Interstate Commerce Commission and Sherman Antitrust Act.

KEY PEOPLE

Review Strategy

See if you can relate these people to their correct context in the "Fast Facts" section.

- "goldbug" Democrats and Republicans

- Greenback Party, Greenback Labor Party, cheap money, unbacked currency

- Mark Hanna

KEY TERMS/IDEAS

Review Strategy

See if you can relate these terms and ideas to their correct context in the "Fast Facts" section.

- bimetalism

- Clayton Antitrust Act, 1914, labor unions

- Dingley Tariff of 1897

- holding company
  "front porch" campaign

- interlocking directorate

- Hepburn Act, 1906, railroad regulation

- McKinley Tariff of 1890

- Specie Resumption Act of 1875, greenbacks "as good as gold"

- Wilson-Gorman Tarriff Bill, House-Senate conference bill, Cleveland's reaction, farmers' support

SECTION 7. THE NATION ABROAD, 1865–1914

In 1867, Secretary of State **William Seward** succeeded in buying **Alaska** from Russia for the United States. It was almost thirty years before the nation added more territory. Between the end of the Civil War and 1900, the nation was occupied settling the West, rebuilding the South, developing industrial power, and becoming an urban nation. It was a time of **isolationism.** However, by the end of the nineteenth century, a new sense of manifest destiny in the form of **imperialism** was catching hold. This desire for territories abroad was fueled by the need for raw materials and new markets for manufactured goods and farm products. It was also an attempt to show Europe that the United States had come of age as a world power.

FAST FACTS

- By 1887 American planters controlled the Hawaiian legislature. When **Liliuokalani** became queen four years later, she attempted to wrest control from the planters. The planters demanded that she renounce the throne. When she refused, the planters set up their own government and asked the United States to annex **Hawaii.** Cleveland, who opposed imperialism, declined. The change in the presidency from Cleveland to McKinley, who embraced imperialism, opened the way for annexation in 1898.

- The year 1898 also saw the short-lived **Spanish-American War.** Fired up by the **yellow journalism** of competing New York newspapers, many Americans demanded that the United States stop Spain's abuses in Cuba. When the U.S.S. *Maine* blew up in Havana harbor, the United States declared war. After an easy victory in the "summer war," the United States and Spain negotiated the **Treaty of Paris.**

- Senate debate over ratification of the treaty focused on the Philippines. Americans were not concerned about tiny Guam, and Puerto Rico was close to the mainland, but the Philippines were 8,000 miles away. Arguments against the treaty included (1) the fear that the United States might be dragged into a war in Asia to defend the Philippines, (2) the problems that would be created by trying to integrate Filipinos into American society if they were granted citizenship and allowed to emigrate to the United States without restriction, (3) the competition that Filipino products would create in U.S. markets if import duties were waived, (4) the concern that the Philippines would request statehood, and (5) the idea that **colonialism** was not compatible with the Constitution. Advocates of the treaty rejected the notion that **"the Constitution follows the flag."** There was no obligation on the part of the United States to establish a process that would lead to statehood for the Philippines. The treaty's advocates won ratification.

- After the war, the United States made Cuba a **protectorate** and passed the **Platt Amendment** to the Cuban constitution. The Amendment (1) forbade interference by any foreign nation in Cuba and (2) stated that the United States had the right to maintain order in Cuba. Cuba became an independent nation in 1934 and the Platt Amendment was withdrawn.

- In 1900, the United States made Puerto Rico a U.S. territory under the **Foraker Act,** which established (1) that trade between Puerto Rico and the United States would not be subject to tariffs and (2)

Review Strategy

This "Fast Fact" relates to China.

Review Strategy

These "Fast Facts" relate to Roosevelt's policies in Latin America.

Review Strategy

This "Fast Fact" relates to Taft's "dollar diplomacy."

that Puerto Ricans would not pay federal taxes. The **Jones Act** in 1917 gave U.S. citizenship to Puerto Ricans.

- The **Open Door policy** of **John Hay** was a clever maneuver to ensure that U.S. business interests in China would be honored. Parts of China had been turned into **spheres of influence** by Russia, Germany, Great Britain, France, and Japan. These nations ran their **foreign concessions** for their own commercial benefit, which concerned U.S. businesses. Hay sent the same note to the American ambassador in each of the capitals of the nations that held a concession in China. The ambassadors were to ask for assurances that the foreign power (1) would not interfere with the privileges accorded other concessions, (2) would not favor their own nationals over others in the fees charged for harbor duties and railroad rates, and (3) would allow the Chinese to continue to collect customs duties. All the foreign powers refused to give Hay these assurances. Hay, however, announced that they had. Rather than be seen as threatening China's independence, the foreign powers remained silent in the face of Hay's lie.

- With the annexation of Hawaii and the addition of Guam and the Philippines to U.S. territory, the United States had a renewed interest in seeing a canal built between the Atlantic and Pacific Oceans. In 1902, President Roosevelt offered **Colombia** $40 million to pay for the work that a French company had already done on a canal. When Colombia refused to sell, Roosevelt aided a rebellion by Panamanians against Colombia. In exchange for guaranteeing the independence of the new nation, the United States signed the **Hay–Bunau-Varilla Treaty** with **Panama,** giving the United States control of the **Panama Canal Zone.**

- Because of growing U.S. business interests in Latin America and the U.S. investment in the Panama Canal, any European intervention in Latin America became an issue for the United States. When several European nations attempted to collect their debts from Venezuela by sending warships, Theodore Roosevelt issued the **Roosevelt Corollary** to the **Monroe Doctrine.** In essence, Roosevelt made the United States the self-appointed policeman of the Western Hemisphere, promising to use force if necessary to keep order and prevent chronic "wrongdoing" by any nation in the hemisphere. Roosevelt invoked the Corollary shortly thereafter to seize customs houses in the Dominican Republic and restore the nation's economic stability so that it could repay its debts to European nations.

- Taft pursued a policy in China and Latin America known as **"dollar diplomacy."** The purpose was (1) to block European and Japanese efforts to take over more of China and (2) to help U.S. businesses invest in China and Latin America. The outcomes were (1) heightened resentment toward the United States on the part of European and Latin American nations and Japan and (2) little in the way of profits for U.S. businesses.

- In contrast to Roosevelt's "big stick" and Taft's "dollar diplomacy," **Woodrow Wilson** began his first term declaring his foreign policy would be based on **"moral diplomacy."** The **Mexican Revolution** tried Wilson's policy, and it was found wanting. Although U.S. business interests supported **General Victoriano Huerta,** Wilson abhorred Huerta's brutal tactics and refused to recognize his government. When the Mexicans did not overthrow Huerta, on a pretext, Wilson sent U.S. marines to seize Veracruz. Wilson had expected that if the Mexican people were given support, they would opt for democracy and oust Huerta. Instead, Mexicans reacted by rioting. European and Latin American nations condemned Wilson's action, and he agreed to mediation by the **ABC powers** (Argentina, Brazil, and Chile).

KEY PEOPLE/TERMS

- **Emilio Aguinaldo, Philippine Insurrection**

- **James G. Blaine, Pan-Americanism, Pan-American Union**

- **Captain Alfred T. Mahan,** *The Influence of Sea Power on History, 1660–1783*

- **American Samoa**

- **"big stick" policy; "Walk softly and carry a big stick"; United States intervention in the Caribbean and Latin America**

- **Boxer Rebellion**

- **Drago Doctrine**

- **Gentlemen's Agreement, school segregation in San Francisco, denial of passports to Japanese laborers**

- **Insular Cases, Congress would determine whether an acquired territory was put on the path to statehood**

- **Nicaragua, "dollar diplomacy," "big stick" policy, Taft**

- **Root-Takahira Agreement, promises not to interfere with each other's territories**

- **Rough Riders**

- **Russo-Japanese War, Treaty of Portsmouth; lack of an indemnity, anti-American rioting**

- **Taft-Katsura Memorandum, United States recognition of Japanese dominance in Korea, Japanese promise not to attack the Philippines**

SECTION 8. THE PROGRESSIVE ERA

The **progressives** sought reform, improvement, and progress through government action. Progressivism was both an attitude and, for a brief time in 1912, a political party. The progressives were repelled by the corruption and **graft** in government, the cutthroat competition in business that reduced the ordinary working family to poverty, and the exploitation of the nation's natural resources.

FAST FACTS

- A certain number of the goals of the progressives could be traced to the **Populist Party,** but there were important differences.

PROGRESSIVES	POPULISTS
Farmers, factory workers, small business owners; college-educated middle- and upper-class urbanites	Farmers, factory workers, small business owners
Urban base	Agrarian base
Progressive Party (1912); worked through established political parties	Basically a political party
Each group had its own issues, such as government reform, regulation of big business, relief for the poor	Tariff and cheap money as major issues
Some success at state and local levels	Issues co-opted by major parties

Review Strategy

These "Fast Facts" and the table relate to differing philosophies of reform.

- The need for reform was publicized through the works of the **muckrakers,** a group of journalists and writers who exposed corruption in government, the evils of big business practices, and the conditions of the cities. Among the muckrakers were: **Lincoln Steffens (***Shame of the Cities***),** Ida M. Tarbell (*History of the Standard Oil Company*), Upton Sinclair (*The Jungle*), Ray Stannard Baker (*Following the Color Line*), John Spargo (*The Bitter Cry of the Children*), and **Gustavus Myers** (*History of the Great American Families*).

- Progressive reforms had some success at the local level and then moved up to the state level. It was only when Theodore Roosevelt became president that the movement was able to accomplish reforms at the national level. Among the changes the progressives brought about were:

    - experiments with different types of city government: **city commission** and **city manager, home rule**

    - adoption of ways to improve government: **direct primary, direct election of U.S. senators (Seventeenth Amendment), initiative, recall, referendum, Australian** or **secret ballot**

    - adoption of a **graduated income tax (Sixteenth Amendment)**

    - **Prohibition (Eighteenth Amendment)**

    - granting of **women's suffrage (Nineteenth Amendment)**

    - more aggressive regulation of big business, including public utilities

    - greater protection for workers

    - regulation of the food and drug industries

    - institutionalization of the **conservation** movement

- **Socialism** presented an alternative for some, in part because of Edward Bellamy's book ***Looking Backward 2000–1887.*** After his arrest and imprisonment in the **Pullman Strike, Eugene V. Debs** organized the **American Socialist Party.** The **Industrial Workers of the World (IWW, Wobblies)** was a radical labor union formed to take control of business. Whereas the Wobblies believed in confrontation, most socialists were more moderate and worked through the system. Debs, for example, ran for President of the United States five times.

Review Strategy

These "Fast Facts" and chart relate to African Americans.

- The period from the Civil War to the 1920s was very difficult for African Americans in the South. Beginning around 1910 and lasting until 1930, the **Great Migration** of African Americans out of the South occurred. They were pushed by (1) the **boll weevil,** (2) several seasons of extreme weather, (3) severe poverty as a result of the **sharecropping system,** (4) fear of **lynching,** and (5) the refusal of white factory owners to hire them.

- In the cities, various organizations developed to serve the newly arrived African Americans. Among them were black churches, newspapers, the **National Urban League,** and the **National Association for the Advancement of Colored People (NAACP).**

The latter developed out of the **Niagara Movement** organized by **W.E.B. Du Bois.** The **Nation of Islam** also began around this time.

- Three major figures of this period were **Booker T. Washington,** Du Bois, and **Marcus Garvey.**

WASHINGTON	DU BOIS	GARVEY
Born a slave	Free born	British subject from Jamaica
Founded **Tuskegee Institute**	Founded Niagara Movement Founded NAACP	Founded **Universal Negro Improvement Association (UNIA)**
Appealed to ordinary African Americans	Appealed to **Talented Tenth**	Appealed to ordinary African Americans
Worked for economic equality, but not social or political equality	Believed in confrontation to achieve complete equality	**Back-to-Africa** movement
Noted for **Atlanta Compromise** Was influential among whites	Noted for writing in the *Crisis* magazine Shared interest in African heritage	Noted for **Pan-Africanism**

Review Strategy

These "Fast Facts" relate to how Roosevelt earned his reputation.

- Theodore Roosevelt earned the title **"trust buster"** as he set out to rein in big business. His administration brought suit against the **Northern Securities Company** and won when the Supreme Court ruled that the **holding company** restrained trade and was, therefore, in violation of the **Sherman Antitrust Act.** In all, Roosevelt's administration prosecuted forty lawsuits against business combinations. Roosevelt was also responsible for Congress passing the **Elkins Act (1903)** and the **Hepburn Act (1906)** to strengthen the **Interstate Commerce Commission.** Congress also passed the **Pure Food and Drug Act,** which helped to establish the precedent that protecting the public welfare was the legitimate business of the federal government. In the coal miners' strike of 1902, Roosevelt became the first President to intervene in a strike on the behalf of labor. Rejecting the opportunity to use the Sherman Antitrust Act against the miners, he attempted to mediate. The attempt failed, but the strike ended soon after both parties agreed to arbitration.

- Roosevelt built his reputation as a **conservationist** on policies such as (1) his withdrawal from sale two hundred million acres of public land, (2) the **Newlands Reclamation Bill** to finance irrigation projects, (3) the establishment of the **Inland Waterways**

Commission, and (4) the **White House Conservation Commission.**

- In the election of 1908, the Republicans had pledged tariff revisions. The **Dingley Tariff of 1897** was still in effect, and many people blamed the tariff for rising prices. Although the Republican Party had favored high tariffs since the election of 1883, Taft said he would reduce tariffs. After an unsuccessful fight to defeat the bill led in the Senate by progressive **Robert La Follette,** the **Payne-Aldrich Tariff** reached Taft's desk. The bill reduced some rates but raised thousands of others. Taft, who had done little to fulfill his campaign promise, signed the bill, praising it as the best tariff bill the Republicans had ever passed. He was concerned that vetoing it would hurt the chances for passage of other legislation that he wanted.

- Claiming that Roosevelt had overstepped his authority, **Richard Ballinger,** the new Secretary of the Interior under Taft and a lawyer, reopened for public sale some of the lands Roosevelt had closed. **Gifford Pinchot,** the chief forester, criticized Ballinger publicly and provided information to the muckraking press about Ballinger's activities. Both a presidential investigation and a Congressional committee found Ballinger innocent of any wrongdoing. Taft fired Pinchot. The progressives in the Republican Party were furious at both the appointment of Ballinger and the firing of Pinchot. This controversy and the Payne-Aldrich Tariff led to a split in the party.

- The split in the Republican Party led to the founding of the **Progressive Party,** or **Bull Moose Party,** which nominated Theodore Roosevelt in the election of 1912. His opponents were Taft, who was renominated by the Republicans; **Woodrow Wilson,** the nominee of the Democratic Party; and Eugene V. Debs, of the Socialist Party who made a strong showing by capturing two million votes.

- The Democrats had promised to revise tariff rates downward if elected. Wilson called a special session of Congress to consider what became known as the **Underwood-Simmons Tariff of 1913.** The bill became locked in debate in the Senate, and Wilson appealed directly to voters. His castigation of lobbyists for big business started a Congressional investigation, and the bill was passed, substantially reducing tariffs for the first time since 1857.

- Wilson also introduced a reform of the banking and currency system. After the **Panic of 1907** forced the closure of a number of banks because they were undercapitalized, Congress established the **Aldrich Commission** to study the nation's monetary practices. In 1913 the Commission reported that (1) the nation's banks lacked stability, (2) the nation's currency supply needed to be more flexible so that it could expand or contract as required by the volume of business, (3) there was no central institution to oversee and regulate banking practices, and (4) that Wall Street (New York City) had too much power over the nation's banking capital. Wilson's answer was the **Federal Reserve Act** that (1) provided money to banks in temporary trouble, (2) eased the inflexibility of the money supply by providing currency in exchange for promissory notes from businesses, and (3) and (4) set up twelve Federal Reserve banks in twelve regions of the country supervised by a Board of Governors whose headquarters were in Washington, D.C., thus removing the power from Wall Street.

- Among Wilson's efforts to regulate big business was creation of the **Federal Trade Commission** and passage of the **Clayton Antitrust Act.** The former could (1) investigate businesses suspected of illegal practices and (2) issue cease-and-desist orders for businesses found guilty of practices as such as mislabeling and adulterating goods and engaging in combinations to fix retail prices. The major significance of the Clayton Antitrust Act was that it specifically exempted labor unions and agricultural cooperatives from antitrust regulations. The law also forbade (1) **interlocking directorates,** (2) **holding companies** for the purpose of creating **monopolies,** (3) **tying contracts,** and (4) price discrimination for the purpose of creating a monopoly.

KEY PEOPLE

Review Strategy

See if you can relate these people to their correct context in the "Fast Facts."

- **Old Guard Republicans, conservatives**
- **Joseph ("Uncle Joe") G. Cannon**
- **William James, pragmatism**

KEY TERMS/IDEAS

Review Strategy

See if you can relate these terms and ideas to their correct context in the "Fast Facts" section.

- *McClure's Magazine*
- **New Freedom, Wilson's philosophy, government should intervene in private business to assert the public interest**
- **New Nationalism, Roosevelt's promise in the election of 1912 "Square Deal," Roosevelt's 1904 campaign promise**

Chapter 10

REVIEWING THE TWENTIETH CENTURY: 1915 TO THE PRESENT

This chapter reviews United States history from the buildup to World War I to the 1992 presidential election. The College Board course guide for the AP United States History Test lists eleven major topics for this era from World War I through the 1920s, the Great Depression, and from World War II through the administrations of Truman, Eisenhower, Kennedy, Johnson, Nixon, Ford, Carter, and Reagan. According to the guide, about one third of the multiple-choice questions will deal with the time between 1915 and the present.

Study Strategy

Check the College Board Web site (www.collegeboard.org/ap) for the time period for your DBQ.

The guide also states that there will be only a "few questions on the period since 1975, [and] neither the DBQ nor any of the four essay questions in Parts B and C will deal exclusively with this period." It does not mean that you should skip reviewing the period from 1975, but it does mean that in proportion to the rest of U.S. history, you will not find many questions about the period from 1975 on the test.

SECTION 1. WILSON AND WORLD WAR I

At the beginning of war in Europe, **President Woodrow Wilson** declared the nation's **neutrality.** While grateful for the expanse of the Atlantic Ocean between the United States and Europe, Americans were still concerned about the fate of Great Britain and especially France because the latter had helped the fledgling United States against the British in the Revolutionary War. As time went on, those who had supported the Germans began to revise their views and become **pro-Ally.** Support for the British and the French intensified.

FAST FACTS

- The declaration of neutrality did not stop private U.S. companies from selling weapons and supplies and making loans to Great Britain and France. This economic activity helped raise the United States out of a recession. Because the British controlled the sea lanes, the Germans could not do business with U.S. companies.

- Both the British and the Germans challenged U.S. neutrality. The British put into effect a series of policies, including laying mines in the North Sea and search and seizure of neutral ships, that endangered U.S. merchant ships and violated their rights under international law. The Germans declared the waters around Great Britain a **war zone** and announced that their submarines, known as **U-boats,** would sink enemy merchantmen on sight. Because British ships sometimes flew the U.S. flag, the Germans said they could not ensure the safety of U.S. ships.

- Wilson protested to both nations, but little came of his protests until a U-boat sank the British passenger ship *Lusitania.* The Germans agreed that in the future U-boats would provide for the safety of the passengers and crew of any ships they sank. After another incident in 1916, the Germans issued the **Sussex Pledge,** stating that they would not sink merchant ships without warning. However, things were going badly for the Germans. In an effort to raise morale and to cut off supplies to the European **Allies,** the Germans decided to resume **unrestricted submarine warfare** in 1917. The Germans realized that this would probably bring the United States into the war, but the Germans decided that they could starve the Allies into defeat before the United States could **mobilize.**

- The backdrop to all this was an internal debate in the United States waged by **pacifists** versus those who advocated **preparedness.** Among the former were **progressives,** who feared that their reform program would founder, and those of German and Irish descent, who did not want to see the United States fight on the side of Great Britain. Among the latter were **nationalists,** who thought that Wilson should be stronger in his response to Germany. Wilson himself wished to keep the nation out of the European war and campaigned in 1916 on the slogan **"He Kept Us Out of War."** However, in 1915, he also asked Congress to authorize a modest **preparedness program.** Faced with harsh opposition from the progressives, Wilson took his campaign to the people and won approval of his proposal.

- In early 1917, when the Zimmerman Note was published asking Mexico to join the German war effort and promising to help recapture Texas, Arizona, and New Mexico, a wave of anger swept the United States. By April 1917, the resumption of unrestricted submarine warfare had severely curtailed shipping; the Allies were nearly exhausted. Wilson called Congress into special session and asked for a declaration of war against Germany. The nation began to mobilize. The **Selective Service** law was passed, which instituted the **draft.** The **War Industries Board,** created to handle the purchasing of materials for the Allies, was one of several such **war boards** established to oversee the management and allocation of industry, labor, and raw materials. To finance the war, the government decided to sell **war bonds,** known as **Liberty bonds,** and organized **Liberty Loan drives** to sell them. Wilson was also given authority to take over industries, requisition supplies, and control distribution in order to further the war effort.

Red Alert!

Remember, the battles may be interesting, but you won't find them on the test.

- At the peace conference that ended World War I, Wilson unveiled his **Fourteen Points,** a set of proposals to eliminate the causes of war. A very moral man, Wilson believed that morality should underlay the conduct of government. His plan called for:

  1. Open rather than secret diplomacy
  2. Freedom of the seas
  3. Removal of as much as possible of tariffs and other trade barriers
  4. Reduction of national armaments to a level consistent with domestic safety
  5. Settlement of colonial claims recognizing the interests of the colonial peoples and the occupying nation
  6. Evacuation of all Russian territory by foreign powers
  7. Evacuation of Belgium and restoration of its sovereignty
  8. Restoration of Alsace-Lorraine to France
  9. Readjustment of the Italian border to recognize nationality
  10. Autonomy for the peoples of Austria-Hungary
  11. Autonomy for Serbia, Montenegro, and Romania—the Balkan states
  12. Autonomy for the subject peoples of the Ottoman Empire
  13. Independence for Poland
  14. An international organization of world nations

- The most important point to Wilson was the fourteenth—a **League of Nations.** Determined to win approval for his plan, Wilson went to the peace conference. Some historians believe he would have been better able to judge the political opposition to his plan at home had he stayed in Washington and even been more likely to win his points at the conference had he been away from the political pressures of the negotiating table. Historians also believe Wilson should have included a prominent Republican or two on his negotiating team to win over the opposition or at least dampen it.

- As it was, Wilson attended the conference to find that while he wanted a peace that would not lead to another war, his Allies wanted revenge and the territories that they had secretly agreed to divide up when they won the war. Most of Wilson's Fourteen Points were ignored. The biggest loss was the Allies' insistence that

Germany pay **reparations.** This insistence would lead to the worldwide depression of the 1920s, the emergence of **Adolf Hitler,** and World War II. Wilson, however, won his League of Nations.

- When Wilson returned with the **Treaty of Versailles,** he faced a fight, not only in the Senate but also in the nation. **Isolationists** denounced the League of Nations because they feared it would force the United States to go to war to preserve other nations' boundaries. Some thought that Great Britain would dominate the League or that the United States would give up its sovereignty to a superstate League. Others thought the Treaty was unjust, especially those who supported Germany or one of the nations that lost territory in the settlement. Some Republicans feared that Wilson would use a victory for the League as an issue in a campaign for a third term. When a number of Republican senators and senators-elect came out against the League, Wilson intemperately denounced them publicly. He took his campaign to the nation in a cross-country tour, but he collapsed partway through the tour and suffered a stroke. The Senate twice refused to ratify the Treaty as it stood and negotiated separate treaties with the **Central Powers.**

Review Strategy

See Chapter 6 for Schenck v. United States.

- The end of the war saw the rise of intolerance and a phenomenon known as the **red scare.** The Russian Revolution of 1917 had stirred up fears in the United States that radicals were trying to take over the government. A series of mail bombs in the early part of 1919 that were addressed to prominent Americans, some of whom had spoken out against subversives or for restrictions on immigration, confirmed for many that these fears had merit. Attorney General **A. Mitchell Palmer** launched an investigation of **Bolsheviks,** raided Communist meetings, seized records, and arrested some 6,000 people without regard to their rights. The courts released most of the accused due to lack of evidence.

Review Strategy

This "Fast Fact" relates to the red scare.

- One of the factors that motivated the red scare was the increasing strength of **labor unions.** During the war, **collective bargaining** had helped to keep the war industries humming, but once **reconversion** was underway, cooperation between business and labor faltered. Prices went up, but wages did not. A series of strikes, thirty-six hundred, swept the nation in 1919, some accompanied by violence. The press carried hostile coverage of the strikes, and some Americans began to see organized labor as un-American, an invitation to **anarchy.**

KEY PEOPLE

Review Strategy

See if you can relate these people to their correct context in the "Fast Facts" section.

- William Jennings Bryan, Theodore Roosevelt
- Eugene V. Debs, "Big Bill" Haywood, deprivation of civil liberties
- David Lloyd George, Georges Clemenceau
- Henry Cabot Lodge, Sr.; William E. Borah
- General John J. Pershing, commander of U.S. troops

KEY TERMS/IDEAS

Review Strategy

See if you can relate these terms and ideas to their correct context in the "Fast Facts" section.

- airplane as a weapon of war, trench warfare, mustard gas
- Article 10, mutual guarantee of political boundaries
- Committee on Public Information, propaganda, anti-German
- contraband
- Espionage Act, Sedition Act
- Food Administration, War Labor Board, War Labor Policies Board, Fuel Administration, Railroad Administration
- moral diplomacy
- National Defense Act, 1916 "peace without victory"

SECTION 2. THE 1920s

The **roaring twenties** coincided with the **"return to normalcy"** promised in the 1920 election by **Warren G. Harding.** It was a time of glittering prosperity mixed with a dark strain of intolerance and injustice.

FAST FACTS

Review Strategy

These "Fast Facts" relate to the business climate of the early 1920s

- Normalcy in business meant a **laissez-faire** attitude toward regulating business and a pro-business attitude (1) in passing the **Fordney-McCumber Tariff,** (2) in promoting foreign trade through providing huge loans to the postwar Allied governments who returned the favor by buying U.S.-produced goods and foodstuffs, and (3) by cracking down on strikes. The Supreme Court helped with a number of rulings favorable to big business, such as allowing antitrust laws to be used as the basis for suits against unions, declaring boycotts by labor to be illegal, and nullifying the minimum wage for women.

- For a time after World War I, farmers participated in the prosperity of the 1920s, but when the federal government cut loans to the Allies early in the decade, the agricultural boom ended. The high tariffs levied by the United States and the Allies' insistence on repayment of war debts hurt the world economy and the market for U.S. farm products. In addition, during the war, farmers had been encouraged to grow as much as they could. Once the war was over, farmers continued that practice and were left with surplus goods. Farmers lobbied for the federal government to buy the excess inventory, but Coolidge vetoed the bill twice. He claimed it would create artificial prices and promote overproduction. In 1929, Congress established the **Farm Board** to buy surpluses and maintain prices, but farmers continued to grow as much as they wanted.

- The Harding administration is remembered for its scandals—from Harding's Attorney General who sold pardons and paroles, to the **Teapot Dome Scandal,** named after a reserve in Wyoming. The reserve land with rich oil deposits had been set aside under the jurisdiction of the Navy Department for years. The scandal involved a member of Harding's cabinet, two oil speculators, and large bribes to open the reserve for drilling.

- The decade of the Twenties was also known as the **Jazz Age.** Jazz is a musical form unique to the United States. It began in the South around the turn of the twentieth century and spread north. It blends West African rhythms, African-American spirituals and blues, and European harmonies. After the war, some jazz musicians and singers found less racial discrimination in Europe and moved abroad.

- The **Great Migration** had transformed parts of some Northern cities into all-black neighborhoods. One of these neighborhoods was Harlem in New York City. It became the center of a flowering of African-American culture called the **Harlem Renaissance.** The **National Urban League,** the **NAACP,** and the **Universal Negro Improvement Association** (led by **Marcus Garvey)** were headquartered in Harlem. Harlem attracted African-American writers, artists, and musicians from around the nation to what was known as the **New Negro Movement.**

- The **Temperance Movement** could trace its beginnings to the reform movements of the early nineteenth century. By 1917, two thirds of the states had passed laws prohibiting the consumption of alcohol, and several others had approved **local-option laws.** With the entrance of the United States into World War I, prohibitionist forces cloaked themselves in the mantle of patriotism to argue that (1) prohibition would shift thousands of tons of grain from liquor manufacture to war uses; (2) alcoholism led to drunkenness, and a drunken man was of no use to the war effort; and (3) most breweries and whiskey distilleries were owned by Germans. In 1917, Congress passed the **Eighteenth Amendment,** and the states ratified it by 1919.

- The amendment was difficult to enforce because most Americans did not support it, including a succession of occupants of the White House. Wilson vetoed the **Volstead Act** that was meant to enforce the amendment, but Congress passed it over his veto. Americans who were tired of the self-sacrifice of the war years circumvented the law through **bootlegging.** The large-scale manufacture and smuggling of alcohol became the business of organized crime. **Prohibition** was repealed in 1933.

- The red scare at the end of war also resulted in legislation restricting immigration. Up until 1875, when the first immigration law was passed, people could freely enter the United States. With the exception of Chinese and Japanese immigrants, this remained true until 1921. In that year, the **Immigration Restriction Act** was passed and in 1924, the **National Origins Act.** These laws were aimed at restricting immigrants from southern and central Europe and Asia. Buoyed by the patriotism generated by the war and fearful of anarchists and Bolsheviks, Americans pressured lawmakers for these laws to keep America for Americans.

- This **nativist** attitude also resulted in a resurgence of the **Ku Klux Klan.** This **white supremacist** organization from the South now spread north and west and added Jews and Catholics to its target list. The organization's goal was to protect white, Anglo-Saxon, Protestant America from African Americans and foreigners.

- Anti-Catholic sentiment was a factor in the 1928 election in which **Al Smith,** the Democratic candidate and a Catholic, faced Herbert Hoover, but historians do not consider it a major factor. Smith had other liabilities. He was a product of the New York City machine and not from a rural background, as most Democratic candidates had been up until then, and he was against Prohibition. Hoover ran on his record of public service and on Republican prosperity. Although Smith lost the **"Solid South,"** he managed to resurrect the Democratic Party from its long eclipse under the Republicans, and he attracted a new constituency to the party. In this election, membership shifted from rural and small-town to urban, Catholic, immigrant, and working class.

KEY PEOPLE

Review Strategy

See if you can relate these people to their correct context in the "Fast Facts" section.

- Romare Bearden, Sargent Johnson, Augusta Savage
- expatriates, "lost generation," alienation, Ernest Heminway, F. Scott Fitzgerald, Gertrude Stein
- Billie Holiday, Duke Ellington, Jelly Roll Morton, Bessie Smith, William Grant Still
- Langston Hughes, Countee Cullen, Zora Neale Hurston, James Weldon Johnson
- Andrew Mellon, cut excess profits tax, tax the poor rather than the rich to stimulate investment

KEY TERMS/IDEAS

Review Strategy

See if you can relate these terms and ideas to their correct context in the "Fast Facts" section.

- anti-Semitism
- consumer culture: the automobile, radio, movies, sports
- Sacco-Vanzetti case
- Scopes trial, evolution, William Cullen Bryan, religious fundamentalism

SECTION 3. THE GREAT DEPRESSION

When Herbert Hoover took office in 1928, there were a number of weaknesses in the U.S. economy that he was either unaware of or ignored. The most visible was the amount of **speculation** in the stock market. But that was just one of a number of problems.

FAST FACTS

Review Strategy

These "Fast Facts" relate to the Stock Market Crash.

- Among the weaknesses in the U.S. economy were: (1) the amount of stock being bought on **margin;** (2) depressed agricultural prices because of large surpluses; (3) the unequal distribution of wealth, so that 5 percent of the population provided the nation's investment capital and the majority of its purchasing power; (4) the tax policies of Andrew Mellon, Secretary of the Treasury, that contributed to the unequal distribution of wealth; (5) the expansion of businesses in response to rapidly increasing profits; (6) easy-to-get

installment credit for consumers; (7) the size and influence on segments of the economy of **holding companies;** (8) the weakness of the banking system because of many small and mismanaged banks; (9) high tariffs that closed off foreign markets to U.S. goods; and (10) the Allies' insistence on collecting war debts that depressed foreign trade, especially for U.S. foodstuffs.

- By the end of the decade, that part of the 95 percent of the population that was buying on credit had overextended its credit or had bought all that it wanted. The larger part of that 95 percent, however, could never afford to buy the new luxury goods of the 1920s. **Overproduction** and **underconsumption** joined to create financial problems for businesses that now found themselves with surplus inventory and their own loans to meet.

- All of these factors came together in the late 1920s to create the backdrop for the **Stock Market Crash of 1929.** By the fall of 1929, more than $7 billion had been borrowed to buy stocks on margin. Based on the profits the companies were earning, many stocks were hugely overvalued. When professional speculators began to cash out of the market in September, it was only a matter of time before **Black Tuesday** and the end of the **Roaring Twenties.**

- After the Crash, many stocks were worthless. People lost their life savings, their jobs, and their homes. Banks foreclosed on loans and mortgages. When their borrowers could not repay their loans, the banks went under. Businesses went bankrupt as inventories piled up because people could not afford anything but necessities. People relied on family members who were better off to take them in. As more businesses closed and more people lost their jobs, the **Great Depression** worsened.

Review Strategy

These "Fast Facts" relate to Hoover's policies in the Depression.

- Hoover believed the Depression would be short-lived. Although he did not believe that the federal government should help the unemployed, he did authorize the funding of the **Home Loan Bank Act** and the **Reconstruction Finance Corporation,** the latter to help businesses. Hoover believed (1) that helping the unemployed was the responsibility of churches, private agencies, and local and state governments; (2) that giving a handout to the unemployed would destroy their self-respect and individual initiative; (3) that a federal relief program would bankrupt the nation; and (4) that a federal relief program would dangerously enlarge the power of the federal government and create a bloated bureaucracy.

- Hoover acted to shore up farm prices by ordering the **Farm Board** to buy surplus farm products to keep prices up. But as warehouses filled, prices fell, and the Farm Board ceased buying surpluses in 1931. Farmers organized **farm committees** to prevent creditors from foreclosing on their neighbors. To keep prices up, the **National Farm Holiday Association** in the Midwest tried to prevent food from being shipped to cities.

- In 1932, some twenty thousand unemployed veterans descended on Washington, D.C., demanding immediate payment of bonus certificates that were not to come due until 1945. The **Bonus Marchers** set up a **Hooverville** just outside the city or camped in empty buildings on Pennsylvania Avenue to await Congress's vote. When Congress rejected the bill, many veterans went home, but some stayed because they had nowhere else to go. After two weeks, Hoover dispatched the capital police to remove the veterans from the abandoned buildings. Somehow, shots were fired, and a mob scene ensued. **General Douglas MacArthur,** who had been told to stand ready in case of trouble, ordered troops and tanks into the fray. The veterans were routed, and the army burned the Hooverville. The sight of unarmed veterans fleeing from U.S. Army tanks hurt Hoover's already damaged credibility.

KEY TERMS/IDEAS

Review Strategy

See if you can relate these terms and ideas to their correct context in the "Fast Facts" section.

- **"self-liquidating projects"**
- **Smoot-Hawley Tariff**

SECTION 4. THE NEW DEAL

Roosevelt's policies to deal with the Great Depression can be categorized as **"relief, recovery, and reform."** The fifteen programs enacted in the first **Hundred Days** were meant to provide relief and begin the nation's recovery. Although some measures in this period dealt with reform of banking and securities businesses, most reform measures came later.

FAST FACTS

- The following table lists some of these major bills and provisions. One agency that was created as the result of a direct order by Roosevelt was the **Civil Works Administration (CWA).** Overseen by **Harry Hopkins/** who also headed **FERA** and later the **WPA,** the CWA pumped a billion dollars into the economy between late 1933 and spring 1934 by providing **work-relief** for more than four-million people from building roads to teaching adult school.

ACT	SOME PROVISIONS
Emergency Banking Act, 1933	• Allowed inspection of bank records to enable financially stable banks to reopen; validated **"bank holiday"** • Permitted **Reconstruction Finance Corporation (RFC)** to buy stocks of banks in trouble, thereby giving the banks an infusion of new capital, an example of **"pump priming"**
Glass-Steagall Banking Act, 1933	Established **Federal Deposit Insurance Corporation (FDIC)** to insure bank deposits (and stabilize the banking system)
Federal Emergency Relief Administration (FERA), 1933	Provided work on projects, such as building roads and airports, schools and playgrounds, and parks
Civilian Conservation Corps (CCC), 1933	Provided jobs related to conservation of natural resources to men between the ages of seventeen and twenty-five
Agricultural Adjustment Act (AAA), 1933	• In order to raise prices, limited farm production by paying **subsidies** to farmers to withhold land from cultivation • Declared unconstitutional in 1936 • Replaced with **Soil Conservation and Domestic Allotment Act** (1936) and second **Agricultural Adjustment Act** (1938) to keep surpluses in check and prices of agricultural commodities and farm incomes up

ACT	SOME PROVISIONS
National Industrial Recovery Act (NIRA), 1933	• Created **National Recovery Administration (NRA)** • Administered codes of fair practices for businesses and industry Declared unconstitutional in *Schechter Poultry Corp.* v. *United States* (Section 7) • Created **Public Works Administration (PWA)** to provide money for construction or improvement of the **infrastructure** and public buildings
Securities Act, 1933	• Gave Federal Trade Commission power to supervise new issues of stock • Required statement of financial information to accompany new stock issues • Made company directors liable—civilly and criminally—for misrepresentation
Tennessee Valley Authority (TVA), 1933	• Bought, built, and operated dams • Generated and sold electrical power • Plan flood control and reforestation projects • Withdrew poor land from farming • Use of TVA rates as a yardstick to gauge rates charged by private utilities controversial
Farm Credit Administration (FCA), 1933	Provided funding for farm mortgages
Home Owners Loan Corporation (HOLC), 1933	Provided funding for home mortgages
Securities and Exchange Act, 1934	• Provided for federal regulation of securities exchanges • Established the **Securities and Exchange Commission (SEC)**
Banking Act of 1935	Reorganized the **Federal Reserve System** to give the **Federal Reserve Board** control over **open-market operations**

ACT	SOME PROVISIONS
National Youth Administration (NYA), 1935	• Provided work-relief, training, and employment to people between the ages of sixteen and twenty-five who were not full-time students • Provided part-time employment for students to enable them to stay in school
Works Progress Administration (WPA), 1935	• Provided employment on infrastructure projects, such as dredging rivers and building highways • Created projects for artists, writers, actors, and musicians
Social Security Act of 1935	• Established unemployment compensation fund • Established old-age pension fund • Set up grants to states for care of needy dependent children, the physically disabled, and women and children in poverty • Did not cover all jobs, such as farmers, farm workers, and domestics, and, therefore, excluded some 80 percent of all African Americans
National Labor Relations Act (also known as **Wagner Act**), 1935	Authorized the **National Labor Relations Board (NLRB)** to oversee union elections and define and prohibit unfair labor practices
Fair Labor Standards Act (also known as **Wages and Hours Act**), 1938	Set maximum of a forty-four hour workweek and a minimum wage of twenty-five cents an hour for workers engaged in interstate commerce or in the production of goods involved in interstate commerce

Review Strategy

See Chapter 6 for more on Schechter Poultry Corp. v. United States.

• In his annual address to Congress in 1935, Roosevelt announced the **Second New Deal.** Admitting that recovery had not helped everyone, Roosevelt ended attempts to balance the budget and shifted the focus of his programs in an attempt to form a new coalition to support both his programs and the Democratic Party. Because of the NRA, business was hostile, so he courted labor, farmers, and African Americans. They joined the traditional backbone of the Democratic Party—Southerners and Northern political machines. The legislation and executive activities of the Second New Deal reflected many of their interests.

- Critics of the New Deal ranged from those who thought it did not do enough to those who thought it did too much. On the left were **Father Charles E.Coughlin,** who attacked Roosevelt for moving too slowly to attack the unequal distribution of the nation's wealth; **Huey Long,** a Louisiana senator, who championed the rural poor and built a national reputation by attacking Roosevelt; and **Dr. Francis Townshend,** who proposed a national pension for the elderly. On the right, business leaders concerned by increasing federal power and the cost of New Deal programs formed the **American Liberty League** to work against Roosevelt and his policies, which they believed were leading the nation into socialism and bankruptcy. Conservative Northern and Western Republicans and conservative Southern Democrats would increasingly oppose Roosevelt's programs as being too liberal.

Review Strategy

See Chapter 9 for more on early labor organizations.

- The **AFL** had been organized in the late 1800s for **crafts workers** and had never attempted to organize the vastly larger group of **industrial workers.** Some members of the AFL believed the labor reforms of the New Deal provided an opportunity for organizing industrial workers. When the leadership of the AFL disagreed, **John L. Lewis** and others founded the **Committee of Industrial Organizations** (later **Congress, CIO**) and began organizing industrial workers, including African Americans. The newly founded CIO was successful in winning contracts from U.S. Steel, General Motors, and the Chrysler Corporation. The CIO used **sit-down strikes** against the two auto makers.

- One of the least successful of Roosevelt's actions was the so-called **court-packing** scheme to put judges who were more sympathetic to the New Deal on the **Supreme Court.** Having had both the AAA and the NIRA and several smaller bills declared unconstitutional, Roosevelt worried about the fate of the NLRA and the Social Security Act. Early in his second term, he asked Congress, in the interest of making the federal judiciary more efficient, to allow him to add judges for those members who chose not to retire at age seventy. He wanted to add no more than forty-four judges to the Circuit Court and six justices to the Supreme Court. The scheme was a blunder on the part of an unusually adept politician. Roosevelt had not prepared the way for his proposal by making it a campaign issue in 1936 or even mentioning it to his own party. Roosevelt played into the hands of Republicans, who criticized him for seeking too much power. Congress voted down Roosevelt's proposal. The issue evaporated when the Court began handing down rulings upholding New Deal legislation, and aging justices began to retire.

- In an effort to offset inflation in 1937, Roosevelt ordered cuts in federal spending, especially in the WPA and in PWA pump-priming activities. In addition, workers and businesses were now paying Social Security taxes. This contraction in **purchasing power** resulted in a **recession** that dragged on into 1938, almost wiping out the economic advances since 1935. By mid-1938, Roosevelt asked for a new spending program, and Congress complied. The recession ended, but no new large-scale relief programs were passed by a Congress that was now controlled by conservatives.

Review Strategy

This "Fast Fact" relates to Native Americans and the New Deal.

- The **Wheeler-Howard Indian Reorganization Act** (1) ended the practice of dividing reservations into individual landholdings; (2) restored to the nations those lands not already given to individuals; (3) guaranteed a measure of self-government for each Native American nation, although real power remained with the secretary of the interior; (4) allowed the practice of traditional customs, beliefs, and crafts; (5) guaranteed the rights of Native Americans to enter into contracts and to sue and be sued in court; (6) established a fund to give loans to Indian corporations for economic development; and (7) provided information on soil conservation and improved methods for raising and selling crops and livestock. Little came of the last or of any of the provisions of the Act. Native Americans still languished in poverty.

Review Strategy

This "Fast Fact" relates to African Americans and the New Deal.

- While Roosevelt's record on African Americans is mixed, his was the first administration since Reconstruction to show concern for them. African Americans participated in FERA, WPA, CCC, and the NYA. However, while federal policy forbade discrimination in New Deal programs, local official ignored it and placed African Americans in segregated groups and did not allow them to do certain jobs. **Mary McCleod Bethune** was the Director of Negro Affairs for the NYA and a member of Roosevelt's informal advisory body known as the **Black Cabinet**. The TVA hurt rather than helped black tenant farmers. Roosevelt did not work for passage of antilynching laws or the end of the poll tax.

KEY PEOPLE

Review Strategy

See if you can relate these people, terms, and ideas to their correct context in the "Fast Facts" section.

- **Louis Brandeis, Supreme Court**

- **Mexicans, repatriation, Hoover administration**

- **Mexican Americans, *mutalistas*, migrant labor, urban jobs and relief programs**

- **Eleanor Roosevelt**

- **sharecroppers, Arkies, Okies, unintended victims of AAA**

KEY TERMS/IDEAS

- **"soak-the-rich" tax, Share the Wealth Clubs**

SECTION 5. DIPLOMACY IN THE 1920s AND 1930s

The diplomacy of the 1930s under Franklin Roosevelt was a dance to ensure that Great Britain and the other nations of Europe who were being menaced by **Adolf Hitler** and **Nazi Germany** were supported, while not antagonizing **isolationists** in Congress and among the voters.

FAST FACTS

Review Strategy

These "Fast Facts" relate to attempts at disarmament and peace.

- There had been several attempts at **disarmament** prior to Roosevelt's first administration. In the **Five-Power Treaty,** signed at the **Washington Conference** in 1921 by the United States, Great Britain, France, Italy, and Japan, the nations agreed to limit their navies to 1921 levels and not to build any large warships for ten years and then only to replace ships that were twenty years old. Although this and other agreements signed at the Washington Conference appeared to create an atmosphere of mutual coopera-tion and desire for peace, no limitations were reached for the size of land forces or for building smaller warships and submarines.

- When Japan overran **Manchuria** and set up **Manchukuo,** Secre-tary of State **Henry L. Stimson** urged President Hoover to issue economic sanctions against Japan. Hoover did not believe that the Japanese were any threat to the United States and refused. He did agree to allow Stimson to issue the **Stimson Doctrine,** which stated that the United States would not recognize any territorial changes or treaties brought about in violation of American rights or by force. The occupation of Manchuria violated the **Nine-Power Treaty,** and, therefore, the United States would not recognize Japan's right to the territory. Other nations did not support the Doctrine, and it did not deter the Japanese.

- The **London Naval Conference** of 1931 extended the ban on shipbuilding until 1936 and included smaller ships in the ban. The **World Disarmament Conference** in 1932 accomplished nothing. Faced with the rise of Nazism and the aggression of Japan, it appeared that disarmament's time had passed.

Review Strategy

This "Fast Fact" relates to the Good Neighbor Policy.

- Roosevelt's articulation of the **Good Neighbor Policy** in 1933 was an effort to enlist the nations of the Western Hemisphere as Allies should war come. The policy was meant to erase the long-standing history of intervention in the affairs of Latin American nations by the United States. The change had begun under Warren Harding and was solidified in the **Clark Memorandum** of Calvin Coolidge's administration. At the **Montevideo Conference,** the United States stated unequivocally that no nation had the right to intervene in the affairs of another state in the Western Hemisphere. In 1936, Roosevelt himself attended the **Inter-American Conference** in **Buenos Aires** to rally support for that part of the **Monroe Doctrine** that pledged nations to resist attacks from abroad. The Roosevelt Corollary was in effect repudiated.

Review Strategy

This "Fast Fact" relates to neutrality legislation.

- Influenced by the **Nye Report** that laid the entrance of the United States into World War I on manipulation by international bankers and arms makers, Congress passed a series of **Neutrality Acts** beginning in 1935. Among other things, the Acts forbade the United States from selling or shipping arms to nations declared in a state of war and banned loans to belligerents. The president could also declare an embargo on arms and ammunition or require a belligerent to pay cash for these goods and transport them on their own ships. Critics of these laws pointed out that the laws did not distinguish between friendly nations and enemy nations. Advocates of the laws believed that the affairs of Europe and the Pacific did not constitute a danger to the security of the United States as long as the nation remained neutral. They also believed that if the **profit motive** for entering into a war was removed, there would be less manipulation of the public interest.

Review Strategy

These "Fast Facts" relate to appeasement and aggression.

- In an effort to avert war in Europe, the leaders of France and Great Britain followed a policy of **appeasement** toward Hitler and **Mussolini**. The climax of French and British concessions was the agreement signed at the **Munich Conference** to allow Hitler to take the part of Czechoslovakia that had a large German population. In exchange, Hitler agreed that he would not interfere with Czechoslovakian sovereignty again. Within six months, he had seized the rest of the nation.

- Talk of neutrality, isolationism, and appeasement was taking place against a backdrop of aggression by what would soon become the **Axis Powers,** Germany, Italy, and Japan.

GERMANY	ITALY	JAPAN
• **Prewar aggression:** Austria, Czechoslovakia, Rhineland • **Wartime invasions:** Poland, Denmark, Norway, Luxembourg, Belgium, Netherlands, France	• **Prewar aggression:** Albania, Ethiopia • **Wartime invasions:** France	• **Prewar aggression:** Manchuria, northern China, most of China's coastal areas • **Wartime invasions:** Indo-China, Guam, Wake Island, Thailand, Singapore, Malaya, Philippine Islands

Review Strategy

These "Fast Facts" relate to United States efforts to aid Great Britain.

- Although Roosevelt declared the neutrality of the United States when Britain and France declared war on Germany and Italy, he wanted to help the Western European nations. He found two ways to do this: the **destroyer deal** and **Lend-Lease.** In exchange for fifty vintage World War I destroyers, the United States received the right to build a string of air and naval bases in British territory in the Western Hemisphere. In the latter deal, the United States would lend Great Britain war matériel rather than the money to buy it. While there was little opposition to the destroyer deal, isolationists considered Lend-Lease a way to pull the United States into war, but they lost their fight against the bill. The program provided some $50 billion worth of supplies to Great Britain and helped to mobilize U.S. industry for war production.

- The **Atlantic Charter,** signed by Roosevelt and **Winston Churchill,** provided a statement of Anglo-American war aims: (1) no extension of territory by either nation, (2) territorial self-determination, (3) the destruction of Nazism, and (4) the establishment of an international organization to promote world peace. The two also promised the **Four Freedoms:** freedom from war, fear, and want and freedom of the seas.

Review Strategy

This "Fast Fact" relates to the Japanese attack on Pearl Harbor.

- The attack on **Pearl Harbor** came after months of trying to find a diplomatic solution to differences between the two nations. Japan would not provide assurances that it would end its aggression in Asia, and in that event, the United States would not promise not to go to war against Japan. When the Japanese overran Indo-China, Roosevelt stopped almost all trade with Japan, including the sale of petroleum, which a resource-poor Japan depended on. The Japanese had expected some small retaliatory action from the United States, but they did not expect anything so forceful, provocative, or damaging to them as ending oil shipments. Japanese military leaders began to prepare for war against the United States. Diplomatic talks continued as a cover for these preparations. The U.S. army had cracked the Japanese code, so the government knew a Japanese attack would come somewhere in the Pacific once diplomatic talks broke down, but it did not know where or when until Japanese bombers roared in over Pearl Harbor on December 7, 1941.

KEY PEOPLE

- **Cordell Hull, secretary of state**
- **General Hideki Tojo**
- **Allies**

KEY TERMS/IDEAS

Review Strategy

See if you can relate these terms and ideas to their correct context in the "Fast Facts" section.

- **blitzkrieg**
- **collective security**
- **Kellogg-Briand Pact, renounced "war as an instrument of national policy"**
- **London Economic Conference, Roosevelt's "bombshell" message, economic nationalism, isolationists' approval**
- **Neutrality Act of 1939, "unrestricted submarine warfare"**
- ***Panay* incident**
- **phony war**
- **Quarantine Speech, major break with isolationists**
- **Russo-German Pact, nonaggression pact**
- **Spanish Civil War, General Franco, fascism**
- **Tripartite Pact**
- **Washington Conference, additional agreements, Four-Power Treaty, Nine-Power Treaty**

SECTION 6. WORLD WAR II

Once war was declared, the United States had to **mobilize.** The army had some 1.6 million men in uniform, and the government instituted a **draft,** eventually registering all men between eighteen and forty-five. Women were allowed to volunteer in special women's branches of the armed forces. African Americans, Hispanics, Native Americans, and Japanese enlisted or were drafted. African Americans in the navy often found themselves relegated to jobs as cooks and stewards. In the army, African Americans were assigned to segregated units. Some six million women took jobs in industry to fill the positions that men gave up to serve in the armed forces.

FAST FACTS

- Shortly after the declaration of war, about 100,000 Japanese Americans, some two thirds of whom had been born in the United States, were evacuated from their homes in California and **interned** in camps in Wyoming, Arizona, and Colorado. Some Americans, including members of the War Department, feared that these Japanese Americans would aid Japan in an invasion of the mainland, so they wanted the Japanese Americans removed from strategic areas. Later, it came to light that some of the Californians pressing for internment had economic motives in wanting the Japanese Americans removed.

- Managing the nation's economic resources came under the authority of the **War Production Board.** It was responsible for mobilizing industry to retool assembly lines to produce war matériel rather than consumer goods. The war was paid for through tax increases and the sale of **war bonds.** As a result, the national debt rose sixfold from 1940 to 1949.

- The war was fought on two fronts, **Europe/North Africa** and the **Pacific.** There was concern that Great Britain might fall if the Germans defeated the Soviet Union and took the Suez Canal. The Allies, therefore, adopted a strategy to defeat Germany and its ally Italy before turning to the Japanese in the Pacific. Short-term goals to accomplish this strategy were (1) control of the sea lanes to keep war matériel moving to Europe, (2) effective use of the Allies' superior air power, and (3) supplying Soviet forces to fight the Nazi assault on the Eastern front.

- Between summer 1942 and May 1943, the Allies had forced the Afrika Korps to surrender, thus ending the war in North Africa. By winter 1941–1942, the Soviets had stopped the German advance into Russia and were on the counterattack. In July 1943, the Allies invaded Italy. On June 6, 1944, the Allies began **Operation Overlord,** their major offensive in Europe. The timing of this invasion had been an area of contention with Stalin since the beginning of the war. Within eleven months, Paris was liberated, U.S. troops fought their way into Germany, Soviet troops continued their advance westward, Hitler committed suicide, and the war in Europe ended on May 7, 1945.

- The Allies developed a two-pronged strategy to defeat the Japanese in the Pacific. **General Douglas MacArthur** would **"leap-frog"**

islands, fighting for control of important islands and going around others on a course from New Guinea to the Philippines. **Admiral Chester Nimitz** would drive through the Central Pacific toward Japan. By 1945, U.S. bombing raids were battering the home islands.

- Allied military experts believed that it could be another year before Japan was conquered, and the fighting could take the lives of another 1 million U.S. troops. At this point, Japan was divided between a civilian government, supported by Emperor **Hirohito,** that was willing to make peace, and the military, which wanted to continue fighting. Through the Soviets, the civilian government offered to end the war but would not accept **unconditional surrender.** When nothing came of the feelers, President Truman ordered the use of the **atomic bomb.** On August 6, 1945, a U.S. plane dropped an atomic bomb on **Hiroshima.** Three days later, in the face of the Japanese government's continuing refusal to surrender, the United States dropped an atomic bomb on **Nagasaki.** The USSR entered the war as promised. Japan surrendered.

Review Strategy

These "Fast Facts" and chart relate to wartime diplomacy.

- While Roosevelt, and to a lesser extent Churchill, believed that the time had come to adopt Wilson's idea for an international organization to ensure the sovereignty of all nations, Stalin had other ideas. However, in order to gain time and war matériel for the Eastern front, Stalin went along with the planning for a **United Nations.** This future organization, the more immediate concerns of European governance after the war, and the conduct of the war itself were the topics of a series of conferences during World War II. The divisions of the **Cold War** could already be seen in the decisions made by the **Big Three.**

CONFERENCE	PURPOSES
Moscow Conference of Foreign Ministers, October 1943 (Great Britain, USSR, United States)	• Agreed to an invasion of France in 1944 • Discussed the future of Poland but reached no agreement • Set up a committee to draft policy for postwar Germany • Agreed to set up an international peace-keeping organization
Teheran, November 1943 (Churchill, Stalin, Roosevelt)	• Agreed on timing of D-Day to coincide with Russian offensive • Renewed promise from Stalin that USSR would join war in Asia after the defeat of Germany • Agreed in vague terms to giving USSR some concessions in Asia for joining the war against Japan • Discussed structure of international peace-keeping organization

CONFERENCE	PURPOSES
Bretton Woods, July 1944 (Forty-four nations represented)	Set up **International Monetary Fund**
Dumbarton Oaks, August–October 1944 (Representatives of China, Great Britain, USSR, United States)	Drafted plans for United Nations, including a **Security Council** as the seat of permanent peace-keeping responsibilities
Yalta, February 1945 (Churchill, Stalin, Roosevelt)	• Agreed to divide Germany into **four military zones of occupation** (France would administer the fourth zone) • Agreed to **free elections** in Poland "as soon as possible" but also agreed to accept the Soviet-dominated **Lublin Committee** as the interim government • Agreed to "broadly representative" interim governments throughout Europe (Communist-backed governments in the areas the Soviets controlled) • Worked out voting procedures in the proposed United Nations for the sixteen Soviet territories • Agreed to call a conference in San Francisco on April 25, 1945, to write a charter for the new international organization **"Secret Agreements"** In exchange for entering the war against Japan and signing a treaty of friendship and alliance with China, Stalin asked for and received: • Recognition of the independence of the Mongolian People's Republic under Soviet protection • Possession of the Kurile Islands, part of Sakhalin Island, an occupation zone in Korea, and rights in Manchuria
Potsdam, July–August 1945 (Churchill replaced by the new Prime Minister, Clement Atlee; Stalin; Truman)	• Agreed to policies for the occupation and administration of Germany, including disarmament, "denazification," democratization, and payment of reparations • Issued **Potsdam Declaration,** demanding Japan's unconditional surrender

• When the "secret agreements" were made known after Roosevelt's death, many critics faulted Roosevelt and Churchill for abandoning Poland, East Germany, the rest of Eastern Europe, and **Nationalist China** to communism. In truth, Soviet forces already occupied **Eastern Europe.** Short of another war, there was little that the Western powers could do to force Stalin to live up to his promises in Europe. In February 1945, the United States and Great Britain were still fighting the war in the Pacific, and British and U.S. troops had not yet entered Germany.

- As World War II ended, the United States found itself in a new role as a world power. Between World Wars I and II, the United States had adopted a policy of **isolationism.** That was no longer possible. As soon as the common enemies were vanquished, the rifts in the wartime alliances began to show. To maintain its own security, the nation had to decide how to (1) safeguard its security and national interests against powerful unfriendly nations; (2) help protect the sovereignty of nations in Europe, Latin America, and Asia without provoking hostile reactions from them or from the **Communist bloc**; (3) establish ties to the newly independent nations of Asia and Africa; and (4) balance the cost of domestic programs with defense needs.

KEY PEOPLE

Review Strategy

See if you can relate these people to their correct context in the "Fast Facts" section.

- **A. Philip Randolph, Brotherhood of Sleeping Car Porters; March on Washington, 1941, Executive Order 8802, Committee on Fair Employment Practices**

- **Kamikaze**

- **Navajo codebreakers**

- **Nisei**

- **Tuskegee Airmen**

KEY TERMS/IDEAS

Review Strategy

See if you can relate these terms and ideas to their correct context in the "Fast Facts" section.

- **Axis**

- **bracero program**

- **Holocaust, concentration camps, anti-Semitism**

- **price controls, rationing, shortages**

- **United Nations Charter, General Assembly, veto power**

- **United Nations Relief and Rehabilitation Administration (UNRRA), relief for Europe and Asia after World War II**

- **Universal Declaration of Human Rights**

- **Zoot suit riots, Mexicans, Mexican Americans**

SECTION 7. TRUMAN AND THE BEGINNING OF THE COLD WAR

The major domestic issues **Harry S Truman** faced after the war were **demobilization** and **reconversion.** Carrying out policies was made more difficult because Truman was faced with a Congress controlled by a conservative coalition of Northern Republicans and Southern Democrats.

FAST FACTS

Review Strategy

This "Fast Fact" relates to demobilization.

- Some 12.5 million members of the armed forces needed to be returned to civilian life, and industries needed to be retooled to produce consumer goods. During the war, 6 million women had entered the labor force in defense industries. Many of these women still needed to work or wanted to continue working, but they often found themselves out of a job, replaced by a returning veteran. However, the trend of women working outside the home has continued since World War II.

Review Strategy

These "Fast Facts" relate to reconversion.

- During the war, the unions had made few wage demands on employers. Once the war was over and the pent-up demand for consumer goods could be satisfied by the items rolling off assembly lines, workers began to demand higher wages. When their demands were not met, a series of strikes in the steel and auto industries occurred in 1945–1946. When the **United Mine Workers** under **John L. Lewis** threatened a strike, Truman seized the mines. He then seized the railroads when railway workers threatened to strike. In the end, workers in both industries won most of their demands.

- Although Truman appeared to be tough on unions with these actions, he vetoed the **Taft-Hartley Act,** which (1) outlawed the **closed shop,** (2) provided **cooling-off periods** before a strike could be called, (3) gave the president the power to ask for an **injunction** to prevent a strike that could be dangerous to the health or safety of the nation, (4) forbade union practices considered unfair (**jurisdictional strikes,** refusal to bargain in good faith, union contributions to political campaigns), and (5) required unions to file annual financial reports. The Act also provided direct benefits to employers by allowing employers (1) to present their side during organizing drives, (2) to ask the **National Labor Relations Board (NLRB)** for elections to determine bargaining agents, and (3) to sue unions for breach of contract. The conservative coalition in Congress passed the bill over Truman's veto, but the Act did not damage unions as badly as had been feared. The Act did, however, cement union support for Truman.

- A liberal Democrat, Truman had come to see the problems that the nation's racism created not only at home but also in dealing with the newly emerging nations of Asia and Africa. He also understood the changing demographics of the nation. As African Americans moved from the South to the North and West, they provided a large bloc of voters that was already sympathetic to the Democratic Party of Roosevelt. Truman set up a series of committees and used their reports to ask Congress (1) to establish a permanent civil rights commission; (2) to set up a permanent **Fair Employment Practices Commission;** (3) to end segregation in schools, transportation, and public accommodations; and (4) to make lynching a federal crime. The conservative coalition in Congress blocked Truman's proposals.

- In the election of 1948, party bosses in Northern and Western states were able to add a strong **civil rights plank** to the Democratic platform. They expected that Truman would lose, but they hoped the civil rights plank would persuade African Americans to vote for lesser Democratic candidates. Truman campaigned hard on this plank, and African Americans responded by reelecting him and electing many other Democrats. Truman then began to fulfill his campaign promise. Although blocked in Congress, Truman used other avenues to promote civil rights, including directing federal agencies to end segregation and to award no federal contracts to businesses that discriminated in employment. He also issued **Executive Order 9981** to end segregation in the armed forces.

- In foreign affairs, Truman adopted the policy of **containment.** According to this idea, the Soviet Union and its **satellites,** if left alone, would change and possibly collapse from internal economic and political pressures. The **free world** only had to keep the Soviet Union from expanding.

- This policy of containment was the basis for the **Truman Doctrine.** When Great Britain announced it could no longer provide economic and military aid to Greece and Turkey to fight Communist takeovers, Truman asked Congress for $400 million in aid. Mindful of the fine line between support and interference, he did not ask for military intervention, stating, "I believe that it must be the policy of the United States to support free people who are resisting attempted subjugation by armed minorities or by outside pressures." Without aid, Greece and Turkey would most probably have fallen to the Communists, and the Soviet Union could then have dominated the eastern Mediterranean.

- Secretary of State **George Marshall** proposed a program that came to be known as the **Marshall Plan** to help European nations rebuild after the war. The Soviet Union and its satellites rejected the offer, but Western European nations agreed to draft a common recovery plan. The Plan met heated resistance in Congress. Opponents claimed it (1) would end any possibility of working with the Soviet Union, (2) would reestablish the United States as an imperialist power, (3) would bankrupt the nation, (4) could be a waste of money or could set up European nations as competitors for American markets, and (5) should be aimed at Asia, not Europe. **Senator Arthur Vandenberg,** a Republican, rose to the defense of the Plan and argued that it was in the nation's self-interest to ensure that Europe did not fall to communism. The Plan was approved.

- In an effort to sabotage the creation of a financially strong, independent, and democratic West Germany, the Soviets manufactured the **Berlin Crisis.** Access to the Western occupation zones of Berlin was through Soviet territory, and there was a written agreement from the Soviets that the path would remain open. However, in June 1948, the Soviets closed the land routes intending either to force the French, British, and Americans to make concessions or to give the Soviets all of Berlin. Instead, the Western Powers decided to institute a massive **airlift** of supplies into Berlin. The Soviets were correct in assuming that the Western Powers did not wish to go to war, but neither did they intend to give up Berlin or their efforts to support a rehabilitated West Germany. The Western Powers believed that the stability of Europe depended on their standing up to the Soviets at this first challenge. The blockade was lifted in 1949.

- Once World War II was over, civil war broke out in China between the **Nationalist Chinese,** led by **Chiang Kai-shek,** and the Communists, or **Kuomintang,** led by **Mao Zedong.** In 1949, the Nationalists fled to **Taiwan** and established what they contended was the government of China, while Mao proclaimed the **People's Republic of China (PRC)** on the mainland. The United States continued to support Chiang and in 1950 broke off diplomatic and trading ties with the PRC.

Review Strategy

These "Fast Facts" relate to the Korean War.

- After World War II, **Korea** was partitioned. In 1948, the United States oversaw free elections in South Korea and pulled out its troops once the new government was installed. Also in 1948, the Soviets installed their own Communist government in North Korea and pulled out. In 1950, North Koreans overran the **38th parallel,** the dividing line between the two nations, and invaded the South. The Soviet Union was boycotting the Security Council because of the United Nations' refusal to admit the PRC, so the Council was able to approve sending UN troops to support the South Koreans. Ninety percent of the troops and support personnel were from the United States. Commanding the forces was U.S. General Douglas MacArthur.

- The fighting moved back and forth, with the North Koreans winning ground and then the South Koreans driving them back. MacArthur was ordered to destroy the North Korean armed forces but not to move into China or the Soviet Union. The UN forces began to move north across the 38th parallel. Within a month, the Chinese had eight divisions in North Korea and began to move south again. MacArthur never agreed with the concept of a **"limited war,"** and publicly disagreed with the president. When Truman removed him from command, MacArthur returned to the United States to plead his case before Congress for total victory, even if that meant war with China. The Joint Chiefs of Staff warned Congress of the danger of war in Asia, and MacArthur's support collapsed. Negotiations to end the war began in mid-1951 and were at a standstill when Eisenhower became president. Stalin died shortly thereafter, and the North Koreans became more flexible in their demands. An armed truce went into effect, and the fighting ended without a peace treaty.

KEY PEOPLE

- **Dixiecrats, "Solid South"**
- **George Kennan, containment**

KEY TERMS/IDEAS

Review Strategy

See if you can relate these terms and ideas to their correct context in the "Fast Facts" section.

- **Arab-Israeli War, Palestinian refugee camps**
- **baby boom**
- **Fair Deal, domestic policies**
- **Four Point Program, technical assistance, capital investment, poor nations of the world**
- **Full Employment Act, Council of Economic Advisers**
- **G.I. Bill of Rights, Servicemen's Readjustment Act**
- **Iron Curtain, cold war**
- **North Atlantic Treaty Organization (NATO), mutual defense pact; did not require immediate declaration of war by all signatories if one attacked, concession for U.S. ratification**

SECTION 8. THE EISENHOWER YEARS

A hero of World War II, **Dwight D. Eisenhower** was drafted in 1952 by the Republican Party to run for president. A conservative in domestic affairs, he had liberal views in world affairs. Although a believer in the free enterprise system and an opponent of enlarging the role of the federal government, Eisenhower made no attempt to undo any of the New Deal legislation.

FAST FACTS

Review Strategy

This "Fast Fact" relates to McCarthyism.

- When Eisenhower took office, **Senator Joseph McCarthy** was still hard at work investigating subversives and **fellow travelers** in the government. McCarthy, a Republican from Wisconsin, had achieved notoriety when he claimed he could identify the country's top spy. When a Senate investigation into his allegations proved them to be groundless, he went after Senator Millard Tydings, a conservative Democrat and the committee chair of the investigation, in his reelection bid. With outside money, McCarthy was able to engineer Tydings' defeat as well as that of another senator who had bucked him. Suddenly, McCarthy had supporters throughout the Republican Party. Eisenhower was incensed at McCarthy's accusations that former General George Marshall was **"soft on communism,"** but counseled patience, believing that McCarthy would eventually "hang himself." The **Army-McCarthy hearings** proved to be his undoing. The Senate **censured** him, and **McCarthyism** gradually subsided.

Review Strategy

These "Fast Facts" relate to civil rights.

Review Strategy

See Section 9, pp. 265–68 for civil rights' activities during Johnson's terms in office.

- During the 1952 campaign, Eisenhower espoused the civil rights ideas of liberal Republicans. Once in office, he began to make changes such as desegregating schools on military bases. In 1956, he sent a civil rights bill to Congress, and although it passed the House, conservative Southern Democrats rejected it in the Senate. Eisenhower tried again in 1957, and this time advocates managed to win approval with the support of **Lyndon Johnson,** the majority leader and Democratic senator from Texas. The **Civil Rights Act of 1957,** the first federal civil rights legislation since 1875, (1) established a permanent Civil Rights Commission, (2) appointed an Assistant Attorney General for civil rights in the Justice Department, and (3) authorized the federal government to issue injunctions in cases where citizens had been denied the right to vote. Little came of the law. The **Civil Rights Act of 1960** was meant to expand voting rights' protection for African Americans by setting up a procedure of findings and referees to add African Americans to voting rolls, but little came of this law either.

Review Strategy

See Chapter 6 for more on Brown v. Board of Education.

Review Strategy

These "Fast Facts" relate to foreign policy.

Review Strategy

See pp. 268-69 for Vietnam.

Review Strategy

See Section 9, p. 268, for information on the Bay of Pigs invasion.

Review Strategy

This "Fast Fact" relates to U.S. society at mid-century.

- One notable Supreme Court ruling was the decision in ***Brown v Board of Education of Topeka, Kansas***. The Supreme Court overturned the **"separate but equal"** decision in ***Plessy v. Ferguson.***

- Eisenhower chose **John Foster Dulles** as his secretary of state. Dulles took a hard line against communism, and his policy became known as **brinkmanship.** His rhetoric called for **massive retaliation** against the Soviets. While Dulles may not have believed in containment and limited war, his conduct of foreign affairs was not much different from that of the Truman administration, except that under the Eisenhower administration, the arsenal of nuclear weapons increased.

- In the 1950s, the United States found itself filling the vacuum in the Middle East created by Great Britain's departure. After the **Suez crisis,** Eisenhower issued what became known as the **Eisenhower Doctrine.** It promised economic and military aid to countries of the Middle East. It also promised that the United States would consider intervening with military force if the sovereignty of any nation was endangered by Communist forces.

- When **Fidel Castro** came to power in **Cuba** in 1959, the U.S. government guardedly hoped that he would launch democratic reforms and rejuvenate the Cuban economy. Instead, he (1) held a series of circus-like trials of former associates of **Fulgencio Batista**, (2) nationalized foreign-owned industries and properties without compensating the owners, (3) mounted an anti-American campaign, (4) signed a series of aid agreements with the Soviet Union, and (5) supported revolutionary activities in several Latin American nations. The United States finally cut all diplomatic and trade relations with Cuba.

- Another **Berlin crisis** occurred between November 1958 and May 1959 when **Nikita Khrushchev** offered the Western powers two alternatives for the future of Berlin. Eisenhower responded that the United States would not agree to any change in the status of Berlin dictated by the Soviets. The United States would stand by its obligations under the **NATO treaty.** It appeared as though the two nations were prepared to go to war. However, the deadline passed without any comment from Khrushchev, and the crisis was over.

- A major social phenomenon of mid-century America was the growth of the **suburbs.** This was made possible by the expansion of the **highway system** under Eisenhower and the proliferation of **tract housing** such as **Levittown, New York,** the first planned suburban development after World War II. The nation was enjoying great prosperity as a result of (1) its natural resources, (2) its educated workforce, (3) its efficiently managed industries, (4) its expanded transportation system, (5) the application of advances in science and technology to industry, and (6) the productivity of its agricultural sector. With a high level of productivity came lower unemployment and higher wages, which led to the development of a **consumer culture.**

KEY PEOPLE

- **Beat Generation**
- **Alger Hiss, Julius and Ethel Rosenberg, witch hunts, Communist Control Act**

KEY TERMS/IDEAS

Review Strategy

See if you can relate these terms and ideas to their correct context in the "Fast Facts" section.

- **arms race, long-range ballistic missiles, nuclear warheads**
- **Hungarian freedom fighters**
- **Nixon's "goodwill tour" of Latin America**
- **Organization of American States, Guatemala, United Fruit Company**
- **Southeast Asia Treaty Organization (SEATO)**
- **space race, *Sputnik,* National Aeronautics and Space Administration (NASA), *Explorer,* Mercury Project, astronauts**
- **U-2 spy plane incident**

SECTION 9. THE KENNEDY/JOHNSON YEARS

John Kennedy became the first Roman Catholic and the youngest man ever elected president. In a very tight race, he defeated **Richard Nixon,** the incumbent vice president. Kennedy's administration became known as the **New Frontier.** He sought domestically to continue the kinds of new programs and reforms that Roosevelt had created in the **New Deal.** Conservative Southern Democrats and conservative Northern Republicans blocked or watered down many of Kennedy's proposals. Some, like **Medicare,** were approved after his **assassination** through the efforts of the new president, **Lyndon Johnson.**

FAST FACTS

Review Strategy

These "Fast Facts" relate to domestic policy.

- When Kennedy assumed office, the nation was mired in a recession. Kennedy requested passage of the **Area Redevelopment Act** to provide grants and loans to communities with chronic economic problems and funding to retrain the unemployed. With this and similar measures, the economy revived but began a downturn again in 1962. Kennedy then sought tax cuts and tax credits in an effort to stimulate the economy. His requests were bogged down in Congress. After Kennedy's assassination, Johnson, using the powers of persuasion and negotiating skills he had honed as **Senate majority leader,** was able to win passage of a **tax cut** bill that promised $11 billion in personal and corporate tax relief to boost spending.

- Johnson's own domestic program was called the **Great Society.** Major legislation included the (1) **Economic Opportunity Act** that launched the **"war on poverty,"** (2) **Medicare,** (3) **Medicaid,** and (4) the **Elementary and Secondary Education Act of 1965.** In time, the escalating **Vietnam War** drained Johnson's energy and strained the national budget. The trade-off symbolized by the phrase **"guns or butter"** became a reality. To push a tax cut through Congress to ease the growing **federal deficit,** Johnson slashed the funding for social programs and effectively ended the "war on poverty."

Review Strategy

These "Fast Facts" and two charts relate to civil rights.

- One of the most far-reaching of Johnson's acts was his issuance of an executive order in 1964 stating that all contractors working on federal projects "take **affirmative action**" to ensure that they did not discriminate in hiring or promoting members of minority groups. This order was meant to enforce the provisions of the **Civil Rights Act of 1964** for federal projects. The concept became institutionalized when President Nixon set specific goals, or quotas, for federally financed construction projects.

Review Strategy

See Chapter 6 for more information on the Warren Court and important Supreme Court decisions.

- During these years, a number of significant pieces of legislation were passed and Supreme Court decisions handed down that expanded civil rights and civil liberties.

LEGISLATION/RULING	SIGNIFICANCE
Civil Rights Act, 1964	• Prohibits discrimination in public accommodations • Authorizes the U.S. Attorney General to intervene on behalf of victims of discrimination • Forbids employers and unions to discriminate against minorities • Enables the federal government to withhold funding from projects in which discrimination exists • Forbids the use of different standards for whites and African Americans applying to register to vote
Twenty-Fourth Amendment	Outlaws the use of a poll tax or any tax to keep African Americans from voting in federal elections
Voting Rights Act, 1965	Allows the federal government to register voters in localities where literacy tests and similar restrictions were in effect as of November 1, 1964, and where less than half the eligible voters had registered and voted in the 1964 federal election (most of the South)
Gideon v. *Wainwright*	Establishes the right of the accused to be represented by counsel
Heart of Atlanta v. *United States*	Upholds the use of the commerce clause as the basis for civil rights legislation
Wesbery v. *Sanders*	Ends pattern of overrepresentation of rural districts and underrepresentation of cities in legislatures; **"one man, one vote"**
Miranda v. *Arizona*	Establishes the right of the accused to be "read his rights;" **Miranda Rule**

• The most prominent civil rights' activist of the late 1950s and 1960s was the **Reverend Martin Luther King, Jr.** The head of the **Southern Christian Leadership Conference (SCLC),** he preached **nonviolence** and led a series of demonstrations and marches to protest racial discrimination until his assassination in 1968. Similar in approach was the **Congress of Racial Equality (CORE),** founded by **James Farmer.** The **Student Nonviolent Coordinating Committee (SNCC)** began with similar objectives and tactics but changed under the leadership of **Stokely Carmichael,** who championed **Black Power.** This caused a split between the SNCC and more mainline organizations like the SCLC and the **NAACP.** Carmichael defined Black Power as a call to African Americans "to unite, to recognize their heritage, to build a sense of community."

Peterson's AP Success: U.S. History

- The following were major civil rights' activities of the 1950s and 1960s:

ACTIVITY	SIGNIFICANCE
Montgomery bus boycott, 1955	• Protested segregation in public buses; lasted more than a year; Supreme Court found bus segregation unconstitutional • Launched Martin Luther King, Jr., as most prominent member of the **Civil Rights Movement**
Desegregation of **Little Rock High School, Arkansas**, 1957	• Governor Orval Faubus blocked enforcement of ***Brown v. Board of Education*** by calling out the Arkansas National Guard to stop students. • Eisenhower took over National Guard and ordered admission of black students.
Greensboro, North Carolina, Sit-in	• A group of integrated college students take over a lunch counter at Woolworth's and request service, which is denied. • Sit-ins spread across the South to protest segregation in public accommodations.
Freedom rides, 1961	• Groups of students rode interstate carriers to protest segregation on interstate buses and in bus terminals. • President Kennedy ordered federal marshals to accompany riders into the **Deep South.** • Federal government issued tougher regulations against segregation on interstate transit.
March on Washington, 1963	Some 250,000 Americans—black and white—marched in Washington to protest segregation. Pressed Congress to pass the civil rights bill that President Kennedy sent Congress.
Freedom Summer, 1964	• Four civil rights organizations join were to lead a **voter registration drive** in the South. • Three volunteers were murdered, and seven **Ku Klux Klan** members were tried and convicted.

- The 1960s also saw the emergence of a civil rights movement among Mexican Americans or **Chicanos/Chicanas.** Led by **César Chávez** and **Dolores Huerta,** Mexican farm workers formed the **National Farm Workers Association (NFWA)** and organized a nationwide boycott of table grapes.

- The **women's movement** emerged in the mid-1960s, seeking equal pay for equal opportunity. A major impetus was the book *The Feminine Mystique* by **Betty Friedan.** The **National Organization for Women (NOW),** founded in 1966, worked for passage of the **Equal Rights Amendment (ERA),** but the amendment was never ratified by the required number of states. Some opponents feared that it would cause women to lose some of the protection they already had under existing laws. Conservatives equated the law with everything from federal funding for abortion to unisex toilets.

Review Strategy

These "Fast Facts" relate to Cuba.

- Shortly after taking office, Kennedy was confronted with the dilemma regarding continued support for an invasion of Cuba by 1,500 **anti-Castro Cubans.** The **Central Intelligence Agency (CIA),** with Eisenhower's approval, had begun the project. Kennedy decided to provide weapons and ships to transport the exiles but no military support. The CIA and the **Cuban exiles** expected Cubans to take up arms and oust Castro, but the insurrection never materialized, and all the exiles were killed or captured. The United States took a great deal of criticism from around the world, especially from Latin American nations, for what became known as the **Bay of Pigs** invasion.

- Kennedy dealt more successfully with the **Cuban Missile Crisis.** The **Soviet Union,** an ally of Castro, had secretly constructed missile sites in Cuba, some 90 miles from the U.S. mainland. Kennedy ordered the U.S. navy to throw up a **blockade** around the island and turn back Soviet ships steaming toward Cuba with missiles to arm the sites. After a week, **Nikita Khrushchev,** the Soviet premier, ordered the ships to return to the USSR without delivering the missiles.

Review Strategy

These "Fast Facts" relate to the Vietnam War.

Review Strategy

See Section 10, pp. 270-71, for the end of the Vietnam War.

- After World War II, France reluctantly gave up its claim to **Vietnam,** and the nation was divided into North and South Vietnam, with Communists in power in the North. **Ngo Dinh Diem** refused to hold free elections in the South in 1956 for fear that the Communists would win. When his regime did not topple but seemed instead to be gaining strength, the Communist **Viet Cong** began a guerrilla campaign to take the South. Eisenhower and then Kennedy, believing in the **domino theory,** sent military advisers to help the government of South Vietnam. Under Kennedy, the United States engineered the ouster of the Diem family and the installation of a civilian as the head of the government. Power would change several more times before the war was over. While the well-organized and highly disciplined Viet Cong were finding support in the countryside, the government in Saigon seemed unable to achieve stability.

- Johnson manufactured the crisis that allowed him to ask Congress to approve the **Gulf of Tonkin resolution.** (The **War Powers Resolution,** passed in 1973, was in direct response to the use of presidential powers in the Vietnam War.) Also believing in the domino theory, Johnson ordered an **escalation** of the war by bombing North Vietnam and sending more U.S. ground troops. Underestimating the resolve of **Ho Chi Minh** and the Communists, Johnson expected this show of force and determination on the part of the United States to compel the Viet Cong to sue for peace within the year. However, the Communists had their own theory that they could outwait the Americans, who would tire of the war and the dissension at home.

- The number of U.S. troops in Vietnam continued to grow and, with it, **antiwar protests** in the United States. These mirrored the dissension and confusion in Congress with **hawks** against **doves.** Ultimately, the escalating war in Vietnam cost Johnson both his Great Society programs and his presidency. Faced with challenges by both antiwar Senators **Eugene McCarthy** and **Robert F. Kennedy,** Johnson (1) ended bombing raids over most of North Vietnam, (2) refused to send any more troops, and (3) withdrew from the 1968 presidential election.

KEY PEOPLE

Review Strategy

See if you can relate these people to their correct context in the "Fast Facts" section.

- **Black Panthers**
- **Rachel Carson,** *Silent Spring*
- **Fannie Lou Hamer, Mississippi Freedom Democratic Party**
- **Malcolm X, Black Nationalism, Nation of Islam**
- **Michael Harrington,** *The Other America*
- **Ralph Nader,** *Unsafe at Any Speed*
- **Rosa Parks, Montgomery, NAACP "silent majority"**

KEY TERMS/IDEAS

Review Strategy

See if you can relate these terms and ideas to their correct context in the "Fast Facts" section.

- **Alliance for Progress, stop the spread of communism, Latin America**
- **American Indian Movement**
- **Berlin crisis, Berlin Wall**
- **Brown Power**
- **Communications Satellite Act, Telstar communications satellite system, private corporation**
- **counterculture, youth culture, antimaterialistic, utopian communes, "Never trust anyone over 30."**

- **Food for Peace**
  "Letter from a Birmingham Jail"
- **NASA: Mercury, Gemini, Apollo space programs**
- **Peace Corps**
- **reverse discrimination**
- **Tet offensive**
- **VISTA, OEO-sponsored**
- **Watts**
- **white backlash**

SECTION 10. THE NIXON YEARS

After his defeat in the 1960 presidential election by **John Kennedy, Richard Nixon** returned to California. When he lost his 1962 bid for the California governorship, he vowed to leave politics forever. However, within two years, Nixon was back on the political scene. He methodically restored his old party ties and won the Republican nomination for president in 1968. The Democrats nominated **Hubert Humphrey.** The presence of third party candidate **George Wallace** made the outcome uncertain, but Nixon won in a very close race. Had Wallace won a few more electoral votes, the election could have been thrown into the House. Then Nixon might have had to negotiate with Wallace for his votes, thus making him beholden to Wallace.

FAST FACTS

Review Strategy

These "Fast Facts" relate to foreign policy.

- With **Henry Kissinger** as his **National Security Adviser,** Nixon set about leaving his mark on world affairs. Impatient with the time involved and the maneuverings inherent in the regular diplomatic channels, Nixon and Kissinger carried on their own high-level negotiations without including the Secretary of State or other officials. The two men believed that the United States' reputation in world affairs had suffered as the Soviet Union had become more powerful. Rather than continue a foreign policy based on moral principles, the United States needed to consider the realities of power and develop policies on a pragmatic basis.

- Nixon, with Kissinger's aid, embarked on finding a solution to the Vietnam War. He announced his **Vietnamization** policy while carrying on a series of negotiating sessions with the North Vietnamese. The talks continued throughout 1970 and 1971, while U.S. troops were withdrawn from Vietnam. On February 27, 1973, after massive bombing of the North, North and South Vietnam and the United States signed a **cease-fire agreement.** A month later the last U.S. troops were gone. The South Vietnamese hung on for another year, but in 1975, the government collapsed, and the North Vietnamese proclaimed a single unified nation. Cambodia and Laos also fell to Communist-backed governments.

- Once a strong supporter of **Nationalist China (Taiwan),** Nixon made an overture to the **People's Republic of China** to establish friendly relations. The United States had severed all diplomatic and trading ties with mainland China after the PRC was established in 1949. Nixon visited the mainland, and both nations agreed to a policy of **peaceful coexistence.** Additional results were (1) resumption of trade, (2) accepting agreement by the United States that Taiwan was part of China, (3) withdrawal of U.S. troops from Taiwan, but (4) continuation of U.S. diplomatic and trade relations with Taiwan.

- Pursuing a policy known as **détente,** Nixon eased tensions with the Soviet Union. As early as 1969, the two nations had signed a **nuclear nonproliferation treaty.** The Soviet Union was interested in relaxing tensions with the United States to strengthen its own position against the PRC and to buy U.S. wheat to ease its food shortages caused by poor harvests. Nixon visited Russia, and signed the first round of the **Strategic Arms Limitation** treaties **(SALT I),** limiting the spread of antiballistic missiles, and agreed to cooperate in health research, space exploration, trade, and pollution control.

Review Strategy

These "Fast Facts" relate to domestic policy.

- In domestic policies, Nixon launched the **New Federalism,** aimed at reducing big government and returning more power to state and local governments. His major tool was **revenue sharing,** which returned to states and municipalities some of the revenue from income taxes. This was in lieu of the federal government's paying directly for programs. A significant provision of revenue sharing was that programs receiving the funds could not engage in racial or ethnic discrimination.

Review Strategy

See Chapter 6 for the landmark decision of the Burger Court, Roe v. Wade.

- Nixon had the opportunity to change the nature of the Supreme Court while president. When Chief Justice **Earl Warren** retired, Nixon nominated **strict constructionist Warren E. Burger** to replace him. Nixon's next two nominees were rejected as unfit, but Nixon ultimately replaced three additional justices, thus turning the court from **judicial activism** to a more conservative reading of the law.

Review Strategy

These "Fast Facts" relate to Watergate.

- Nixon was brought down by the **Watergate Scandal.** It began early in the 1972 election with an attempt to bug Democratic National Headquarters in the Watergate office complex. Surprised in the act, the seven "burglars" were arrested, tried, and convicted. The trail led back to the **Republican campaign committee to reelect Nixon.** Top administration officials began to resign as the details of a **cover-up** unfolded. It was learned that Nixon had routinely taped conversations in the Oval Office, and a court fight ensued over the tapes. When transcripts of some of the tapes were made public, it appeared certain that Nixon had participated in the cover-up. Impeachment proceedings began in the House, and the **House Judiciary Committee** voted to send three **articles of impeachment** to the House for formal debate. The articles accused the president of (1) obstructing justice in the Watergate cover-up, (2) abusing presidential power, and (3) attempting to block the impeachment process by withholding evidence. Tapes played during the debate showed that Nixon approved the cover-up six days after the burglary. Nixon then admitted publicly that he had known about the cover-up, but he said that it did not merit impeachment. With urging by Republican Party leaders in Congress, Nixon resigned.

- In addition to the cover-up, Nixon had been found to have evaded taxes, used tax information against political "enemies," and bugged the telephones of some members of Congress and the press. The attempt to wiretap Democratic Party headquarters was an attempt to subvert the electoral process.

Key People

Review Strategy

See if you can relate these people to their correct context in the "Fast Facts" section.

- **Archibald Cox, special prosecutor, "Saturday Night Massacre"**
- **John Dean, President's counsel, testimony on taping of the Oval Office**
- **Sam Ervin, senator, Ervin Committee**
- **Leon Jaworski, special prosecutor**
- **John Sirica, judge**

KEY TERMS/IDEAS

Review Strategy

See if you can relate these terms and ideas to their correct context in the "Fast Facts" section.

- *University of California* v. *Bakke,* **affirmative action** "Christmas bombing"
- **Ellsberg break-in**
- **Kent State, National Guard, incursion into Cambodia**
- **shuttle diplomacy**
- **"peace with honor," extrication of United States from Vietnam**
- **superpowers**
- **"Two China" policy**
- **wage and price controls**

SECTION 11. THE UNITED STATES SINCE 1974

A major phenomenon of the late 1970s and 1980s was the emergence of the **New Right.** Members of the movement believe that **liberalism** is responsible for much of the nation's current social problems. According to them, liberals have taken over the federal government, corporations, the banking system, the media, and labor unions and are wielding their power to make and enforce policies that weaken the moral and social fabric of the nation as well as its political and economic well-being. The election of Ronald Reagan to the presidency in 1980 and 1984 was brought about in large part by a coalition of the New Right and **fundamentalist groups** with whom he shared certain views, such as reversing the right to abortion and enacting legislation that would allow **school prayer.**

FAST FACTS

Review Strategy

This "Fast Fact" relates to the Ford/Rockefeller term.

- Among the important facts to remember about the **Gerald Ford/ Nelson Rockefeller** administration are:
    - Gerald Ford and Nelson Rockefeller are the only two un-elected president and vice president to serve in those offices. Ford was nominated to replace Nixon's vice president, **Spiro Agnew,** and when Nixon resigned, Ford became president and nominated Nelson Rockefeller as vice president.
    - Ford granted Nixon an **unconditional pardon** for all crimes he may have committed while in office. When Ford explained this would save the nation the agony of a trial, critics pro-

tested. It would be a number of years before Nixon began the process of rehabilitating his reputation.

- The relations between Ford and the Democratic–controlled Congress were tense from the beginning but worsened over differences in how to fight the **recession.** While Ford's concerns were inflation and dependence on foreign oil, Congress worried about unemployment and the low level of **GDP** (then **GNP**).

- Ford continued the policy of **détente,** signed the **Helsinki Accords,** and watched helplessly while Congress refused to aid Cambodia and South Vietnam, both of which fell to Communist-led insurgents.

Review Strategy

This "Fast Fact" relates to the Carter/Mondale term.

- Among the important facts to remember about the **Jimmy Carter/ Walter Mondale** administration are:

  - Faced with rising oil prices as a result of actions by the **Organization of Petroleum Exporting Companies (OPEC)** and a genuine concern about Americans' consumption of oil, a nonrenewable resource, Carter declared an **energy crisis** and tried to enlist Americans in a **"moral war"** against energy consumption. His approach failed with the public and with Congress when he asked for a tax on oil imports and the authority to impose gasoline rationing.

  - Rising energy prices brought on **double-digit inflation**. When the **Federal Reserve Board** raised interest rates to curb inflation, a recession resulted. Unemployment and prices continued to rise during Carter's Presidency.

  - A major foreign policy coup was the **Camp David Accords** that brought peace between Egypt and Israel. The two nations agreed to (1) the establishment of diplomatic relations, (2) a phased withdrawal of Israeli forces from the Egyptian Sinai, and (3) further discussions to resolve the question of Palestinian self-rule.

  - A major problem was the **Iranian hostage crisis.** The United States had supported the Shah of Iran during his thirty-eight–year reign. Forced to flee after a year of increasingly violent antigovernment demonstrations, the Shah sought refuge in the United States for cancer treatment, and Carter agreed. In retaliation, a mob of Iranians stormed the U.S. Embassy in Teheran and took 63 American employees hostage. A series of negotiations and an attempted military rescue failed. After agreeing to accept $8 billion dollars in Iranian assets that had been frozen in the United States, the Iranian government released the hostages some thirty minutes after Carter left office in January 1981.

- Other important elements of Carter's foreign policy were (1) recognition of the People's Republic of China; (2) the signing of the **Strategic Arms Limitation Treaty (SALT II),** although the Senate did not ratify it; (3) an embargo on grain shipments to the USSR and a boycott of the Summer Olympics in Moscow in retaliation for the Soviet invasion of Afghanistan; and (4) treaties abolishing the **Panama Canal Zone** and turning over control of the area to Panama.

Review Strategy

This "Fast Fact" relates to the two terms of Reagan and Bush.

- Some of the major facts to remember about the two terms in office of **Ronald Reagan/George Bush** are:

  - Reagan's election in 1980 was significant because it showed the shift to **conservatism** among the nation's voters, including many blue-collar Democrats. It was the first election of a conservative to the presidency since Calvin Coolidge. Americans relating to Reagan's call for smaller government gave him a Republican-controlled Senate and so large a number of Republican representatives that Democrats retained only a slim margin in the House.

  - Faced with the continuing recession, Reagan called for tax reductions and spending cuts. He based his policies, called **Reaganomics,** on **supply-side economics.** Many people objected to his cuts in social programs like food stamps and Medicare. However, with the support of Southern Democrats, Reagan's measures were passed. An economic recovery began and unemployment dropped.

  - While advocating cuts in social programs, Reagan pushed for increases in the defense budget, especially for the development of a space-based antiballistic missile defense system, the **Strategic Defense Initiative (SDI, "Star Wars").** Democrats refused to agree to Reagan's cuts in social programs. Because of the cost of social programs coupled with Reagan's defense requests, the **federal budget deficit** mushroomed. Few social programs actually ended during Reagan's administration, and some, like Medicare, were actually strengthened and expanded.

  - In foreign affairs, Reagan signed the **Intermediate Nuclear Force (INF) Treaty** with the Soviet Union. He, however, opposed a **nuclear freeze.**

  - The **Iran-contra affair** was, to a degree, a result of Reagan's "hands-off" management style. **Sandinistas,** socialist revolutionaries, had overthrown the dictatorship in **Nicaragua** and set up a government. Reagan backed a second revolutionary group, the **Contras**, who opposed the Sandinistas. Members of Congress who disagreed with Reagan's policy passed a measure banning aid to the Contras. Several high-level members of Reagan's staff continued to supply the Contras with money. They sold weapons to so-called Iranian moderates to obtain the release of three hostages and used the profits for the Contras. (1) The arms sale violated U.S. policy. (2) The financial support to the Contras violated the Congressional ban. (3) Several administration officials were charged with conspiracy, fraud, lying, and withholding information.

Review Strategy

This "Fast Fact" relates to deregulation.

- During both the Carter and Reagan administrations, a number of industries were **deregulated** beginning with the airline industry in 1978 and including interstate bus companies and financial institutions. The trend continued into the 1990s with the telecommunication industry among others. The goals of deregulation were to (1) increase competition, (2) cut the costs associated with the enforcement of regulation, and thereby (3) decrease consumer prices.

Review Strategy

This "Fast Fact" relates to the Bush/Quayle term.

- The major achievements of the **George Bush/Dan Quayle** administration were in foreign affairs. Bush seemed to lack the experience or the skill to deal successfully with domestic issues. The wrangle over **"no new taxes"** and the ever-worsening federal deficit created the impression among voters that Bush's domestic programs had little direction. In the election of 1992, **Bill Clinton** combined his own appeal to the **Baby Boomers** with Bush's economic problems to win a close election.

  - The **Persian Gulf War** brought together a coalition of nations to oust Iraq from Kuwait. In **Operation Desert Storm,** they bombarded military installations in Iraq and in Kuwait. After six weeks, the international force began an invasion. While the Iraqi were forced from Kuwait, which was returned to its former status as an independent state, Saddam Hussein remained in power.

Review Strategy

These "Fast Facts" relate to ethnic groups.

  - Although more African Americans and Hispanics were elected to public office on the state and local levels, little headway was made on the national level. **Bilingual education** and **affirmative action** became major social and political issues of the 1980s and 1990s.

  - **Hispanics** became the fastest growing ethnic group in the United States in the late 1980s and 1990s. Most Hispanics are of **Mexican descent.**

- The **1986 Immigration Reform and Control Act** naturalized illegal aliens. The **1990 Immigration Act** revised past quotas and loosened restrictions for those with special employment skills.

KEY PEOPLE

- **Jesse Jackson, presidential bids**
- **Mikhail Gorbachev**
- **Menachem Begin, Anwar Sadat**

KEY TERMS/IDEAS

Review Strategy

See if you can relate these terms and ideas to their correct context in the "Fast Facts" section.

- **El Salvador, human rights, civil war**
- **end of the Cold War, fall of the Berlin Wall**
- *glasnost, perestroika*
- **Gramm-Rudman Act, across-the-board federal spending cuts**
- **Grenada**
- **Carter: human-rights policy, national malaise**
- **War Powers Act, reassertion of Congressional power, backlash to Vietnam**

PRACTICE TEST 1

AP UNITED STATES HISTORY

On the front page of your test booklet, you will find some information about the test. Because you have studied this book, none of it should be new to you, and much of it is similar to other standardized tests you have taken.

The page will tell you that the following exam will take 3 hours and 5 minutes—55 minutes for the multiple-choice section and 2 hours and 10 minutes for the three essays. Fifteen minutes of the time for Section II is a mandatory reading period, primarily for the DBQ. There are two booklets for this exam, one for the multiple-choice section and one for the essays.

The page in your test booklet will also say that SECTION I

- is 55 minutes.

- has 80 questions.

- counts for 50 percent of your total grade.

Then you will find a sentence in capital letters telling you not to open your exam booklet until the monitor tells you to open it.

Other instructions will tell you to be careful when you fill in the ovals on the answer sheet. Fill in each oval completely. If you erase an answer, erase it completely. If you skip a question, be sure to skip the answer oval for it. You will not receive any credit for work done in the test booklet, but you may use it for making notes.

You will not only find a paragraph about the guessing penalty—a deduction of one-quarter point for every wrong answer—but also words of advice about guessing if you know something about the question and can eliminate several of the answers.

The final paragraph will remind you to work effectively and to pace yourself. You are told that not everyone will be able to answer all the questions and it is preferable to skip questions that are difficult and come back to them if you have time.

SECTION I

Time—55 minutes
80 questions

Directions: Each question or incomplete statement is followed by five suggested responses. Choose the best answer and fill in the correct oval on the answer sheet.

---

1. All of the following were part of James I's charter to the Virginia Company EXCEPT

    (A) to bring Christianity and civilization to the native people

    (B) to build a commonwealth based on God's word

    (C) to explore for precious metals

    (D) to trade with the native people

    (E) to find a Northwest Passage

2. The only Native Americans who were able to unite and become strong enough to resist the English colonists successfully were the

    (A) Powhatan Confederacy

    (B) Seminoles

    (C) Iroquois League

    (D) Pequots

    (E) Wampanoag

3. The revenue from which of the following acts was to be used to pay the salaries of royal governors, thus negating the power of the purse?

    (A) Tea Act

    (B) Stamp Act

    (C) Sugar Act

    (D) Currency Act

    (E) Townshend Acts

4. The major achievement of the government under the Articles of Confederation was

    (A) defeat of the Whiskey Rebellion

    (B) levying of the nation's first protective tariff

    (C) establishment of the procedure for settling the Northwest Territory

    (D) the negotiation of the treaty with Spain giving the United States the right of deposit at New Orleans

    (E) removal of the Native American threat in the Ohio Valley

5. Passage of the Twelfth Amendment was a direct result of

    (A) the controversy that arose when the election of 1824 was settled in the House of Representatives

    (B) the difficulties that resulted from not having separate presidential and vice presidential elections in the electoral college in the election of 1800

    (C) the revolution of 1800

    (D) the one-man, one-vote system of the electoral college

    (E) the loss of the 1888 presidential election by Grover Cleveland to Benjamin Henry Harrison

6. The issue of protective tariffs led to fierce debate in Andrew Jackson's administration over

   (A) internal improvements

   (B) Indian removal

   (C) states' rights

   (D) popular sovereignty

   (E) specie circular

7. The Kansas-Nebraska Act nullified part of the

   (A) Compromise of 1850

   (B) Great Compromise

   (C) Wilmot Proviso

   (D) Missouri Compromise

   (E) Dred Scott decision

8. The primary issue in Reconstruction about which Lincoln and Congress disagreed was

   (A) Lincoln's veto of the Wade-Davis bill

   (B) Congress's division of the South into five military districts

   (C) Congress's refusal to honor Lincoln's promise of "forty acres and a mule"

   (D) Lincoln's recognition of state governments without Congressional approval

   (E) Lincoln's assertion that Reconstruction was part of the war effort and, therefore, his responsibility as commander in chief

Question 9 refers to the following photograph.

9. All of the following are most likely true about the people in this photograph EXCEPT

   (A) the workers exemplify the doctrine of Social Darwinism

   (B) the workers are recent immigrants

   (C) the workers are doing piecework

   (D) the workers are nonunion

   (E) the workers are working in a sweatshop

10. Which of the following statements about the labor market in the second half of the nineteenth century is not true?

   (A) Union strikes and boycotts were considered "conspiracies in restraint of trade."

   (B) The national labor market was highly competitive because of the movement of people from farms to cities and the influx of immigrants.

   (C) The AFL effectively recruited and organized immigrants.

   (D) A series of economic depressions drove wages down.

   (E) Installment of new machines sometimes resulted in technological unemployment.

11. In the 1950s, all of the following resulted in long-term social changes EXCEPT

   (A) the development of rock and roll

   (B) the development of suburbia

   (C) *Brown* v. *Board of Education of Topeka*

   (D) shift from permissiveness to more traditional child-rearing practices

   (E) the baby boom

12. All of the following were elements of the "war on poverty" EXCEPT

   (A) Voting Rights Act of 1965

   (B) Office of Economic Opportunity

   (C) Medicare

   (D) Elementary and Secondary School Act

   (E) Volunteers in Service to America (VISTA)

13. The primary reason the British government was interested in chartering Georgia was to

   (A) earn profits for its proprietors who were friends of the king

   (B) provide a buffer between South Carolina and Spanish Florida

   (C) establish a colony for the poor who were imprisoned for debt

   (D) establish a colony of small farms rather than slave-run plantations

   (E) experiment with rice agriculture

14. Which of the following colonies was self-governing?

   (A) Maryland

   (B) Pennsylvania

   (C) Rhode Island

   (D) Georgia

   (E) New York

15. All of the following were elements of U.S. foreign relations with Great Britain in the first half of the nineteenth century EXCEPT

   (A) Rush-Bagot Agreement

   (B) War of 1812

   (C) settlement of the boundary dispute over Oregon

   (D) purchase of Alaska

   (E) Webster-Ashburton Treaty

16. The Monroe Doctrine was issued

   (A) to protect U.S. business interests in Latin America

   (B) to warn that the United States would not tolerate any attempt by European nations to intervene in affairs of their former colonies in the Western Hemisphere

   (C) to assert that the United States had the right to ensure that acceptable governments were in power in nations of the Western Hemisphere

   (D) as part of the recall of troops from Nicaragua and Haiti

   (E) to forestall a similar declaration by France

17. Which of the following best describes the purpose of the Freedmen's Bureau?

   (A) to oversee the distribution of land and supplies to former slaves

   (B) to help freed slaves adjust to their new lives

   (C) to sign up former slaves to run for public office

   (D) to feed, clothe, and educate former slaves

   (E) to assist former slaves in finding work and to negotiate fair terms

18. "The working class and the employing class have nothing in common. There can be no peace so long as hunger and want are found among millions of working people and the few, who make up the employing class, have all good things in life."
The above quotation is most likely from the constitution of the

(A) Greenback Party

(B) Knights of Labor

(C) The Grange

(D) Industrial Workers of the World

(E) CIO

19. The U.S. Senate did not ratify the Treaty of Versailles principally because

(A) Wilson agreed to the end of the Ottoman Empire in the Middle East

(B) Wilson waffled but then agreed to require Germany to repay the Allies for their costs in fighting the war

(C) Wilson insisted that the League of Nations be part of the peace treaty

(D) Wilson would not agree to the division of Austria-Hungary

(E) of Wilson's intemperate remarks about the "narrow, selfish, provincial purposes" of his critics in Congress

20. The Harlem Renaissance can best be described as a period in which

(A) a wide audience was exposed to jazz

(B) white as well as black audiences became interested in African-American literature, art, and music

(C) the concept of the "New Negro" underlay African-American cultural works

(D) poets and novelists wrote about black pride and black protest

(E) African-American painters and sculptors exhibited their works to appreciative audiences

21. "If you are scared to go to the brink, you are lost" reflects the foreign policy of

(A) President Dwight D. Eisenhower

(B) President John F. Kennedy

(C) John Foster Dulles, Secretary of State

(D) Madeline Albright, Secretary of State

(E) Neville Chamberlain, British Prime Minister

22. Jimmy Carter won the 1976 election for all of the following reasons EXCEPT

(A) his ability to put together a coalition of the industrial Northeast and the South

(B) his strategy of campaigning as an outsider

(C) the Watergate scandal

(D) his promise to balance the budget

(E) his promise to lower inflation by raising employment

23. The Proclamation of 1763 contributed to growing tension between the colonies and Great Britain because the Proclamation

(A) forbade settlers from moving into the land west of the Appalachians until treaties could be signed with the Native Americans

(B) set the boundary between Canada and Maine, Vermont, and New York

(C) outlawed land speculation in the trans-Appalachians but not the purchase of land by settlers

(D) declared martial law on the western frontier of the thirteen colonies

(E) established the presence of a standing British army in the colonies

24. All of the following were true of the Declaration of Independence EXCEPT

(A) the Declaration was based on the philosophy of the Enlightenment

(B) all references to George III's part in the slave trade were deleted in the final version

(C) by declaring independence the new nation established that the rules of war had to be observed and thus protected its soldiers

(D) the Declaration listed various ways in which George III had taken away the rights of the colonists

(E) the Declaration established the organization of the new nation

25. "What good man would prefer a country covered with forests and ranged by a few thousand savages to our extensive Republic, studded with cities, towns, and prosperous farms embellished with all the improvements which art can devise or industry execute, occupied by more than 12,000,000 happy people. . ."
The above statement would most likely have been written in support of

(A) Confederate secession

(B) *Cherokee Nation* v. *The State of Georgia*

(C) the Indian Removal Act of 1830

(D) establishment of the Indian Territory

(E) a request for Oklahoma statehood

26. All of the following contributed to the growth of U.S. industry between 1800 and 1850 EXCEPT

(A) the availability of a large pool of immigrant labor

(B) the introduction of the factory system

(C) the introduction of the cotton gin

(D) a series of protective tariffs

(E) passage of federal internal improvement bills

27. Great Britain came to the brink of entering the Civil War in support of the Confederacy as a direct result of

(A) the Union's seizure of two Confederate representatives from the British ship *Trent*

(B) John Slidell's mission to gain French support for the Confederacy

(C) the Union's blockade of Southern ports that closed off the supply of cotton to English mills

(D) the Emancipation Proclamation

(E) the Union's refusal to lower tariffs

28. The Grange movement did all of the following EXCEPT

(A) successfully lobby for passage of laws in several states that set maximum railroad passenger and freight rates

(B) win *Munn* v. *Illinois*

(C) support *laissez-faire* capitalism

(D) organize businesses such as mills, banks, and grain elevators

(E) admit women on an equal basis with men

29. All of the following contributed to the Great Depression EXCEPT

(A) buying stocks on margin

(B) consumer installment buying

(C) underconsumption of goods

(D) underproduction of goods

(E) United States insistence on collecting its war debts

30. " . . . We whose names are underwritten, . . . having undertaken, for the glory of country, a voyage to plant the first colony in the Northern parts of Virginia, do . . . solemnly and mutually in the presence of God, and one of another, covenant and combine ourselves together into a civil body politic . . . ; and by virtue hereof to enact, constitute, and frame such just and equal laws, ordinances, acts, and constitutions, and offices, from time to time, as shall be thought most meet and convenient for the general good of the Colony. . . ."
The above statement was most probably written by the founders of

(A) Massachusetts Bay

(B) Maryland

(C) Plymouth Colony

(D) Pennsylvania

(E) Georgia

31. The major stumbling block between the colonies and Great Britain was

(A) King George's refusal to believe the colonists were loyal subjects

(B) Parliament's insistence on the theory of virtual representation

(C) the Boston Tea Party

(D) the Townshend Acts

(E) the Proclamation of Rebellion

32. The American System favored all of the following EXCEPT

(A) development of U.S. industrial capacity

(B) relaxation of the quota system for immigrants

(C) lessening of sectional divisions

(D) a charter for the Second Bank

(E) a protective tariff

Questions 33 and 34 refer to the following map.

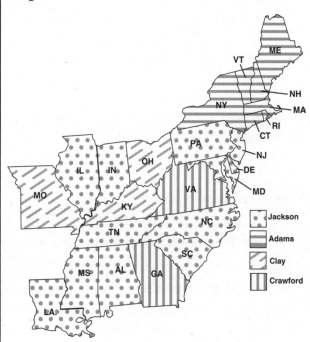

33. In the election of 1824, which two candidates won the Western states?

(A) Adams and Jackson

(B) Clay and Crawford

(C) Adams and Clay

(D) Clay and Jackson

(E) Crawford and Jackson

34. In which region of the country was Adams the strongest?

(A) Western

(B) Southern

(C) New England

(D) Middle Atlantic

(E) frontier

35. The election of 1824 was decided in the House of Representatives because

(A) of the corrupt bargain

(B) Jackson did not have a majority of the popular vote

(C) each state has only one vote in the electoral college

(D) Jackson did not have a majority of the electoral vote

(E) the Twelfth Amendment had not yet been ratified

36. Andrew Johnson vetoed the Civil Rights Act of 1866 because he believed

(A) its provisions were already covered in the Fourteenth Amendment

(B) it violated states' rights

(C) it should have included women's rights

(D) it would be unnecessary once Reconstruction went into effect

(E) it was not strong enough to counteract the black codes

37. In 1904, the Supreme Court ruled that which of the following was a "combination in restraint of trade"?

(A) Sherman Antitrust Act

(B) AFL

(C) Grange Movement

(D) Standard Oil Company

(E) Northern Securities Company

38. The most significant result of the Bonus Army March was

(A) the passage in 1936 of a law allowing World War I veterans to cash in their certificates nine years early

(B) the show of support veterans received from the active army

(C) the image it created of Hoover's apparent disregard for human suffering

(D) the additional money the Reconstruction Finance Corporation gave to state governments for relief efforts

(E) the demolition of the veterans' Hooverville

39. All of the following are characteristic of the 1960s EXCEPT

(A) failure to make progress in eliminating racial inequalities

(B) conservative backlash against civil rights and antiwar demonstrators

(C) "war on poverty"

(D) inability to balance the cost of social programs and the war in Vietnam

(E) deepening government commitment to an unpopular war in Vietnam

40. Passage of the Alliance for Progress program was in response to

(A) requests by Cuban exiles

(B) the threat of Soviet missiles in Cuba

(C) the appeal of the Communist government of Fidel Castro to other Latin American nations

(D) the presence of Peace Corps volunteers in Latin America

(E) OAS intervention in the Dominican Republic

41. The significance of the Annapolis Convention lay in

(A) its agreement on uniform trade regulations for the new states

(B) its decision to send troops to end Shay's Rebellion

(C) its ratification of the Northwest Ordinance

(D) its decision to request another convention to discuss the weaknesses of the Articles of Confederation

(E) its nomination of George Washington for president

42. All of the following are true about the Cherokee EXCEPT

(A) the Cherokee adopted farming and converted to Christianity

(B) the Cherokee had a written constitution and a form of government similar to that of the United States

(C) Jackson sided with the Cherokee against Georgia

(D) in *Worcester* v. *Georgia* the Supreme Court ruled in favor of the Cherokee

(E) the Cherokee supported the Confederacy in the Civil War

43. Reconstruction ended in the South as a direct result of

(A) the collapse of the remaining carpetbag governments in Florida, South Carolina, and Louisiana

(B) ratification of the Fifteenth Amendment

(C) increased activities of white supremacist groups

(D) Democrats' acceptance of Hayes as President in exchange for the withdrawal of troops from the South

(E) general Northern fatigue with the programs of the Radical Republicans

44. The Gilded Age can best be described as a period of

(A) intense political activity by the presidents

(B) political agitation by Western farmers

(C) labor unrest and combinations of businesses

(D) unbridled use of the spoils system and unregulated business competition

(E) *laissez-faire* attitude by government toward business

45. The significance of the Open Door Policy for the United States lay in its

(A) providing a use for the Philippines as a way station between China and the United States

(B) moving the American public away from isolationism and toward the view of the nation as a world power

(C) keeping Japan from annexing Formosa

(D) guarantees from leasehold nations that they would keep their Chinese ports open to all nations

(E) obtaining the right to build a railroad in China

46. "No race can prosper until it learns that there is as much dignity in tilling a field as in writing a poem. It is at the bottom of life we must begin, and not at the top."

The above statement reflects the philosophy of which of the following African Americans?

(A) Paul Laurence Dunbar

(B) W.E.B. Du Bois

(C) Langston Hughes

(D) Booker T. Washington

(E) Ralph Ellison

47. The term "conspicuous consumption" was used to describe the life of the upper classes in *The Theory of the Leisure Class* written by

(A) Eugene V. Debs

(B) Karl Marx

(C) Thorstein Veblen

(D) Mark Twain

(E) Henry George

48. Which of the following was not a result of Andrew Mellon's economic policies?

(A) Taxes took a disproportionate share of the wages of middle- and lower-class wage earners.

(B) The lack of places to invest large amounts of money contributed to an overheated stock market.

(C) The high tariff reduced markets for U.S. goods.

(D) A higher proportion of taxes was paid by the wealthy.

(E) Corporations and the rich accumulated large amounts of capital for investment.

49. In *Schechter Poultry Corp.* v. *United States,* the Supreme Court ruled that the Constitution gave Congress the power to control interstate but not intrastate commerce, thus finding which of the following unconstitutional?

(A) Glass–Steagall Act

(B) Rural Electrification Administration

(C) Tennessee Valley Authority

(D) Agricultural Adjustment Act

(E) National Industrial Recovery Act

50. Executive Order 9981 guaranteeing equal opportunity in the military was issued by

(A) General Douglas MacArthur

(B) Franklin Roosevelt

(C) Harry Truman

(D) Dwight Eisenhower

(E) Lyndon Johnson

51. An important work that contributed to the awareness of the need for the "war on poverty" was

(A) Michael Harrington's *The Other America*

(B) Rachel Carson's *Silent Spring*

(C) Ralph Nader's *Unsafe at Any Speed*

(D) Hinton Helper's *The Impending Crisis in the South*

(E) John Kenneth Galbraith's *The Affluent Society*

52. César Chávez used which of the following tactics in the National Farm Workers Association strike against grape owners in California?

(A) sit-down strike

(B) injunction

(C) huelga

(D) national consumer boycott of grapes

(E) jurisdictional strike

Questions 53 and 54 refer to the following charts.

State	Voting For	Voting Against
1. Delaware	30	0
2. Pennsylvania	46	23
3. New Jersey	38	0
4. Georgia	26	0
5. Connecticut	128	40
6. Massachusetts	187	168
7. Maryland	63	11
8. South Carolina	149	73
9. Rhode Island	34	32
10. New Hampshire	57	47
11. Virginia	89	79
12 New York	30	27
13. North Carolina	194	77

53. Which two states ratified the Constitution with the narrowest vote?

(A) New York and Pennsylvania

(B) Rhode Island and New Hampshire

(C) Virginia and New Hampshire

(D) New York and Rhode Island

(E) New Hampshire and New York

54. How many states were needed to ratify the Constitution in order for it to become law?

(A) seven

(B) all thirteen states

(C) nine

(D) the four most populous states

(E) three quarters of the states

55. All of the following were obstacles to ratification of the Constitution EXCEPT

(A) lack of a Bill of Rights

(B) the federal structure established by the Constitution that placed the national government over state government

(C) Rhode Island's boycott of the Constitutional Convention

(D) ratification by a special convention in each state rather than by the states' legislatures

(E) lack of leadership among Federalists

56. The reason that the Mexican government gave for restricting the settlement of Americans in Texas was

(A) the settlers had brought slaves with them in violation of Mexican law

(B) American settlers had attacked General Santa Anna's forces at the Alamo

(C) the U.S. government was agitating for control of East Texas

(D) Mexico was concerned that the settlers would demand independence

(E) Stephen Austin had protested the Mexican government's actions to collect customs duties on trade across the Texas–United States border

57. Organized labor would have supported which of the following demands in the "Omaha Platform" of the Populist Party in the 1892 election?

(A) an increase in currency resulting from the free and unlimited coinage of silver

(B) government ownership of railroads

(C) eight-hour workday

(D) graduated income tax

(E) direct election of Senators

58. At Yalta, Roosevelt, Churchill, and Stalin agreed to all of the following EXCEPT

(A) a combined United States–British invasion of France

(B) the holding of free elections in postwar Europe

(C) veto power for permanent members of the Security Council

(D) the Soviet Union's entrance into the war against Japan

(E) Stalin's supporting the Nationalist Chinese

59. The Truman Doctrine was issued in support of "free peoples who are resisting attempted subjugation by armed minorities or by outside pressure" in

(A) Turkey and Greece

(B) Poland and Hungary

(C) Albania and Yugoslavia

(D) East Germany

(E) Cyprus

60. What policy of the Federal Reserve Board to curb inflation in the late 1970s resulted in a severe business recession?

(A) The Fed "primed the pump."

(B) The Fed took no action.

(C) The Fed raised interest rates.

(D) It imposed a windfalls-profit tax.

(E) It discouraged borrowing.

61. Anglicanism was the established church in

(A) Pennsylvania

(B) Maryland

(C) Massachusetts Bay

(D) Connecticut

(E) Georgia

62. All of the following were provisions of the Constitution as originally ratified EXCEPT

(A) indirect election of Senators

(B) the counting of three-fifths of slaves for purposes of determining representation in the House

(C) abolition of the internal slave trade

(D) enumerated powers

(E) the elastic clause

63. Which of the following was not a cause of the War of 1812?

(A) Macon's Bill No. 2

(B) Westerners' interest in seizing Canada

(C) impressment of U.S. sailors

(D) United States attack on the *Chesapeake*

(E) British repeal of the Orders in Council

64. All of the following presidents acquired territory for the United States EXCEPT

(A) Andrew Jackson

(B) William McKinley

(C) James K. Polk

(D) James Monroe

(E) Andrew Johnson

65. The upturn in the economy around 1880 was significant because it

(A) put an end to lobbying for expansion of the currency system

(B) renewed pressure for free and unlimited coinage of silver

(C) resulted in passage of the Bland-Allison Act

(D) caused the decline of the Greenback Party

(E) demonetized silver

66. The most significant change in higher education at the end of the nineteenth century was

(A) the introduction of courses in the social and natural sciences

(B) the widespread introduction of the elective system

(C) the founding of colleges devoted to technical training

(D) the building of state university systems, often through the Morrill Act

(E) coeducation as a common practice in colleges and universities

67. "You come to us and tell us that the great cities are in favor of the gold standard. We reply that the great cities rest upon our broad and fertile plains. Burn down your cities and leave our farms, and your cities will spring up again as if by magic; but destroy our farms, and the grass will grow in the streets of every city in the country."
The above reflects the philosophy in the election of 1896 of a

(A) Silver Democrat

(B) Republican

(C) Gold Democrat

(D) Wall Street banker

(E) Greenback Party member

68. The most significant effect of "dollar diplomacy" was

(A) the Panama Canal

(B) intervention in domestic elections in Nicaragua

(C) suspicion and mistrust of the United States

(D) large profits for United States banks from Latin American investments

(E) the reduction of U.S. protective tariffs

69. The Zimmerman Note

(A) requested U.S. neutrality in World War I

(B) offered Canada an alliance

(C) announced that all vessels near Great Britain, France, and Italy would be sunk without warning by U-boats

(D) promised Mexico that in exchange for an alliance, it would return Texas, New Mexico, and Arizona at the end of the war

(E) revoked the Sussex Pledge

70. "To resist without bitterness; to be cursed and not reply" reflects the philosophy of

(A) Booker T. Washington in the Atlanta Compromise

(B) Malcolm X and the Black Muslims

(C) Stokely Carmichael and Black Power

(D) Martin Luther King and the Southern Leadership Conference

(E) W.E.B. Du Bois and the NAACP

71. The most significant result of the French and Indian War was that

(A) France gave Spain the Louisiana Territory in payment for its debts

(B) France lost its remaining territories in North America

(C) the Native Americans in the Ohio Valley lost their French allies

(D) the colonists learned to work together and realized the benefits of cooperation

(E) Pontiac's Rebellion

72. Which of the following was not true of the British position in the American Revolution?

(A) The war was unpopular in Great Britain.

(B) The hit-and-run tactics of the Americans made it difficult for the British to plan and execute their strategies.

(C) The British were well supplied by both their navy and by Loyalist farmers.

(D) Secure in their empire, the British were able to focus their resources and attention on the American Revolution.

(E) The British had a well-trained army led by professional soldiers.

73. The Webster-Hayne debate

(A) centered on the issue of slavery

(B) resulted in a rebuttal of the Freeport Doctrine

(C) shifted from discussing a limit on Western land sales to the protective tariff

(D) shifted from discussing a limit on Western land sales to states' rights and nullification

(E) was settled in a compromise by the Force Bill

74. The most significant fact about free African Americans in the North before the Civil War was

(A) custom rather than law kept whites and blacks separated

(B) African Americans could not attend public schools

(C) African Americans faced competition in the job market from European immigrants with fewer skills

(D) in most Northern states African Americans could not vote, serve on juries, or testify against a white person

(E) free African Americans were free and not free

75. The system of laws and customs in Southern states from the 1880s to the 1950s that segregated African Americans from whites is known as

(A) Jim Crow

(B) black codes

(C) *Plessy* v. *Ferguson*

(D) New South

(E) *de facto* segregation

Peterson's AP Success: U.S. History

76. "This perennial rebirth, this fluidity of American life, this expansion westward with its new opportunities, its continuous touch with the simplicity of primitive society, furnish the forces dominating American character. The true point of view in the history of this nation is not the Atlantic coast, it is the great West."
The above statement reflects the attitude of

(A) Charles Beard

(B) Frederick Jackson Turner

(C) James Fenimore Cooper

(D) Theodore Roosevelt

(E) George Catlin

77. *Living Well Is the Best Revenge* would be an appropriate title for a literary work of which of the following movements?

(A) romanticism

(B) Beat Generation

(C) realism

(D) Lost Generation

(E) nationalism

78. All of the following are true about the report of the Nye Committee EXCEPT

(A) it contributed to Congress's resolve to look at ways to limit U.S. economic aid to belligerents

(B) it fed isolationist fears

(C) it was a factor in the passage of the Neutrality Acts of 1935, 1936, and 1937

(D) it was a factor in Roosevelt's adoption of the Good Neighbor Policy

(E) it blamed U.S. entrance into World War I on U.S. bankers and weapons manufacturers

79. President Nixon resigned rather than face Articles of Impeachment accusing him of

(A) income tax evasion

(B) using income tax records against political enemies

(C) ordering a cover up of the break-in and attempt to wiretap Democratic National Party headquarters

(D) obstruction of justice, abuse of power, and refusal to supply subpoenaed information

(E) the use of campaign funds to buy the silence of the Watergate burglars

80. In *Bakke* v. *Regents of the University of California,* the Supreme Court ruled

(A) that affirmative action programs were unconstitutional

(B) that President Johnson had erred in issuing his executive order requiring those who received federal money to hire and promote members of minorities

(C) that while strict racial quotas were unconstitutional in determining admissions, race could be taken into consideration

(D) that bilingual education was not mandatory

(E) that the Civil Rights Act of 1964 prohibiting discrimination in hiring and firing, wages, and promotion based on sex, race, religion, or place of birth was constitutional

END OF SECTION I.

If you have time, you may go back and review your answers.

SECTION II
PART A
(Suggested writing time–45 minutes)

Directions: The following question asks you to write a cohesive essay incorporating your interpretation of Documents A to H and your knowledge of the period stated in the question. To earn a high score, you must cite key evidence from the documents and use your outside knowledge of United States history.

1. The United States became a major player in world affairs at the end of the nineteenth century. The majority supported American expansion as a national and moral imperative; others disagreed. Evaluate the validity of each position. Include long-term consequences of each point of view.

   Use the following documents and your knowledge of United States history from 1880 to 1900 to construct your essay.

Document A

Source: Josiah Strong, Secretary of the Home Missionary Society, *Our Country,* 1885

. . . It seems to me that God, with infinite wisdom and skill, is training the Anglo-Saxon race for an hour sure to come in the world's future. Heretofore there has always been in the history of the world a comparatively unoccupied land westward, into which the crowded countries of the East have poured their surplus populations. But the widening waves of migration, which millenniums ago rolled east and west from the valley of the Euphrates, meet today on our Pacific coast. There are no more new worlds. The unoccupied arable lands of the earth are limited, and will soon be taken. The time is coming when the pressure of population on the means of subsistence will be felt here as it is now felt in Europe and Asia. Then will the world enter upon a new stage of its history—*the final competition of races, for which the Anglo-Saxon is being schooled.* Long before the thousand millions are here, the mighty *centrifugal* tendency, inherent in this stock and strengthened in the United States, will assert itself. Then this race of unequaled energy, with all the majesty of numbers and the might of wealth behind it—the representative, let us hope, of the largest liberty, the purest Christianity, the highest civilization—having developed peculiarly aggressive traits calculated to impress its institutions upon mankind, will spread itself over the earth. If I read not amiss, this powerful race will move down upon Mexico, down upon Central and South America, out upon the islands of the sea, over upon Africa and beyond. And can any one doubt that the result of this competition of races will be the "survival of the fittest"?

Document B

Source: Senator Albert Beveridge, 1889

American factories are making more than the American people can use. American soil is producing more than they can consume. Fate has written our policy for us: the trade of the world must and shall be ours. . . . We will establish trading-posts throughout the world as distributing points for American products. We will cover the oceans with our merchant marine. Great colonies, . . . flying our flag and trading with us, will grow about our posts of trade. . . . American law, American order, American civilization, and the American flag will plant themselves on shores hitherto bloody and benighted. . . .

Document C

Source: Henry Cabot Lodge, "Our Blundering Foreign Policy," *Forum* magazine, 1895

The tendency of modern times is toward consolidation. It is apparent in capital and labor alike, and it is also true of nations. Small States are of the past and have no future. The modern movement is all toward the concentration of people and territory into great nations and large dominions. The great nations are rapidly absorbing for their future expansion and their present defence all the waste places of the earth. It is a movement which makes for civilization and the advancement of the race. As one of the great nations of the world, the United States must not fall out of the line of march.

Document D

Source: William McKinley's War Message to Congress, April 11, 1898

Yesterday, and since the preparation of the foregoing message, official information was received by me that the latest decree of the Queen Regent of Spain directs General Blanco, in order to prepare and facilitate peace, to proclaim a suspension of hostilities, the duration and details of which have not yet been communicated to me.

This fact, with every other pertinent consideration, will, I am sure, have your just and careful attention in the solemn deliberations upon which you are about to enter. If this measure attains a successful result, then our aspirations as a Christian, peace-loving people will be realized. If it fails, it will be only another justification for our contemplated action.

Document E

Source: Walter Hines Page, an editorial, "The War with Spain and After," *Atlantic Monthly,* 1898

. . . Are we, by virtue of our surroundings and institutions, become a different people from our ancestors, or are we yet the same race of Anglo-Saxons, whose restless energy in colonization, in conquest, in trade, in "the spread of civilization," has carried their speech into every part of the world, and planted, their habits everywhere?

Within a week such a question, which we had hitherto hardly thought seriously to ask during our whole national existence, has been put before us by the first foreign war that we have had since we became firmly established as a nation. Before we knew the meaning of foreign possessions in a world ever growing more jealous, we have found ourselves the captors of islands in both great oceans; and from our home-staying policy of yesterday we are brought face to face with world-wide forces in Asia as well as in Europe, which seem to be working, by the opening of the Orient, for one of the greatest changes in human history. Until a little while ago our latest war dispatches came from Appomattox. Now our latest dispatches (when this is written) come from Manila. The news from Appomattox concerned us only. The news from Manila sets every statesman and soldier in the world to thinking new thoughts about us, and to asking new questions. And to nobody has the change come more unexpectedly than to ourselves. Has it come without our knowing the meaning of it? The very swiftness of these events and the ease with which they have come to pass are matters for more serious thought than the unjust rule of Spain in Cuba, or than any tasks that have engaged us since we rose to commanding physical power.

Document F

Source: Carl Schurz, "The Policy of Imperialism," Liberty Tracts Number 4, 1899

We hold that the policy known as imperialism is hostile to liberty and tends toward militarism, an evil from which it has been our glory to be free. We regret that it has become necessary in the land of Washington and Lincoln to reaffirm that all men, of whatever race or color, are entitled to life, liberty, and the pursuit of happiness. We maintain that governments derive their just powers from the consent of the governed. We insist that the subjugation of any people is "criminal aggression" and open disloyalty to the distinctive principles of our government.

Document G

Source: From the Platform of the American Anti-Imperialist League, October 17, 1899

We propose to contribute to the defeat of any person or party that stands for the forcible subjugation of any people. We shall oppose for re-election [sic] all who in the white house [sic] or in congress [sic] betray American liberty in pursuit of un-American ends. We still hope that both of our great political parties will support and defend the declaration of independence in the closing campaign of the century.

We hold with Abraham Lincoln, that "no man is good enough to govern another man without that other's consent. When the white man governs himself, that is self-government, but when he governs himself and also governs another man, that is more than self-government—that is despotism. Our reliance is in the love of liberty which God has planted in us. Our defense is in the spirit which prizes liberty as the heritage of all men in all lands. Those who deny freedom to others deserve it not for themselves, and under a just God cannot long retain it."

We cordially invite the co-operation of all men and women who remain loyal to the declaration of independence and the constitution of the United States.

Document H

Source: Woodrow Wilson, Appeal for Neutrality, 1914

The people of the United States are drawn from many nations, and chiefly from the nations now at war. It is natural and inevitable that there should be the utmost variety of sympathy and desire among them with regard to the issues and circumstances of the conflict. Some will wish one nation, others another, to succeed in the momentous struggle. It will be easy to excite passion and difficult to allay it. Those responsible for exciting it will assume a heavy responsibility, responsibility for no less a thing than that the people of the United States, whose love of their country and whose loyalty to its Government should unite them as Americans all, bound in honor and affection to think first of her and her interests, may be divided in camps of hostile opinion, hot against each other, involved in the war itself in impulse and opinion if not in action.

Such divisions amongst us would be fatal to our peace of mind and might seriously stand in the way of the proper performance of our duty as the one great nation at peace, the one people holding itself ready to play a part of impartial mediation and speak the counsels of peace and accommodation, not as a partisan, but as a friend.

SECTION II
PARTS B AND C
(Suggested planning and writing time–70 minutes)

PART B

> **Directions:** You are to answer ONE question from this group. The suggested planning time is 5 minutes with 30 minutes to write. State a thesis, cite relevant evidence, and use logical, clear arguments to support your generalizations.

2. Many issues contributed to the development of the two earliest political parties, the Federalists and the Democratic-Republicans. Discuss how their views on foreign relations and national economic policy differed.

3. Beginning in 1763, colonists faced a series of conflicts that led to the break with Great Britain. Discuss these crises, stressing the role of each in the growth of the independence movement.

PART C

> **Directions:** You are to answer ONE question from this group. The suggested planning time is 5 minutes with 30 minutes to write. State a thesis, cite relevant evidence, and use logical, clear arguments to support your generalizations.

4. The history of each ethnic group in the United States is distinctive, and yet the struggles of diverse peoples to achieve freedom and equality exhibit common elements. Evaluate the accuracy of this statement by discussing the immigrant experience of two of the following:

- Jewish immigrants during the late nineteenth century

- Italian immigrants during the late nineteenth and early twentieth centuries

- Japanese immigrants during the late nineteenth and early twentieth centuries

Peterson's AP Success: U.S. History

5. Franklin Roosevelt's New Deal included strong measures. The effects of these strong programs were mostly positive. Defend this position.

 END OF TEST.

ANSWERS AND EXPLANATIONS

QUICK-SCORE ANSWERS

1. B	11. D	21. C	31. B	41. D	51. A	61. E	71. D
2. C	12. A	22. E	32. B	42. C	52. D	62. C	72. D
3. E	13. B	23. A	33. D	43. D	53. D	63. E	73. D
4. C	14. C	24. E	34. C	44. D	54. C	64. A	74. E
5. B	15. D	25. C	35. D	45. B	55. E	65. A	75. A
6. C	16. B	26. E	36. B	46. D	56. A	66. D	76. B
7. D	17. B	27. A	37. E	47. C	57. C	67. A	77. D
8. E	18. D	28. C	38. C	48. D	58. A	68. C	78. D
9. A	19. C	29. D	39. A	49. E	59. A	69. D	79. D
10. C	20. B	30. C	40. C	50. C	60. C	70. D	80. C

EXPLANATION OF ANSWERS

Test-Taking Strategy

For not/except *questions, ask yourself if the answer is true. If it is, cross it off and go on.*

1. **The correct answer is (B).** King James's charter included all the elements except choice (B). Although it was a commercial charter, it did include the stipulation to bring Christianity and civilization to the native people, choice (A), because religion was very much a part of seventeenth-century life. However, the concept of building a commonwealth based on the Bible was the founding principle of the Massachusetts Bay Colony, choice (B). The first colonists in Jamestown spent so much time looking for precious metals, choice (C), that the colony almost died out— "the starving time"—and had it not been for help from the Powhatan Confederacy, it would have collapsed. It was many years before Europeans gave up the idea of finding a way through the North American continent rather than around it to reach Asia, choice (E).

2. **The correct answer is (C).** Made up of five, and after 1722 six, nations (Mohawk, Oneida, Onondaga, Cayuga, Seneca, and later Tuscarora), the Iroquois were members of the Iroquoian linguistic group and were able to unite because of a common language, common traditions, and a common enemy. They were able to play one European enemy against another—the French against

the British—to get weapons and to maintain their lands for more than 150 years. The Powhatan Confederacy, choice (A), was also a political union of some 30 groups under the leadership of Powhatan, but English weapons proved too powerful, and after Powhatan's death, the confederacy was not able to resist the encroaching English settlers. *Seminole,* choice (B), was the name given to the coalition that developed in Florida of Creeks escaping from British settlers in Georgia, fugitive slaves from the Southern slave owners, and native Appalachee Indians. They fought two Seminole wars, one against Andrew Jackson from 1817 to 1818, and the second from 1835 to 1842 that resulted in their forced removal to Indian Territory. Both the Pequots, choice (D), and the Wampanoag, choice (E), had been decisively defeated by English colonists in New England by 1675 and lost their lands, the latter in a bloody war known as Metacom's War.

3. **The correct answer is (E).** The power of the purse was the only hold that the colonies had over the royal governors' actions. The purpose of choice (A) was to give the East India Company a monopoly on the tea trade in the colonies. The significance of choice (B) was that it placed a tax on goods made and sold in the colonies and, therefore, did not support mercantilism. The significance of choice (C) was in Great Britain's announcement that it would be strictly enforced; it meant that Great Britain was abandoning its policy of salutary neglect. Choice (D) tightened Great Britain's financial hold on the colonies by requiring that all taxes be paid in gold or silver and forbidding the colonies to print their own paper money.

Test-Taking Strategy

This is a question where chronology can help you eliminate some answers.

4. **The correct answer is (C).** The Whiskey Rebellion, choice (A), did not occur until Washington's first term in office (it was Shays' Rebellion under the government of the Articles). Pinckney's Treaty, choice (D), and the Treaty of Greenville, choice (E), also did not occur until Washington's administration. Choice (B) is incorrect because the central government under the Articles did not have the power to levy taxes.

5. **The correct answer is (B).** The election of 1800 was determined in the House because both Aaron Burr and Thomas Jefferson had the same number of electoral votes. Although Burr had run for the vice presidency, he wanted to be president, but because there was no separate election, there was no way to distinguish votes. The election of 1824 was decided in the House because no candidate for president had a majority of electoral votes, choice (A); the issue was different because the Twelfth Amendment had been ratified by 1804. Choice (C) is a term given to the peaceful change in the political party in power in

the election of 1800. Choice (D) is incorrect; each state's electoral vote is the sum of the number of its senators and members of the House. Choice (E) is the wrong time frame for the question.

6. **The correct answer is (C).** Choices (A), (B), (D), and (E) have nothing to do with protective tariffs. Choices (A) and (B) were issues during Jackson's administrations but do not involve the protective tariff (except indirectly as a source of revenue for government activities). Because the South did not want a high tariff for fear of damaging its profitable trade in cotton, Southerners in Congress opposed the tariff with the argument that states could nullify any federal law that they found to be unjust and unconstitutional.

7. **The correct answer is (D).** The Missouri Compromise, choice (D), had set the Northern boundary for slavery at 36° 30' and Kansas and Nebraska lay north of this line, thus nullifying the law. Choice (A) did not deal with Kansas and Nebraska, but did admit California as a free state; prohibit the slave trade in Washington, D.C.; propose a stricter Fugitive Slave Law; defer the discussion of slavery in Utah and New Mexico until they requested statehood; and agree to pay Texas to give up much of its western land to the federal government. Choice (B) refers to the compromise in the writing of the Constitution that resulted in two members from each state in the Senate and proportional representation in the House. Choice (C) is the proposal, never accepted, that would have banned slavery in any territory purchased as a result of the Mexican War. Choice (E) ruled that slave owners' rights to their property (slaves) was protected.

8. **The correct answer is (E).** Both choices (A) and (E) are correct, but Lincoln used the argument in choice (E) to justify his control of Reconstruction, preventing Congress's harsh stand. The Wade-Davis Bill was a Congressional plan for Reconstruction. Choice (B) occurred after Lincoln's death, as did choice (D)— Andrew Johnson recognized the Southern governments while Congress was in recess. Choice (C) is incorrect.

9. **The correct answer is (A).** Social Darwinism was a theory of the nineteenth century that sought to explain social inequalities by Darwin's theory of survival of the fittest. The workers in the photograph are most likely recent immigrants, doing piecework in a nonunion sweatshop, choices (B), (C), (D), and (E).

Test-Taking Strategy

The key word is primary. *Knowing the time frame will also help you eliminate some answer choices.*

Test-Taking Strategy

For a not/except *question, ask yourself if the answer is true. If it is, cross it off and go to the next answer.*

Peterson's AP Success: U.S. History

10. **The correct answer is (C).** The AFL was a craft union, and most immigrants were unskilled or semiskilled labor rather than craft workers. AFL's refusal to recruit unskilled and semiskilled workers led in 1935 to the establishment of the Congress of Industrial Organizations, made up of industrial unions rather than craft unions. Although choice (E) is true, it often meant that when one job was mechanized, another job opened up.

11. **The correct answer is (D).** Choice (D) is the opposite of what occurred. Parents turned away from traditional child-rearing practices and embraced permissiveness. The leading advocate of more liberal practices was Dr. Benjamin Spock, who wrote *Common Sense Book of Baby and Child Care.*

12. **The correct answer is (A).** Choice (A) had a political rather than economic purpose: to enforce the voting rights of all Americans, most notably African Americans. Choice (D) was part of the "war on poverty" because it gave federal aid to public and parochial schools to improve educational opportunities for all children, including the poorest and African Americans.

13. **The correct answer is (B).** Spanish Florida was a problem because Native Americans staged raids into South Carolina from there and slaves escaped into La Florida, as it was known. Having a population center closer to La Florida would make it easier to defend British interests. Although Choices (A), (C), and (D) were goals of the proprietors, they were not goals of the British government. Choice (E) is incorrect.

14. **The correct answer is (C).** Rhode Island and Connecticut were the only two self-governing colonies. Unlike Maryland, choice (A); Pennsylvania, choice (B); Georgia, choice (D); and, for a time, New York, choice (E); they were not governed by proprietors. They had been founded by dissenters from Massachusetts Bay, and each colony elected its own governor and representatives to the upper and lower legislative houses.

15. **The correct answer is (D).** The United States bought Alaska in 1867 from Russia for $7.2 million. Choice (A) agreed to the mutual disarmament of the Great Lakes by the United States and Canada. Choice (C) refers to the Treaty of 1846, and choice (E), to the settlement of the boundary between Maine and New Brunswick Province.

16. **The correct answer is (B).** For the time period, choice (A) is incorrect. Choice (C) relates to the Roosevelt Corollary issued by Theodore Roosevelt. Choice (D) refers to the Good Neighbor Policy of Franklin Roosevelt. Choice (E) is incorrect; Great Britain was interested in issuing a joint declaration with the United States, but Secretary of State John Quincy Adams convinced

President James Monroe to issue the statement in the name of the United States alone.

Test-Taking Strategy

The key words are purpose *and* best described.

17. **The correct answer is (B).** Choices (A), (B), (D), and (E) are all true, but choice (B) contains all the elements of the other three choices and thus is the best description of the purpose of the Freedmen's Bureau. Choice (C) is incorrect.

Test-Taking Strategy

Eliminating choices can lead you to an educated guess.

18. **The correct answer is (D).** Clues are the phrases *working class* and *employing class* and the aggressive tone of the quotation. Choice (A) was made up largely of farmers, so it can be eliminated. Choice (B) was a conservative labor union that believed in the use of arbitration rather than strikes, so it can be eliminated. Choice (C) was a cooperative farm organization and not a labor union. Choice (E) can be eliminated because the CIO was not organized until 1935, and this question fits between the 1860s and 1919. The Industrial Workers of the World (IWW) was organized by socialist radicals in 1905 and championed revolution rather than reform. Its slogan was "Workers of the World, Unite!"

19. **The correct answer is (C).** In order to win concessions from the Allies at the peace conference that would benefit American interests, Wilson agreed as stated in choices (A) and (B). He also agreed to the division of Austria-Hungary, so choice (D) is incorrect. Wilson made his remarks, choice (E), after thirty-nine senators and senators-elect signed a statement objecting to the League of Nations; his remarks undoubtedly did not help his side, but they did not cause the problem.

20. **The correct answer is (B).** Choices (A), (B), (C), (D), and (E) are all true about the Harlem Renaissance, but choice (B) incorporates all the elements of the other four. It includes the music—jazz, choice (A); the "New Negro," choice (B); the subject matter of poets and novelists, choice (D); and the interest in the arts, choice (E). In addition, it mentions the audience for the works of the Harlem Renaissance.

Test-Taking Strategy

Knowing the time frame will help you eliminate choices choices (D) and (E).

21. **The correct answer is (C).** John Foster Dulles is known for his "brinkmanship" foreign policy, his threat of "massive retaliation" against communism, and his articulation of the domino theory. If one nation in a region fell to communism, they all would. Eisenhower, choice (A), under whom Dulles served, was more cautious. Albright, choice (D), as secretary of state under Bill Clinton is in the wrong time frame. Chamberlain, choice (E), also in the wrong time frame, was the opposite of Dulles and is known for his appeasement policy toward Hitler. Choice (B) is incorrect.

Peterson's AP Success: U.S. History

22. **The correct answer is (E).** Carter became the first Southerner, choice (A), elected president since Zachary Taylor. Choice (E) is the correct answer because in a time of high inflation, Carter campaigned on a promise not to decrease inflation by allowing unemployment to increase. Choice (E) is also incorrect because increasing employment tends to make inflation rise rather than decline.

23. **The correct answer is (A).** Choices (B), (C), and (D) are incorrect. Choice (E) may sound familiar but is not quite correct. Pontiac's Rebellion, which resulted in the Proclamation of 1763, convinced the British that a standing army was needed in the colonies.

24. **The correct answer is (E).** The Second Continental Congress managed the government of the states during the early days of the war and oversaw the establishment of a new government under the Articles of Confederation, which took effect in 1781. Choice (B) occurred because the delegates to the Continental Congress were afraid that any references to the slave trade would diminish Southerners' support for independence.

Review Strategy

See Chapter 6 for more information on two decisions relating to the Cherokee.

25. **The correct answer is (C).** The clues are *savages* and *12,000,000.* Choice (A) can be eliminated because Confederate secession does not have anything to do with Native Americans, whom the writer calls savages. If you did not know the population of the United States at any given time, you could still eliminate choices (D) and (E) because both came after 1850, the time frame for the next question. Time frame will also eliminate choice (A). The question prompt asks you to identify the answer that the quotation supported. Choice (B) ruled against the Cherokees' standing to bring a case to the Supreme Court but upheld their right to their lands, so choice (B) is incorrect because the writer of the quotation opposed the right of Native Americans to the land. Choice (C) then is correct; the quotation was written by Andrew Jackson seeking support for the Indian Removal Act.

Test-Taking Strategy

For not/except questions, ask yourself if the answer is true. If it is, cross it off and go on to the next answer.

26. **The correct answer is (E).** After passage of the bill to begin construction of the National Road, later appropriations were defeated because of the issue of states' rights. Choice (C) aided industrial development by making possible large supplies of raw cotton to feed the growing capacity of textile mills.

27. **The correct answer is (A).** John Slidell was one of the Confederate representatives who was seized aboard the *Trent*, but it was not the reason the British almost entered the war. He was on his way to seek French support, so choice (B) is incorrect. The British welcomed choice (D) because they had recently

abolished slavery. Although choice (C) was a problem, the British decided it was not worth going to war over. Choice (E) is incorrect.

28. **The correct answer is (C).** *Laissez-faire* capitalism opposes government intervention in economic affairs and was the opposite of what the Grange advocated. Choice (B) was an important victory because the Supreme Court ruled that public utilities like railroads and grain elevators had to submit to public regulation for the public good. The Grange recognized the importance of women, choice (E), to farm life and welcomed them into the movement.

Test-Taking Strategy

For not/except *questions, ask yourself if the answer is true. If it is, cross it off and go on to the next answer.*

29. **The correct answer is (D).** The problem was overproduction, not underproduction, choice (D), combined with underconsumption, choice (C). Early in the 1920s, people had used installment credit, choice (B), to purchase big-ticket items, and by the end of the decade the demand was decreasing, but not the supply. Factories were turning out more than Americans could buy, and the high tariffs (Fordney-McCumber) along with the United States's insistence on collecting its war debts, choice (E), decreased foreign markets. The amount of loans made to cover stocks bought on margin, choice (A), caused professional speculators to begin to sell their stocks, and the downward economic spiral began.

Test-Taking Strategy

The jump back in time is your clue that number 30 begins a new and more difficult set of questions.

30. **The correct answer is (C).** The clue is *first colony in the Northern parts of Virginia.* Of the five choices, only the Pilgrims set out to establish a colony, Plymouth, choice (C), in northern Virginia. This quotation is from their Mayflower Compact. Another way to eliminate three choices is to consider that choices (B), (D), and (E) all had proprietors and, therefore, the colonists would not be drawing up an agreement about governing themselves. Choice (A) might be true, but the clue and the fact that Plymouth was the first colony to establish self-government would rule out choice (A).

Test-Taking Strategy

The key words are the major stumbling block.

31. **The correct answer is (B).** The underlying premise of all Parliament's dealings with the colonies was the theory of virtual representation, that is, the House of Commons was sworn to represent every person, voter and nonvoter alike, in England and the empire. The colonists, on the other hand, believed in direct or actual representation. Although choice (A) was true—and with good reason—it was not the basic issue. Choices (C) and (D) were results of the conflict, but neither was a cause. George III issued the *Proclamation of Rebellion,* choice (E), to rally his loyal supporters in the colonies; it was not a proclamation issued by the colonists as you may think from the title.

32. **The correct answer is (B).** Like Hamilton's financial program, Clay and Calhoun's American System favored choices (A), (D), and (E). The two Congressmen hoped that choice (C) would be an outcome of their program. Choice (B) is the correct answer because the first immigration law was not passed until 1875.

33. **The correct answer is (D).** You could have answered this question without reading the electoral map. Logic dictates that, as Westerners, Clay and Jackson would probably have carried the frontier states.

34. **The correct answer is (C).** This is another question that you could have answered without the electoral map. It is logical that as a New Englander, Adams would have won New England.

35. **The correct answer is (D).** Although Jackson did not have a majority of the popular vote, choice (B), that is not the reason that the election was decided in the House. The winning presidential candidate must have a majority of electoral votes, and no candidate in 1824 did, choice (D). Choice (A) is the term Jackson's supporters gave to what they considered the deal Adams and Clay made. In return for being named secretary of state, Clay swung his support to Adams for president. Choice (C) is incorrect; each state's electors equal the sum of the number of its senators and representatives. Choice (E) is incorrect; the Twelfth Amendment was ratified in 1804.

36. **The correct answer is (B).** Choice (A) is true, but the Fourteenth Amendment was not drafted and ratified until after the Civil Rights Act was passed over Johnson's veto. Because others shared Johnson's concern that the act was unconstitutional, Congress drafted the amendment. Choices (C), (D), and (E) are incorrect.

37. **The correct answer is (E).** The Northern Securities Company had been formed in 1902 when competing combinations had been unable to win control of the Northern Pacific Railroad. J.P. Morgan and James J. Hill joined with E. H. Harriman and the banking house of Kuhn, Loeb to create a holding company with a monopoly over rail transportation from Lake Michigan to the Pacific. This Supreme Court case was the first in a series under Theodore Roosevelt to rein in trusts and combinations. Choice (B) may have given you a moment's pause because strikes and boycotts by labor unions had once been considered against the law, but choice (B) is incorrect in this context. Choice (A) was the federal law under which the Northern Securities case was prosecuted. Choices (C) and (D) are incorrect.

Test-Taking Strategy

The key words are most significant.

38. The correct answer is (C). Choices (A), (C), and (E) are true, but in the larger context of United States history, choice (C) is the most significant. The pictures of the active army demolishing the veterans' Hooverville added to the belief that Hoover was indifferent to those suffering in the Depression, an unfair assessment of the man, but one that contributed to his losing the 1932 election. The RFC, choice (D), did provide additional money for relief, but it was unrelated to the Bonus Army. Choice (B) is incorrect; the United States Army destroyed the veterans' makeshift camp.

39. The correct answer is (A). Although some may disagree with the extent of desegregation efforts in the 1960s, progress was made, so choice (A) is correct. With this progress came a backlash, choice (B), a certain amount of it from blue-collar, white ethnic workers. Choices (C), (D), and (E) resulted in high inflation, increased taxes, and a legacy of mistrust of government on the part of many citizens.

40. The correct answer is (C). In an effort to help those living in great poverty in Latin America and to head off any attempted revolutions inspired by Castro's Communist reforms in Cuba, President John Kennedy proposed the Alliance for Progress. Choice (B) occurred after the Alliance was established. Choice (D) is irrelevant, and the information in choices (A) and (E) is incorrect.

41. The correct answer is (D). The Annapolis Convention was called to discuss trade regulations across the new states, but ended in requesting a convention to address the weaknesses of the Articles, choice (D). No trade agreements were reached, so choice (A) is incorrect. The Confederation Congress accomplished choice (C). Massachusetts put down Shay's Rebellion, so choice (B) is incorrect. Choice (E) is incorrect.

Review Strategy

Check Chapter 6 for more information on these two Supreme Court cases.

42. The correct answer is (C). Even though the Supreme Court ruled in favor of the Cherokee in *Cherokee Nation* v. *The State of Georgia* and *Worcester* v. *Georgia,* Jackson, the old "Indian Fighter," sided with Georgia. Because of the Indian Removal Act of 1830 and his refusal to aid the Cherokee, Jackson, and later, President Martin Van Buren, oversaw the transfer of thousands of Native Americans from the Southeast to the Indian Territory.

Test-Taking Strategy

The key word is direct.

43. The correct answer is (D). Although choice (E) was a contributing factor, the deal reached to make Hayes president, choice (D), was the direct cause of the end of Reconstruction. Choice (A) occurred once the military had moved out of Florida, South Carolina, and Louisiana. States that did not have reconstructed governments by 1870 had to ratify the Fifteenth as well as the

Fourteenth Amendment, but choice (B) had no bearing on the end of Reconstruction, nor did choice (C).

44. The correct answer is (D). Choices (B), (C), (D), and (E) are all characteristics to a certain extent of the period from the end of the Civil War to 1880, but choice (D) is the most correct description of the term "Gilded Age." Although all the events in choices (B), (C), (D), and (E) occurred, the term refers to the political corruption and unrestrained business competition of the era. Choice (A) is incorrect; this period was notable for its lack of presidential leadership.

45. The correct answer is (B). Choices (A), (B), and (D) are true about the Open Door Policy, but the importance of the policy lay in choice (B). Between the War of 1812 and the Spanish-American War of 1898, the United States had been able to rely on its location to keep it out of European conflicts. After the United States's victory in the Spanish-American War and the acquisition of an overseas empire, the United States viewed itself as a world power. United States businessmen, fearing they would be forced out of China, demanded a change in policy. The Open Door Policy established terms in such a way that nations had to agree. Japan had already annexed Formosa in 1895, choice (C). The information in choice (E) is incorrect.

46. The correct answer is (D). The statement was written by Booker T. Washington as part of the *Atlanta Compromise.* The clue is the phrase "as much dignity in tilling a field." This should signal that Washington was the author because of his espousal of vocational education and labor versus the arts and sciences. Dunbar, choice (A), was a poet and writer who often wrote about African-American rural life. Du Bois, choice (B), had views directly opposed to those of Washington. Hughes, choice (C), was a poet and writer who used the rhythm of African-American music in his works. Ellison, choice (E), won the National Book Award for his first novel, *Invisible Man.*

47. The correct answer is (C). Veblen was an economist and social theorist at the turn of the twentieth century who devised a theory that people acquire goods to enhance their status rather than for the goods' usefulness or value. Debs, choice (A), was a socialist, labor leader, founder of the Socialist Party, and United States presidential candidate. Marx, choice (B), was a social and economic theorist who posited that capitalism would eventually decline and be replaced by socialism and then communism, an economic theory in which all labor, capital, and the means of production would belong to the workers. Twain, choice (D), was a writer and social satirist who along with a co-author coined the term "Gilded Age." George, choice (E), was a journalist who believed that the cause of inequality was the possession of land; he proposed a single tax on land.

48. **The correct answer is (D).** Mellon believed that the wealthy should pay a smaller proportion of taxes so that they could accumulate wealth that would then be invested back into business, so choice (D) is incorrect. Choices (A), (B), and (C) fed the Depression and the stock market crash.

49. **The correct answer is (E).** Choice (D) was also ruled unconstitutional on similar grounds: agriculture was an intrastate activity and not subject to federal regulation. Choice (A) established the Federal Deposit Insurance Corporation (FDIC) to insure individual deposits in banks. Choice (B) lent money to areas to set up power lines. Choice (C) was empowered to buy, build, and operate dams in the Tennessee Valley; to sell power; and to manage flood control and reforestation. The constitutionality of choices (A) and (B) was not tested, and in a 1936 case, the Supreme Court ruled that in establishing the TVA the federal government had not exceeded its constitutional powers.

50. **The correct answer is (C).** Truman signed the Executive Order in 1948, but by 1950 only the Air Force was desegregating its forces to any extent. It was not until the Korean War that the military began actively integrating its units.

51. **The correct answer is (A).** Harrington was a socialist and writer who is credited with making visible the "invisible poverty" in the United States. Carson, choice (B), was a marine biologist and science writer who wrote about the dangers of environmental pollution. Nader, choice (C), is a lawyer and consumer advocate whose work has resulted in investigations and regulations to protect consumers. Helper's book, choice (D), was written in the 1850s and attacked slavery on economic grounds. Galbraith, choice (E), was an economist who urged government spending to fight unemployment and the use of private wealth to help the needy.

52. **The correct answer is (D).** Choice (A) was usually used in factories. Choice (B) is used against strikers. Choice (C) is the Spanish word for strike. Choice (E) is a disagreement between unions over which union should represent workers in a company or an industry.

53. **The correct answer is (D).**

54. **The correct answer is (C).** Although the Constitution would go into effect when nine states ratified it, supporters knew that the new nation would not succeed if all thirteen did not approve it. Debate in Virginia and New York was especially heated. When

Review Strategy

Check Chapter 6 for more information on Schechter Poultry Corp. *v.* United States.

Peterson's AP Success: U.S. History

they ratified, only North Carolina and Rhode Island remained outside the nation. Those states ratified in November 1789 and May 1790, respectively.

55. **The correct answer is (E).** The Federalists had strong leadership in Alexander Hamilton, John Jay, and James Madison, who co-authored *The Federalist*. Choices (B) and (D) were concerns of the Anti-Federalists. Having a special convention in each state seemed to usurp the power of the states.

56. **The correct answer is (A).** One of the provisions that Mexico had insisted on in welcoming American settlers was that they obey Mexican law, and slavery was against Mexican law. Until Americans outnumbered Mexicans in Texas by about 6 to 1, Mexico did not enforce the law. Choice (E) occurred as a result of choice (A); the Mexican government included enforcement of customs duties in its new regulations. Choice (D) was probably the ulterior reason for choice (A). Choice (B) is the reverse of what occurred. Choice (C) did not occur until after Texas won its independence.

57. **The correct answer is (C).** The other four planks were more representative of the interests of the farmers, miners, and small business owners who also made up the Populist Party.

58. **The correct answer is (A).** D-Day, the Normandy invasion of France, choice (A), had occurred in 1944, a year before the Yalta Conference. To obtain Stalin's agreement to enter the war against Japan once the war in Europe had ended, choice (D), and his pledge to make a treaty with Chiang Kai-shek, choice (E), Churchill and Roosevelt agreed to allow Russia to retake the Kurile Islands and southern Sakhalin, to keep Outer Mongolia, and to recognize Russia's trading interests in Darien. These last three are the elements of a secret bargain that the three struck to keep Stalin in the war. Choice (C) was part of the general negotiations for a new world organization that had begun in 1944.

59. **The correct answer is (A).** Choices (B), (C), and (D) were already in Communist hands by the end of World War II. Greece was fighting a Communist takeover when the British announced they could no longer provide aid to Greece or Turkey. A judgment was made that if Greece fell, Turkey would also. The Russians would then be able to control sea traffic from the Black Sea into the Mediterranean. Truman announced immediate aid to both Greece and Turkey, choice (A), to strengthen their governments and fight off the Communists. Choice (E) is irrelevant. It did not become an independent nation until 1960 when the British turned over the government.

Test-Taking Strategy

Be sure both parts of an answer are correct. A partially correct answer is a partially incorrect answer—and a quarter-point deduction.

60. **The correct answer is (C).** Raising rates normally lowers inflation, but for much of the 1970s the action of the Fed caused stagflation. Inflation continued, and economic growth declined. Choice (A) means putting government money into circulation through loans and federal programs to get the economy moving. Only Congress can levy taxes, so choice (D) is incorrect. Choice (E) was an outcome of choice (C); rising interest rates discourage people from borrowing because of the amount of money they will have to pay back. Choice (B) is incorrect.

61. **The correct answer is (E).** Established religion in this sense means the religion that is supported by the state. Pennsylvania, choice (A), was set up as a haven for Quakers, so there was no established religion. Maryland, choice (B), practiced religious toleration. Congregationalism was the state-supported religion in Massachusetts Bay, while Connecticut had no established religion. Georgia was chartered by George II and became a royal colony. The Church of England is Anglican.

62. **The correct answer is (C).** The Constitution forbid the importation of slaves after 1808, but said nothing about the internal slave trade, which grew dramatically in the following decades with the spread of cotton agriculture.

63. **The correct answer is (E).** The British repeal of the Orders in Council, which had forbidden neutral ships to trade with European nations unless the ships stopped in British ports first, was meant to avoid hostilities with the United States. However, the United States had already declared war on Great Britain.

64. **The correct answer is (A).** Only Andrew Jackson did not add any territory to the United States during his terms in office. McKinley, choice (B), annexed Hawaii, the Philippines, and Guam. Polk, choice (C), oversaw the addition of Texas, California, and New Mexico Territory. Monroe, choice (D), acquired East Florida from the Spanish. Johnson's, choice (E), Secretary of State, William Seward, purchased Alaska.

65. **The correct answer is (A).** Choice (B) is the opposite of what occurred. The end of the lobby to expand the currency system meant an end to the lobby for free and unlimited coinage of silver. The Bland-Allison Act, choice (C), had been passed before the economy improved, had done little to expand the money supply, had brought little relief to debtors, and had made little profit for silver miners. Choice (D) had already begun after the election of 1878. The demonetization of silver, choice (E), was known as the "Crime of 1873" and is irrelevant to this period.

66. The correct answer is (D). All five responses are correct, but choices (A), (B), (C), and (E) would not have been widespread without the building of state university systems such as the University of California and Michigan State.

67. The correct answer is (A). The clues are *gold standard* as well as the high regard for farms and disdain for cities. The quotation is from William Jennings Bryan's speech at the 1896 Democratic convention. Choices (B), (C), and (D) would not have spoken against gold. Greenback Party members, choice (E), wanted paper money backed by neither gold nor silver.

68. The correct answer is (C). The legacy of William Howard Taft's "dollar diplomacy" was mistrust and suspicion of the United States's motives toward Latin American nations. Choice (A) occurred before Taft's administration. The United States intervened in Nicaragua several times, including once during Taft's administration, but choice (B) is not broad enough to be correct. Choices (D) and (E) are incorrect.

69. The correct answer is (D). Wilson tried to use the note to secure broad authority from Congress to protect United States ships engaged in peaceful pursuits. Wilson planned to arm merchant ships so they could fight off German U-boats. Regardless of the outrage over the note, the isolationists in Congress blocked the vote. Choice (C) was a provision of the Sussex Pledge, choice (E). Choices (A) and (B) are incorrect.

70. The correct answer is (D). This quotation reflects the philosophy of nonviolence that Dr. Martin Luther King brought to the SCLC and the civil rights movement. It is the antithesis of the beliefs of Stokely Carmichael, choice (C), who believed in aggressive confrontation, and Malcom X, choice (B), who advocated revolution. Du Bois, choice (E), also believed in peaceful resistance, but the NAACP waged its campaigns more through lobbying legislators, its publications, and court cases. Washington, choice (A), proposed that African Americans should seek progress through economic efforts and not political protest, so choice (A) would not apply.

71. The correct answer is (D). All five choices are correct, but choice (D) is the most important in terms of the larger context of American history. Spain had to cede the Louisiana Territory back to France at the end of the American Revolution, choice (A), so there is little long-term importance to this. Choice (B) was important to France, but not particularly to the British colonies or to the later United States, which dealt with Great Britain rather than France. Choice (C) was important to settlers on the frontier, but during the American Revolution and for a time afterwards, the British armed the Native Americans, so the long-term importance of choice (C) was minimal. Choice (E) was a contributing factor to the development of colonial resistance to Great Britain, but not as lasting as the ability of colonists to work together.

72. **The correct answer is (D).** One of the reasons that the British imposed extra taxes on the colonies and began to enforce the Navigation Acts after the French and Indian War was to force the colonies to pay for the war. The British empire stretched around the globe so that the British government was faced with subduing and governing large parts of the world that did not wish to be governed as colonies. Its resources were overextended.

73. **The correct answer is (D).** What began as a debate about limiting the sale of Western land in order to keep factory workers in the Northeast turned into a full-scale discussion of states' rights and nullification with Webster upholding the Union. Choice (C) is partially correct in that the debate did shift to tariffs but then shifted again to states' rights, and that was the greater significance of the debate. Choices (A) and (B) are incorrect. The Force Bill, choice (E), did not represent a compromise and relates to a later tariff and secession attempt by South Carolina.

Test-Taking Strategy

The key words are most significant.

Review Strategy

See Chapter 6 for more information on Plessy v. Ferguson.

74. **The correct answer is (E).** All five choices are correct, but choice (E) is the most inclusive and, therefore, matches the key words.

75. **The correct answer is (A).** The same name, "black codes," choice (B), was given to laws passed before and after the Civil War in the South to regulate the rights of blacks. After the Civil War, the laws were one cause of the imposition of Congressional or Radical Reconstruction. Choice (D) is the name given to the reconstructed South. Choice (E) is segregation that exists not by law but by custom and economic conditions; *de jure* segregation is segregation by law.

76. **The correct answer is (B).** Turner's *The Frontier in American History* is the classic work on the closing of the frontier. Beard, choice (A), was an economic historian. Cooper, choice (C), was a writer of the early nineteenth century who used the frontier as the setting for his novels. Roosevelt, choice (D), as president added more than 200 million acres to the nation's forests and established such programs as the Inland Waterways Commission. Catlin, choice (E), was a painter known for his works showing Native Americans and frontier life.

Test-Taking Strategy

Knowing the time frame will help you eliminate four choices.

77. The correct answer is (D). The title is from a work about two members of the Lost Generation, Sara and Gerald Murphy, rich Americans whose only claim to fame was knowing and entertaining authors like Ernest Hemingway and F. Scott Fitzgerald. Romanticism, choice (A), is a literary and artistic style of the mid-nineteenth century that focused on emotion, intuition, imagination, and individualism. The "Beats," choice (B), were writers of the 1950s who protested what they saw as smug, self-satisfied, middle-class American life. Realism, choice (C), is a style of the late nineteenth century that described people in realistic detail. Nationalism, choice (E), inspired the cultural developments of the new nation in the early nineteenth century.

78. The correct answer is (D). Isolationism was strong in the United States in the 1930s, and the conflicts in Europe fed those fears. Roosevelt adopted the Good Neighbor Policy in an attempt to better relations with other nations in the Western Hemisphere should war be declared. His actions, however, were not a direct consequence of the Nye Report; they were a consequence of the policy of intervention that the United States had adopted earlier in the century.

79. The correct answer is (D). Choices (A), (B), (C), and (E) are all true of Nixon's actions in office. However, choice (A) had already been settled and Nixon had agreed to pay back taxes. Choice (D) covers the information in choices (B), (C), and (E) and is, therefore, the most complete choice.

80. The correct answer is (C). The *Bakke* decision had a limited application and was not applied to all affirmative action programs, so choice (A) is incorrect. Choice (B) is incorrect; the decision did not overrule Johnson's executive order. Choice (D) is incorrect and does not relate to affirmative action. Choice (E) is incorrect; the constitutionality of the law was not questioned.

SUGGESTIONS FOR THE DOCUMENT-BASED QUESTION, PART A

Study Strategy

Revise your essay using points from this list that will strengthen it.

Be sure that you evaluated both sides of the arguments for and against expansion and imperialism. Notice that you were asked to relate these ideas to consequences in the twentieth century. You might have noticed that the documents were in chronological order, but you do not need to write about them in that order. You should incorporate references to them in your essay in the order in which they support your thesis. You might have chosen the following points about Documents A through H to discuss in your essay on the growth of the United States as a world power. Consider them as you complete your self-evaluation.

Document A

Josiah Strong, as you can see in Document (A), was a man of great prejudice. This selection reveals his belief that the Anglo-Saxon race, particularly the American branch, will dominate the earth in the future. At a time when others were concerned with national economic development, expansion westward, and immigration, he advocated a future for the United States as an expanding imperialist nation and a dominant international power.

This document is an extremely strong statement of the concept of American superiority that drove much of the imperialist policy of the period. Ask yourself what this document reveals about American thinking. How logical are the arguments? How does this relate to United States foreign policy during the twentieth century?

Document B

Like Josiah Strong, Senator Beveridge argued for the potential of American expansion and emergence as an imperial nation. However, he bases his argument mainly on economic reasons. He states that the United States produces more than it consumes and so the United States needs more markets, which it can create only by expanding throughout the world. In order to rally patriots to his cause, he promises that United States culture and values will follow trade.

The value of business was paramount during the late 1880s. Advocacy of capitalism became almost a religion and used religious and scientific "theories" as supports. Consider the relation of the business philosophy of the late 1800s to the policy of multinational corporations in the twentieth century. How did and does United States foreign policy reflect these dominant economic ideas?

Document C

Document C presents another argument for American imperialism. Henry Cabot Lodge, along with others such as Theodore Roosevelt, believed that expansion overseas was crucial to the future of the United States. They proposed an aggressive foreign policy that included economic expansion, acquisition of territories for military stations, and entrance into the imperialist race against European powers. In the article from which this excerpt is taken, the writer attacks President Cleveland for his conservative position opposing annexation of Hawaii. In this selection, Lodge sets up the thesis that small countries are not viable; hence, large, powerful countries such as the United States may rightfully acquire them. Such actions are inevitable and advance civilization.

Fascinated with struggles for power throughout history, Lodge called for a larger navy, annexation of Hawaii, a canal through Central America, and purchase of the Dutch West Indies to protect that canal. His political ideas complemented those of Captain Alfred Thayer Mahan. Mahan theorized that the United States had to sell its products in foreign countries in order to be strong and consequently needed to build a strong navy in order to protect its presence abroad. Compare the ideas of Lodge and Mahan with twentieth-century concepts of the domino theory or the arms races. What other twentieth-century foreign policy ideas are similar to Henry Cabot Lodge's idea?

Document D

The speech from which Document D is excerpted was presented to Congress on April 11, 1898. McKinley reluctantly brought the issue of war with Spain to the legislature. He did not want war, but mounting support for Cuba's struggle for independence, provoked by the yellow press, forced his hand. Most of the speech reviewed the background of the struggle in Cuba. However, in the speech's last two paragraphs (the selection presented here), McKinley notes that Spain had offered to accede to major United States demands. Such an offer warranted reopening of negotiations to establish a peaceful settlement. In spite of this, Congress passed resolutions that recognized Cuba as an independent nation. Spain declared war, and the United States then followed the next day with its own declaration of war. Some historians believe that if McKinley had had more courage, he could have kept the United States out of war.

This document raises issues about the United States' increasing involvement in the affairs of Latin America and the world. Concern regarding the safety of United States business interests and support for the freedom movement indicate Americans' belief in the right of the United States to determine the future of other countries. The war of intervention indicated that the country was ready to join the race for empire. Ask yourself what were the results of the Spanish-American War. What did the United States gain or lose on the world stage? How did other nations look at the United States as a result of the war? Consider the yellow press. What role has the media played in influencing foreign policy in the twentieth century?

Study Strategy

Be sure to complete the "Self-Evaluation Rubric" on pp. 326-27 for each essay.

Document E

Written by the editor of the *Atlantic Monthly,* Document E is excerpted from an editorial that appeared in June 1898. In the article, Page examines the meaning of the United States victory in Manila. He analyzes the turn toward imperialism that the United States was taking as a result of the Spanish-American War. Since the article is an editorial, you know that this selection expresses the writer's personal view—United States expansion is a positive, in fact, a necessary development. The result he anticipates is a strengthening of morale in the United States.

You may have noticed that these documents have been arranged chronologically. Did you recognize that the arguments have also grown more subtle? How might the acquisition of the Philippines have affected United States business? The people of the Philippines had begun fighting for independence well before the Spanish-American War. What long-term effects have resulted from the United States takeover of the Philippines? How might other Asian countries have viewed United States actions?

Document F

In this excerpt, Carl Schurz, an influential journalist and staunch Republican, argued against expansionism. Dewey's victory in Manila created a dilemma for the people of the United States. Should the United States stay in the Philippines or leave the islands to the Filipinos? Schurz argues that to remain in the Philippines, and expansionism itself, is morally and politically inconsistent with traditional United States principles.

In spite of strong opposition, the expansionists prevailed. The peace treaty with Spain, ratified in 1899, gave the United States important territories in the Caribbean and the Pacific. Was Schurz correct to say imperialism was immoral? How does this philosophy relate to United States neutrality before both world wars?

Document G

The annexation of the Philippines disturbed some Americans a great deal. People such as Mark Twain, Jane Addams, and Andrew Carnegie worried about the United States ruling other people. They saw expansion as a departure from America's ideals of self-government and the protection of human rights (note that this did not extend to African Americans or Asian immigrants). In addition, many feared that expansion in the Pacific might lead to war with Japan. Such people became known as anti-imperialists. In 1899, they formed the Anti-Imperialist League and adopted a platform from which Document F is taken.

This document represents an opposing view to the belief in United States imperial destiny then being popularized in the nation and a view adopted by the Democrats and their candidate William Jennings Bryant in the election of 1900. Consider the outcome of the McKinley versus Bryant presidential election. Ask yourself what happened because the United States "pacified" the Philippines. Were the anti-imperialists correct in fearing eventual war with Japan over United States acquisition of territory in the Pacific? What were the long-term consequences of the United States takeover in Cuba and Puerto Rico?

Document H

Document H is an excerpt from President Wilson's formal proclamation of neutrality at the beginning of World War I. He asked that neutrality not be simply a matter of law but of spirit as well. However, impartiality was not possible, even for the president.

Most Americans were drawn to the British side, although millions favored the Central powers. Ask yourself how neutrality at the beginning of World War I could be considered a part of the policy of imperialism. How might it relate to the ideas and ideals of those who opposed imperialism?

Other points to consider:

- **Open-Door Policy**
- **Puerto Rico**
- **Cuba**
- **Panama Canal**
- **Roosevelt Corollary**
- **Russo-Japanese War**
- **The Root-Takahira Agreement**
- **Dollar Diplomacy**
- **Mexico**

SUGGESTIONS FOR FREE RESPONSE ESSAYS, PART B

ESSAY 2

You might have chosen the following points about the Federalists and the Democratic-Republicans to discuss in your essay on the development of the first two United States political parties. Consider them as you complete your self-evaluation.

Federalists	Democratic-Republicans
Economy	**Economy**
• Constitutional provisions for national economy	• Jefferson and his supporters: belief in an agrarian way of life
• Secretary of the Treasury Alexander Hamilton responsible for implementation of new program of growth	• Desired western expansion to increase farming base
• Hamilton's belief in the need for the support of rich and well-born people	• United States credit: feared unreasonable profits by speculators; rewarded states that had not paid their debts
• United States credit: pay war debts of states and national government	• Premise: nation to remain agrarian; buy manufactured goods from other nations
• Premise: commerce and manufacturing as keys to economic prosperity	• Considered National Bank unconstitutional
• Protectionism: use of tariff but never considered by Congress	• Whiskey Rebellion: caused shift in support to Democratic-Republicans
• National Bank: stability and paper currency	
• Excise tax on whiskey to raise money	
Foreign Policy	**Foreign Policy**
• Pro-British: neutrality proclamation in 1793; used Genêt's actions and propaganda against the French	• Pro-French: considered them allies; British forts in Northwest; trade restrictions
• Jay's Treaty: some settlement with Britain; divided country	• Jay's Treaty: sacrifice national honor for commerce; its pro-British stance interpreted as monarchical

ESSAY 3

Review Strategy

Check Chapters 5 through 10 to review content you are not sure about.

You might have chosen the following points to discuss in your essay on the development of the colonial movement for independence. Consider them as you complete your self-evaluation.

Proclamation of 1763

- To prevent fighting between colonists and Native Americans; confined colonists to existing settlements until treaties could be signed; settlement west of the Appalachians forbidden

- Displeased colonists who wanted to go west for land (tobacco) and money (real estate); land speculators as well as settlers

Sugar Act, Currency Act, and Stamp Act

- Colonists to pay fair share of war costs; generate revenue for Britain; exert greater control over colonies; established vice-admiralty courts

- Aggravated depression, increased concern about increasing control; feared loss of tradition of self-taxation; removed court jurisdiction from colonists; Otis's argument for representation in Parliament or more self-government; united some colonies; Sons of Liberty; Daughters of Liberty

- Repealed; the Declaratory Act instituted

Townshend Acts

- Taxes on British goods paid the salary for tax collectors; more courts; suspended New York legislature for refusing to supply British troops

- Massachusetts asked all assemblies to protest together; forbidden by Britain to discuss issue; rallies and boycotts

- Britain repealed all but tea duty; British still stationed in Boston

- Boston Massacre: propaganda; soldiers fired on innocent bystanders; bystanders threw rocks

Boston Tea Party, Intolerable Acts, Quebec Act, First Continental Congress

- Committees of Correspondence: information shared among colonies, encouraged citizens to be active in cause

- New taxes to support East India Tea Company: colonists refused to let ships unload; dumped tea in harbor

- Intolerable Acts in retaliation; tightened British control; colonists to house soldiers; felt semi-autonomy had ended

- Quebec Act: greater liberties for Catholics; prevented westward growth

- Continental Congress: in most spheres, colonists to rule themselves

Battles of Lexington and Concord, Second Continental Congress

- Provided rallying point for cause of independence

- Printed money, established offices

- Battle of Bunker Hill

Publication of *Common Sense,* Declaration of Independence

- *Common Sense:* advocated independence; republicanism over monarchy

- Declaration of Independence: colonists' grievances, principle of individual liberty, government's responsibility to serve people

SUGGESTIONS FOR FREE RESPONSE ESSAYS, PART C

ESSAY 4

Review Strategy

Be sure to use the "Self-Evaluation Rubric" on pp. 326–27.

You might have chosen the following points about Jewish, Italian, or Japanese immigrants to discuss in your essay on the immigrant experience at the turn of the twentieth century. Consider them as you complete your self-evaluation.

Jewish immigrants during the late nineteenth century

- Most from Eastern Europe; especially Russia and Poland

- Escaping religious persecution and pogroms

- Swamped existing United States Jewish community, especially New York

- Poor or destitute, less educated than other immigrant groups, provincial

- Orthodox, Yiddish language embarrassment to some American Jews

- Jewish philanthropic organizations to aid and Americanize immigrants

- Lived in crowded apartments in close-knit communities, many rarely venturing out

- Growing anti-Semitism from Christians; "Help Wanted— Christian"

- Manual labor—skilled and unskilled; especially garment trade, contract work in homes and sweatshops; rarely servants

- High regard for education; language a problem

- Children rarely worked full time, so they had time for education

- Upward movement in later generations: entertainment, the arts, science, and medicine

Italian immigrants during the late nineteenth and early twentieth centuries

- Most from southern Italy; mostly men; many planned to return to Italy; birds of passage

- Economic problems, famines, political revolts

- Mostly laborers; women worked but not often as servants; home sweatshops; active in labor unions (virtually no English speakers)

- California: agricultural entrepreneurs; padrone system supplied labor to United States industry; interpreters

- Southern Italians repudiated by earlier Northern Italian immigrants

- Immigrants from same villages lived together; mutual aid societies based on regions

- Family is the strongest social institution; lack of identification with Italians from other regions; coexisted well with other ethnic and cultural groups

- Education slow to be accepted; children had to work

Japanese immigrants during the late nineteenth and early twentieth centuries

- Overpopulation and dislocation in Japan; source of cheap farm labor; determined to be good Americans; some returned to Japan

- Ambitious young men with limited finances; money sent to Japan

- Japanese associations; organized immigrants

- Initially welcomed in United States and Hawaii; worked together; virtues of hard work turned other laborers against them; refused union membership

- Education valued

- Alien Land Law

- Prospered through small businesses

ESSAY 5

Review Strategy

Be sure to use the "Self-Evaluation Rubric" on pp. 326–27.

You might have chosen the following points about the New Deal programs for your essay defending the value of Roosevelt's New Deal programs. Consider them as you complete your self-evaluation.

- The three goals of the New Deal: *relief, recovery,* and *reforms* to prevent another depression

- Some New Deal programs:

    - Civilian Conservation Corps: jobs for conservation

- Tennessee Valley Authority: built dams for power in seven Southern states to produce electricity, control floods
- Federal Emergency Relief Administration: employment for needy and unemployed
- Agricultural Adjustment Administration: paid farmers to keep land out of production; ruled unconstitutional; replaced by Soil Conservation and Domestic Allotment Act
- National Recovery Administration: enforced regulations on wages, prices, child labor, and working conditions; ruled unconstitutional
- Public Works Administration: provided employment building schools, dams, bridges, parks, public buildings
- Federal Deposit Insurance Corporation: insured bank accounts
- Rural Electrification Administration: provided funds for rural electrification
- Works Progress Administration: employed people in the creative arts; also built infrastructure
- Social Security Act: set up pensions, unemployment insurance, and funds for the disabled

- Critics of the New Deal: Liberty League, Huey Long, Father Coughlin, Francis Townsend

- Supreme Court: overturns several of the New Deal programs; "court packing" fails; Roosevelt able to appoint judges who supported his plans

SELF-EVALUATION RUBRIC FOR THE ADVANCED PLACEMENT ESSAYS

	8–9	5–7	2–4	0–1
Overall Impression	Demonstrates excellent understanding of U.S. history and outstanding writing; thorough and effective; incisive	Demonstrates good understanding of U.S. history and good writing competence	Reveals simplistic or incomplete thinking and/or immature understanding of U.S. history; fails to respond adequately to the question; little or no analysis	Very little or no understanding of U.S. history; unacceptably brief; fails to respond to the question; little clarity
Understanding of U.S. History	Scholarly; excellent understanding of the question; effective and incisive; in-depth critical analysis; includes many apt, specific references; acknowledges opposing views	Mostly historically accurate; good understanding of the question; often perceptive; includes specific references and critical analysis	Some historical inaccuracies; superficial understanding and treatment of the question; some misreading of documents and lack of historical evidence; mechanical; overgeneralized	Serious historical errors; extensive misreadings and little supporting evidence; completely off the topic
Development	Original, unique and/or intriguing thesis; excellent use of documents and historical knowledge; thoroughly developed; conclusion shows applicability of thesis to other situations	Adequate thesis; satisfactory use of documents and/or historical knowledge; competent development; acceptable conclusion	Inadequate, irrelevant or illogical thesis; little use of documents and/or historical knowledge; some development; unsatisfactory, inapplicable, or nonexistent conclusion	Lacking both thesis and conclusion; little or no use of historical documents or knowledge; no distinguishable development
Organization/Conventions of English	Meticulously and thoroughly organized; coherent and unified; virtually error free	Reasonably organized; mostly coherent and unified; some errors	Somewhat organized; some incoherence and lack of unity; some major errors	Little or no organization; incoherent and void of unity; extremely flawed

Rate yourself in each of the categories below. Enter the numbers on the lines below. Be as honest as possible so you will know what areas need work. Then calculate the average of the four numbers to determine your final score. It is difficult to score yourself objectively, so you may wish to ask a respected friend or teacher to assess your essays for a more accurate reflection of their strengths and weaknesses. On the AP test itself, a reader will rate your essays on a scale of 0 to 9, with 9 being the highest.

Each category is rated 9 (high) to 0 (incompetent).

DBQ

SELF-EVALUATION

Overall Impression _____

Understanding of U.S. History _____

Development _____

Organization/Conventions
   of English _____

TOTAL _____

   Divide by 4 for final score. _____

DBQ

OBJECTIVE EVALUATION

Overall Impression _____

Understanding of U.S. History _____

Development _____

Organization/Conventions
   of English _____

TOTAL _____

   Divide by 4 for final score. _____

FREE RESPONSE 1

SELF-EVALUATION

Overall Impression _____

Understanding of U.S. History _____

Development _____

Organization/Conventions
   of English _____

TOTAL _____

   Divide by 4 for final score. _____

FREE RESPONSE 1

OBJECTIVE EVALUATION

Overall Impression _____

Understanding of U.S. History _____

Development _____

Organization/Conventions
   of English _____

TOTAL _____

   Divide by 4 for final score. _____

FREE RESPONSE 2

SELF-EVALUATION

Overall Impression _____

Understanding of U.S. History _____

Development _____

Organization/Conventions
   of English _____

TOTAL _____

   Divide by 4 for final score. _____

FREE RESPONSE 2

OBJECTIVE EVALUATION

Overall Impression _____

Understanding of U.S. History _____

Development _____

Organization/Conventions
   of English _____

TOTAL _____

   Divide by 4 for final score. _____

PRACTICE TEST 2

AP UNITED STATES HISTORY

On the front page of your test booklet, you will find some information about the test. Because you have studied this book, none of it should be new to you, and much of it is similar to other standardized tests you have taken.

The page will tell you that the following exam will take 3 hours and 5 minutes—55 minutes for the multiple-choice section and 2 hours and 10 minutes for the three essays. Fifteen minutes of the time for Section II is a mandatory reading period, primarily for the DBQ. There are two booklets for this exam, one for the multiple-choice section and one for the essays.

The page in your test booklet will also say that SECTION I

- is 55 minutes.

- has 80 questions.

- counts for 50 percent of your total grade.

Then you will find a sentence in capital letters telling you not to open your exam booklet until the monitor tell you to open it.

Other instructions will tell you to be careful when you fill in the ovals on the answer sheet. Fill in each oval completely. If you erase an answer, erase it completely. If you skip a question, be sure to skip the answer oval for it. You will not receive any credit for work done in the test booklet, but you may use it for making notes.

You will also find a paragraph about the guessing penalty—deduction of one-quarter point for every wrong answer—but also words of advice about guessing if you know something about the question and can eliminate several of the answers.

The final paragraph will remind you to work effectively and to pace yourself. You are told that not everyone will be able to answer all the questions and it is preferable to skip questions that are difficult and come back to them if you have time.

SECTION I

Time–55 minutes
80 questions

> **Directions:** Each question or incomplete statement is followed by five suggested responses. Choose the best answer and fill in the correct oval on the answer sheet.

1. The major significance of the Great Awakening of the 1700s was

   (A) it inadvertently helped to nurture the seeds of independence by emphasizing the individual's freedom to choose his or her own religion

   (B) it was led by Englishman George Whitefield and Jonathan Edwards from Massachusetts

   (C) it led to divisions within churches that gave rise to different Presbyterian and Congregationalist sects

   (D) it led to the establishment of colleges to train ministers

   (E) it created a need for religious toleration to deal with the diversity of religions

2. All of the following are true about the Albany Plan of Union EXCEPT

   (A) each state legislature would select representatives to a Grand Council

   (B) it was based on the Iroquois League of Six Nations

   (C) the plan was the first step toward uniting the colonies

   (D) a purpose of the Union was to organize and act together for common defense

   (E) the Grand Council would elect the governor-general

3. The Judiciary Act of 1789

   (A) established the principle of judicial review

   (B) designated the Supreme Court as the court to hear disputes involving federal laws

   (C) established the office of Attorney General and the Department of Justice

   (D) created the federal court system

   (E) was invoked by Andrew Jackson in the dispute over enforcement of *Worcester* v. *State of Georgia*

4. Hamilton's financial program and the American System had all of the following in common EXCEPT

   (A) money for internal improvements

   (B) a protective tariff

   (C) programs for each of the sections of the country in order to draw them together

   (D) regulation of labor unions

   (E) a national bank

5. Both the Force Bill and the Tariff Act of 1833 were passed to deal with the crisis that developed over

(A) the Webster-Hayne Debate

(B) South Carolina's Ordinance of Nullification

(C) *South Carolina Exposition* published anonymously by John Calhoun

(D) Tariff of Abominations

(E) the Maysville Road veto

6. "We hold these truths to be self-evident; that all men and women are created equal. . . Now, in view of this entire disfranchisement of one half of the people of this country, their social and religious degradation . . . and most fraudulently deprived of their most sacred rights, we insist that they have immediate admission to all the rights and privileges which belong to them as citizens of the United States."
This was most probably written in behalf of:

(A) free blacks

(B) enslaved blacks

(C) women

(D) Native Americans

(E) Mexicans in the Southwest

7. All of the following were part of Congressional Reconstruction EXCEPT

(A) the Southern states were organized into five military districts

(B) the Southern states had to ratify the Fourteenth Amendment

(C) the governments of the Southern states except for Tennessee were declared illegal

(D) the Southern states were to write new constitutions to guarantee suffrage to African-American men

(E) former Confederate officials could participate in the state conventions if they paid a fine

8. The Crédit Mobilier scandal involved

(A) an attempt by Congress to raise its own pay and to collect two years' back pay

(B) a bribe by an Indian trader to William Belknap, the Secretary of State

(C) "Boss Tweed" and the building of a courthouse in New York City

(D) the awarding of construction contracts on the Union Pacific Railroad by a group of stockholders to their own company at inflated prices

(E) a ring of whiskey distillers and blackmailers who had been defrauding the federal government of taxes on whiskey

9. All of the following were results of the Spanish-American War EXCEPT

(A) interest in having a U.S. naval presence in the Pacific as well as the Atlantic Ocean

(B) renewed interest in building the Panama Canal

(C) establishment of a protectorate in Cuba

(D) the Supreme Court ruling that unincorporated possessions such as Puerto Rico were not destined for statehood

(E) the Monroe Doctrine was modified

10. The roots of U.S. isolationism lay in

(A) the belief that Great Britain was strong enough to check any war advances by Germany and Japan

(B) disillusionment with the results of World War I

(C) a belief that World War I had been "the war to end all wars"

(D) the desire to collect U.S. war debts and, therefore, an unwillingness to see the reality of the situation in Europe and Asia

(E) the belief that neutrality would protect the nation

11. In the English colonies in the 1600s, the role of Africans shifted from that of indentured servant to slave for life because

(A) European indentured servants were no longer interested in coming to the colonies

(B) agricultural colonies like Maryland were looking for a cheap, plentiful labor supply

(C) Africans found it difficult to cope with European ways

(D) New England merchants found that they could profitably transport Africans on the Africa-to-Caribbean leg of the trans-Atlantic trade

(E) the English believed that they were superior to the Africans

12. One result of the rapid settlement of Western lands between 1789 and 1803 was

(A) the exodus of British soldiers from forts in the Ohio Valley

(B) extension of suffrage by eliminating property qualifications for voting

(C) loss of French and British allies arming Native Americans on the frontier

(D) the Whiskey Rebellion

(E) the adoption of the Northwest Ordinance

13. The War of 1812 is considered a turning point in U.S. history because

(A) the nation embarked on its policy of manifest destiny

(B) the United States began to intervene militarily in Latin American nations

(C) Great Britain entered a period when it would not cooperate with the United States

(D) the United States no longer allowed events in Europe to shape U.S. foreign and domestic policies

(E) War Hawks were able to gain enough support to declare war

14. Labor did not think of itself as a powerful force in the U.S. economy in the 1830s and 1840s because

(A) immigrants were willing to work for low wages

(B) the Panic of 1837 caused many people to lose their jobs

(C) only Massachusetts recognized the legality of labor unions

(D) Americans were used to working on their own as farmers or skilled craft workers

(E) women who made up a significant part of the work force of early factories were reluctant to join unions

15. Agriculture prospered during the Civil War, as a result of all of the following EXCEPT

(A) rising prices for farm products

(B) the Homestead Act of 1862

(C) development of laborsaving machines such as the McCormick reaper

(D) expansion of railroads

(E) contraction of the money supply

16. Division of labor in factories resulted in

(A) the manufacture of interchangeable parts

(B) the factory system

(C) mass production of goods

(D) the Bessemer steel process

(E) development of the electric dynamo

17. In the election of 1912, Theodore Roosevelt wanted Progressives to abandon which of the following beliefs?

(A) The federal government should use its resources to aid the needy.

(B) The federal government should strike down all legal challenges to free-market competition.

(C) The tariff system should be reformed to aid workers.

(D) Monopolies are never in the public interest.

(E) The federal government should prohibit child labor through federal law.

18. The Howard-Wheeler, or Indian Reorganization, Act failed in its aim of

(A) raising the living standards of Native Americans

(B) restoring tribal ownership to those reservation lands that had not been divided into individual parcels

(C) returning local self-government to nations who wished it

(D) ridding the reservations of squatters

(E) re-establishing traditional beliefs, crafts, and customs

19. Which of the following did not contribute to the growth of suburbia after World War II?

    (A) the availability of low-cost housing

    (B) the development of a national highway system

    (C) low-interest loans to veterans

    (D) a boom in the construction of schools, factories, offices, and government buildings

    (E) the railway system

20. All of the following occurred during Eisenhower's two terms in office EXCEPT

    (A) the war in Korea ended in a stalemate

    (B) approval of economic aid and military assistance to Middle Eastern nations in an attempt to thwart Communist plans in the region

    (C) Alaska and Hawaii were admitted to statehood

    (D) the National Aeronautics and Space Administration (NASA) was created

    (E) Eisenhower sent troops to Little Rock, Arkansas, to keep peace and end the crisis over the integration of the high school

21. Which of the following helped England become a major power in the Americas?

    (A) exploration of North America by Frobisher, Hudson, and Cabot

    (B) the exploits of "sea dogs" like Sir Francis Drake against the Spanish

    (C) the defeat of the Spanish Armada

    (D) the rivalry between Spain and France

    (E) the triangle trade route

22. Which of the following rebellions was caused by frontier settlers and landless former indentured servants angered by the policies of Virginia's government?

    (A) the Stono Uprising

    (B) Nat Turner's Rebellion

    (C) the Whiskey Rebellion

    (D) Shay's Rebellion

    (E) Bacon's Rebellion

23. The Declaratory Act

    (A) asked the loyal subjects of George III to oppose rebellion

    (B) was a precursor to the Declaration of Independence

    (C) stated Parliament's position that it had the right to make laws for the colonies in all matters

    (D) was drafted by the Massachusetts legislature and urged the other colonies to resist the Townshend Acts

    (E) drafted by the First Continental Congress listed the basic rights of the colonists as British subjects

24. The Treaty of Fort Laramie stated that

    (A) Native Americans would not attack settlers crossing their lands

    (B) former Mexican settlers in the newly acquired New Mexico Territory would be guaranteed all the rights of U.S. citizens

    (C) the U.S. Army would not build any more forts in the West

    (D) the Black Hills would be closed to white settlers

    (E) the United States would pay $10 million to the Mexican government for the southern right-of-way for a transcontinental railroad

25. The major reason for the economic rebuilding of the South was

(A) high railway rates for freight

(B) the alliance between Southern businessmen and Northern financiers

(C) because Southern factory owners paid
lower wages than in the North

(D) the large number of African Americans
who were employed as sharecroppers

(E) the Supreme Court's attitude toward
separate but equal accommodations

**Questions 26 and 27 refer to the following
cartoon.**

26. King Monopoly would most likely have
favored all of the following EXCEPT

(A) labor unions

(B) a high protective tariff

(C) cheap money

(D) U.S. expansionism

(E) unregulated immigration

27. The cartoonist who drew this picture would
most likely have been in favor of which of
the following laws?

(A) Bland-Allison Act

(B) Interstate Commerce Act

(C) Pendleton Act

(D) Sherman Antitrust Act

(E) Sherman Silver Purchase Act

28. All of the following were criticisms of the
nation's banking and currency system before
enactment of the Federal Reserve Act
EXCEPT

(A) during crises the banking system lacked
stability

(B) the amount of currency in circulation
was not pegged to the investment needs
of the country

(C) the money supply should be backed
by gold

(D) no central bank set banking practices

(E) Wall Street controlled too much bank
capital

29. The end of Communist governments in
Eastern Europe in the late 1980s proved the
wisdom of

(A) the domino theory

(B) the Eisenhower Doctrine

(C) the Truman Doctrine

(D) the policy of containment

(E) the Marshall Plan

30. The Pueblo people adapted to the environment of the

(A) Woodlands

(B) Great Plains

(C) Southeast

(D) Southwest

(E) Pacific Northwest

31. The major significance of the delegated powers listed in the U.S. Constitution is

    (A) the powers correct areas of weakness in the Articles of Confederation

    (B) Congress is given the power to levy and collect taxes

    (C) the delegated powers relate to matters of common concern across the states

    (D) the states reserve some powers to themselves

    (E) the Tenth Amendment asserts that powers not given to the states reside with the federal government

32. The unstated purpose of the Alien and Sedition Acts was

    (A) to unite the nation in time of danger

    (B) to deport immigrants who were becoming too numerous

    (C) to protect freedom of the press from misuse by Anti-Federalists

    (D) to silence advocates of states' rights

    (E) to weaken the Democratic-Republican Party

33. Martin Van Buren's belief during the Panic of 1837 that "the less the government interferes with private pursuits, the better for the general prosperity" could also be attributed to

    (A) Franklin Roosevelt

    (B) John Maynard Keynes

    (C) Theodore Roosevelt

    (D) Herbert Hoover

    (E) Grover Cleveland

34. Which of the following statements best describes the United States at the end of the nineteenth century?

    (A) The nation had shifted from an agrarian, rural economy to an industrial, urban one.

    (B) The development of a vast transportation system was a major factor in the industrialization of the Midwest.

    (C) The closing of the frontier marked the end of the era of manifest destiny.

    (D) Cities had undergone a vast change with the growth of urban services and infrastructures.

    (E) Widespread use of the telegraph and telephone had created a giant communications network that linked the nation.

35. All of the following contributed to the period of intolerance after World War I EXCEPT

    (A) fear of Bolsheviks

    (B) Sacco-Vanzetti case

    (C) anti-immigration laws

    (D) anti-Semitism and Catholic-baiting

    (E) power of organized labor

36. Roosevelt's stated purpose in proposing the alleged "court packing" bill was

    (A) to avoid Supreme Court rulings against the National Labor Relations Act and the Social Security Act

    (B) to remove judges who were still living in the "horse-and-buggy era"

    (C) to increase the efficiency of the federal judicial system

    (D) to establish a "Roosevelt court"

    (E) to preserve the constitutional system of checks and balances

37. The ruling in *Miranda* v. *Arizona* established

    (A) the principle of judicial review

    (B) the right to be represented by counsel

    (C) the principle of clear and present danger

    (D) the rights of a suspect under questioning

    (E) that the defendant had been rightfully convicted for failure to relocate

38. A major characteristic of colonial British society on the eve of the revolution was

    (A) the lack of free Africans in the colonies

    (B) the ability of indentured servants to move into the middle class after they served their term of indenture

    (C) the relatively low position of women

    (D) the value placed on education

    (E) the lack of diversity among the population

39. Which of the following best describes the British response to the colonies?

    (A) Parliament levied a series of taxes that it then had to enforce on belligerent colonists.

    (B) Great Britain continued to use old policies to solve new problems.

    (C) Parliament insisted on the theory of virtual representation in the face of colonial demands for direct representation.

    (D) The position of the British was undermined by the violence that occurred in Boston.

    (E) The British were caught in a cycle of action-reaction-action with no escape.

40. The painters and novelists of the new nation took the inspiration for their works from all of the following EXCEPT

    (A) European Romantics

    (B) Native Americans

    (C) factory life

    (D) nature

    (E) colonial life

Questions 41 and 42 refer to the following map.

41. The Compromise of 1850 affected which of the following?

    (A) California

    (B) California and the Utah and New Mexico Territories

    (C) Kansas and Nebraska Territories

    (D) Minnesota Territory

    (E) Oregon Territory and Washington Territory

42. Popular sovereignty was to be used to decide the question of slavery in

    (A) Utah and New Mexico Territories
    (B) Kansas and Nebraska Territories
    (C) California
    (D) Utah, New Mexico, Kansas, and Nebraska Territories
    (E) Texas

43. All of the following influenced the nature of Congressional Reconstruction EXCEPT

    (A) concern for the rights of African Americans
    (B) political conciliation
    (C) concern that the Republicans would become the minority party when Southerners returned to Congress
    (D) belief that it was Congress's responsibility to direct Reconstruction
    (E) doubt about the loyalty to the Union of ex-Confederate officials

44. Rebates and pooling were abusive practices of

    (A) the canal industry
    (B) the railroad industry
    (C) the oil industry
    (D) farmers on the Great Plains
    (E) the steel industry

45. The "Crime of 1873" refers to

    (A) the rise in the ratio of silver to gold from 16 to 1 to 18 to 1
    (B) the falling price of silver on the open market
    (C) passage of the Bland-Allison Act
    (D) Congress's decision to stop coining silver
    (E) the decline of the Greenback Party

46. Which of the following applied pressure to Franklin Roosevelt to ensure that defense industries did not discriminate against African-American workers in hiring and employment practices?

    (A) Martin Luther King
    (B) Marcus Garvey
    (C) Ralph Abernathy
    (D) A. Philip Randolph
    (E) Mary McCleod Bethune

47. U.S. immigration policies in the 1950s reflected all of the following EXCEPT

    (A) the desire to help displaced persons and children orphaned by World War II
    (B) fear of immigrants who might subvert the U.S. government
    (C) the goal of equalizing immigration between Asian nations and European nations
    (D) the desire to provide a haven for those fleeing Communist governments
    (E) the need to hurry development of the U.S. missile program by admitting a selected number of scientists and technicians

48. Which of the following was not part of Nixon's foreign policy initiatives?

    (A) Iran-contra
    (B) "Two China" policy
    (C) "peace with honor"
    (D) détente
    (E) shuttle diplomacy

49. *Durante vita* was the term applied to

   (A) the offer of land as an inducement to attract people to Virginia

   (B) the contract of indenture

   (C) the status of Africans after the 1660s in Maryland

   (D) compromise Puritans reached to allow baptized children of church members to baptize their children

   (E) another name for the Great Awakening

50. The Fourth Amendment grew out of the colonists' grievance against the British practice of

   (A) quartering troops at the expense of the colonists

   (B) writs of assistance

   (C) strict libel laws

   (D) courts of admiralty

   (E) supporting the Church of England as the established church

51. Reduction of the tariff, restoration of the independent treasury, settlement of the Oregon boundary, and acquisition of California were the four goals of

   (A) James K. Polk

   (B) William Henry Harrison

   (C) Henry Clay

   (D) Daniel Webster

   (E) Franklin Pierce

52. Which of the following was Theodore Roosevelt's most significant use of his "big stick" policy?

   (A) The United States established a protectorate in Cuba after the Spanish-American War.

   (B) The United States sent marines to occupy Veracruz and keep President Huerta from receiving weapons from Germany.

   (C) Roosevelt legitimized the "big stick" policy by issuing the Good Neighbor Policy toward Latin America.

   (D) The United States supported Panamanian rebels in their revolt against Colombia.

   (E) The United States intervened in the internal affairs of the Dominican Republic when that nation could not repay its foreign debts.

53. Because of Cleveland's stand on tariffs and silver, which of the following groups supported him?

   (A) Western farmers and miners

   (B) Eastern big business

   (C) Eastern big business, farmers, shop owners, and workingmen

   (D) Southern Democrats

   (E) Southern and Western Democrats

54. Which of the following novelists of the early twentieth century wrote about the hypocrisy and materialism of small-town life?

   (A) Sinclair Lewis

   (B) Ernest Hemingway

   (C) Edith Wharton

   (D) Frederick Lewis Allen

   (E) Langston Hughes

55. Which of the following was a U.S. program meant to provide aid to poverty-stricken countries anywhere in the world fighting communism?

   (A) Marshall Plan
   (B) NATO
   (C) Square Deal
   (D) Point Four
   (E) Alliance for Progress

56. By the mid-1700s, the largest city in the colonies was

   (A) New York
   (B) Boston
   (C) Philadelphia
   (D) Charleston
   (E) Wilmington, Delaware

57. "This kingdom . . . has always bound the colonies by her laws, her regulations . . . in every thing except that of taking their money out of their pockets without their consent. Here I would draw the line."
   The above statement was most likely spoken by

   (A) Benjamin Franklin
   (B) Edmund Andros
   (C) Patrick Henry
   (D) William Pitt
   (E) Alexis de Tocqueville

58. The defeat of which Native American leader made William Henry Harrison's presidential ambitions possible?

   (A) The Prophet
   (B) Tecumseh
   (C) Cochise
   (D) Chief Joseph
   (E) Blue Jacket

59. Which of the following recommended that the United States offer Spain $120 million for Cuba and if rebuffed, take the island by force?

   (A) Hay–Bunau-Varilla Treaty
   (B) Ballinger-Pinchot Controversy
   (C) Ostend Manifesto
   (D) Gadsden Purchase
   (E) Seward's Folly

60. Which of the following was not one of Lincoln's beliefs about reconstructing the South?

   (A) Reconstruction was part of his responsibility as commander in chief; it was not Congress's responsibility.
   (B) Congress did not have the authority to abolish slavery; a Constitutional amendment was needed to end slavery.
   (C) Lincoln wanted a generous practical policy of reconstruction in order "to bind up the nation's wounds" with "malice toward none, with charity for all."
   (D) Lincoln believed that the rebellion had been caused by individuals; the Southern states had never left the Union.
   (E) The right of African Americans to vote should be guaranteed in each new Southern state constitution.

61. African Americans were disenfranchised in Southern states by all the following practices EXCEPT

   (A) poll tax
   (B) literacy test
   (C) property test
   (D) white primary elections
   (E) separate but equal ruling in *Plessy* v. *Ferguson*

62. Which of the following is not true about the Washington Conference?

(A) The conference gave Americans a false sense of peace and security.

(B) Through the Four-Power Treaty, the signatories agreed to respect one another's possessions in the Pacific.

(C) The conference lessened tensions in the Pacific in the short term.

(D) Through the Nine-Power Treaty, the signatories agreed to respect one another's trading rights in China.

(E) Agreements were reached on limiting land forces and the building of smaller warships like submarines.

63. All of the following statements are true about Latinos' experiences in World War II EXCEPT

(A) unlike African Americans, Latinos fought in integrated units

(B) Latino youths were the target of Zoot Suit riots in several major cities

(C) Puerto Ricans were not allowed to enlist in the U.S. armed forces

(D) through the bracero program, Mexicans were brought to the United States to work in agriculture

(E) Latinos and Latinas found work in defense industries as a result of the Fair Employment Practices Commission

Questions 64 and 65 refer to the following charts.

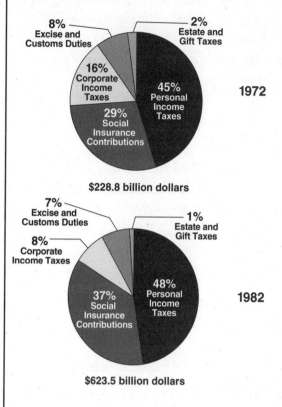

$228.8 billion dollars

$623.5 billion dollars

Department of Commerce

64. According to the two pie charts, the fastest growing source of government revenue is

(A) Personal Income Taxes

(B) Social Insurance Contributions

(C) Corporate Income Taxes

(D) Excise and Customs Duties

(E) Estate and Gift Taxes

65. Social Insurance Contributions (FICA) include

(A) Old Age, Survivors, and Disability Insurance; Medicare; Unemployment Insurance

(B) Old Age, Survivors, and Disability Insurance and Medicare

(C) Old Age, Survivors, and Disability Insurance; Medicare; and Medicaid

(D) Worker's Compensation

(E) Unemployment Insurance

66. Federal personal income taxes are

(A) proportional

(B) regressive

(C) progressive

(D) proportional and regressive

(E) progressive and proportional

67. According to the Navigation Acts,

(A) goods did not have to be shipped through England so long as customs duties were paid

(B) enumerated goods could be sold only to England

(C) hatmakers in the colonies could sell their beaver hats to England or to the colonies

(D) colonists could export raw wool, yarn, or wool cloth to countries other than England if customs duties were paid

(E) smugglers would be tried in admiralty courts

68. The underlying cause for the depression that lingered after the Panic of 1837 was

(A) the high tariff

(B) cheap money

(C) overspeculation in Western lands

(D) a corresponding depression in European markets

(E) Van Buren's independent treasury system

69. Which of the following issues cost both Hayes and Arthur their party's renomination as president?

(A) tariff reform

(B) cheap money

(C) proposed regulation of big business

(D) civil service reform

(E) their use of federal troops to intervene in strikes

70. Which of the following agreements renounced war as a vehicle of national policy?

(A) Five-Power Treaty

(B) Treaty of Versailles

(C) United Nations Charter

(D) Kellogg-Briand Pact

(E) Rush-Bagot Agreement

71. Truman and Congress differed over

(A) raising the minimum wage

(B) passage of the National Housing Act of 1949

(C) establishing farm price supports

(D) expansion of the Reclamation Bureau's work in flood control and the building of hydroelectric plants

(E) enactment of national health care

342   *Peterson's AP Success: U.S. History*

72. Critics of Reagan's economic program

   (A) complained that an increase in taxes would damage economic growth

   (B) advised "priming the pump"

   (C) were supply-siders

   (D) believed that he was passing the problem of the huge federal deficit to future generations

   (E) urged a tax cut to jump-start the economy

73. The writings of which of the following led to the end of the encomienda system?

   (A) King Ferdinand

   (B) Fray Junípero Serra

   (C) Sor Juana Inés de La Cruz

   (D) Bartolomé de Las Casas

   (E) Fray Eusebio Kino

74. "Everything that is right or reasonable pleads for separation. The blood of the slain, the weeping voice of nature cries, 'Tis Time to Part!' "
   The above statement, which deeply affected the delegates to the Second Continental Congress, is from

   (A) *Letters from a Farmer in Pennsylvania* by John Dickinson

   (B) *Poor Richard's Almanack* by Ben Franklin

   (C) *Letters from an American Farmer* by Hector St. John de Crevécoeur

   (D) *Common Sense* by Thomas Paine

   (E) A letter from Abigail Adams

75. All of the following are examples of the concept that third parties often develop out of some radical approach to a problem EXCEPT

   (A) Populists

   (B) Progressives

   (C) Know-Nothings

   (D) Democrats (Andrew Jackson era)

   (E) Republicans (founded 1854)

76. All of the following were among the reforms inspired by progressives at the state and local level EXCEPT

   (A) setting the maximum working hours for women at 10 hours a day

   (B) regulation of child labor

   (C) women's suffrage

   (D) establishment of worker's compensation funds

   (E) regulation of railroad rates

77. The major difference between W.E.B. Du Bois and his fellow African Americans Booker T. Washington and Marcus Garvey was Du Bois's

   (A) appeal to the Talented Tenth

   (B) belief that education alone would correct all injustices

   (C) disinterest in all things African

   (D) focus on economic equality

   (E) use of white politicians to gain an audience for African-American causes

78. Roosevelt would have preferred that the Neutrality Acts of 1935, 1936, and 1937

(A) limited U.S. economic aid to belligerents

(B) banned loans to warring nations in the Western Hemisphere

(C) distinguished between aggressor nations and victim nations

(D) banned the sale of nuclear weapons

(E) allowed the sale of weapons after a certain period of time

79. All of the following were writers of the "Beat Generation" EXCEPT

(A) William Burroughs

(B) Allen Ginsberg

(C) Laurence Ferlinghetti

(D) Jack Kerouac

(E) Jasper Johns

80. Who are the only two vice presidents to have gained office through the Twenty-Fifth Amendment?

(A) Lyndon Johnson and Gerald Ford

(B) Nelson Rockefeller and Harry Truman

(C) Gerald Ford and Nelson Rockefeller

(D) Theodore Roosevelt and Lyndon Johnson

(E) Lyndon Johnson and Harry Truman

END OF SECTION I.

If you have time, you may go back and review your answers.

SECTION II
PART A
(Suggested writing time—45 minutes)

Directions: The following question asks you to write a cohesive essay incorporating your interpretation of Documents A through I and your knowledge of the period stated in the question. To earn a high score, you must cite key evidence from the documents and use your outside knowledge of United States history.

1. Reform movements, westward expansion, and states' rights forced the United States to face the issue of slavery. Evaluate the relative importance of each influence as a cause of the Civil War.

   Use the following documents and your knowledge of United States history from 1850 to 1861 to construct your essay.

Document A

Source: Senator Salmon P. Chase, "Appeal of the Independent Democrats," January 19, 1854

Whatever apologies may be offered for the toleration of slavery in the States, none can be offered for its extension into Territories where it does not exist, and where that extension involves the repeal of ancient law and the violation of solemn compact. Let all protest, earnestly and emphatically, by correspondence, through the press, by memorials, by resolutions of public meetings and legislative bodies, and in whatever other mode may seem expedient, against this enormous crime.

For ourselves, we shall resist it by speech and vote, and with all the abilities which God has given us. Even if overcome in the impending struggle, we shall not submit. We shall go home to our constituents, erect anew the standard of freedom, and call on the people to come to the rescue of the country from the domination of slavery. We will not despair; for the cause of human freedom is the cause of God.

Document B

Source: Chief Justice C. J. Taney, *Dred Scott* v. *Sanford*, 1857

The rights of private property have been guarded with equal care. Thus the rights of property are united with the rights of person, and placed on the same ground by the fifth amendment to the Constitution. . . . An Act of Congress which deprives a person of the United States of his liberty or property merely because he came himself or brought his property into a particular Territory of the United States, and who had committed no offense against the laws, could hardly be dignified with the name of due process of law. . .

Upon these considerations, it is the opinion of the court that the Act of Congress the Missouri Compromise which prohibited a citizen from holding and owning property of this kind in the territory of the United States north of the line therein mentioned, is not warranted by the Constitution and is therefore void; and that neither Dred Scott himself, nor any member of his family, were made free by being carried into this territory; even if they had been carried there by the owner, with the intention of becoming a permanent resident. . . .

Document C

Source: Senator James Henry Hammond, Speech printed in the *Congressional Globe*, March 4, 1858

In all social systems there must be a class to do the mean duties, to perform the drudgery of life. . . Fortunately for the South, she found a race adapted to that purpose. . . We call them slaves. . . We do not think that whites should be slaves either by law or necessity. Our slaves are black, of another and inferior race. . . They are elevated from the condition in which God first created them, by being made our slaves. . . . They are happy, content, unaspiring, and utterly incapable, from intellectual weakness, ever to give us any trouble.

Document D

Source: Comments on the Lincoln-Douglas Freeport Debate, the *Chicago Tribune*, September 4, 1858

According to Senator Douglas, the Territorial Legislatures, though prohibited by the Constitution from abolishing slavery within their respective jurisdictions, may lawfully abstain from enforcing the rights of slaveholders and so extinguish the institution by voluntary neglect . . . In the name of common sense and common fairness, if slavery is to be prohibited or abolished in the Territories by any legislative tribunal, let it be done by one in which the whole nation is represented, and not by one composed of the representatives of the first stragglers from some over-burdened city or restless border State who happen to squat on the public domain. If slavery is to be prohibited in the Territories by legislation at all, let it be done by the people of the United States. If we must have sovereignty in the case, apart from the Constitution, give us the sovereignty of the American people, not squatter sovereignty. Senator Douglas, as we have seen, gives us the latter—Mr. Lincoln the former. Between the two, no intelligent, discerning patriot can hesitate a moment. Mr. Lincoln's position, aside from its virtually speculative cast, is infinitely less unfriendly to the constitutional rights and just interests of the South. When, furthermore, we reflect that the Supreme Court has pronounced this identical position unconstitutional, and would nullify any Congressional legislation in pursuance of it, the practical consequence of Mr. Lincoln's error vanishes into a political dream. But if it were as vital as it is lifeless, it would be immeasurably less pernicious than the reckless and shameless heresy of Douglas.

Document E

Source: Abraham Lincoln, reply to Stephen Douglas, October 15, 1858

That is the real issue. That is the issue that will continue in this country when these poor tongues of Judge Douglas and myself shall be silent. It is the eternal struggle between these two principles—right and wrong—throughout the world. They are the two principles that have stood face to face from the beginning of time and will ever continue to struggle. The one is the common right of humanity, and the other the divine right of kings. It is the same principle in whatever shape it develops itself. It is the same spirit that says, "You work and toil and earn bread, and I'll eat it." No matter in what shape it comes, whether from the mouth of a king who seeks to bestride the people of his own nation and live by the fruit of their labor, or from one race of men as an apology for enslaving another race, it is the same tyrannical principle. . .

Document F

Source: From an editorial in the *Daily Nashville Patriot,* Nashville, Tennessee, November 19, 1860

Secession, therefore, by the people of a State, is a nullity in law, and every citizen of the State continues, in spite of secession, still a citizen of the Union, liable to the penalties of the laws of the Union; and every act of resistance to the laws of the government, either by one man or one hundred thousand, is a crime, and can only be made innocent by the people of the United States. The contrary doctrine would give us a government without law, without order, without safety either for life, liberty, or property—just no government at all. The violation of a law by a single individual is simply a crime; if there be organized resistance to the law by many, it may be rebellion; and if by a State, it is called secession. . .

Document G

Source: "South Carolina Declaration of Causes of Secession," December 24, 1860

. . . We hold that the Government thus established is subject to the two great principles asserted in the Declaration of Independence; and we hold further, that the mode of its formation subjects it to a third fundamental principle, namely, the law of compact. We maintain that in every compact between two or more parties, the obligation is mutual; that the failure of one of the contracting parties to perform a material part of the agreement, entirely releases the obligation of the other; and that, where no arbiter is provided. Each part is remitted to his own judgment to determine that fact of failure, with all its consequences.

. . . A geographical line has been drawn across the Union, and all the States north of that line have united in the election of a man to the high office of President of the United States whose opinions and purposes are hostile to Slavery. He is to be entrusted with the administration of the common Government, because he has declared that "Government cannot endure permanently half slave, half free," and that the public mind must rest in the belief that Slavery is in the course of ultimate extinction.

We, therefore, the people of South Carolina . . . have solemnly declared that the Union heretofore existing between this State and the other States of North America is dissolved, and that the State of South Carolina has resumed her position among the nations of the world, as a separate and independent state, with full power to levy war, conclude peace, contract alliances, establish commerce, and to do all other acts and things which independent States may of right do.

Document H

Source: Abraham Lincoln, Inaugural Address, March 4, 1861

In your hands, my dissatisfied fellow countrymen, and not in mine, is the momentous issue of civil war. The government will not assail you. You can have no conflict without being yourselves the aggressors. You have no oath registered in heaven to destroy the government, while I shall have the most solemn one to "preserve, protect, and defend" it.

I am loath to close. We are not enemies, but friends. We must not be enemies. Though passion may have strained, it must not break, our bonds of affection. The mystic cords of memory, stretching from every battlefield and patriot grave to every living heart and hearthstone all over this broad land, will yet swell the chorus of the Union when again touched, as surely they will be, by the better angels of our nature.

Document I

Source: Jefferson Davis, Message to the Confederate Congress, April 29, 1861

Strange, indeed, must it appear to the impartial observer, but it is nonetheless true that all these carefully worded clauses proved unavailing to prevent the rise and growth of the Northern States of a political school which has persistently claimed that the government thus formed was not a compact between States, but in effect a national government, set up above and over the States. An organization created by the States to secure the blessings of liberty and independence against foreign aggression, has been gradually perverted into a machine for their control in their domestic affairs. . . . The people of the Southern States, whose almost exclusive occupation was agriculture, early perceived a tendency in the Northern States to render the common government subservient to their own purposes. . . .

Finally a great party was organized for the purpose of obtaining the administration of the Government, with the avowed object of using its power for the total exclusion of the slave States from all participation in the benefits of the public domain acquired by all the States in common, whether by conquest or purchase; of surrounding them entirely by States in which slavery should be prohibited; of thus rendering the property in slaves so insecure as to be comparatively worthless, and thereby annihilating in effect property worth thousands of millions of dollars. This party, thus organized, succeeded in the month of November last in the election of its candidate for the Presidency of the United States.

SECTION II
PARTS B AND C
(Suggested planning and writing time–70 minutes)

PART B

Directions: You are to answer ONE question from this group. The suggested planning time is 5 minutes with 30 minutes to write. State a thesis, cite relevant evidence, and use logical, clear arguments to support your generalizations.

2. In the 1740s, Great Britain and France realized that a struggle for control of North America was inevitable. Accept or refute this statement and cite evidence to support your position.

3. In the 1840s, the idea of manifest destiny appealed to many Americans. Define the concept and explain the effects on the policies of the United States government and on its citizens.

PART C

Directions: You are to answer ONE question from this group. The suggested planning time is 5 minutes with 30 minutes to write. State a thesis, cite relevant evidence, and use logical, clear arguments to support your generalizations.

4. Compare the contributions of two of the following to the economy and society of the United States from the late nineteenth to the early twentieth century.

   - Cornelius Vanderbilt
   - Andrew Carnegie
   - Ida Tarbell
   - Samuel Gompers

5. From 1960 to 1980, rivalry between the United States and the Union of Soviet Socialist Republics dominated world affairs. Explain how United States foreign policy changed from Cold War to détente, only to cool again in the late 1970s.

 END OF TEST.

Peterson's AP Success: U.S. History

ANSWERS AND EXPLANATIONS

EXPLANATORY ANSWERS

Test-Taking Strategy

The key words are major significance.

Test-Taking Strategy

For not/except *questions, ask yourself if the answer is true. If it is, cross it off and go on to the next answer.*

1. **The correct answer is (A).** All five choices present true information, but only choice (A) looks at the Great Awakening in the larger context of U.S. history. The other four choices deal with details of the movement.

2. **The correct answer is (E).** The Albany Plan of Union, proposed by Benjamin Franklin, called for choices (A), (B), (C), and (D), but the Crown would appoint the governor-general, so choice (E) is the correct answer. If the question had asked about the significance of the Albany Plan of Union, then choice (D) would have been correct.

3. **The correct answer is (D).** *Marbury* v. *Madison* established the principle of judicial review, choice (A). The Constitution established choice (B). The First Congress created the office of Attorney General, but the Justice Department was not created until 1870, choice (C). Choice (E) is incorrect; Jackson ignored the Supreme Court's ruling in this case.

4. **The correct answer is (D).** Labor unions were in their infancy at the beginning of the new nation.

5. **The correct answer is (B).** All five choices were part of a series of events that culminated in the Force Bill and the Tariff Act of 1833, but the direct cause of the two bills was choice (B).

The Webster-Hayne Debate, choice (A), began as a discussion of limiting the sale of western lands to keep workers in the Northeast and progressed to a discussion of the tariff. The Tariff of Abominations, choice (D), or the Tariff of 1828, angered South Carolinians who were faced with a depressed cotton market and blamed high tariff rates. They found voice in Calhoun's paper, choice (C). Jackson's veto of the Maysville Road Bill in 1830, choice (E), on the grounds that it encroached on the sovereignty of a state, seemed to signal to advocates of nullification that he would support states' rights in a showdown with South Carolina. However, Jackson issued a statement to South Carolina after it passed the Ordinance of Nullification, choice (B), that nullification was equal to treason. The Force Bill gave Jackson the power to use force in South Carolina to prevent dissolution, and a new tariff lowered rates, thus averting the crisis.

Test-Taking Strategy

Knowing the time frame will help you eliminate choices (B) and (D).

6. **The correct answer is (C).** The clues are *women, one half of the people,* and *citizens.* If you did not recognize this quotation from the Seneca Falls "Declaration of Sentiments and Resolutions," you could eliminate several of the choices by educated guessing. The time frame for this question is after 1833 and before Reconstruction, so that neither choice (B) nor choice (D) were citizens. Choices (A) and (E) could not account for "one half of the people of this country," even though free blacks could not necessarily vote, so choice (C) must be the answer.

7. **The correct answer is (E).** According to the Congressional Reconstruction plan and the Fourteenth Amendment, former Confederate officials could not participate in the state constitutional conventions or vote. Any state that had not organized a new government by 1870 also had to ratify the Fifteenth Amendment to be readmitted.

8. **The correct answer is (D).** All five choices describe actual scandals of the post–Civil War period, but only choice (D) describes Crédit Mobilier. Choice (A) was known as the "salary grab." Belknap, choice (B), wanted to award the lucrative Indian trading rights at Fort Sill, Oklahoma, to a friend, but the current trader offered a bribe to both Belknap and the friend to keep his trading rights. "Boss" Tweed, choice (C), and his Tammany Hall machine were responsible for much of the graft and corruption in New York City government, including ballot stuffing, kickbacks for city jobs, and bribery. The "whiskey ring," choice (E), operated to blackmail distillers who found it cheaper to pay blackmail than to pay federal taxes on whiskey.

9. The correct answer is (E). President Theodore Roosevelt later issued the Roosevelt Corollary that modified the Monroe Doctrine to suit U.S. business interests in Latin America, but the Spanish-American War did not result in any changes to it. Once in possession of territories in the Pacific, the United States realized that it needed to be able to defend them, and that realization resulted in choices (A) and (B). The Insular Cases, choice (D), resulted in a ruling that unincorporated territories like Puerto Rico and the Philippines did not have the constitutional protection of incorporated territories such as Hawaii, but the residents were guaranteed due process.

10. The correct answer is (B). Americans were disillusioned by the quarrels among European nations that occurred after World War I (known as the Great War), the tariff wars, and the Europeans' failure to disarm. The Nye Committee report on the huge wartime profits by U.S. bankers and munitions makers was another cause of disillusionment. While choice (C) was the belief of many people, it was not a cause of isolationist feelings. Choice (A) is incorrect. Choice (D) is incorrect, although many in government and outside it insisted on collecting war debts and therefore added to the worldwide depression. Choice (E) may have been a result of isolationism, but it was not a cause.

11. The correct answer is (B). Choice (D) is also based on economics, but was a secondary effect of the Southern colonies' need for cheap and plentiful labor. Choice (A) is incorrect; colonists found enslaved Africans had several advantages over indentured servants. Africans could not escape by blending into the population, were not free when their term of indenture was over, and were well suited to the hot climate of the South. There also seemed to be an endless supply of Africans. Choice (E) is a rationalization that the English used to justify their enslavement of Africans. Choice (C) is an example of something a slave owner might say to justify slavery.

12. The correct answer is (B). Choices (A), (C), and (E) contributed to choice (B), so they were causes of, rather than the result of, settlement. Choice (D) occurred on the frontier, but was a result of Hamilton's excise tax on whiskey.

13. The correct answer is (D). Choice (A) is incorrect because the term "manifest destiny" was not coined until 1845 in the midst of the debate over annexation of Texas and the Oregon boundary line. Choice (B) is incorrect; the United States did not begin its interventions until 1898. Choice (C) is incorrect; Great Britain wanted to issue what became known as the Monroe Doctrine jointly. The information in choice (E) is true, but irrelevant.

14. **The correct answer is (D).** Choices (A), (B), and (C) were weaknesses of labor unions in this period, but not the reason why labor was unaware of its power. Only later did laborers discover that by banding together they could force employers to improve working conditions, shorten working hours, and raise pay—all basic demands of later unions. Choice (E) is incorrect; the efforts of the women in the Lowell factories to unionize in the 1840s illustrates the opposite.

15. **The correct answer is (E).** During the Civil War, inflation—the opposite of a tight money supply—was a great problem, so choice (E) is the correct answer. If you were not sure of the answer, you could make an educated guess based on the fact that farmers, or any debtors, prefer cheap, or inflated, money because they can repay their loans with money that is worth less than when they borrowed it.

16. **The correct answer is (C).** First came the factory system, choice (B), and then the development of interchangeable parts, choice (A), by Eli Whitney among others. These resulted in the division of labor that, in turn, resulted in the mass production of goods, choice (C). Mass production was facilitated by the development of the electric motor, choice (E). Choice (D) is irrelevant.

17. **The correct answer is (D).** Roosevelt never wished to abandon choices (A), (C), or (E). He had come to believe, however, that monopolies were not inherently bad. Some actually could work for the benefit of consumers, for example, by using economies of scale to produce goods and lower prices. Also, combinations and big business enterprises were inevitable. Roosevelt did believe that business needed to be policed, and he proposed a federal trade commission to oversee business practices. Wilson campaigned on choice (B).

18. **The correct answer is (A).** Efforts were made to teach soil conservation and better ways to raise crops and livestock, but with little success. As a result, the program did not raise the standard of living of Native Americans on reservations, as had been intended. Choices (B), (C), and (E) were goals that were met. Choice (D) is incorrect.

19. **The correct answer is (E).** Railroads lost business to long-distance trucks and to passenger cars. Even though commuter trains, mainly in the Northeast, still carried people to work from the suburbs, the railroads operated at a great loss. By the 1960s, many had filed for bankruptcy. Choice (C), in combination with choice (A), allowed many to buy homes in subdivisions such as Levittown.

20. **The correct answer is (A).** The war was at a stalemate when Eisenhower took over the presidency from Truman. Eisenhower put pressure on the North Koreans to resume negotiations, and a truce was reached by mid-1953. Choice (B) was known as the Eisenhower Doctrine and also stated that the United States would intervene if any Middle Eastern nation came under attack by Communist forces.

Test-Taking Strategy

Knowing the timeframe will help you eliminate choice (E).

21. **The correct answer is (C).** Although the facts in choices (A) and (B) are true, neither is the main reason that England became a major power. The defeat of the Spanish Armada greatly hindered Spain's ability to keep English ships off the seas. Knowing that the trans-Atlantic triangle trade did not begin until the late 1600s will help you eliminate choice (E). Choice (D) is irrelevant.

22. **The correct answer is (E).** Bacon's Rebellion helped convince Virginia planters that Africans enslaved for life would be less trouble than indentured servants who might not be able to make a living after they were free. Both choices (A) and (B) were rebellions of enslaved blacks. The Stono Uprising, choice (A), occurred in 1739 near Charleston, South Carolina, and resulted in the deaths of twenty or thirty whites and most of the twenty slaves. In 1831, Nat Turner, choice (B), led some sixty slaves in rebellion in Virginia, and they killed approximately sixty whites before they were captured. The Whiskey Rebellion, choice (C), occurred on the Pennsylvania frontier in response to the excise tax on whiskey levied as part of Alexander Hamilton's fiscal program for the new nation. Shay's Rebellion, choice (D), occurred in Massachusetts during the Confederation period in response to high taxes and the practice of foreclosing and imprisoning debtors.

23. **The correct answer is (C).** Choice (A) refers to the *Proclamation of Rebellion* issued by George III. Choice (B) relates to Lee's Resolution, which was introduced into the Second Continental Congress and debated while the Declaration of Independence was being written. Choice (D) relates to the Circular Letter, and choice (E) to the Declaration of Rights and Grievances.

24. **The correct answer is (A).** The treaty signed in 1851 by the representatives of Native American nations and the U.S. government was never ratified by the Senate, although the United States paid $50,000 a year for fifteen of the fifty years that the treaty called for. In exchange, the Native Americans kept their side of the treaty until after the Civil War. Choice (C) is the opposite of a provision in the treaty. The Treaty of Guadalupe Hidalgo covered choice (B). The federal government had set aside the

Black Hills, choice (D), as the Sioux reservation, but when gold was found in the mountains in the 1870s, the area was opened to whites. Choice (E) refers to the Gadsden Purchase.

25. **The correct answer is (B).** The alliance provided capital for Southern factory owners. Choice (A) worked against the development of the Southern economy and was one cause of the low wages Southern factories paid, choice (C). The information in choices (D) and (E) is true but irrelevant.

26. **The correct answer is (A).** Choice (B) discourages foreign competition. Choice (C) means people have more money to spend. Choice (D) meant more markets for U.S. goods, and choice (E) would mean a larger pool of cheap labor.

27. **The correct answer is (D).** Choice (A) is related to the purchase and coinage of small amounts of silver. Choice (B) related to the regulation of railroads; it set up the Interstate Commerce Commission, the first regulatory body in the nation's history. Choice (C) regulated the federal civil service system. Choice (E) authorized the government to purchase silver; this law was passed almost twenty years after the Bland-Allison Act.

Test-Taking Strategy

Knowing the time frame will help you eliminate (E).

28. **The correct answer is (C).** Choice (C) is incorrect and irrelevant; the money supply at the time was backed by gold reserves. The Federal Reserve Act established the Federal Reserve System, the monetary side of the nation's economic policies, by setting up twelve Federal Reserve Banks in twelve regions around the nation. Through member banks, the Fed provided money to banks in temporary trouble, choice (A). It eased the inflexibility of the money supply, choice (B), by providing Federal Reserve notes in exchange for promissory notes from member banks. The Fed also controlled the amount of money in circulation, choice (D). The Federal Reserve Board that governed the system was appointed by the president and approved by the Senate for fourteen-year terms, choice (E).

29. **The correct answer is (D).** Containment theory, first used by Truman, stated that the United States should take an aggressive posture toward the Soviet Union, short of instigating a third world war. In time, the Soviet Union would become less belligerent or would change. The end of communism in Eastern Europe—and the Soviet Union—seems to have proven this theory. Choice (A) refers to the idea that if one country in Asia fell to communism, they all would. Choice (B) promised military and economic aid to nations in the Middle East and potential U.S. intervention against communist aggression. Choice (C) provided aid to Turkey and Greece after World War II to fight off commu-

nist takeovers. Choice (E) provided materials and financial aid to seventeen European countries to rebuild after World War II.

30. **The correct answer is (D).** So named by the Spanish because they lived in villages (*pueblos*), Pueblo people still live in the Southwestern United States. Descended from the Anasazi cliff dwellers, the Pueblos were and continue to be sedentary farmers with great skill in basket weaving and pottery.

Test-Taking Strategy

The key words are major significance.

Review Strategy

See Chapter 6 for more information on the Supreme Court.

31. **The correct answer is (C).** Choices (A), (B), (C), and (D) are true, but choice (D) does not relate to the delegated powers, so it can be eliminated. Of the other three choices, choices (A) and (B) are very specific. Choice (C) is a general view of delegated powers and thus a better answer. Choice (E) is the opposite of what the Tenth Amendment says. All powers not specifically delegated to the federal government reside with the states.

32. **The correct answer is (E).** Choice (A) was the stated purpose of these acts, but choice (E) was the Federalists' underlying goal. The acts were aimed at French immigrants, most of whom joined the Democratic-Republican Party, which favored U.S. intervention in the European wars on the side of France. Federalists may have used choice (C) as a rationalization, but the Sedition Act interfered with both the freedom of the press and freedom of speech. Both choices (B) and (D) are incorrect.

33. **The correct answer is (D).** As the Depression worsened, Hoover followed his theory of "rugged individualism" and "decentralized local responsibility." Franklin Roosevelt, choice (A), on the other hand, with the advice of Keynes, choice (B), believed in "priming the pump"—putting government money into the economy to provide relief and jobs. Theodore Roosevelt, choice (C), as a progressive, also believed that government should help people. As the Panic of 1893 worsened, Cleveland accepted the offer of J. P. Morgan and a group of bankers to lend the federal government money to shore up the sagging dollar.

Test-Taking Strategy

The key words are best describes.

34. **The correct answer is (A).** While choices (A), (B), (D), and (E) are true of the period, choice (A) is the most inclusive choice. It contains the elements of the other three answers. Widespread transportation and communications networks, the growth of industries and markets for industrial goods, and large-scale urban development that provided workers—all transferred the center of power, influence, and wealth from farms to cities. Choice (C) is arguably true of the period but irrelevant to the question. Americans shifted from a belief in manifest destiny on the U.S. continent to a philosophy of imperialism, or worldwide colonialism.

35. The correct answer is (C). This is a cause-and-effect question. Choices (A), (B), (D), and (E) all contributed to the intolerance of the period, while choice (C) was a result of it. Choices (A) and (E) were related in many Americans' minds. These people feared that the Bolshevik Revolution of 1917, which toppled the czar in Russia, would inspire the radicals in the United States to overthrow the government. A series of mail bombs thought to have been sent by radicals fueled suspicions. At the same time, labor unions organized a series of strikes in 1919 that resulted in violence. Choice (B) was used as an excuse to push through laws in 1921 and 1924 restricting immigration. Jews and Catholics were seen as clannish and divided in their loyalties, and their customs and traditions were unfamiliar and, therefore, seen as odd and potentially menacing, choice (D). Racism is another element of intolerance that could have been included in the list.

36. The correct answer is (C). In offering his proposal, which included the request to appoint lower-level federal judges as well as to enlarge the Supreme Court, Roosevelt used choice (C) as his reason. His unstated purposes were choices (A) and (B). These, in turn, would have created choice (D). As Supreme Court justices retired between 1937 and 1940, the new Court upheld New Deal measures, including the National Labor Relations Act and the Social Security Act. Choice (E) was the reason people gave in opposing Roosevelt's proposal.

37. The correct answer is (D). *Marbury* v. *Madison* established choice (A). *Gideon* v. *Wainwright* established choice (B). Choice (C) was the principle in *Schenck* v. *United States*. *Korematsu* v. *United States* is the case referred to in choice (E).

38. The correct answer is (B). Perhaps the defining characteristic of the colonies was social mobility. Choice (A) is an example of an absolute statement; it is not logical to expect that there were no free blacks in any of the colonies, so choice (A) should be eliminated. Choice (C) is the opposite of the situation. Women were highly regarded for their contributions to the welfare and economic life of the colonies. Choice (D) is incorrect; even as late as the mid-1800s there was no general belief in the need for universal education. Choice (E) is incorrect; by 1775 slightly less than half the colonial population was English. The Middle Colonies had the greatest diversity.

39. The correct answer is (B). All five choices are true about British policies in the colonies, but choice (B) is the most inclusive. The old policy in choice (A) is the levying of taxes; the new problem is the strong reaction of the colonists after the French and Indian War. The theory of virtual representation is the way Parliament had always considered its colonies, while direct or actual representation was the new view of the colonists, choice (C). Choice (D) is undoubtedly true, but irrelevant to the question. The British were in a cycle in which they passed a law, the colonists reacted, and the British passed another law, rescinded the first law, issued a proclamation, shut down a legislature, and so on, choice (E). Whether the cycle was inescapable is arguable.

40. **The correct answer is (C).** The factory system did not exist in the United States until the nineteenth century. Influenced by the themes of European Romanticism, choice (A), the artists and writers of the early republic set out to establish a national identity through their works. For example, James Fenimore Cooper in his novels and George Caleb Bingham and George Catlin in their paintings used Native Americans, frontier life, and nature as themes, choices (B) and (D). Writers like Washington Irving and Nathaniel Hawthorne used the colonial past for themes, choice (E).

41. **The correct answer is (B).** The Compromise of 1850 affected all the territory received from Mexico at the end of the Mexican War. Choice (C) and much of choice (D) were part of the Louisiana Territory. Washington Territory was created from part of the Oregon Territory, choice (E), after the Treaty of 1846 fixed the border with Canada.

Test-Taking Strategy

A partially correct answer is a partially incorrect answer—and a quarter-point deduction.

42. **The correct answer is (D).** Choices (A) and (B) are only partially correct. While admitting California as a free state, choice (C), the Compromise of 1850 called for Utah and New Mexico Territories to delay statehood until they had determined for themselves if they would be free or slave. The Kansas-Nebraska Act of 1854 called for popular sovereignty to determine the issue in those two territories as well. The Compromise had no effect on Texas's admission as a slave state.

43. **The correct answer is (B).** Many Republicans, including moderate Republicans, were truly concerned about ensuring the political, legal, and economic rights of African Americans. But choice (C) also figured to an extent in the thinking of some Republicans. Choice (D) was the major area of contention between Congress and both Lincoln and Johnson. Some Republicans also worried about the loyalty of former Confederates, choice (E).

Test-Taking Strategy

Knowing the time frame will help you eliminate choice (A).

44. **The correct answer is (B).** Question 43 is about the early period of Reconstruction, so the canal industry, choice (A), cannot be the correct response since the canals' usefulness was eclipsed by railroads in the 1850s. Logic says that choice (D) is

incorrect because the farmers in the late 1800s were the victims of industry, not the perpetrators of abuses. A rebate was a refund to a favored shipper of part of the advertised rate that the shipper paid. Pooling was the practice whereby the railroads in an area agreed to maintain high prices for shipping goods. Some pools even divided the profits among member railroads. Choices (C) and (E) are incorrect.

45. **The correct answer is (D).** The "Crime of 1873" is the term given to Congress's decision not to coin silver by silver miners who were burdened with huge new silver mines and debtors who wanted cheap money with which to repay their debts. Choices (A) and (B) meant that it would have been more profitable for owners of silver mines to sell their silver to the government at the government's old ratio of 16 to 1. This prompted their calling the demonetizaton of silver in 1873 the "Crime of 1873." Choice (C) was a response to the call for cheap money, but helped little in enlarging the money supply and reducing the value of the dollar. Choice (E) is irrelevant; the Party survived into the 1880s.

46. **The correct answer is (D).** To head off a march through Washington, D.C., by an estimated 50,000 African Americans, Roosevelt met with A. Philip Randolph, the head of the Brotherhood of Sleeping Car Porters, and agreed to establish the Fair Employment Practices Commission to ensure that African Americans were not discriminated against in defense industries. King, choice (A), was the head of the Southern Christian Leadership Conference in the 1950s and 1960s. Abernathy, choice (C), took King's place after his assassination. Garvey, choice (B), founded the Universal Negro Improvement Association and a "back-to-Africa" movement. Bethune, choice (E), headed the National Youth Administration under Roosevelt and was a member of his informal "Black Cabinet."

47. **The correct answer is (C).** Although the Walter-McCarran Immigration and Nationality Act removed the ban on immigrants from Asia, it continued the quota or national preference system, which discriminated against non-Northern and non-Western Europeans.

48. **The correct answer is (A).** Iran-contra refers to a scandal in the Reagan administration that involved the selling of arms to supposed moderates in Iran and diverting the profits to the Contras fighting the Sandinistas in Nicaragua. The activities were carried on by officials high in the administration in violation of national policy and a Congressional ban. Choice (B) refers to the Uniteid States's recognition of the Republic of China while

maintaining ties with Taiwan. Choice (C) was the policy Nixon and his Secretary of State Henry Kissinger pursued in an attempt to end the war in Vietnam. Choice (D) was the relaxation of strained relations between the United States and the Soviet Union. Choice (E) accomplished a new era of peace in the Middle East between Israel and Egypt.

49. **The correct answer is (C).** The first Africans had been considered indentured servants, but as tobacco became the major crop and planters looked for a stable and cheap labor force, Maryland passed a law in 1663 to make Africans slaves "for life." Choice (A) describes the practice of headright. Choice (D) is known as the Half-Way Covenant. Choices (B) and (E) are incorrect.

50. **The correct answer is (B).** The Fourth Amendment prohibits unlawful searches and seizures and was aimed at the British use of writs of assistance to search for smuggled goods. The Third Amendment rectifies choice (A). The seeds of responses to choices (D) and (E) can be seen in various provisions of the Constitution, such as the right to a speedy trial by one's peers and separation of church and state, choice (E). The American principle of assessing the truthfulness of statements to determine libel was established in the trial of John Peter Zenger, choice (C).

51. **The correct answer is (A).** When he took office, Polk told historian George Bancroft that these were his four goals. Logic tells you Webster, choice (D), cannot be the answer, because he would not have wanted to reduce the tariff. If you knew that Pierce became president in 1852 and that the Oregon boundary and the annexation of California had already been accomplished, you could eliminate choice (E). Choices (B) and (C) are incorrect.

52. **The correct answer is (D).** Choices (A), (D), and (E) state correct information. Choice (A) refers to the Platt Amendment, choice (D) to the establishment of Panama, and choice (E) to a situation that caused Roosevelt to use the Roosevelt Corollary to the Monroe Doctrine for the first time. Of these three, the most significant effect in the long-term history of the United States and the world was the assigning of the right to build a canal across the isthmus of Panama to the United States, so choice (D) is the best answer. Choice (B) is an action of President Wilson. Choice (C) is only partially correct. Theodore Roosevelt legitimized the "big stick" policy through the Roosevelt Corollary, while Franklin Roosevelt adopted the Good Neighbor Policy to Latin America.

53. **The correct answer is (C).** First, you need to know that Cleveland opposed "free and unlimited silver," which choice (A) supported. Choice (B) is only partially correct. The groups in

Test-Taking Strategy

Educated guessing can help you when you don't know the answer immediately.

Test-Taking Strategy

The key words are most significant.

choice (C) feared unlimited silver coinage as a Western threat to stability and supported Cleveland. Choices (D) and (E) supported the Populist program of silver and cheap money.

54. **The correct answer is (A).** Lewis's best-known works are *Babbit* and *Main Street.* Hemingway, choice (B), was a member of the "lost generation." Wharton, choice (C), wrote about New York society around the turn of the twentieth century. Allen, choice (D), was a journalist and social historian. Hughes, choice (E), was a writer and poet of the Harlem Renaissance.

55. **The correct answer is (D).** Choice (A) provided aid to war-torn Europe after World War II. Choice (B) was established after World War II to provide for the mutual defense of non-Communist nations in Europe. Choice (C) was the name Theodore Roosevelt gave to his domestic program. Choice (E) was Kennedy's program to halt the spread of communism in Latin America.

56. **The correct answer is (C).** By 1754, Philadelphia was the second-largest city in the British Empire after London. New York, choice (A), was the second-largest city in the North American colonies and Boston, choice (B), the third. Charleston, choice (D), was an important port for the South. Wilmington, choice (E), was an important port in the southern Middle Colonies. Note that all these cities were ports.

57. **The correct answer is (D).** One clue is the use of the third person (*their*) in referring to the colonies. That eliminates choices (A) and (C); logic says that they would have spoken in the first person. Choice (B) can be eliminated because Andros was removed after he antagonized the colonists of New England. Choice (E) was French, so he would not be speaking of "this kingdom." William Pitt the Elder did speak these words in defense of the colonies' rights.

58. **The correct answer is (A).** Do not be confused because The Prophet, choice (A), was the spiritual leader and Tecumseh, choice (B), was the warrior. Tecumseh was not in the village of Tippecanoe when Harrison's troops attacked, so choice (A) is correct. Choice (C) was an Apache chief who was captured in 1871. Choice (D) was a chief of the Nez Perce who surrendered to the U.S. Army in 1877. Choice (E) led the Shawnee and their allies against General Anthony Wayne at the Battle of Fallen Timbers in 1794.

59. **The correct answer is (C).** Southern slave owners pushed for purchase or annexation of Cuba to add more slaveholding territory to the United States, but nothing came of the offer. Choice (A) ceded to the United States what became the Panama

Canal Zone. Choice (B) involved Taft's Secretary of the Interior Richard Ballinger and Gifford Pinchot, the chief forester, over Ballinger's opening of lands in Montana, Wyoming, and Alaska for private purchase. Choice (D) was the purchase of land from Mexico in order to secure a Southern route for a transcontinental railroad. Choice (E) was the derisive name given to the purchase of Alaska; Secretary of State William Seward arranged for the sale.

Test-Taking Strategy

For not/except questions, ask yourself if an answer is true. If it is, cross it off and go on to the next answer.

60. **The correct answer is (E).** Suffrage for African Americans was never part of Lincoln's official plan for Reconstruction. Lincoln believed choice (D), while Charles Sumner espoused the theory of state suicide on one hand and on the other, Thaddeus Stevens advocated the theory of conquered provinces.

61. **The correct answer is (E).** Choice (E) relates to public accommodations. According to choice (A), African Americans had to pay a tax to vote; many did not have the money. Because African Americans' access to education was limited, choice (B) was discriminatory. Few owned property, making choice (C) discriminatory as well. Because the Fifteenth Amendment did not cover primary elections, African Americans were not always allowed to vote in them.

62. **The correct answer is (E).** Choice (E) is one of the reasons why the Conference had only short-term effects, choice (C); no such agreements were reached. There were no provisions for enforcing choices (B) or (D), so choice (A) proved true for the nation, but is wrong as the answer.

63. **The correct answer is (C).** Puerto Ricans had been made U.S. citizens in 1917 under the Jones Act. Puerto Ricans served in World War I and another 65,000 served in World War II. Although choice (A) is true, Latinos often served in units that originated in states with high concentrations of Latinos, such as New Mexico.

64. **The correct answer is (B).**

65. **The correct answer is (B).** Unemployment insurance and worker's compensation are not included in FICA, so choices (A), (D), and (E) are incorrect. Medicaid, choice (C), is a state-funded program and not part of FICA.

66. **The correct answer is (C).** Federal personal income taxes take a larger share of higher incomes than lower ones. Federal corporate income taxes are also progressive. Choice (A) takes the same percentage of all incomes. State or local sales taxes are regressive, choice (B), in that they take a larger proportion of lower incomes than higher ones. FICA is both proportional, because it takes the same percentage of tax out of everyone's income up to a maximum wage, and regressive, because it takes

a larger percentage out of smaller incomes. Choice (E) is incorrect.

67. **The correct answer is (B).** Choice (A) is the opposite of what the Navigation Acts stated. According to the Hat Act, choice (C), beaver hats could be sold only in the colonies. The Woolen Act, choice (D), forbade the export of wool to other colonies or to England to protect English manufacturing. Choice (E) was a later provision under George Grenville.

68. **The correct answer is (C).** The effects of Jackson's release of several million acres of Western land, the destruction of the Second Bank, and the issuing of credit by unstable state banks were felt for a number of years. Choice (A) had been reduced after the bitter fight in 1833. Choice (B) became an issue in the second half of the 1800s. Choices (D) and (E) are incorrect.

69. **The correct answer is (D).** Hayes appointed people to positions because of their qualifications rather than their party affiliation and insisted that government positions be filled by competitive examination. This alienated both the Halfbreeds and the Stalwarts in the Republican Party. Arthur pushed for civil service reform and supported passage of the Pendleton Act. Arthur supported choice (A). Hayes opposed the issuance of greenbacks and vetoed the Bland-Allison Act, which became law over his veto, choice (B). Choice (C) is incorrect. Hayes set a precedent for choice (E).

70. **The correct answer is (D).** Ultimately, sixty-two nations signed the Pact. It had little practical effect since there were no provisions for enforcing it other than popular opinion. Choice (A) was signed as part of the Washington Conference; the signatories agreed to limit production of large warships. Choice (B) included the charter for the League of Nations, which would settle international disputes peacefully and punish errant nations. Choice (C) established a world organization to promote peace and cooperation and to work to improve the welfare of poor countries. Choice (E) was an agreement between the United States and Great Britain for mutual disarmament of the Great Lakes.

71. **The correct answer is (E).** It was not until Lyndon Johnson's presidency that a national medical care program—for the elderly, the disabled, and the poor—was signed into law as Medicare and Medicaid. Choices (A), (B), (C), and (D) were part of Truman's Fair Deal program and were passed by Congress.

72. **The correct answer is (D).** Reagan increased defense spending greatly, cut domestic programs, and cut taxes, creating a huge deficit and high interest rates and giving rise to choice (D).

Reagan's policy was known as supply-side economics, so choice (C) is illogical. Choice (B) would only have added to the deficit, so it is also illogical. Reagan cut taxes, so choice (A) is illogical. Choice (E) is what Reagan was doing, so it is incorrect.

73. **The correct answer is (D).** By protesting the ill treatment of Native Americans, de Las Casas unwittingly aided in the enslavement of Africans. A king need simply to decree that the system end, so choice (A) is illogical. Choice (B) established a series of missions in California in the late 1700s. Choice (C) was a poet and scholar in Mexico in the late 1600s. Choice (E) explored the Spanish borderlands, establishing some twenty-five missions and mapping the territory in the late 1600s and early 1700s.

74. **The correct answer is (D).** The clues are the tone and the reference to the Second Continental Congress. Choice (A) was written in 1767 and 1768, so it was too early to be an influence on the delegates. More importantly, although a delegate to the Continental Congress, Dickinson was against independence. Choice (B) is illogical given the nature of the *Almanack*. Choice (C) was written in 1782 and is a description of the period, not a political tract. Although Abigail Adams was influential, she wrote private letters, so it is doubtful that the delegates would have read these words.

75. **The correct answer is (D).** The purpose of the Jacksonian Democrats was to elect Jackson; there was no particular social, political, or economic problem they wished to solve. Choice (A), Progressives, were interested in reforms aimed at helping farmers, such as coinage of silver. Choice (B) advocated a number of reforms at all levels of society: government, business, social mores, politics. Choice (C) formed to limit immigration and keep Catholics and naturalized citizens out of government. Choice (E) formed from the Whig and Free Soil Parties and abolitionists.

76. **The correct answer is (E).** Choices (A), (B), (C), and (D) were all reforms at the local and state levels before they became national laws. National regulation was needed to regulate railroads because they were interstate.

Test-Taking Strategy

Always read the question carefully. Underline or circle important words and ideas.

77. **The correct answer is (A).** Both Washington and Garvey addressed their messages to ordinary African Americans. None of them believed in choice (B). Both DuBois and Garvey celebrated their African heritage, Garvey with his "back-to-Africa" movement and DuBois with Pan-Africanism. Choice (D) was Washington's focus. Choice (E) was also true of Washington's approach.

78. **The correct answer is (C).** Choice (A) is the opposite of the Acts; the United States could provide aid only to nonbelligerents.

Choices (B), (D), and (E) are incorrect. Choice (D) is easy to eliminate because there were no nuclear weapons in this time period.

79. **The correct answer is (E).** Johns was a painter of the 1950s. Choices (A) and (D) were novelists, and choices (B) and (C) were poets.

Review Strategy

See Chapter 6 for more information on the Constitution.

80. **The correct answer is (C).** After Spiro Agnew was forced to resign, Nixon nominated Ford as vice president. When Nixon was forced to resign, Ford nominated Rockefeller as vice president. These are the only two times Section 2 of the Twenty-Fifth Amendment has been used. Choices (D) and (E) are instances of the normal succession of the vice president upon the death of the president as stated in Section 1 of Article II.

SUGGESTIONS FOR THE DOCUMENT-BASED QUESTION, PART A

Study Strategy

Revise your essay using points from this list that will strength it.

Be sure you recognized that the issues of reform movements, westward expansion, and states' rights were key political elements, especially in the elections of 1856 and 1860. These controversies forced the United States to face the issue of slavery. Notice that the articles are arranged in chronological order, although you need not use them in that order. You should incorporate references to documents in the order in which they best support your thesis. In developing your argument, you might have chosen the following points about Documents A through I. Consider them as you complete your self-evaluation. Use the *Self-Evaluation Rubric* on pp. 000 and 000 to score your essays.

Document A

Document A is an excerpt from Senator Chase's angry protest over the Kansas-Nebraska Bill then being debated in Congress. Chase states that those who are opposed to slavery will not give in; indeed, they will fight. Abolitionism is a holy crusade, since the end of slavery is one of God's causes. In spite of vociferous opposition, the bill, written by Stephen Douglas, passed—in essence nullifying the Missouri Compromise.

While Chase's purpose was to rally parts of the Democratic Party to the cause of abolition, in reality this widely reproduced document helped provide the impetus for the organization of the Republican Party. As a result of the anger against the Kansas-Nebraska Act, the guiding principle for the new political party was resistance to the spread of slavery into the territories. Republicans called slavery "a great moral, social, and political evil" and vowed to concentrate all their efforts to battle against the extension of slavery. Republican political success in the 1856 election struck fear in the heart of the South. How can you relate the slavery debate to westward expansion? Would the dilemma of free versus slave states have existed without expansion? You could discuss slavery as a moral issue and as an economic issue.

Document B

This document, from the majority opinion regarding the Dred Scott decision, declares the Missouri Compromise to be unconstitutional. The law violated the Fifth Amendment because it deprived persons of their property without due process of law. the decision also ended the idea of popular sovereignty.

The decision exacerbated sectional tensions. Although moderates had hoped that the Compromise of 1850 would resolve the divisive issue of slavery in the territories, it did not. From 1855 on, the bloody struggle between free-soilers and proslavery forces in Kansas further divided the North and South. Then, in 1857, antislavery proponents received a major setback with the Dred Scott decision. Many people feared that the Supreme Court was conspiring to extend slavery not only into new territories but also into older free states. Why was this Court decision such a turning point? How can you use the Dred Scott decision to argue the influence of reformers and westward expansion on the outbreak of the Civil War?

Document C
Document C and the document that follows it demonstrate the virulence of the debate about slavery. Abolitionists were not above publishing propaganda, invoking Christian tenets, twisting facts, and using inflammatory language. Abolitionists were more interested in telling horror stories than painting an accurate picture of slavery and the South. Attempts to correct the picture by Southern slave owners resulted in speeches and documents like this.

Unfortunately, Northerners, especially those opposed to slavery, developed a skewed view of the South. Hatred easily spread from the institution of slavery to Southerners in general, even though most Southerners did not own slaves. How did these misunderstandings and stereotypes hamper relations between North and South? Did it really matter that so few Southerners owned slaves when Southerners in general believed the propaganda of their leaders about the "Southern way of life"?

Document D
Document D contains some interesting points. Although it was reproduced in a Northern newspaper, it was originally printed in the South. The selection demonstrates that some Northerners and Southerners agreed that popular sovereignty—"squatter sovereignty"— was unacceptable. The better solution was Congressional action since the Supreme Court decision in the Dred Scott case had nullified popular sovereignty.

Lincoln lost the senatorial election by only a slim margin. However, he attracted national interest, which laid the foundation for his presidential bid in 1860. Because Lincoln was able to get Douglas to contrive the Freeport Doctrine, Douglas lost support among Southern Democrats whom he had hoped to court in his presidential campaign. This division aided Lincoln's election in 1860. Ask yourself why Americans from other states were interested in the Lincoln-Douglas debates. How did this issue and the election of Lincoln influence decisions made by Southern legislatures?

Document E

A portion of the October 15 debate of the seven Lincoln-Douglas debates, Document E frames Lincoln's thinking about the institution of slavery. Unlike Douglas, Lincoln and the Republican Party saw it as more than a political issue. For them, slavery was a moral evil of such magnitude that the nation must take a firm stand against its expansion. Lincoln believed that the Founders had recognized slavery as an evil but had tolerated it for political reasons. Therefore, he would tolerate slavery where it existed but firmly oppose its expansion.

Lincoln's position on slavery during the debates placed him in the forefront for the Republican nomination. Southerners believed that his nomination and subsequent election meant they no longer had a voice in the federal government. The Republican victory made the South feel as if the president and the Congress were set against Southern interests. How did these events lead to sectional conflict? Was the South correct to fear Lincoln's presidency?

Document F

What is most interesting about this document is that although it was written by a Southern newspaper editor, it opposes secession. The editorial compares secession to a crime. Every citizen of a seceding state remains a citizen of the United States. Acts against the nation are crimes whether they are committed by an individual or members of a larger group. Any other position results in no law and therefore no government. Finally, secession and rebellion are deemed criminal behavior.

Until the winter of 1860 and 1861, many people in both the North and the South thought that the nation might avoid armed conflict. Even after the election, Congress made a desperate effort to work out another compromise between the North and the South. The proposed "unamendable amendments" would have forbidden the federal government from interfering with slavery in the states and would have extended the Missouri Compromise line to California. The effort failed. Republicans felt their bold stand would draw Southern Unionists to their side and work against the secessionists. What is the importance of this stand against secession among some Southerners? Were the Republicans right to stand firm against expansion of slavery? To what extent can you hold the Republicans responsible for the Civil War?

Document G

Prepared by Christopher G. Memminger, this manifesto refers to South Carolina as an independent nation and claims the privilege of a state to dissolve a compact if the other parties fail to live up to the agreement—the theory of states' rights. The document explains that with the election of a hostile President whose goal is to abolish slavery, the state's economy and culture are threatened.

Secessionists were not rejecting the American democratic experiment. In fact, they believed that they were preserving it as the Founders had intended. Secessionists felt that Northern states had continually violated the Constitution when it came to slavery. The North had abandoned the ideal of limited government and had threatened the property rights of slaveholders. How does this contrast with Lincoln's view in Document E? What does Document F say about sentiments surrounding Lincoln's election? How does Southern bias contribute to the coming conflict? What relation does this view have with westward expansion?

Document H

In Abraham Lincoln's first inaugural address, the new president restates his belief that secession was illegal, reaffirms his position that federal property in the South must be defended, and vows to deliver U.S. mail in the Southern states. However, he appeals to longtime friendship among the states, promising no force will be used and that there will be no interference with slavery where it exists. He makes any outbreak of hostilities the responsibility of the South.

Interestingly, the final paragraph was suggested and outlined by William H. Seward, the nominated secretary of state. Seward, a controversial opponent of slavery, wanted Lincoln to soften the harsh ending. Elsewhere in the speech, Lincoln offers to support an amendment protecting slavery in existing states. What does this say about Lincoln's concern for the Union? Why would Lincoln want to point out the South was bringing war on itself?

Document I

As provisional president of the Confederacy, Jefferson Davis addressed the provisional Congress of the Confederacy at the end of April, 1861. His message is a well-developed, logical statement of the South's case and a historical justification for secession. He argues that the original government established for the United States was developed for mutual protection against a common enemy. Its purpose was not to bind the states together in a federal government that exercised power over individual member states. However, the government the Confederacy created demonstrated many similarities to that of the Union.

The Confederacy's population was nine million to the Union's twenty-two million. There were fewer railroads, a smaller industrial base, and a weak banking system. Contrast this position with that of the Northern states. How would you evaluate the states' rights argument as motivation for secession or as a legal excuse to do so?

Other points to consider:

- The Mexican War and its results

- The election of 1856

- The Kansas-Nebraska Act

- Abolitionist activities: abolitionist societies, *Uncle Tom's Cabin,* the Underground Railroad, John Brown's raid on Harper's Ferry

- Attack on Fort Sumter

SUGGESTIONS FOR FREE RESPONSE ESSAYS, PART B

ESSAY 2

Study Strategy

Be sure to complete the "Self-Evaluation Rubric" for each essay.

You might have chosen the following points about Great Britain and France for your essay on the struggle for control of North America. Consider these points as you complete your self-evaluation.

- Rivalries among European powers spread to the Americas.

- France, England, Spain, and the Netherlands were in a worldwide contest to control trade and commerce.

- In North America the greatest struggle was between Great Britain and France.

- After the Treaty of Aix-la-Chapelle, France began to consolidate its position in the Ohio Valley.

- British trappers and traders from New York and Pennsylvania moved into the Ohio River Valley to try to take over French trade with the Indians.

- France built forts along the Ohio, Mississippi, and Missouri Rivers as well as the Great Lakes to protect its territory.

- The government in France sent orders to the officials in New France to remove by force, if necessary, any British colonials in the Ohio River Valley.

- Most of the French in the Ohio Valley were trappers and traders who worked with and needed the Native Americans.

- The British, on the other hand, were farmers who wanted to push Native Americans out of the area.

- After Washington's failure to reclaim the Ohio Valley from the French, Virginia asked Britain for help.

- In retaliation, France and its Native American allies attacked and a long and costly war ensued.

ESSAY 3

Study Strategy

Revise each essay using suggested points from the list that will strengthen it.

You might have chosen the following points about people's attitude toward U.S. acquisition of territory to discuss in your essay on Manifest Destiny. Consider these points as you complete your self-evaluation.

- Manifest destiny is the concept that the United States had not only the right but the duty to settle all the territory between the Atlantic and Pacific Oceans.

- Racism was inherent within this concept, which, as it developed during the nineteenth century, became problematic for some Americans.

- In 1844, Polk was elected president on a platform of expansion of U.S. territory. His election signaled acceptance of the annexation of Texas after a war with Mexico.

- Polk had four goals as he began his presidency—two related to territory: to settle the Oregon boundary and to annex California. He accomplished both these goals.

- The Mexican Cession, part of the Treaty of Guadalupe Hidalgo that ended the Mexican War, gave California and most of New Mexico Territory to the United States for $15 million.

- By the Gadsden Purchase in 1853, the United States acquired from Mexico a strip of land in New Mexico and Arizona for $10 million to give the United States a Southern route for a transcontinental railroad.

- The acquisitions of these lands added Mexicans and Native Americans to the United States, Mexicans as citizens and Native Americans as wards. White Americans acted toward them with superior attitudes and attempted to destroy their cultures and take their lands, sometimes in a misguided attempt to improve their lives but often out of greed.

SUGGESTIONS FOR FREE RESPONSE ESSAYS, PART C

ESSAY 4

Study Strategy

Be sure to complete the "Self-Evaluation Rubric" for each essay.

You might have chosen the following points about the two individuals that you chose to discuss in your essay. Consider these points as you complete your self-evaluation.

Vanderbilt:

- Vanderbilt earned his first fortune in the steamship business and then bought and consolidated railroad lines in the Northeast.

- He ended up owning most of the railroads between Chicago and Buffalo, New York.

- He was often ruthless. In an effort to force another railroad to sell to him, he did not allow passengers to transfer from that line to one he owned, stranding the passengers.

- The railroad system benefited the nation by providing transportation for goods and passengers, which was an economic advantage.

- As a monopoly, it also cut out competition and placed control of a vital resource in the hands of a limited group.

- It was also antilabor.

Carnegie:

- Carnegie, a Scottish immigrant, first began investing in iron foundries and then began acquiring steel mills.

- He integrated his company vertically by buying iron suppliers and railroads to ship his steel.

- While he gave jobs to thousands, he was not a supporter of labor. The Homestead Strike took place in his steelworks, and its end signaled the end of unionism in steel mills for forty years.

- He gave millions of dollars to charities including money to build 2,800 local libraries. The foundations he created continue to give money to worthy causes.

Tarbell:

- A muckraker, her articles targeted big business.

- Her best-known work, *History of the Standard Oil Company*, pointed out the unfair practices used by Standard Oil.

- Her work contributed to tighter regulatory controls on trusts and benefits to consumers.

Gompers:

- Gompers helped found the American Federation of Labor (AFL).

- He stressed higher wages, a shorter workday, and safer working conditions.

- The AFL combined many trade unions but did not organize unskilled and semiskilled workers, African Americans, or women. Because it only organized craftworkers, most immigrants were also left out.

ESSAY 5

Study Strategy

Check Chapters 5 through 10 to review content you are not sure about.

You might have chosen the following points about the Cold War and détente for your essay on how the United States changed its policies during this time. Consider these points as you complete your self-evaluation.

- Symbols and evidence of the Cold War:

  - Arms race

  - Soviet invasion of Hungary

  - Berlin Wall

  - U-2 incident

  - Cuban missile crisis

  - Containment

  - Summitry

- Nixon, previously a major critic of the Chinese government, made secret overtures to the Chinese for improved relations and ultimately recognized the People's Republic of China in an effort to play the Soviet Union and the PRC against each other.

  - ping-pong diplomacy

  - Kissinger's meetings with the Chinese

  - Establishment of diplomatic relations

- Evidence of détente with the Soviet Union:

  - Strategic Arms Limitation Talks I (SALT) agreement

- Soviets' purchase of wheat from the United States

- Joint space missions

- Following the invasion of Afghanistan by the Soviet Union, relations between the countries deteriorated.

  - SALT II was not ratified by the United States Senate.

- President Jimmy Carter had the United States Olympic team withdraw from the Moscow Olympics.

SELF-EVALUATION RUBRIC FOR THE ADVANCED PLACEMENT ESSAYS

	8–9	5–7	2–4	0–1
Overall Impression	Demonstrates excellent understanding of U.S. history and outstanding writing; thorough and effective; incisive	Demonstrates good understanding of U.S. history and good writing competence	Reveals simplistic or incomplete thinking and/or immature understanding of U.S. history; fails to respond adequately to the question; little or no analysis	Very little or no understanding of U.S. history; unacceptably brief; fails to respond to the question; little clarity
Understanding of U.S. History	Scholarly; excellent understanding of the question; effective and incisive; in-depth critical analysis; includes many apt, specific references; acknowledges opposing views	Mostly historically accurate; good understanding of the question; often perceptive; includes specific references and critical analysis	Some historical inaccuracies; superficial understanding and treatment of the question; some misreading of documents and lack of historical evidence; mechanical; overgeneralized	Serious historical errors; extensive misreadings and little supporting evidence; completely off the topic
Development	Original, unique and/or intriguing thesis; excellent use of documents and historical knowledge; thoroughly developed; conclusion shows applicability of thesis to other situations	Adequate thesis; satisfactory use of documents and/or historical knowledge; competent development; acceptable conclusion	Inadequate, irrelevant or illogical thesis; little use of documents and/or historical knowledge; some development; unsatisfactory, inapplicable, or nonexistent conclusion	Lacking both thesis and conclusion; little or no use of historical documents or knowledge; no distinguishable development
Organization/Conventions of English	Meticulously and thoroughly organized; coherent and unified; virtually error free	Reasonably organized; mostly coherent and unified; some errors	Somewhat organized; some incoherence and lack of unity; some major errors	Little or no organization; incoherent and void of unity; extremely flawed

Rate yourself in each of the categories below. Enter the numbers on the lines below. Be as honest as possible so you will know what areas need work. Then calculate the average of the four numbers to determine your final score. It is difficult to score yourself objectively, so you may wish to ask a respected friend or teacher to assess your essays for a more accurate reflection of their strengths and weaknesses. On the AP test itself, a reader will rate your essays on a scale of 0 to 9, with 9 being the highest.

Each category is rated 9 (high) to 0 (incompetent).

DBQ

SELF-EVALUATION

Overall Impression _____

Understanding of U.S. History _____

Development _____

Organization/Conventions
of English _____

TOTAL _____

    Divide by 4 for final score. _____

DBQ

OBJECTIVE EVALUATION

Overall Impression _____

Understanding of U.S. History _____

Development _____

Organization/Conventions
of English _____

TOTAL _____

    Divide by 4 for final score. _____

FREE RESPONSE 1

SELF-EVALUATION

Overall Impression _____

Understanding of U.S. History _____

Development _____

Organization/Conventions
of English _____

TOTAL _____

    Divide by 4 for final score. _____

FREE RESPONSE 1

OBJECTIVE EVALUATION

Overall Impression _____

Understanding of U.S. History _____

Development _____

Organization/Conventions
of English _____

TOTAL _____

    Divide by 4 for final score. _____

FREE RESPONSE 2

SELF-EVALUATION

Overall Impression _____

Understanding of U.S. History _____

Development _____

Organization/Conventions
of English _____

TOTAL _____

    Divide by 4 for final score. _____

FREE RESPONSE 2

OBJECTIVE EVALUATION

Overall Impression _____

Understanding of U.S. History _____

Development _____

Organization/Conventions
of English _____

TOTAL _____

    Divide by 4 for final score. _____

ANSWER SHEET FOR DIAGNOSTIC TEST

Completely darken bubbles with a No. 2 pencil.
If you make a mistake, be sure to erase mark completely. Erase all stray marks.

1 ⊂A⊃ ⊂B⊃ ⊂C⊃ ⊂D⊃ ⊂E⊃	28 ⊂A⊃ ⊂B⊃ ⊂C⊃ ⊂D⊃ ⊂E⊃	55 ⊂A⊃ ⊂B⊃ ⊂C⊃ ⊂D⊃ ⊂E⊃
2 ⊂A⊃ ⊂B⊃ ⊂C⊃ ⊂D⊃ ⊂E⊃	29 ⊂A⊃ ⊂B⊃ ⊂C⊃ ⊂D⊃ ⊂E⊃	56 ⊂A⊃ ⊂B⊃ ⊂C⊃ ⊂D⊃ ⊂E⊃
3 ⊂A⊃ ⊂B⊃ ⊂C⊃ ⊂D⊃ ⊂E⊃	30 ⊂A⊃ ⊂B⊃ ⊂C⊃ ⊂D⊃ ⊂E⊃	57 ⊂A⊃ ⊂B⊃ ⊂C⊃ ⊂D⊃ ⊂E⊃
4 ⊂A⊃ ⊂B⊃ ⊂C⊃ ⊂D⊃ ⊂E⊃	31 ⊂A⊃ ⊂B⊃ ⊂C⊃ ⊂D⊃ ⊂E⊃	58 ⊂A⊃ ⊂B⊃ ⊂C⊃ ⊂D⊃ ⊂E⊃
5 ⊂A⊃ ⊂B⊃ ⊂C⊃ ⊂D⊃ ⊂E⊃	32 ⊂A⊃ ⊂B⊃ ⊂C⊃ ⊂D⊃ ⊂E⊃	59 ⊂A⊃ ⊂B⊃ ⊂C⊃ ⊂D⊃ ⊂E⊃
6 ⊂A⊃ ⊂B⊃ ⊂C⊃ ⊂D⊃ ⊂E⊃	33 ⊂A⊃ ⊂B⊃ ⊂C⊃ ⊂D⊃ ⊂E⊃	60 ⊂A⊃ ⊂B⊃ ⊂C⊃ ⊂D⊃ ⊂E⊃
7 ⊂A⊃ ⊂B⊃ ⊂C⊃ ⊂D⊃ ⊂E⊃	34 ⊂A⊃ ⊂B⊃ ⊂C⊃ ⊂D⊃ ⊂E⊃	61 ⊂A⊃ ⊂B⊃ ⊂C⊃ ⊂D⊃ ⊂E⊃
8 ⊂A⊃ ⊂B⊃ ⊂C⊃ ⊂D⊃ ⊂E⊃	35 ⊂A⊃ ⊂B⊃ ⊂C⊃ ⊂D⊃ ⊂E⊃	62 ⊂A⊃ ⊂B⊃ ⊂C⊃ ⊂D⊃ ⊂E⊃
9 ⊂A⊃ ⊂B⊃ ⊂C⊃ ⊂D⊃ ⊂E⊃	36 ⊂A⊃ ⊂B⊃ ⊂C⊃ ⊂D⊃ ⊂E⊃	63 ⊂A⊃ ⊂B⊃ ⊂C⊃ ⊂D⊃ ⊂E⊃
10 ⊂A⊃ ⊂B⊃ ⊂C⊃ ⊂D⊃ ⊂E⊃	37 ⊂A⊃ ⊂B⊃ ⊂C⊃ ⊂D⊃ ⊂E⊃	64 ⊂A⊃ ⊂B⊃ ⊂C⊃ ⊂D⊃ ⊂E⊃
11 ⊂A⊃ ⊂B⊃ ⊂C⊃ ⊂D⊃ ⊂E⊃	38 ⊂A⊃ ⊂B⊃ ⊂C⊃ ⊂D⊃ ⊂E⊃	65 ⊂A⊃ ⊂B⊃ ⊂C⊃ ⊂D⊃ ⊂E⊃
12 ⊂A⊃ ⊂B⊃ ⊂C⊃ ⊂D⊃ ⊂E⊃	39 ⊂A⊃ ⊂B⊃ ⊂C⊃ ⊂D⊃ ⊂E⊃	66 ⊂A⊃ ⊂B⊃ ⊂C⊃ ⊂D⊃ ⊂E⊃
13 ⊂A⊃ ⊂B⊃ ⊂C⊃ ⊂D⊃ ⊂E⊃	40 ⊂A⊃ ⊂B⊃ ⊂C⊃ ⊂D⊃ ⊂E⊃	67 ⊂A⊃ ⊂B⊃ ⊂C⊃ ⊂D⊃ ⊂E⊃
14 ⊂A⊃ ⊂B⊃ ⊂C⊃ ⊂D⊃ ⊂E⊃	41 ⊂A⊃ ⊂B⊃ ⊂C⊃ ⊂D⊃ ⊂E⊃	68 ⊂A⊃ ⊂B⊃ ⊂C⊃ ⊂D⊃ ⊂E⊃
15 ⊂A⊃ ⊂B⊃ ⊂C⊃ ⊂D⊃ ⊂E⊃	42 ⊂A⊃ ⊂B⊃ ⊂C⊃ ⊂D⊃ ⊂E⊃	69 ⊂A⊃ ⊂B⊃ ⊂C⊃ ⊂D⊃ ⊂E⊃
16 ⊂A⊃ ⊂B⊃ ⊂C⊃ ⊂D⊃ ⊂E⊃	43 ⊂A⊃ ⊂B⊃ ⊂C⊃ ⊂D⊃ ⊂E⊃	70 ⊂A⊃ ⊂B⊃ ⊂C⊃ ⊂D⊃ ⊂E⊃
17 ⊂A⊃ ⊂B⊃ ⊂C⊃ ⊂D⊃ ⊂E⊃	44 ⊂A⊃ ⊂B⊃ ⊂C⊃ ⊂D⊃ ⊂E⊃	71 ⊂A⊃ ⊂B⊃ ⊂C⊃ ⊂D⊃ ⊂E⊃
18 ⊂A⊃ ⊂B⊃ ⊂C⊃ ⊂D⊃ ⊂E⊃	45 ⊂A⊃ ⊂B⊃ ⊂C⊃ ⊂D⊃ ⊂E⊃	72 ⊂A⊃ ⊂B⊃ ⊂C⊃ ⊂D⊃ ⊂E⊃
19 ⊂A⊃ ⊂B⊃ ⊂C⊃ ⊂D⊃ ⊂E⊃	46 ⊂A⊃ ⊂B⊃ ⊂C⊃ ⊂D⊃ ⊂E⊃	73 ⊂A⊃ ⊂B⊃ ⊂C⊃ ⊂D⊃ ⊂E⊃
20 ⊂A⊃ ⊂B⊃ ⊂C⊃ ⊂D⊃ ⊂E⊃	47 ⊂A⊃ ⊂B⊃ ⊂C⊃ ⊂D⊃ ⊂E⊃	74 ⊂A⊃ ⊂B⊃ ⊂C⊃ ⊂D⊃ ⊂E⊃
21 ⊂A⊃ ⊂B⊃ ⊂C⊃ ⊂D⊃ ⊂E⊃	48 ⊂A⊃ ⊂B⊃ ⊂C⊃ ⊂D⊃ ⊂E⊃	75 ⊂A⊃ ⊂B⊃ ⊂C⊃ ⊂D⊃ ⊂E⊃
22 ⊂A⊃ ⊂B⊃ ⊂C⊃ ⊂D⊃ ⊂E⊃	49 ⊂A⊃ ⊂B⊃ ⊂C⊃ ⊂D⊃ ⊂E⊃	76 ⊂A⊃ ⊂B⊃ ⊂C⊃ ⊂D⊃ ⊂E⊃
23 ⊂A⊃ ⊂B⊃ ⊂C⊃ ⊂D⊃ ⊂E⊃	50 ⊂A⊃ ⊂B⊃ ⊂C⊃ ⊂D⊃ ⊂E⊃	77 ⊂A⊃ ⊂B⊃ ⊂C⊃ ⊂D⊃ ⊂E⊃
24 ⊂A⊃ ⊂B⊃ ⊂C⊃ ⊂D⊃ ⊂E⊃	51 ⊂A⊃ ⊂B⊃ ⊂C⊃ ⊂D⊃ ⊂E⊃	78 ⊂A⊃ ⊂B⊃ ⊂C⊃ ⊂D⊃ ⊂E⊃
25 ⊂A⊃ ⊂B⊃ ⊂C⊃ ⊂D⊃ ⊂E⊃	52 ⊂A⊃ ⊂B⊃ ⊂C⊃ ⊂D⊃ ⊂E⊃	79 ⊂A⊃ ⊂B⊃ ⊂C⊃ ⊂D⊃ ⊂E⊃
26 ⊂A⊃ ⊂B⊃ ⊂C⊃ ⊂D⊃ ⊂E⊃	53 ⊂A⊃ ⊂B⊃ ⊂C⊃ ⊂D⊃ ⊂E⊃	80 ⊂A⊃ ⊂B⊃ ⊂C⊃ ⊂D⊃ ⊂E⊃
27 ⊂A⊃ ⊂B⊃ ⊂C⊃ ⊂D⊃ ⊂E⊃	54 ⊂A⊃ ⊂B⊃ ⊂C⊃ ⊂D⊃ ⊂E⊃	

BE SURE TO ERASE ANY ERRORS OR STRAY MARKS COMPLETELY.

ANSWER SHEET FOR PRACTICE TEST 1

Completely darken bubbles with a No. 2 pencil.
If you make a mistake, be sure to erase mark completely. Erase all stray marks.

1 ⊂A⊃ ⊂B⊃ ⊂C⊃ ⊂D⊃ ⊂E⊃	28 ⊂A⊃ ⊂B⊃ ⊂C⊃ ⊂D⊃ ⊂E⊃	55 ⊂A⊃ ⊂B⊃ ⊂C⊃ ⊂D⊃ ⊂E⊃
2 ⊂A⊃ ⊂B⊃ ⊂C⊃ ⊂D⊃ ⊂E⊃	29 ⊂A⊃ ⊂B⊃ ⊂C⊃ ⊂D⊃ ⊂E⊃	56 ⊂A⊃ ⊂B⊃ ⊂C⊃ ⊂D⊃ ⊂E⊃
3 ⊂A⊃ ⊂B⊃ ⊂C⊃ ⊂D⊃ ⊂E⊃	30 ⊂A⊃ ⊂B⊃ ⊂C⊃ ⊂D⊃ ⊂E⊃	57 ⊂A⊃ ⊂B⊃ ⊂C⊃ ⊂D⊃ ⊂E⊃
4 ⊂A⊃ ⊂B⊃ ⊂C⊃ ⊂D⊃ ⊂E⊃	31 ⊂A⊃ ⊂B⊃ ⊂C⊃ ⊂D⊃ ⊂E⊃	58 ⊂A⊃ ⊂B⊃ ⊂C⊃ ⊂D⊃ ⊂E⊃
5 ⊂A⊃ ⊂B⊃ ⊂C⊃ ⊂D⊃ ⊂E⊃	32 ⊂A⊃ ⊂B⊃ ⊂C⊃ ⊂D⊃ ⊂E⊃	59 ⊂A⊃ ⊂B⊃ ⊂C⊃ ⊂D⊃ ⊂E⊃
6 ⊂A⊃ ⊂B⊃ ⊂C⊃ ⊂D⊃ ⊂E⊃	33 ⊂A⊃ ⊂B⊃ ⊂C⊃ ⊂D⊃ ⊂E⊃	60 ⊂A⊃ ⊂B⊃ ⊂C⊃ ⊂D⊃ ⊂E⊃
7 ⊂A⊃ ⊂B⊃ ⊂C⊃ ⊂D⊃ ⊂E⊃	34 ⊂A⊃ ⊂B⊃ ⊂C⊃ ⊂D⊃ ⊂E⊃	61 ⊂A⊃ ⊂B⊃ ⊂C⊃ ⊂D⊃ ⊂E⊃
8 ⊂A⊃ ⊂B⊃ ⊂C⊃ ⊂D⊃ ⊂E⊃	35 ⊂A⊃ ⊂B⊃ ⊂C⊃ ⊂D⊃ ⊂E⊃	62 ⊂A⊃ ⊂B⊃ ⊂C⊃ ⊂D⊃ ⊂E⊃
9 ⊂A⊃ ⊂B⊃ ⊂C⊃ ⊂D⊃ ⊂E⊃	36 ⊂A⊃ ⊂B⊃ ⊂C⊃ ⊂D⊃ ⊂E⊃	63 ⊂A⊃ ⊂B⊃ ⊂C⊃ ⊂D⊃ ⊂E⊃
10 ⊂A⊃ ⊂B⊃ ⊂C⊃ ⊂D⊃ ⊂E⊃	37 ⊂A⊃ ⊂B⊃ ⊂C⊃ ⊂D⊃ ⊂E⊃	64 ⊂A⊃ ⊂B⊃ ⊂C⊃ ⊂D⊃ ⊂E⊃
11 ⊂A⊃ ⊂B⊃ ⊂C⊃ ⊂D⊃ ⊂E⊃	38 ⊂A⊃ ⊂B⊃ ⊂C⊃ ⊂D⊃ ⊂E⊃	65 ⊂A⊃ ⊂B⊃ ⊂C⊃ ⊂D⊃ ⊂E⊃
12 ⊂A⊃ ⊂B⊃ ⊂C⊃ ⊂D⊃ ⊂E⊃	39 ⊂A⊃ ⊂B⊃ ⊂C⊃ ⊂D⊃ ⊂E⊃	66 ⊂A⊃ ⊂B⊃ ⊂C⊃ ⊂D⊃ ⊂E⊃
13 ⊂A⊃ ⊂B⊃ ⊂C⊃ ⊂D⊃ ⊂E⊃	40 ⊂A⊃ ⊂B⊃ ⊂C⊃ ⊂D⊃ ⊂E⊃	67 ⊂A⊃ ⊂B⊃ ⊂C⊃ ⊂D⊃ ⊂E⊃
14 ⊂A⊃ ⊂B⊃ ⊂C⊃ ⊂D⊃ ⊂E⊃	41 ⊂A⊃ ⊂B⊃ ⊂C⊃ ⊂D⊃ ⊂E⊃	68 ⊂A⊃ ⊂B⊃ ⊂C⊃ ⊂D⊃ ⊂E⊃
15 ⊂A⊃ ⊂B⊃ ⊂C⊃ ⊂D⊃ ⊂E⊃	42 ⊂A⊃ ⊂B⊃ ⊂C⊃ ⊂D⊃ ⊂E⊃	69 ⊂A⊃ ⊂B⊃ ⊂C⊃ ⊂D⊃ ⊂E⊃
16 ⊂A⊃ ⊂B⊃ ⊂C⊃ ⊂D⊃ ⊂E⊃	43 ⊂A⊃ ⊂B⊃ ⊂C⊃ ⊂D⊃ ⊂E⊃	70 ⊂A⊃ ⊂B⊃ ⊂C⊃ ⊂D⊃ ⊂E⊃
17 ⊂A⊃ ⊂B⊃ ⊂C⊃ ⊂D⊃ ⊂E⊃	44 ⊂A⊃ ⊂B⊃ ⊂C⊃ ⊂D⊃ ⊂E⊃	71 ⊂A⊃ ⊂B⊃ ⊂C⊃ ⊂D⊃ ⊂E⊃
18 ⊂A⊃ ⊂B⊃ ⊂C⊃ ⊂D⊃ ⊂E⊃	45 ⊂A⊃ ⊂B⊃ ⊂C⊃ ⊂D⊃ ⊂E⊃	72 ⊂A⊃ ⊂B⊃ ⊂C⊃ ⊂D⊃ ⊂E⊃
19 ⊂A⊃ ⊂B⊃ ⊂C⊃ ⊂D⊃ ⊂E⊃	46 ⊂A⊃ ⊂B⊃ ⊂C⊃ ⊂D⊃ ⊂E⊃	73 ⊂A⊃ ⊂B⊃ ⊂C⊃ ⊂D⊃ ⊂E⊃
20 ⊂A⊃ ⊂B⊃ ⊂C⊃ ⊂D⊃ ⊂E⊃	47 ⊂A⊃ ⊂B⊃ ⊂C⊃ ⊂D⊃ ⊂E⊃	74 ⊂A⊃ ⊂B⊃ ⊂C⊃ ⊂D⊃ ⊂E⊃
21 ⊂A⊃ ⊂B⊃ ⊂C⊃ ⊂D⊃ ⊂E⊃	48 ⊂A⊃ ⊂B⊃ ⊂C⊃ ⊂D⊃ ⊂E⊃	75 ⊂A⊃ ⊂B⊃ ⊂C⊃ ⊂D⊃ ⊂E⊃
22 ⊂A⊃ ⊂B⊃ ⊂C⊃ ⊂D⊃ ⊂E⊃	49 ⊂A⊃ ⊂B⊃ ⊂C⊃ ⊂D⊃ ⊂E⊃	76 ⊂A⊃ ⊂B⊃ ⊂C⊃ ⊂D⊃ ⊂E⊃
23 ⊂A⊃ ⊂B⊃ ⊂C⊃ ⊂D⊃ ⊂E⊃	50 ⊂A⊃ ⊂B⊃ ⊂C⊃ ⊂D⊃ ⊂E⊃	77 ⊂A⊃ ⊂B⊃ ⊂C⊃ ⊂D⊃ ⊂E⊃
24 ⊂A⊃ ⊂B⊃ ⊂C⊃ ⊂D⊃ ⊂E⊃	51 ⊂A⊃ ⊂B⊃ ⊂C⊃ ⊂D⊃ ⊂E⊃	78 ⊂A⊃ ⊂B⊃ ⊂C⊃ ⊂D⊃ ⊂E⊃
25 ⊂A⊃ ⊂B⊃ ⊂C⊃ ⊂D⊃ ⊂E⊃	52 ⊂A⊃ ⊂B⊃ ⊂C⊃ ⊂D⊃ ⊂E⊃	79 ⊂A⊃ ⊂B⊃ ⊂C⊃ ⊂D⊃ ⊂E⊃
26 ⊂A⊃ ⊂B⊃ ⊂C⊃ ⊂D⊃ ⊂E⊃	53 ⊂A⊃ ⊂B⊃ ⊂C⊃ ⊂D⊃ ⊂E⊃	80 ⊂A⊃ ⊂B⊃ ⊂C⊃ ⊂D⊃ ⊂E⊃
27 ⊂A⊃ ⊂B⊃ ⊂C⊃ ⊂D⊃ ⊂E⊃	54 ⊂A⊃ ⊂B⊃ ⊂C⊃ ⊂D⊃ ⊂E⊃	

BE SURE TO ERASE ANY ERRORS OR STRAY MARKS COMPLETELY.

ANSWER SHEET FOR PRACTICE TEST 2

Completely darken bubbles with a No. 2 pencil.
If you make a mistake, be sure to erase mark completely. Erase all stray marks.

1 ⊂A⊃ ⊂B⊃ ⊂C⊃ ⊂D⊃ ⊂E⊃	28 ⊂A⊃ ⊂B⊃ ⊂C⊃ ⊂D⊃ ⊂E⊃	55 ⊂A⊃ ⊂B⊃ ⊂C⊃ ⊂D⊃ ⊂E⊃
2 ⊂A⊃ ⊂B⊃ ⊂C⊃ ⊂D⊃ ⊂E⊃	29 ⊂A⊃ ⊂B⊃ ⊂C⊃ ⊂D⊃ ⊂E⊃	56 ⊂A⊃ ⊂B⊃ ⊂C⊃ ⊂D⊃ ⊂E⊃
3 ⊂A⊃ ⊂B⊃ ⊂C⊃ ⊂D⊃ ⊂E⊃	30 ⊂A⊃ ⊂B⊃ ⊂C⊃ ⊂D⊃ ⊂E⊃	57 ⊂A⊃ ⊂B⊃ ⊂C⊃ ⊂D⊃ ⊂E⊃
4 ⊂A⊃ ⊂B⊃ ⊂C⊃ ⊂D⊃ ⊂E⊃	31 ⊂A⊃ ⊂B⊃ ⊂C⊃ ⊂D⊃ ⊂E⊃	58 ⊂A⊃ ⊂B⊃ ⊂C⊃ ⊂D⊃ ⊂E⊃
5 ⊂A⊃ ⊂B⊃ ⊂C⊃ ⊂D⊃ ⊂E⊃	32 ⊂A⊃ ⊂B⊃ ⊂C⊃ ⊂D⊃ ⊂E⊃	59 ⊂A⊃ ⊂B⊃ ⊂C⊃ ⊂D⊃ ⊂E⊃
6 ⊂A⊃ ⊂B⊃ ⊂C⊃ ⊂D⊃ ⊂E⊃	33 ⊂A⊃ ⊂B⊃ ⊂C⊃ ⊂D⊃ ⊂E⊃	60 ⊂A⊃ ⊂B⊃ ⊂C⊃ ⊂D⊃ ⊂E⊃
7 ⊂A⊃ ⊂B⊃ ⊂C⊃ ⊂D⊃ ⊂E⊃	34 ⊂A⊃ ⊂B⊃ ⊂C⊃ ⊂D⊃ ⊂E⊃	61 ⊂A⊃ ⊂B⊃ ⊂C⊃ ⊂D⊃ ⊂E⊃
8 ⊂A⊃ ⊂B⊃ ⊂C⊃ ⊂D⊃ ⊂E⊃	35 ⊂A⊃ ⊂B⊃ ⊂C⊃ ⊂D⊃ ⊂E⊃	62 ⊂A⊃ ⊂B⊃ ⊂C⊃ ⊂D⊃ ⊂E⊃
9 ⊂A⊃ ⊂B⊃ ⊂C⊃ ⊂D⊃ ⊂E⊃	36 ⊂A⊃ ⊂B⊃ ⊂C⊃ ⊂D⊃ ⊂E⊃	63 ⊂A⊃ ⊂B⊃ ⊂C⊃ ⊂D⊃ ⊂E⊃
10 ⊂A⊃ ⊂B⊃ ⊂C⊃ ⊂D⊃ ⊂E⊃	37 ⊂A⊃ ⊂B⊃ ⊂C⊃ ⊂D⊃ ⊂E⊃	64 ⊂A⊃ ⊂B⊃ ⊂C⊃ ⊂D⊃ ⊂E⊃
11 ⊂A⊃ ⊂B⊃ ⊂C⊃ ⊂D⊃ ⊂E⊃	38 ⊂A⊃ ⊂B⊃ ⊂C⊃ ⊂D⊃ ⊂E⊃	65 ⊂A⊃ ⊂B⊃ ⊂C⊃ ⊂D⊃ ⊂E⊃
12 ⊂A⊃ ⊂B⊃ ⊂C⊃ ⊂D⊃ ⊂E⊃	39 ⊂A⊃ ⊂B⊃ ⊂C⊃ ⊂D⊃ ⊂E⊃	66 ⊂A⊃ ⊂B⊃ ⊂C⊃ ⊂D⊃ ⊂E⊃
13 ⊂A⊃ ⊂B⊃ ⊂C⊃ ⊂D⊃ ⊂E⊃	40 ⊂A⊃ ⊂B⊃ ⊂C⊃ ⊂D⊃ ⊂E⊃	67 ⊂A⊃ ⊂B⊃ ⊂C⊃ ⊂D⊃ ⊂E⊃
14 ⊂A⊃ ⊂B⊃ ⊂C⊃ ⊂D⊃ ⊂E⊃	41 ⊂A⊃ ⊂B⊃ ⊂C⊃ ⊂D⊃ ⊂E⊃	68 ⊂A⊃ ⊂B⊃ ⊂C⊃ ⊂D⊃ ⊂E⊃
15 ⊂A⊃ ⊂B⊃ ⊂C⊃ ⊂D⊃ ⊂E⊃	42 ⊂A⊃ ⊂B⊃ ⊂C⊃ ⊂D⊃ ⊂E⊃	69 ⊂A⊃ ⊂B⊃ ⊂C⊃ ⊂D⊃ ⊂E⊃
16 ⊂A⊃ ⊂B⊃ ⊂C⊃ ⊂D⊃ ⊂E⊃	43 ⊂A⊃ ⊂B⊃ ⊂C⊃ ⊂D⊃ ⊂E⊃	70 ⊂A⊃ ⊂B⊃ ⊂C⊃ ⊂D⊃ ⊂E⊃
17 ⊂A⊃ ⊂B⊃ ⊂C⊃ ⊂D⊃ ⊂E⊃	44 ⊂A⊃ ⊂B⊃ ⊂C⊃ ⊂D⊃ ⊂E⊃	71 ⊂A⊃ ⊂B⊃ ⊂C⊃ ⊂D⊃ ⊂E⊃
18 ⊂A⊃ ⊂B⊃ ⊂C⊃ ⊂D⊃ ⊂E⊃	45 ⊂A⊃ ⊂B⊃ ⊂C⊃ ⊂D⊃ ⊂E⊃	72 ⊂A⊃ ⊂B⊃ ⊂C⊃ ⊂D⊃ ⊂E⊃
19 ⊂A⊃ ⊂B⊃ ⊂C⊃ ⊂D⊃ ⊂E⊃	46 ⊂A⊃ ⊂B⊃ ⊂C⊃ ⊂D⊃ ⊂E⊃	73 ⊂A⊃ ⊂B⊃ ⊂C⊃ ⊂D⊃ ⊂E⊃
20 ⊂A⊃ ⊂B⊃ ⊂C⊃ ⊂D⊃ ⊂E⊃	47 ⊂A⊃ ⊂B⊃ ⊂C⊃ ⊂D⊃ ⊂E⊃	74 ⊂A⊃ ⊂B⊃ ⊂C⊃ ⊂D⊃ ⊂E⊃
21 ⊂A⊃ ⊂B⊃ ⊂C⊃ ⊂D⊃ ⊂E⊃	48 ⊂A⊃ ⊂B⊃ ⊂C⊃ ⊂D⊃ ⊂E⊃	75 ⊂A⊃ ⊂B⊃ ⊂C⊃ ⊂D⊃ ⊂E⊃
22 ⊂A⊃ ⊂B⊃ ⊂C⊃ ⊂D⊃ ⊂E⊃	49 ⊂A⊃ ⊂B⊃ ⊂C⊃ ⊂D⊃ ⊂E⊃	76 ⊂A⊃ ⊂B⊃ ⊂C⊃ ⊂D⊃ ⊂E⊃
23 ⊂A⊃ ⊂B⊃ ⊂C⊃ ⊂D⊃ ⊂E⊃	50 ⊂A⊃ ⊂B⊃ ⊂C⊃ ⊂D⊃ ⊂E⊃	77 ⊂A⊃ ⊂B⊃ ⊂C⊃ ⊂D⊃ ⊂E⊃
24 ⊂A⊃ ⊂B⊃ ⊂C⊃ ⊂D⊃ ⊂E⊃	51 ⊂A⊃ ⊂B⊃ ⊂C⊃ ⊂D⊃ ⊂E⊃	78 ⊂A⊃ ⊂B⊃ ⊂C⊃ ⊂D⊃ ⊂E⊃
25 ⊂A⊃ ⊂B⊃ ⊂C⊃ ⊂D⊃ ⊂E⊃	52 ⊂A⊃ ⊂B⊃ ⊂C⊃ ⊂D⊃ ⊂E⊃	79 ⊂A⊃ ⊂B⊃ ⊂C⊃ ⊂D⊃ ⊂E⊃
26 ⊂A⊃ ⊂B⊃ ⊂C⊃ ⊂D⊃ ⊂E⊃	53 ⊂A⊃ ⊂B⊃ ⊂C⊃ ⊂D⊃ ⊂E⊃	80 ⊂A⊃ ⊂B⊃ ⊂C⊃ ⊂D⊃ ⊂E⊃
27 ⊂A⊃ ⊂B⊃ ⊂C⊃ ⊂D⊃ ⊂E⊃	54 ⊂A⊃ ⊂B⊃ ⊂C⊃ ⊂D⊃ ⊂E⊃	

BE SURE TO ERASE ANY ERRORS OR STRAY MARKS COMPLETELY.

NOTES

NOTES

NOTES

NOTES

NOTES

NOTES

NOTES

NOTES

NOTES

NOTES

NOTES

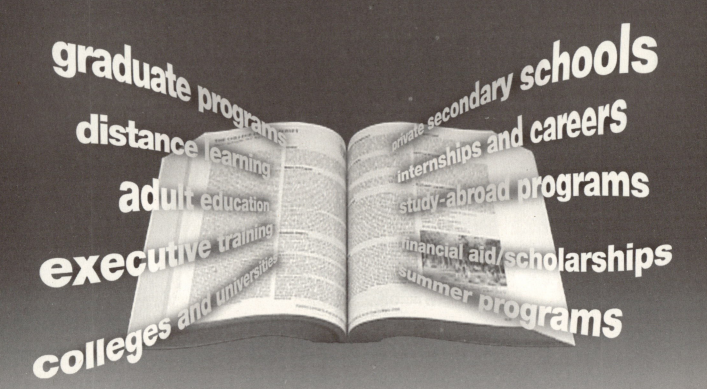